MICROSOFT®
EXCEL
2003

MEREDITH FLYNN

Bowling Green University
Bowling Green, Ohio

EMCParadigm
PUBLISHING

Project Editor	Sonja Brown
Developmental Editor	Courtney Kost
Senior Designer	Leslie Anderson
Copyeditor	Susan Capecchi
Cover Designer	Jennifer Wreisner
Desktop Production Specialists	Desktop Solutions; Erica Tava, Lisa Beller
Proofreader	Kathryn Savoie
Technical Reviewer	Desiree Faulkner
Indexer	Nancy Fulton
Photo Researcher	Paul Spencer

Publishing Team—George Provol, Publisher; Janice Johnson, Director of Product Development and Instructional Design; Tony Galvin, Acquisitions Editor; Lori Landwer, Marketing Manager; Shelley Clubb, Electronic Design and Production Manager

Acknowledgments—The publisher, author, and editors wish to thank the following instructors for their technical and academic contributions:

- Susan Lynn Bowen, Valdosta Technical College, Valdosta, Georgia, for testing the assessment material
- Ann Lewis, Ivy State Technical College, Evansville, Indiana, for preparing Chapter Challenges as part of the chapter assessment sections
- Rob Krumm, Diablo Valley College, Pleasant Hill, California, for creating the XML material
- Michael Feeney, Fanshawe College, London, Ontario, for reviewing the XML material
- Denise Seguin, Fanshawe College, London, Ontario, for writing the introductions to Word 2003, Access 2003, Excel 2003, and PowerPoint 2003, as well as providing content review

Photo Credits: E1, Jon Feingersh/CORBIS, CORBIS; E2, CORBIS; E4, CORBIS

Library of Congress Cataloging-in-Publication Data

Flynn, Meredith.
   Microsoft Excel 2003. Expert / Meredith Flynn.
     p. cm. -- (Benchmark series)
   Includes index.
   ISBN 0-7638-2051-2 (text)
1. Microsoft Excel (Computer file) 2. Business--Computer programs. 3. Electronic
spreadsheets. I. Title. II. Benchmark series (Saint Paul, Minn.)

HF5548.4.M523R884 2004
005.54--dc22
                                                                      2003060316

Text: ISBN 0-7638-0751-2
Product Number 05619

© 2004 by Paradigm Publishing, Inc.
      Published by **EMC**Paradigm
      875 Montreal Way
      St. Paul, MN 55102

      (800) 535-6865
      E-mail: educate@emcp.com
      Web site: www.emcp.com

CONTENTS

WELCOME

You are about to begin working with a textbook that is part of the Benchmark Office 2003 Series. The word *Benchmark* in the title holds a special significance in terms of *what* you will learn and *how* you will learn. *Benchmark*, according to *Webster's Dictionary*, means "something that serves as a standard by which others may be measured or judged." In this text, you will learn the Microsoft Office Specialist skills required for certification on the Specialist and/or Expert level of one or more major applications within the Office 2003 suite. These skills are benchmarks by which you will be evaluated, should you choose to take one or more certification exams.

The design and teaching approach of this textbook also serve as a benchmark for instructional materials on software programs. Features and commands are presented in a clear, straightforward way, and each short section of instruction is followed by an exercise that lets you practice using the new feature. Gradually, as you move through each chapter, you will build your skills to the point of mastery. At the end of a chapter, you are offered the opportunity to demonstrate your newly acquired competencies—to prove you have met the benchmarks for using the Office suite or an individual program. At the completion of the text, you are well on your way to becoming a successful computer user.

EMC/Paradigm's Office 2003 Benchmark Series includes textbooks on Office 2003, Word 2003, Excel 2003, Access 2003 and PowerPoint 2003. Each book includes a Student CD, which contains documents and files required for completing the exercises. A CD icon and folder name displayed on the opening page of each chapter indicates that you need to copy a folder of files from the CD before beginning the chapter exercises. *(See the inside back cover for instructions on copying a folder.)*

Introducing Microsoft Office 2003

Microsoft Office 2003 is a suite of programs designed to improve productivity and efficiency in workplace, school, and home settings. A suite is a group of programs that are sold as a package and are designed to be used together, making it possible to exchange files among the programs. The major applications included in Office are Word, a word processing program; Excel, a spreadsheet program; Access, a database management program; and PowerPoint, a slide presentation program.

Using the Office suite offers significant advantages over working with individual programs developed by different software vendors. The programs in the Office suite use similar toolbars, buttons, icons, and menus, which means that once you learn the basic features of one program, you can use those same features in the other programs. This easy transfer of knowledge decreases the learning time and allows you to concentrate on the unique commands and options within each program. The compatibility of the programs creates seamless integration of data within and between programs and lets the operator use the program most appropriate for the required tasks.

New Features in Office 2003

Users of previous editions of Office will find that the essential features that have made Office popular still form the heart of the suite. New enhancements include improved templates for both business and personal use. The Smart Tags introduced in Office XP also have been enhanced in Office 2003 with special customization options. One of the most far-reaching changes is the introduction of XML (eXtensible Markup Language) capabilities. Some elements of this technology were essentially hidden behind the scenes in Office XP. Now XML has been brought to the forefront. XML enables data to be used more flexibly and stored regardless of the computer platform. It can be used between different languages, countries, and across the Internet. XML heralds a revolution in data exchange. At the same time, it makes efficient and effective use of internal data within a business.

Structure of the Benchmark Textbooks

Users of the Specialist Certification texts and the complete application textbooks may begin their course with an overview of computer hardware and software, offered in the *Getting Started* section at the beginning of the book. Your instructor may also ask you to complete the *Windows XP* and the *Internet Explorer* sections so you become familiar with the computer's operating system and the essential tools for using the Internet.

Instruction on the major programs within the Office suite is presented in units of four chapters each. Both the Specialist and Expert levels contain two units, which culminate with performance assessments to check your knowledge and skills. Each chapter contains the following sections:

- performance objectives that identify specifically what you are expected to learn
- instructional text that introduces and explains new concepts and features
- step-by-step, hands-on exercises following each section of instruction
- a chapter summary
- a knowledge self-check called Concepts Check
- skill assessment exercises called Skills Check
- a case study exercise called Chapter Challenge

Exercises offered at the end of units provide writing and research opportunities that will strengthen your performance in other college courses as well as on the job. The final activities simulate interesting projects you could encounter in the workplace.

Benchmark Series Ancillaries

The Benchmark Series includes some important resources that will help you succeed in your computer applications courses:

Snap Training and Assessment

A Web-based program designed to optimize skill-based learning for all of the programs of Microsoft Office 2003, Snap is comprised of:

- a learning management system that creates a virtual classroom on the Web, allowing the instructor to schedule tutorials and tests and to employ an electronic gradebook;
- over 200 interactive, multimedia tutorials, aligned to textbook chapters, that can be used for direct instruction or remediation;
- a test bank of over 1,800 performance skill items that simulate the operation of Microsoft Office and allow the instructor to assign pretests, to administer chapter posttests, and to create practice tests to help students prepare for Microsoft Office Specialist certification exams; and
- over 6,000 concept items that can be used in combined concepts/application courses to monitor student understanding of technical and computer literacy knowledge.

Online Resource Center

Internet Resource Centers hosted by EMC/Paradigm provide additional material for students and instructors using the Benchmark books. Online you will find Web links, updates to textbooks, study tips, quizzes and assignments, and supplementary projects.

Class Connection

Available for both WebCT and Blackboard, EMC/Paradigm's Class Connection is a course management tool for traditional and distance learning.

What does this logo mean?

It means this courseware has been approved by the Microsoft® Office Specialist program to be among the finest available for learning Microsoft Excel 2003. It also means that upon completion of this courseware, you may be prepared to take an exam for Microsoft Office Specialist qualification.

What is a Microsoft Office Specialist?

A Microsoft Office Specialist is an individual who has passed exams for certifying his or her skills in one or more of the Microsoft Office desktop applications such as Microsoft Word, Microsoft Excel, Microsoft PowerPoint, Microsoft Outlook, Microsoft Access, or Microsoft Project. The Microsoft Office Specialist Program typically offers certification exams at the Specialist and Expert skill levels. The Microsoft Office Specialist Program is the only program in the world approved by Microsoft for testing proficiency in Microsoft Office desktop applications and Microsoft Project. This testing program can be a valuable asset in any job search or career advancement.

More Information

- To learn more about becoming a Microsoft Office Specialist, visit www.microsoft.com/officespecialist
- To learn about other Microsoft Office Specialist approved courseware from EMC/Paradigm Publishing, visit www.emcp.com

---

MICROSOFT® EXCEL

Complex analysis of numerical data is made easier with the advanced features in Microsoft Excel 2003. Learn to use the various tools to assist with projecting, analyzing, consolidating, and managing data. By getting accurate results more efficiently, you can use your time to focus on the meaning of the numbers, which will lead to sound decision making and, in the final analysis, a competitive edge for you and your company.

Organizing Information

Naming ranges means you can assign user-friendly names to cells for use in formulas. Using the range name in a calculation makes it easier to understand how a result was obtained. Consider how much easier it is to read the formula =*HoursWorked*PayRate* than to read =*D22*$E$12*. And, the significance of the formula quickly becomes clear, thanks to the name.

The expression "no one is perfect" fits more often than we like to admit, but with the error checking tools in Excel, perfect work is more attainable. When Excel detects an error in a cell, the Trace Error button becomes active with options for helping you find the source of the problem. Turn on the Auditing toolbar and use the Trace Precedents and

Display the Auditing toolbar to help find errors in formulas. In this worksheet, the red and blue arrows are drawn between dependent cells

EXPERT

Making EXCEL Work for YOU!

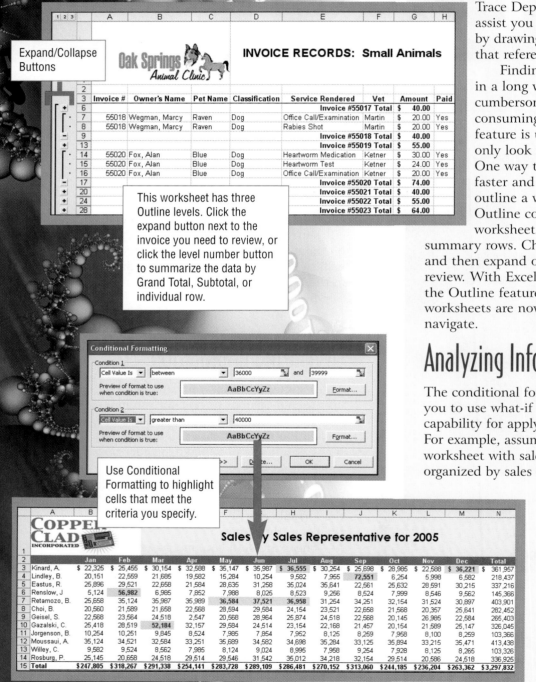

Expand/Collapse Buttons

This worksheet has three Outline levels. Click the expand button next to the invoice you need to review, or click the level number button to summarize the data by Grand Total, Subtotal, or individual row.

Use Conditional Formatting to highlight cells that meet the criteria you specify.

Trace Dependents buttons to assist you with troubleshooting by drawing arrows between cells that reference each other.

Finding specific information in a long worksheet can become cumbersome and time consuming. Using the Find feature is useful but you can only look for one item at a time. One way to locate information faster and more easily is to outline a worksheet. Excel's Outline command organizes the worksheet by displaying only the summary rows. Check the summaries and then expand only those you want to review. With Excel's Subtotal feature and the Outline feature, those long worksheets are now much easier to navigate.

Analyzing Information

The conditional formatting feature allows you to use what-if decision making capability for applying formats to cells. For example, assume you have a worksheet with sales for the entire year organized by sales representative. At a glance, you want to see in each month which salesperson performed the best by exceeding a certain target. Rather than pore over the data yourself, use conditional formatting to instruct Excel to apply a different color and/or fill to highlight the top performers.

Within seconds, those sales representatives stand out in the crowd.

Today's employers often require that two or more people at the same or different workplace work together on financial spreadsheets, research data, or other tracking of numerical information. Excel features that accommodate this collaboration among workers include the ability to share a workbook, track changes, accept and reject changes made by multiple authors, and merge multiple versions of the same workbook.

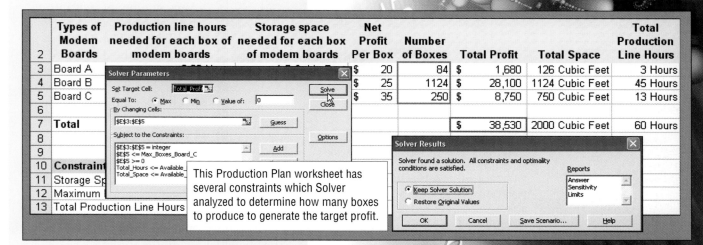

Here Goal Seek is used to determine what the Selling Price should be to achieve $8.00 Profit.

This Production Plan worksheet has several constraints which Solver analyzed to determine how many boxes to produce to generate the target profit.

While using these tools to help facilitate a team project, you and your managers can rest assured that the confidential information is secure by protecting cells, worksheets, and workbooks, assigning passwords, or attaching a digital signature for authentication.

Excel's Goal Seek, Solver, and Scenario Manager tools assist decision makers by calculating solutions to problems. In each case, you specify the cells containing the constraints or variables and instruct Excel on how to arrive at the result you are looking for. Use Goal Seek to calculate a result when you have only one variable. When more than one factor affects your decision, use

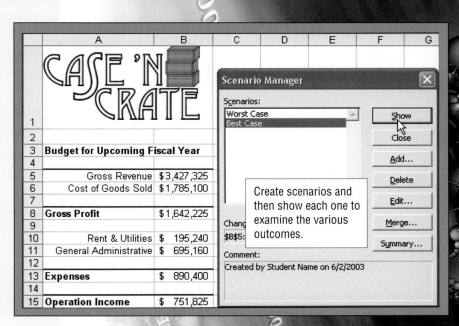

Create scenarios and then show each one to examine the various outcomes.

the Solver add-in to calculate the "best" solution to a problem. Finally, when you want to consider several different outcomes based on a set of criteria, consider using Scenario Manager to define each set of circumstances to see how each affects the final outcome. Help with those difficult decisions is just a few mouse clicks away!

Presenting Information

PivotTables and PivotCharts present information by condensing and summarizing a large number of cells into a small table or chart. A PivotTable or PivotChart summarizes the data based on the rows and columns you specify that you want consolidated. For example, assume a worksheet contains a long list of orders placed at various stores. You want to view a summary of the total value of orders by store and by model ordered. To do this on your own would take a significant effort. However, using the PivotTable and PivotChart Wizard, the summary is created in seconds!

Publishing interactive worksheets to the Web is simple using the Publish as Web Page dialog box in Excel. Choose whether you want spreadsheet functionality or PivotTable functionality. Placing Excel data within a browser interface that is more familiar to users is one way to expand access to information within an organization.

The expert features in Microsoft Excel are invaluable tools with which to manage the deluge of information that workers face each day. Learning how to use these features will save time and effort— a worthwhile goal at which you will want to *excel!*

	A	B	C	D	E	F	G	H	I	J	K	L
3	**Store**	**Model**	**Quarter**	**Units**	**Price**	**Total**		Sum of Price	Model			
4	Water Sports	Pathfinder	1st	6	$1,149.00	$ 6,894.00		Store	Excursion	Pathfinder	Trekker	Grand Total
5	Adventures Unlimited	Trekker	1st	5	$1,199.00	$ 5,995.00		Adventures Unlimited	2,716	3,447	3,597	9,760
6	Outdoor Sporting Goods	Excursion	1st	2	$ 679.00	$ 1,358.00		Backwoods Country	2,037	4,596	2,398	9,031
7	The Canoe Shop	Trekker	1st	8	$1,199.00	$ 9,592.00		Camping and More	2,037	1,149	4,796	7,982
8	Water Sports	Trekker	1st	10	$1,199.00	$11,990.00		NorthWest Camping	2,716	3,447	1,199	7,362
9	Outdoor Adventures	Excursion	1st	2	$ 679.00	$ 1,358.00		Outdoor Adventures	2,716	2,298	2,398	7,412
10	NorthWest Camping	Pathfinder	1st	7	$1,149.00	$ 8,043.00		Outdoor Sporting Goods	2,716	1,149	2,398	6,263
11	Adventures Unlimited	Excursion	1st	9	$ 679.00	$ 6,111.00		The Canoe Shop		1,149	3,597	4,746
12	Backwoods Country	Excursion	1st	15	$ 679.00	$10,185.00		Water Sports	3,395	4,596	2,398	10,389
13	Camping and More	Trekker	1st	32	$1,199.00	$38,368.00		**Grand Total**	**18,333**	**21,831**	**22,781**	**62,945**
14	NorthWest Camping	Pathfinder	1st	9	$1,149.00	$10,341.00						
15	Water Sports	Excursion	1st	7	$ 679.00	$ 4,753.00						
16	Outdoor Sporting Goods	Excursion	1st	4	$ 679.00	$ 2,716.00						
17	Outdoor Adventures	Pathfinder	1st	30	$1,149.00	$34,470.00						
18	Camping and More	Excursion	1st	9	$ 679.00	$ 6,111.00						
19	Water Sports	Excursion	1st	8	$ 679.00	$ 5,432.00						
20	Backwoods Country	Trekker	1st	5	$1,199.00	$ 5,995.00						
21	Adventures Unlimited	Trekker	2nd	12	$1,199.00	$14,388.00						
22	Outdoor Adventures	Excursion	2nd	18	$ 679.00	$12,222.00						
23	Water Sports	Excursion	2nd	4	$ 679.00	$ 2,716.00						
24	Backwoods Country	Pathfinder	2nd	3	$1,149.00	$ 3,447.00						
25	NorthWest Camping	Excursion	2nd									
26	Camping and More	Trekker	2nd									
27	Outdoor Sporting Goods	Trekker	2nd									
28	Camping and More	Excursion	2nd									
29	Adventures Unlimited	Pathfinder	2nd									
30	Backwoods Country	Pathfinder	2nd									
31	NorthWest Camping	Excursion	2nd									
32	Outdoor Adventures	Excursion	2nd									

The PivotTable above was created from the list of data shown at the left. Using the PivotTable and PivotChart Wizard, the report was created in just a few steps. At a glance, you can see the total price value by model order at each store.

Provide access to Excel data in a browser by publishing a worksheet as a Web page. Adding interactivity provides spreadsheet functionality.

Manager Worksheet for Calculating Earnings - Microsoft Internet Explorer

File   Edit   View   Favorites   Tools   Help

Back   Search   Favorites

Address   C:\My Documents\CNCEarnings.mht

Manager Worksheet for Calculating Earnings

	A	B	C	D	E	F	G
1	**Case 'N Crate**						
2	**Worksheet for Calculating Weekly Earnings**						
3							
4	**Sales Rep**	**Category**	**Total Sales**	**Commission Rate**	**Commission**	**Salary**	**Total Earnings**
5	McBride	1	$ 22,368	10.00%	$ 2,236.80	$ 200.00	$ 2,436.80
6	Bachman	2	$ 15,891	8.25%	$ 1,311.01	$ 200.00	$ 1,511.01
7	Malone	3	$ 25,024	10.75%	2,690.08	450.00	
8	Landis	2	$ 19,562	9.25%	$ 1,809.49	$ -	$ 1,809.49
9	Lalonde	4	$ 27,023	11.25%	$ 3,040.09	$ -	$ 3,040.09
10	Levinson	1	$ 30,251	12.00%	$ 3,630.12	$ 200.00	$ 3,830.12
11	Rainwater	3	$ 15,352	8.25%	$ 1,266.54	$ -	$ 1,266.54
12	Santiago	4	$ 23,054	10.25%	$ 2,363.04	$ -	$ 2,363.04

Sheet1

Done   My Computer

EXPERT

MICROSOFT®
EXCEL

Expert Level Unit 1: Advanced Formatting and Functions

➤ Formatting Excel Worksheets Using Advanced Formatting Techniques

➤ Working with Templates and Workbooks

➤ Using Advanced Functions

➤ Working with Lists

BENCHMARK MICROSOFT® EXCEL 2003

MICROSOFT OFFICE SPECIALIST
EXPERT SKILLS—UNIT 1

Reference No.	Skill	Pages
XL03E-1 Organizing and Analyzing Data		
XL03E-1-1	Use Subtotals	
	Adding subtotals to worksheet data	E151-E155
XL03E-1-2	Define and apply advanced filters	
	Creating and applying advanced filters	E159-E165
XL03E-1-3	Group and outline data	
	Grouping and outlining data	E147-151
XL03E-1-4	Use data validation	
	Adding data validation criteria to cells	E133-E139
XL03E-1-5	Create and modify list ranges	
	Creating and modifying list ranges	E165-E166
		E168-E170
XL03E-1-9	Use Lookup and Reference functions	
	Using Lookup and Reference functions	E113-E116
XL03E-1-10	Use Database functions	
	Creating and editing Database functions	E166-E170
XL03E-1-14	Define, modify and use named ranges	
	Naming one or more cell ranges	E112-E113
	Using a named range reference in a formula	E113
XL03E-2 Formatting Data and Content		
XL03E-2-1	Create and modify custom data formats	
	Creating and applying custom number formats	E9-E11
XL03E-2-2	Use conditional formatting	
	Using conditional formatting	E27-E28
XL03E-2-3	Format and resize graphics	
	Using cropping and rotating tools	E44-E47,
		E49-E51
	Controlling image contrast and brightness	E48-E51
	Scaling and resizing graphics	E47-E51
XL03E-2-4	Format charts and diagrams	
	Applying formats to charts and diagrams	E51-E55
XL03E-3 Collaborating		
XL03E-3-3	Share workbooks	
	Creating and modifying shared workbooks	E83-E89
XL03E-4 Managing Data and Workbooks		
XL03E-4-4	Create and edit templates	
	Creating a workbook template	E68-E70
	Creating a new workbook based upon a user-defined template	E71-E72
	Editing a workbook template	E71-E72
XL03E-4-5	Consolidate data	
	Consolidating data from two or more worksheets	E78-E80
XL03E-4-6	Define and modify workbook properties	
	Managing workbook properties	E72-E74
XL03E-5 Customizing Excel		
XL03E-5-3	Modify Excel default settings	
	Modifying default font settings	E19-E20
	Setting the default number of worksheets	E20
	Changing the default file location	E20

1

FORMATTING EXCEL WORKSHEETS USING ADVANCED FORMATTING TECHNIQUES

PERFORMANCE OBJECTIVES

Upon successful completion of Chapter 1, you will be able to:

➤ Apply accounting, fraction, and scientific formats
➤ Create and apply custom number formats
➤ Format large labels
➤ Automatically adjust column widths and row heights
➤ Create, apply, and edit styles
➤ Use the Format Painter
➤ Format a worksheet by adding borders and shading
➤ Turn off zeros
➤ Modify default font settings
➤ Set the default number of worksheets
➤ Change the default working folder
➤ Apply formatting to a worksheet using one of Excel's predesigned AutoFormats
➤ Create and use conditional formatting
➤ Adjust the layout of a worksheet
➤ Use the Paste Special command
➤ Hide and unhide rows, columns, and sheets
➤ Rename sheets
➤ Select colors for worksheet tabs
➤ Format large worksheets
➤ Format and resize graphics
➤ Apply formats to charts and diagrams

ChapterO1E
EXCEL

Excel includes many formatting features beyond the basic options found on the Formatting toolbar. Although worksheets are commonly used to manipulate financial data, they are also used in many other fields, including science and engineering.

Some of these specialized fields use Excel's more advanced formatting features, such as fraction and scientific number formats. In some cases, the numbering format that is needed for a particular worksheet may not be included as one of Excel's preset number formats, in which case a custom format can be created. In other cases, a particular format may be needed only in certain circumstances, in which case a conditional format can be created. An especially large worksheet can also present a formatting challenge as you try to fit the worksheet on as few pages as possible while making it easy to read and understand.

In this chapter you will learn many advanced formatting techniques that will help you manage not only the most complex or challenging worksheet but also the most basic worksheet. These techniques will help save you time and will help to make your worksheets as readable as possible.

Applying Number Formats

HINT

Three frequently used number formats, Currency, Comma, and Percent, are available as buttons on the Formatting toolbar.

In Excel there are 12 categories by which numbers can be formatted. These categories are found in the Format Cells dialog box, which is accessed either by clicking Format and then Cells or by right-clicking the cell to be formatted and then clicking Format Cells from the shortcut menu. Click the Number tab on the Format Cells dialog box, and all the available categories are displayed in the *Category* list box, as shown in Figure 1.1.

FIGURE

1.1 **Excel's Number Formats**

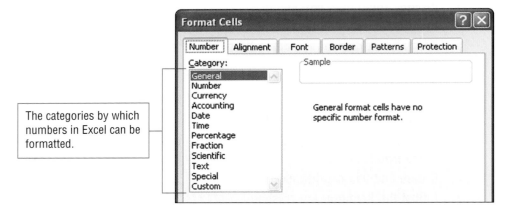

The categories by which numbers in Excel can be formatted.

The first three categories listed, General, Number, and Currency, are probably the three most frequently used categories. But some of the more specialized categories, such as Accounting, Fraction, and Scientific, are quite useful as well. The difference between the Currency and Accounting formats is that the Accounting format lines up the currency symbols and the Currency format does not. The Fraction format enables you to choose how fractions are displayed in the cells. The Scientific format is used for very large or very small numbers. Engineers and scientists often use the Scientific format, which is also called scientific notation. For example, the Andromeda galaxy (the closest one to our Milky Way galaxy) contains at least 200,000,000,000 stars. Scientists commonly work with such large numbers, so they must use an easier way to write them rather than entering

QUICK STEPS

Apply Number Format
1. Right-click cell(s) to be formatted.
2. Click Format Cells, then click the Number tab.
3. Choose a category.
4. Click OK.

all those zeros. If you entered the number 250,000,000,000, for example, and formatted it as Scientific, it would look like 2.5E+11 on the worksheet. The number after the *E* refers to how many places to the right you have to move the decimal point.

Creating Custom Formats

The last option in the *Category* list box on the Format Cells dialog box is *Custom*. This option allows you to create your own format. To create a custom format, first select the cells to which you want the format applied, right-click one of the selected cells, click Format Cells from the shortcut menu, and then click the Number tab. Click *Custom*, the last option in the *Category* list box. The *Type* box is displayed, as shown in Figure 1.2. The default data that is entered into the *Type* box depends on the current format of the selected cells.

HINT

A custom numeric format can have up to four parts: a positive number format, a negative number format, a format for zeros, and a format for text. Semicolons are used to separate the parts.

FIGURE

1.2 *The* Custom *Option from the* Category *List Box*

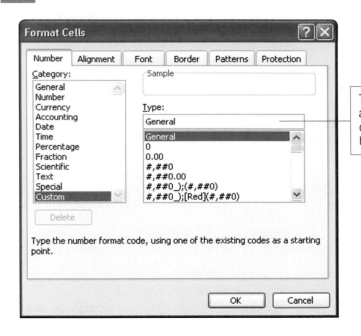

The *Type* box becomes available when the *Custom* option from the *Category* list box is selected.

To create a custom format, enter the desired format in the Type box. If you are entering text that you want to appear, you must enclose the text with quotation marks. For example, you want to create a custom format that uses the text *meters*. You would place the insertion point to the right of the last entry in the Type box, press the spacebar once, and then enter "meters" as shown in Figure 1.3.

QUICK STEPS

Create Custom Format
1. Right-click cell(s) to be formatted.
2. Click Format Cells, then click the Number tab.
3. Click the *Custom* option in the *Category* list box.
4. Enter the desired format in the *Type* list box.
5. Click OK.

1.3 *Creating a Custom Format in the* Type *Box*

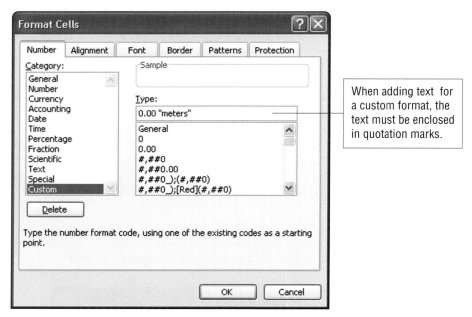

When adding text for a custom format, the text must be enclosed in quotation marks.

Numeric, date, and time formatting codes can be used when creating custom formats. These codes are listed in Table 1.1. As is shown in Figure 1.4, once you have created a custom format, it is added to the end of the *Type* list box so that you can use it again. If you want to delete a custom format that you have created, select the format you want to delete from the *Type* list box and then click the Delete button.

TABLE

1.1 *Numeric, Date, and Time Formatting Codes*

Code	Description
Numeric Formatting Codes	
#	Used to hold the place for a digit. Insignificant zeros are not displayed
0	Used to hold the place for a digit; zeros are displayed
?	Used to hold the place for a digit; insignificant zeros are represented by a space
.	Decimal point
,	Thousands separator
%	Percentage sign, entry is multiplied by 100
;	Used to separate positive number format from negative number format
_	Used to skip the width of the next character, for example, entering _) skips the width of the right parenthesis character
/	Used as a separator for fractions
"text"	Quotation marks are used to insert specified text
[color]	Braces are used to format entry as specified color
@	Used to hold the place where user-input text is to appear

Code	Description

Date Formatting Codes

m	Displays the month as a number (1, 2, 3, …10, 11, 12)
mm	Displays the month as a number with a leading zero (01, 02, 03…)
mmm	Displays the month as a three-letter abbreviation (Jan, Feb, Mar…)
mmmm	Displays the month as a complete name (January, February, March…)
d	Displays the day of the month as a number (2, 18, 29)
dd	Displays the day of the month as a number with a leading zero (01, 04, 08)
ddd	Displays the day of the week as a three-letter abbreviation (Mon, Tue, Wed)
dddd	Displays the day of the week as a complete name (Monday, Tuesday, Wednesday)
yy	Displays the year as a two-digit number (92, 94, 98)
yyyy	Displays the year as a complete number (1994, 1998, 2000)

Time Formatting Codes

h	Displays the hour as a number (1, 8, 10)
hh	Displays the hour as a number with a leading zero (03, 05, 08)
m	Displays the minutes as a number (5, 38, 46)
mm	Displays the minutes as a number with a leading zero (03, 06, 09)
s	Displays the seconds as a number (7, 34, 56)
ss	Displays the seconds as a number with a leading zero (03, 05, 08)
AM/PM	Displays either AM or PM to indicate AM or PM time
A/P	Displays either A or P to indicate AM or PM time

FIGURE

1.4 **Applying and Deleting a Custom Format**

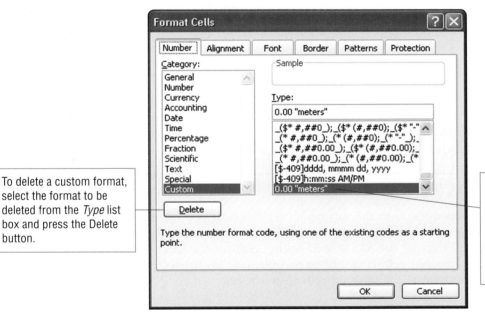

To delete a custom format, select the format to be deleted from the *Type* list box and press the Delete button.

When you create a custom format, it is added to the end of the *Type* list. To apply the format elsewhere in the worksheet, simply select the custom format from the *Type* list box.

Formatting Large Labels

Merge and Center

Labels are used as headings to identify the contents of a row or column. If a label on a worksheet is quite large, it may make the worksheet's format look awkward. For example, if the longest entry in a column is only 5 digits, but the label for that column is 50 characters, there will be a lot of wasted space, since the column has to be wide enough to accommodate the label.

HINT

If at a later time you wish to undo the effects of using the Merge and Center button, right-click the merged cell, click Format Cells, click the Alignment tab, click the *Merge cells* check box so that it is no longer selected, and click OK.

Large labels can be handled a couple of different ways in Excel. First, if the label does not have to be confined to one column, the Merge and Center button is useful for centering a label across several columns. To use the Merge and Center button, first enter the label and then select all the cells across which the label is to be centered. Next, click the Merge and Center button. All the cells that were selected are merged into one cell and the label is centered within that one cell. The Merge and Center button is useful, for example, for centering a label over an entire worksheet that is made up of many columns.

Large labels can be handled in several ways, which are found on the Alignment tab of the Format Cells dialog box, shown in Figure 1.5. To access these options, right-click the cell containing the label and then click Format Cells on the shortcut menu. On the Format Cells dialog box, click the Alignment tab.

FIGURE

1.5 *The Format Cell Dialog Box with Alignment Tab Selected*

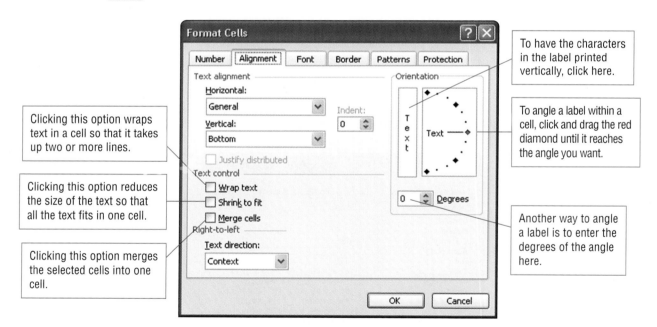

HINT

Adjust the column to the width you want it to be *before* issuing the command to Wrap Text.

The options in the *Text control* section help you manage large labels. Selecting the *Wrap text* option wraps the label within the cell so that it takes up two or more lines. Selecting the *Shrink to fit* option reduces the label as necessary to make it all fit within one cell. If two or more cells have been selected, selecting the *Merge cells* option merges the selected cells into one cell.

The *Orientation* section offers another way to handle large labels. By clicking and dragging the red diamond, you can angle the label within the cell. As you drag the red diamond, the degrees of the angle are displayed in the *Degrees* box. You can also just enter the degrees of the angle for the label in the *Degrees* box. If you want the text in the label to be printed vertically, with one character directly underneath another, click the third option in the *Orientation* section.

If in the *Orientation* section, you choose to have the labels displayed vertically, you should also make a selection from the *Vertical* drop-down list, in the *Text alignment* section. A vertical label can be placed within a cell at the top, in the center, at the bottom, or justified.

Automatically Adjusting Column Widths and Row Heights

The AutoFit option allows you to automatically adjust the width of one or more columns or the height of one or more rows to fit the longest or highest entry. To use this option to adjust the width of columns, first select all the columns to be adjusted. Click Format and then point to Column. Click AutoFit Selection on the Column submenu. The columns are automatically adjusted so that each column is wide enough to display the widest entry in that particular column. To use the AutoFit option to adjust the height of rows, first select all the rows to be adjusted. Click Format and then point to Row. Click Autofit on the Row submenu. The rows are automatically adjusted so that each row is high enough to display the highest entry in that row.

You can also automatically adjust the width of columns by double-clicking on the right column heading border. If you want to use this method to automatically adjust the width of several columns at one time, first select the columns and then double-click on the right heading border of any one of the selected columns. Each column is automatically adjusted to display the widest entry in that column. This method also works for automatically adjusting row heights. Simply double-click the bottom row heading border and the row will automatically adjust to display the highest entry in that row. To adjust the height of several rows at a time, select the rows to be adjusted and double-click the bottom row heading border of any one of the selected rows. Each row is automatically adjusted to display the highest entry in that row. If you want to specify an exact column width or row height, click either Format, Column, and Width or Format, Row, and Height and type the desired dimension in the dialog box that is displayed.

(Note: Before completing Exercise 1, copy to your disk the ExcelChapter01E subfolder from the Excel2003Expert folder on the CD that accompanies this textbook. Steps on how to copy a folder are presented on the inside of the back cover of this textbook. Do this every time you start a chapter's exercises.)

exercise

APPLYING SCIENTIFIC AND CUSTOM FORMATS, ADJUSTING COLUMN WIDTHS, AND FORMATTING LARGE LABELS

1. Open Excel.
2. Open **Excel Worksheet01**.
3. Save the file using the Save As command and name it **eec1x01**.
4. Create a custom header by completing the following steps:
   a. Click File and then click Page Setup.

b. Click the Header/Footer tab.

c. Click the Custom Header button.

d. Enter your name in the *Left section* text box.

e. Click the *Right section* text box to select it. Click the File name button. This will automatically insert the name of the file.

f. Click the OK button twice.

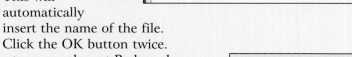

Step 4b

Step 4c

Step 4e

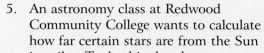

5. An astronomy class at Redwood Community College wants to calculate how far certain stars are from the Sun in miles. To do this they have to convert the distance measured in light-years into miles. The formula to accomplish this is the number of light-years multiplied by the speed of light times seconds in a minute, times minutes in an hour, times hours in a day, times days in a year. Type the following formula in cell C4:

$$=B4*186000*60*60*24*365.25$$

6. The number is too large to be displayed. Widen the column by completing these steps:
   a. Position the mouse pointer on the column boundary between columns C and D until it turns into a double-headed arrow pointing left and right.
   b. Double-click.

7. The number that is displayed is very large and would be more appropriately displayed in scientific notation. Change the format of this number to scientific notation by completing the following steps:
   a. Right-click cell C4.
   b. On the shortcut menu, click Format Cells.
   c. At the Format Cells dialog box, click the Number tab if necessary.
      1) Click *Scientific* in the *Category* list box.
      2) Click OK.

8. Copy the formula in cell C4 to cells C5 through C16 by completing the following steps:
   a. Select cell C4.
   b. Place the mouse pointer over the AutoFill fill handle in the lower right corner of cell C4. The mouse pointer should look like a plus sign.
   c. Double-click on the AutoFill fill handle in the lower right corner of cell C4.

9. Create the custom format *ly*, which stands for light-years, for the numbers in column B by completing the following steps:
   a. Select cells B4 through B16.
   b. Right-click one of the selected cells.
   c. On the shortcut menu, click Format Cells.
   d. On the Format Cells dialog box, click the Number tab if necessary.

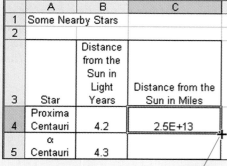

	A	B	C
1	Some Nearby Stars		
2			
3	Star	Distance from the Sun in Light Years	Distance from the Sun in Miles
4	Proxima Centauri	4.2	2.5E+13
5	α Centauri	4.3	

Step 8b

1) In the *Category* list box, click *Custom*.
2) In the *Type* box, click to the right of the last zero.
3) Press the spacebar once and then type "**ly**". Be sure to include both sets of quotation marks.
4) Click OK. The label *ly* now appears in cells B4 through B16.

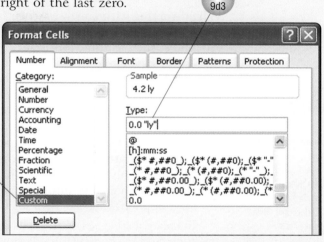

Step 9d3

Step 9d1

10. Create the custom format *miles* for the numbers in column C by completing the following steps:
   a. Select cells C4 through C16.
   b. Right-click one of the selected cells.
   c. At the shortcut menu, click Format Cells.
   d. At the Format Cells dialog box, click the Number tab if necessary.
      1) In the *Category* list box, click *Custom*.
      2) In the *Type* text box, click to the right of the last zero.
      3) Press the spacebar once and then type "**miles**". Be sure to include both sets of quotation marks.
      4) Click OK. The label *miles* now appears in cells C4 through C16.
11. Format the three column labels so that they are at an angle by completing the following steps:
   a. Select cells A3 through C3.
   b. Right-click one of the selected cells.
   c. At the shortcut menu, click Format Cells.
   d. Click the Alignment tab.
      1) Click and drag the red diamond in the *Orientation* section until 45 is displayed in the *Degrees* box.
      2) Click OK.

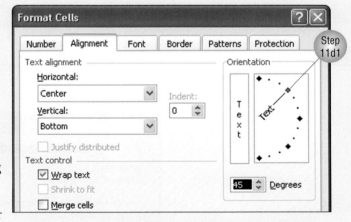

Step 11d1

12. Apply the Merge and Center command on cells A1 through D1 by completing the following steps:
   a. Select cells A1 through D1.
   b. Click the Merge and Center button.
13. Change the formatting of the title "Some Nearby Stars" by completing the following steps:
   a. Select cell A1 if necessary.
   b. Click the Bold button.
   c. Change the font size to 12.
14. Save the worksheet with the same name (**eec1x01**).
15. Print and then close **eec1x01**.

Creating, Applying, and Editing Styles

When working with large worksheets or a workbook that has many worksheets, it is a good idea to apply formatting using styles. A style is a predefined set of formatting attributes, such as font, font size, alignment, color, borders, and so on. In fact, all the options available from the Format Cells dialog box can be defined as part of a particular style. Once a style has been defined, that style can be applied to any cell in a worksheet. Applying formatting using styles has several advantages. First, styles help to assure that the formatting from one worksheet to another is consistent. Second, all the attributes for a particular style have to be defined one time only. If you decide to use the same formatting over and over, you do not have to keep redefining each attribute of the format. Third, if a change needs to be made to the style, you only have to make that change one time in the style's definition, and then that change is automatically reflected in all the cells to which the style has been applied, thus saving a lot of time.

To create a style, select the cells to which the style is to be applied. Click Format and then Style. The Style dialog box, as shown in Figure 1.6, is displayed. Each one of the check boxes on the Style dialog box corresponds to one of the tabs on the Format Cells dialog box. To create a new style, enter the name of the style in the *Style name* box. If any of the options listed in the Style dialog box are not going to be part of the style you are going to create, click in the check boxes next to those options so that they are no longer selected. Click the Modify button and the Format Cells dialog box appears. Make the selections you want for the style from the Format Cells dialog box and then click OK. The Style dialog box is displayed, and the attributes you selected will be listed. Click OK again, and the style will be applied to the selected cells. To apply the style to other cells, simply select those cells, click Format, and then click Style. Click the down-pointing arrow to the right of the *Style name* box and select the name of the style you want to apply from the drop-down list. Click OK and the style is applied to the selected cells. To delete a style, click the down-pointing arrow to the right of the *Style name* box, select the name of the style to be deleted, and then click the Delete button.

QUICK STEPS

Create and Apply a Style
1. Select cell(s) to which the style will be applied.
2. Click Format, Style.
3. Make the style selections.
4. Click OK.

HINT

The Normal style applies to all unformatted cells in the worksheet. If you modify the Normal style, all the unformatted cells in the worksheet will be changed to reflect whatever modification you make.

FIGURE

1.6 *The Style Dialog Box*

The options in the Style dialog box correspond to the tabs in the Format Cells dialog box.

Using the Format Painter Button

Format Painter

The Format Painter button allows you to copy the format of one or more cells and apply it to other cells in the worksheet. To use the Format Painter button, select the cell or cells with the formatting you want to copy. Click the Format Painter button on the Standard toolbar. The mouse pointer changes to a paintbrush next to a cross, as shown in Figure 1.7. Select the cells to which you want the copied formatting applied. Clicking the Format Painter button one time allows you to apply the copied formatting one time. If you double-click the Format Painter button, you can apply the copied formatting as many times as you want. When you have finished applying the copied formatting, click the Format Painter button again to turn the feature off.

> **HINT**
>
> When using the Format Painter, the target cell or cells (the cells to which the copied format is to be applied) can be in a different worksheet.

FIGURE

1.7 *Using the Format Painter Button*

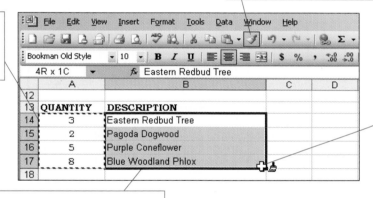

Step 2
Click the Format Painter button.

Step 1
Select the cells with the formatting you want to copy.

Step 3
The mouse pointer changes to the Format Painter symbol.

Step 4
Select the cells to which you want the copied formatting applied.

Applying Borders and Shading

Borders and shading can be applied to cells in a worksheet in three ways. You can use either a dialog box or a button on the toolbar, or you can draw them. To apply borders using a dialog box, select the cells to which you want to add borders, right-click one of the selected cells, click Format Cells on the shortcut menu, and then click the Border tab. You can make border selections from the dialog box shown in Figure 1.8. You can also apply shading to a cell from this dialog box.

You must select the line style and line color (found in the *Line* section of the dialog box) before selecting a border style (the buttons in the *Presets* and *Border* sections of the dialog box). Any line style or color you select after selecting the border style will not go into effect.

> **QUICK STEPS**
>
> **Apply Borders and Shading**
> 1. Select cell(s) to which the borders and/or shading will be applied.
> 2. Right-click a selected cell.
> 3. Click Format Cells, then click the Border tab.
> 4. Make the border and/or shading selections.
> 5. Click OK.

1.8 Applying Borders and Shading Using the Dialog Box

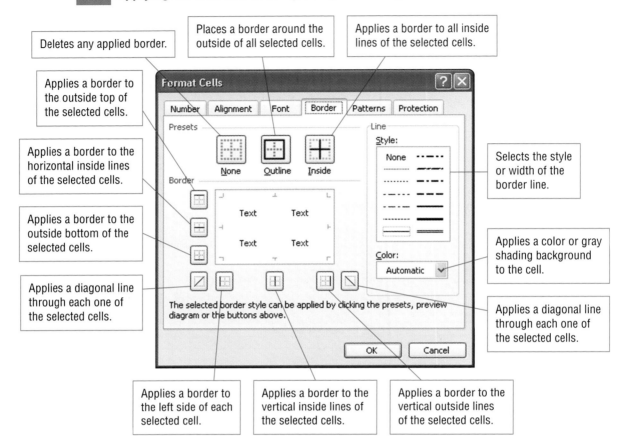

Deletes any applied border.

Places a border around the outside of all selected cells.

Applies a border to all inside lines of the selected cells.

Applies a border to the outside top of the selected cells.

Applies a border to the horizontal inside lines of the selected cells.

Applies a border to the outside bottom of the selected cells.

Applies a diagonal line through each one of the selected cells.

Selects the style or width of the border line.

Applies a color or gray shading background to the cell.

Applies a diagonal line through each one of the selected cells.

Applies a border to the left side of each selected cell.

Applies a border to the vertical inside lines of the selected cells.

Applies a border to the vertical outside lines of the selected cells.

HINT

Border colors other than black are most effective with thicker lines.

To apply borders using the toolbar, click the down-pointing arrow to the right of the Borders button on the Formatting toolbar and the border options shown in Figure 1.9 are displayed. Click the button that represents the border style you want. The last selected border style becomes the default for the button on the toolbar. To apply the style that appears on the button on the toolbar, simply click the button. You can click and drag on the menu options blue title bar, and the menu will become a floating palette that you can place anywhere on the worksheet. The palette will be displayed until you click the close button in the upper right corner of the palette.

1.9 Applying Borders Using the Toolbar

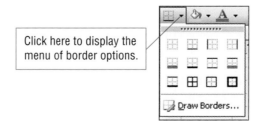

Click here to display the menu of border options.

To create a cell border by drawing it, click the Draw Borders option at the bottom of the Borders drop-down menu. The mouse pointer changes to the shape of a pencil. Any cell you "draw" around will have a border.

To apply shading using the toolbar, click the down-pointing arrow to the right of the Fill Color button on the Formatting toolbar and the options shown in Figure 1.10 are displayed. Click the option that represents the shading you want to apply. The last selected color becomes the default for the button on the toolbar. To apply the color that appears on the button on the toolbar, simply click the button. As with the borders menu, you can click and drag on the menu options blue title bar, and the menu will become a floating palette that remains on the worksheet until you click the Close button in the upper right corner of the window.

FIGURE

1.10 *Applying Shading Using the Toolbar*

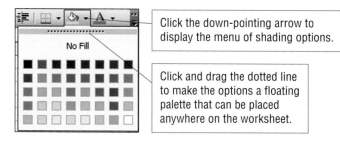

Click the down-pointing arrow to display the menu of shading options.

Click and drag the dotted line to make the options a floating palette that can be placed anywhere on the worksheet.

Turning Off Zeros

If a formula is entered into a cell and the cells being referenced by the formula are empty, a zero will be placed in the cell. In some situations, you may not want this zero to be displayed. To turn off zeros in a worksheet, click Tools and then Options. From the Options dialog box that appears, click the View tab. In the *Window options* section, there is a check box for *Zero values*. If you do not want zeros to be displayed in a worksheet, this check box should be empty. Click the check box so that it is not selected and then click OK.

Another way to hide zeros is to select the range of cells where you do not want zeros to be displayed, right-click the selected cells, click Format Cells from the shortcut menu, click the Number tab, click Custom in the *Category* list box, and type # in the *Type* box. Click OK.

Turn Off Zeros
1. Click Tools, Options.
2. Click the View tab.
3. Click the *Zero values* check box so it is not selected.
4. Click OK.

Modifying Default Font Settings

The default font setting in Excel is Arial, size 10. To change this default setting, click Tools and then Options. From the Options dialog box that appears, click the General tab. As shown in Figure 1.11, the two drop-down lists next to the *Standard font* option allow you to change the default font and font size. Once you click OK, the warning box appears letting you know that you must exit and then restart Microsoft Excel in order for the changes to the standard font to take effect. Click OK. Exit Excel and then restart it and the changes you made to the font settings will take effect.

Modify Default Font Setting
1. Click Tools, Options.
2. Click the General Tab.
3. Make the necessary changes to the *Standard font* options.
4. Click OK.

1.11 *Modifying Default Font Settings*

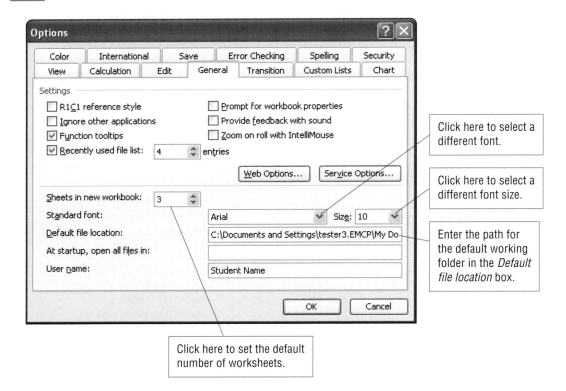

Click here to select a different font.

Click here to select a different font size.

Enter the path for the default working folder in the *Default file location* box.

Click here to set the default number of worksheets.

QUICK STEPS

Set Default Number of Worksheets
1. Click Tools, Options.
2. Click the General Tab.
3. Set the number of worksheets using the *Sheets in new workbook* option.
4. Click OK.

Setting the Default Number of Worksheets

When a workbook is opened, the default setting for the number of worksheets within the workbook is three. This default setting can be changed by clicking Tools and then Options. Click the General tab on the Options dialog box that appears. As shown in Figure 1.11, the *Sheets in new workbook* option allows you to set the default number of worksheets in a workbook.

Changing the Default Working Folder

Often the default location for opening and saving Excel files is in the My Documents folder on the C drive. You may want to store your files elsewhere. To change the default working folder, click Options from the Tools menu. Click the General tab. Refer to Figure 1.11 to locate the *Default file location* option. Enter the path for the folder you want Excel to go to automatically when opening a file and to save to automatically when saving a file.

exercise 2

1. Open **ExcelWorksheet02**.
2. Save the file using the Save As command and name it **eec1x02**.
3. Create a custom header that has your name left-aligned and the name of the file right-aligned.
4. This worksheet is an invoice used by Greenspace Architects. Greenspace Architects is a nursery that sells plants and flowers and provides landscaping services. The invoice needs to be formatted. Add some lines for filling in the information at the top of the invoice by completing the following steps:

   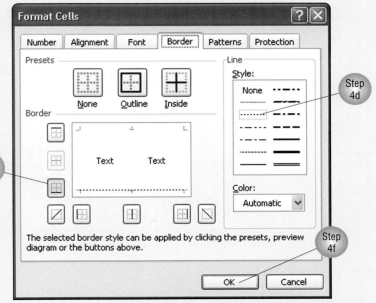

   a. Select cells B3 through E3 and right-click one of the selected cells.
   b. Click Format Cells on the shortcut menu.
   c. Click the Border tab on the Format Cells dialog box.
   d. Click the third option in the first column in the *Style* list box.
   e. Click the button to apply a border to the bottom of the cell.
   f. Click OK.
5. Use the Format Painter button to apply the border to the other cells where it is needed at the top of the invoice by completing the following steps:
   a. Select cell B3.
   b. Double-click the Format Painter button.
   c. Select cell G2.
   d. Select cells B4 through E4.
   e. Select cells B5 through C5.
   f. Select cells B6 through C6.
   g. Select cell E5.
   h. Select cells G5 through G6.
   i. Select cells E8 through F10.
   j. Click the Format Painter button to turn it off.
6. The cells next to the labels MC (for MasterCard), V (for Visa), and AX (for American Express) are supposed to be check boxes. Place a border around these cells by completing the following steps:
   a. Right-click cell C8.
   b. Click Format Cells on the shortcut menu.
   c. If necessary, click the Border tab on the Format Cells dialog box.

d. Click the second option in the first column in the *Style* box.

e. In the *Presets* section, click the Outline button.

f. Click OK.

g. Double-click the Format Painter button.

h. Select cells C9 through C11.

i. Click the Format Painter button to turn it off.

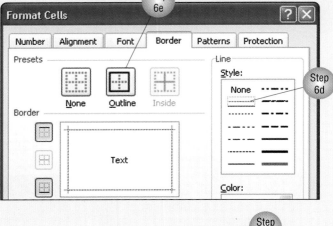

7. Place borders around the ordering information to make it easier to read by completing the following steps:

a. Select cells A14 through A27.

b. Click the down-pointing arrow to the right of the Borders button.

c. Click the Outside Borders button, the third button from the left in the last row.

d. Each block of cells that is to be outlined by the border has to be selected separately. Select cells B14 through E27, hold down the Ctrl key, and select cells F14 through F27, cells G14 through G27, G28 through G30, and G31 and then release the Ctrl key. The Outside Borders button is now the active Border button on the Formatting toolbar. Click the Borders button to apply the outside borders format.

8. Create a style called Label 1 to be used on some of the labels on the invoice by completing the following steps:

a. Select cell A3.

b. Click Format and then Style.

c. Change the name in the *Style name* box to *Label 1*.

d. Click the *Number* check box so that there is no longer a check mark in it.

e. Click the Modify button.

f. Click the Alignment tab and from the *Horizontal* drop-down list, select *Right (Indent)*.

g. Click the Font tab and then in the *Font Style* list box click *Bold*.

h. Click the down-pointing arrow to the right of the *Color* option box and click Green, the fourth button from the left in the second row.

i. Click the OK button twice.

9. Apply the Label 1 style to the invoice by completing the following steps:

a. Select cells A4 through A6, hold down the Ctrl key, select the following cells, and then release the Ctrl key: D5, F5, F6, B8, B9, B10, B11, D8, D9, D10, F28, F29, F30.

b. Click Format and then Style.

c. Click the down-pointing arrow to the right of the *Style name* box and select *Label 1*.

d. Click OK.

10. You want to create another style that is similar to the Label 1 style. The easiest way to do this is to start by selecting a cell that uses the Label 1 style. Many of the options you want for the new style will automatically be selected. Create a style called Label 2 by completing the following steps:

a. Select cell A3.

b. Click Format and then Style.

c. Change the name in the *Style name* box to *Label 2*.

    d.   Click the *Number* check box so that there is no longer a check mark in it.

    e.   Click the Modify button.

    f.   Click the Alignment tab and from the *Horizontal* drop-down list, select *Center*.

    g.   Click the OK button twice.

    h.   Change the style of cell A3 back to Label 1 by clicking Format and then Style, and then selecting *Label 1* from the *Style name* list box.

    i.   Click OK.

11. Apply the Label 2 style to the invoice by completing the following steps:

    a.   Select cells A13 through G13.

    b.   Click Format and then Style.

    c.   Click the down-pointing arrow to the right of the *Style name* box and click *Label 2*.

    d.   Click OK.

12. Create a style called Label 3 to be used on some of the labels on the invoice by completing the following steps:

    a.   Select cell E2.

    b.   Click Format and then Style.

    c.   Change the name in the *Style name* box to *Label 3*.

    d.   Click the *Number* check box so that there is no longer a check mark in it.

    e.   Click the Modify button.

    f.   Click the Alignment tab and from the *Horizontal* drop-down list, select *Right (Indent)*.

    g.   Click the Font tab.

        1) From the *Font style* list box, select *Bold*.

        2) From the *Size* list box, select *12*.

        3) Click the down-pointing arrow to the right of the *Color* box and select White, the last option in the fifth row.

    h.   Click the Patterns tab and select the green color that is the fourth option from the left in the second row.

    i.   Click the OK button twice.

13. Apply the Label 3 style to cell F31 by selecting cell F31, clicking Format and then Style, selecting *Label 3* from the *Style name* list box and then clicking OK.

14. You decide that the font size for the style Label 1 is too large and you want to change it. Edit the Label 1 style by completing the following steps:

    a.   Select cell A3.

    b.   Click Format and then Style. Make sure that *Label 1* is in the *Style name* box.

    c.   Click the Modify button.

    d.   Click the Font tab.

    e.   From the *Size* list box, select *9*.

    f.   Click the OK button twice.

15. You are going to format the numbers on the invoice so that they are displayed as prices by creating a custom format for the Number format. You want to include one space to the right of any entry formatted as Number. Complete the following steps:

    a.   Select cells F14 through F27.

    b.   Right-click one of the selected cells.

    c.   Select Format Cells on the shortcut menu.

    d.   Click the Number tab.

        1) You want your custom format to be based on the Number format, so first select *Number* from the *Category* list box and then select *Custom*.

2) The *Type* box displays
   0.00. You want to
   include a space equal to
   the size of the right
   parenthesis character to
   the right of the entry.
   The symbol for
   inserting this space is
   _). Place the insertion
   point to the right of the
   last zero in the *Type* box
   and press the underline
   key and then the right
   parenthesis key.

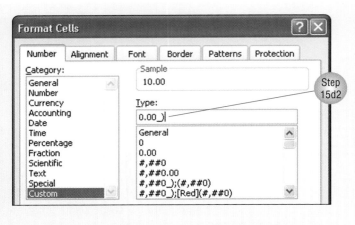

Step 15d2

e. Click OK.
f. Select cells G14 through G31. Right-click one of the selected cells. Click Format cells. Select *Custom* from the *Category* list box. Scroll to the bottom of the *Type* list box. Click on the last entry in the list, which is the custom format you just created. Click OK.

16. You want the first value in a list to be displayed with a dollar sign in front of it. Apply the Accounting format to these cells by completing the following steps:
   a. Select cell F14, hold down the Ctrl key, and select cells G14, G28, and G31.
   b. Right-click one of the selected cells.
   c. Select Format Cells on the shortcut menu.
   d. Click the Number tab and select *Accounting* from the *Category* list box. Make sure *2* is displayed in the *Decimal places* box and a dollar sign is displayed in the Symbol box. If necessary, click the down-pointing arrow to the right of the *Symbol* box and select the dollar sign.
   e. Click OK.

17. The formulas in some of the cells in column G do not have any corresponding data for making the calculations, so zeros are displayed. Turn off these zeros by completing the following steps:
   a. Click Tools and then Options.
   b. Click the View tab.
   c. Click the *Zero values* check box so that there is no longer a check mark in it.
   d. Click OK.

Step 18b

18. You want to make the prices in the *Amount* column stand out by adding some shading. Complete the following steps:
   a. Select cells G14 through G31.
   b. Click the down-pointing arrow next to the Fill color button on the Formatting toolbar.
   c. Click the palest green color, the fourth option from the left in the last row.

Step 18c

19. Make sure that none of the outside borders you set in Step 7 have been lost. There should be an outside border around the following cells: A14:A27, B14:E27, F14:F27, G14:G27, G28:G30, and G31. Reset any missing borders.

20. Save the worksheet with the same name (**eec1x02**).

21. Print and then close **eec1x02**.

EXCEL

exercise 3

1. Open a new Excel worksheet.
2. Create a custom header that has your name left-aligned and the name of the file, **eec1x03**, right-aligned.
3. Change the default working folder by completing the following steps:
   a. Click Tools and then Options.
   b. Click the General tab.
   c. On a piece of paper, write down the path location currently in the *Default file location* box. At the end of the exercise you will change the path back to this current entry.
   d. Highlight the current contents of the *Default file location* box to select it.
   e. If your student data disk is in drive A, type: A:\. If it is not in drive A, type whatever the path is to your student data disk, and then click OK.
4. Change the default font setting by completing the following steps:
   a. Click Tools and then Options.
   b. Click the General tab.
   c. Use the drop-down lists next to the *Standard font* option to change the font to Times New Roman and the font size to 12.
5. With the Options dialog box still open, set the default number of worksheets by completing the following steps:
   a. Select the current entry for the *Sheets in new workbook* option and type 1.
   b. Click OK.
   c. A warning box opens saying you have to quit and restart Excel for the font to take effect. Click OK.

6. Save and then exit Excel.
7. Restart Excel. Notice that the column letters and row numbers are now Times New Roman 12. Also notice there is only one worksheet in the workbook.
8. Enter the following data into the worksheet:

Cell	Data	Cell	Data
A1	Greenspace Architects	B5	4.95
A2	Perennial Plants	C5	3
A4	Plant	D5	=B5*C5
B4	Unit Price	A6	Chinese Foxglove
C4	Quantity	B6	4.25
D4	Total	C6	6
A5	Branched Coneflower		

9. Copy the formula in D5 to D6.
10. Widen the column A by completing the following steps:

a. Position the mouse pointer on the column boundary between columns A and B until it turns into a double-headed arrow pointing left and right and then double-click.

11. Bold and center the labels in cells A4 through D4.

12. Save the worksheet using the name **eec1x03**.

13. Print and then close **eec1x03**.

14. Open a new workbook. Change the default settings back to what they were by completing the following steps:

   a. Click Tools and then Options.

   b. Click the General tab.

   c. Referring to the path name you wrote down for Step 3c, highlight the entry in the *Default File location* box to select it, and type the original default file location path.

   d. Use the drop-down lists next to the *Standard font* option to change the font to Arial and the font size to 10.

   e. Select the current entry for the *Sheets in new workbook* option and type 3.

   f. Click OK.

   g. A warning box opens saying you have to quit and restart Excel for the font to take effect. Click OK.

15. Exit Excel.

QUICK STEPS

Using AutoFormat

Use AutoFormat
1. Select cells to be formatted.
2. Click Format, AutoFormat.
3. Select a format.
4. Click OK.

Excel includes many predesigned formats that can easily be applied to a worksheet. To use a predesigned format, select the cells to which the format is to be applied. Click Format and then AutoFormat. The AutoFormat dialog box is shown in Figure 1.12. A preview of what each format looks like is displayed. To select a format, click its preview. Seventeen different predesigned formats are available. Use the scroll bar to see more of the formats.

FIGURE

1.12 **The AutoFormat Dialog Box**

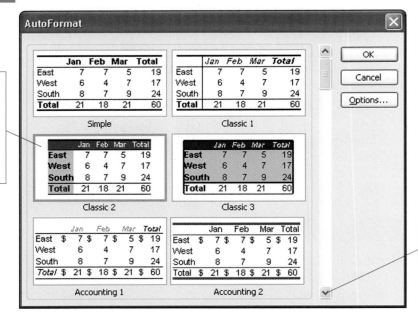

To select a format, click on its preview. To select the Classic 2 format, for example, click here.

Click here to see more formats.

Using Conditional Formatting

There may be times when you want to format cells in a particular way only if they meet a specific condition. For example, you may want to be alerted if sales figures dip below a specific number and therefore want only those entries to be displayed in red. Conditional formatting allows you to specify how cells that meet a specific condition should be formatted. To use conditional formatting, first select the cells to which the formatting should apply. Click Format and then Conditional Formatting. The Conditional Formatting dialog box, as shown in Figure 1.13, is displayed.

Use Conditional Formatting
1. Select cells to be formatted.
2. Click Format, Conditional Formatting.
3. Set the conditions by which the cells should be formatted.
4. Click OK.

FIGURE

1.13 *The Conditional Formatting Dialog Box*

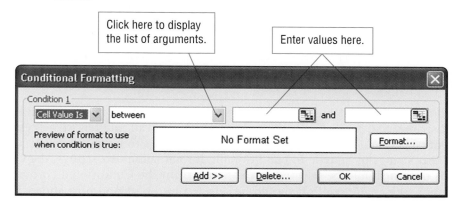

The default entry for the first box is *Cell Value Is*. This is the option you will want in most cases, particularly if the formula in the cell results in a value. If, however, the formula in the cell produces a result such as true or false, you would want to click the down-pointing arrow at the right side of the first box and select the *Formula Is* option. The second box enables you to select the argument. Click the down-pointing arrow at the right side of the box to see the list of arguments, which includes *between, not between, equal to, not equal to, greater than, less than, greater than or equal to*, and *less than or equal to*. In the remaining box or boxes you enter a constant value or formula if the *Cell Value Is* option is selected. If a formula is entered, it must begin with an equal sign. If the *Formula Is* option is selected, enter a formula that evaluates to a logical value of true or false.

To set the formatting for the cells that meet the condition you have defined, click the Format button. The Format Cells dialog box appears. Using this dialog box you can set options for Font style, Underline, Color, Strikethrough, Border, and Patterns. Once you click the OK button on the Format Cells dialog box, the Conditional Formatting dialog box appears again. A preview of what the entries in the cells that meet the condition will look like is displayed in the box called *Preview of format to use when condition is true*. If you want to set up a second condition, click the Add button. The dialog box expands to include a section for defining the second condition, as shown in Figure 1.14. You can define formatting for up to three conditions.

HINT

When using conditional formatting, the Number, Alignment, and Protection tabs are not available on the Format Cells dialog box. The options from these tabs cannot be changed using conditional formatting.

1.14 *Adding a Second Condition for Conditional Formatting*

A preview of what the formatting will look like in cells where the condition is true is displayed here.

When you click the Add button, a section for defining another condition is displayed.

Conditional Formatting

Condition 1

Cell Value Is ▾ | less than ▾ | 5000

Preview of format to use when condition is true: AaBbCcYyZz   Format...

Condition 2

Cell Value Is ▾ | between ▾ | and

Preview of format to use when condition is true: No Format Set   Format...

Add >>   Delete...   OK   Cancel

To add another condition, click the Add button.

To delete a condition, click the Delete button.

Use conditional formatting sparingly. If most of the cells in a worksheet use conditional formatting, nothing will really stand out and catch your eye.

Conditional formatting can also be used for formatting nonnumeric data, such as text strings. Say, for example, the words "Pass" and "Fail" are text strings entered in a worksheet, and you want all the "Pass" text strings to be green and all the "Fail" text strings to be red. To conditionally format these text strings, the *Cell Value Is* option should be selected in the first box on the Conditional Formatting dialog box, the *equal to* option should be selected in the second box, and either **Pass** or **Fail** should be entered in the third box.

To delete a condition, click the Delete button. The Delete Conditional Format dialog box shown in Figure 1.15 is displayed. Simply select the condition you want to delete and click OK.

1.15 *The Delete Conditional Format Dialog Box*

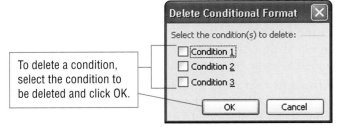

To delete a condition, select the condition to be deleted and click OK.

Delete Conditional Format

Select the condition(s) to delete:

☐ Condition 1
☐ Condition 2
☐ Condition 3

OK   Cancel

The distance entered in the *Header* and *Footer* boxes must be less than the distance entered in the *Top* and *Bottom* margin boxes or else the data in the worksheet will overlap the header or footer when the worksheet is printed.

Adjusting the Layout of a Worksheet

To have a worksheet print on one page, adjustments to the layout of the worksheet are often necessary. You can do several things to adjust the layout of a worksheet to have it print on one page. First, you can make the margins smaller by clicking File and then Page Setup. On the Page Setup dialog box, click the Margins tab. As shown in Figure 1.16, there is a box for the Top, Bottom, Left, and Right margins.

To change the margins, you can either select the current entry and enter a new margin setting, or click the up- or down-pointing arrow to the right of the box to make the margin larger or smaller. You can also adjust the distance of the header from the top of the page and the footer from the bottom of the page. In the *Center on page* section, you can select the *Horizontally* check box to have the worksheet centered horizontally on the page or the *Vertically* check box to have the worksheet centered vertically on the page.

QUICK STEPS

Set Worksheet Margins
1. Click File, Page Setup.
2. Click the Margins tab.
3. Set the desired margins.
4. Click OK.

FIGURE

1.16 *The Page Setup Dialog Box with Margins Tab Selected*

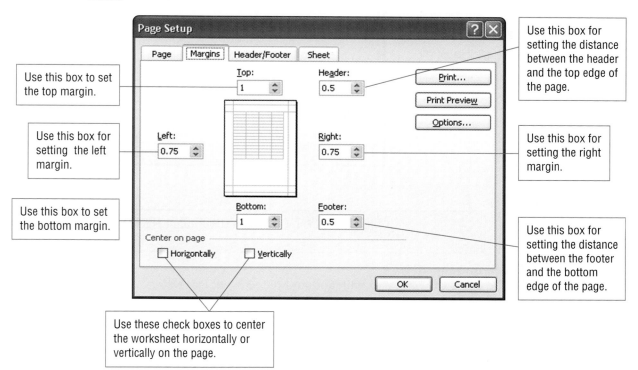

Use this box to set the top margin.

Use this box for setting the left margin.

Use this box to set the bottom margin.

Use this box for setting the distance between the header and the top edge of the page.

Use this box for setting the right margin.

Use this box for setting the distance between the footer and the bottom edge of the page.

Use these check boxes to center the worksheet horizontally or vertically on the page.

In many cases, worksheets are wider than they are long and would be more appropriately printed in landscape rather than portrait. With portrait orientation, the narrowest edge of the page is at the top. With landscape orientation, the widest edge of the page is at the top. To change the orientation of the page, click File and then Page Setup. On the Page Setup dialog box, click the Page tab. As shown in Figure 1.17, the options for *Portrait* and *Landscape* orientation are on this tab. You can also scale the size of the worksheet. To reduce the worksheet size by a specific percentage of its full size, either select the current entry in the *Adjust to* box and enter a new scaling percentage, or click the up- or down-pointing arrow to the right of the *Adjust to* box to increase or reduce the scaling percentage. Use the *Fit to* option to fit the worksheet onto a specified number of pages.

QUICK STEPS

Set Worksheet Orientation and Scaling
1. Click File, Page Setup.
2. Click the Page tab.
3. Select either *Portrait* or *Landscape*.
4. Make necessary scaling adjustments.
5. Click OK.

FIGURE

1.17 *The Page Setup Dialog Box with Page Tab Selected*

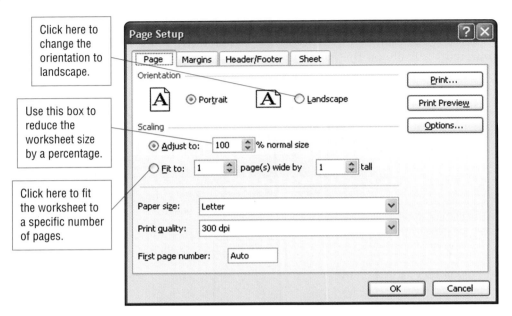

Click here to change the orientation to landscape.

HINT

Column widths, row heights, page margins, and page breaks determine the number of columns and rows that print on a page. Another way to adjust exactly what data fits on a printed page is to adjust the settings for these options.

Use this box to reduce the worksheet size by a percentage.

Click here to fit the worksheet to a specific number of pages.

exercise 4

USING AUTOFORMAT, CREATING A CONDITIONAL FORMAT, AND ADJUSTING THE LAYOUT OF THE WORKSHEET

1. Open **ExcelWorksheet04**.
2. Save the file using the Save As command and name it **eec1x04**.
3. Create a custom header that has your name left-aligned and the name of the file right-aligned.
4. Copper Clad Incorporated is a manufacturing company that designs and manufactures printed circuit boards. The company has a sales force of 12 sales representatives who are responsible for selling their printed circuit boards across the United States. This worksheet records each sales representative's sales for each month in the year 2004. Format the worksheet using AutoFormat by completing the following steps:
   a. Select cells A5 through N18 by completing the following steps:
      1) Click cell A5 to select it.
      2) Move the mouse pointer to the bottom edge of cell A5. The mouse pointer should turn into an arrow, with a four-headed arrow attached.
      3) Press the Shift key. While holding down the Shift key, double-click the bottom edge of cell A5. Cells A5 through A18 should be selected.
      4) Move the mouse pointer to the right edge of the selected cells. The mouse pointer should turn into an arrow, with a four-headed arrow attached.
      5) Press the Shift key. While holding down the Shift key, double-click the right edge of the selected cells. Cells A5 through N18 should now be selected.
   b. Click Format and then AutoFormat.

c. Select the Accounting 2 style.
d. Click OK.

5. This worksheet would be more useful if you could tell at a glance when sales figures were over or under a certain amount. If a sales representative's sales figures in a month are over $35,000, you want the entry to be displayed in green. If a

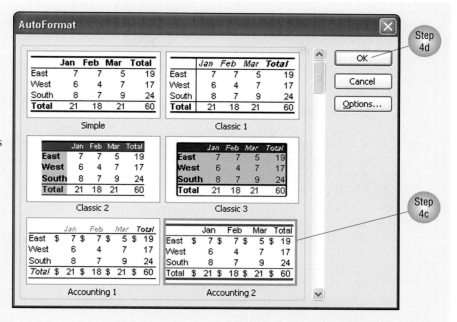

sales representative's sales figures in a month are under $8,000, you want the entry to be displayed in red. Format the worksheet using conditional formatting by completing the following steps:

a. Select cells B6 through M17.
b. Click Format and then Conditional Formatting.
c. Click the down-pointing arrow to the right of the second box in the Conditional Formatting dialog box and select *greater than*.
d. Type **35000** in the third box.
e. Click the Format button.
f. If necessary, click the Font tab.
   1) Click *Bold* in the *Font style* list box.
   2) Click the down-pointing arrow at the right side of the *Color* box.
   3) Click the Sea Green color, the fourth color from the left in the third row.
   4) Click OK. In the *Preview of format to use when condition is true* box, the letters should be green.
g. Click the Add button.

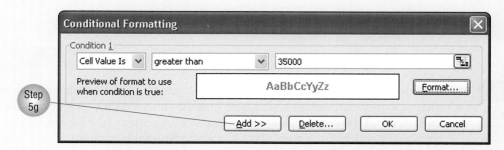

h. Under Condition 2, click the down-pointing arrow to the right of the second box in the Conditional Formatting dialog box and select *less than*.
i. Type **8000** in the third box.

j.   Click the Format button.
k.   If necessary, click the Font tab.
  1) Click *Bold* in the *Font style* list box.
  2) Click the down-pointing arrow at the right side of the *Color* box.
  3) Click the Red color, the first color in the third row.
  4) Click OK. In the *Preview of format to use when condition is true* box, the letters should be red.
l.   Click OK.
6.   As it is currently formatted, the worksheet will not fit on one page. Complete the following steps to adjust the worksheet so that it will fit onto one page:
a.   Click File and then Page Setup.
b.   Click the Page tab if necessary.
c.   Click the *Landscape* option.
d.   Click the Margins tab.
  1) Select the current setting in the *Top* text box and enter .75 and then press Tab.
  2) Type .5 in the *Bottom* text box, and the press Tab.
  3) Type .5 in the *Left* text box, and the press the Tab.
  4) Type .5 in the *Right* text box, and then click OK.
e.   Click the Print Preview button. The worksheet still will not fit on one page.
f.   Click the Close button.
g.   To save room, you do not want any decimal places displayed. Select cells B6 through N18. Click the Decrease Decimal button twice.
h.   You want to automatically adjust the widths of the columns now that the numbers in the cells are not as wide. With cells B6 through N18 still selected, click Format, point to Column, and then click AutoFit Selection.
i.   Click the Print Preview button. The worksheet still does not fit on one page, but it is getting close. Click the Close button.
j.   Click File and then Page Setup.
k.   Click the Page tab if necessary.
l.   In the *Scaling* section, click the *Fit to* option. The *page(s) wide by* box and *tall* box should both display *1*.
m.   Click OK.
7.   Save the worksheet with the same name (**eec1x04**).
8.   Print and then close **eec1x04**.

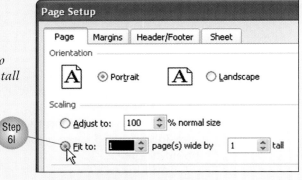

Step 6l

Using the Paste Special Command

When you use the Paste command, the entire contents of the cell or cells, including formulas and formats, are pasted. There may be times when you want to copy the contents of a cell, but you do not want to paste its format or you want to paste just the values and not the formulas. The Paste Special command allows you to do this. To access the Paste Special command, you first have to copy some cells and then click Edit and Paste Special. Or, after copying some cells, you can click the down-pointing arrow next to the Paste button and click Paste Special. The Paste Special dialog box, as shown in Figure 1.18, is displayed.

EXCEL

1.18 *The Paste Special Dialog Box*

The Paste Special dialog box provides options for many unique pasting situations. Table 1.2 describes all the options on the Paste Special dialog box. All the options in the *Paste* section relate to what is going to be pasted. All the options in the *Operation* section relate to how the copied cells are to be combined with the cells to which they are being copied. The copied cells could, for example, be added to the cells into which they are pasted. As shown in Figure 1.19, some of the options in the Paste Special dialog box are included on the drop-down menu that is displayed when you click the down-pointing arrow next to the Paste button.

F I G U R E

1.19 *Paste Button Drop-Down Menu*

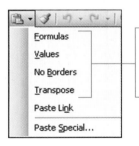

Some of the options that appear in the drop-down menu for the paste button are the same options found in the Paste Special dialog box.

T A B L E

1.2 *Paste Special Dialog Box Options*

Option	Description
Paste	
All	Pastes the cell's contents and formatting attributes
Formulas	Pastes only formulas; does not paste formatting attributes

Continued on next page

Option	Description
Values	Pastes values and formula results; does not paste formulas
Formats	Pastes formats only; does not paste formulas, values, or formatting attributes
Comments	Pastes comment notes only
Validation	Pastes data validation criteria only
All except borders	Pastes the cell's contents and all formatting attributes except borders
Column widths	Pastes the column widths only; does not paste formulas, values, or formatting attributes
Formulas and number formats	Pastes only formulas and all number formatting options from the selected cells
Values and number formats	Pastes only values and all number formatting options from the selected cells

Operation

None	The contents of the copied cells replace the contents of the cells into which they are being pasted.
Add	The contents of the copied cells are added to the contents of the cells into which they are being pasted.
Subtract	The contents of the copied cells are subtracted from the contents of the cells into which they are being pasted.
Multiply	The contents of the copied cells are multiplied by the contents of the cells into which they are being pasted.
Divide	The cells into which the copied cells are being pasted are divided by the copied cells.
Skip blanks	Any blank cells that are copied will not replace the contents of the cells into which they are pasted.
Transpose	The contents of rows are formatted into columns and the contents of columns are formatted into rows.

Hiding and Unhiding Rows, Columns, and Sheets

HINT

Another way to hide a row is by dragging the bottom border of the row heading to the top border of the row heading. A column can be hidden by dragging the right border of the column heading to the left border of the column heading.

At times you may not want certain columns displayed. Say, for example, you have a worksheet open that contains confidential payroll information. You could hide specific columns so that the confidential information would not be visible to anyone passing by your computer. To hide a column or columns, first select the columns to be hidden. Click Format, point to Column, and then click Hide. The columns are then hidden. You can tell if a column is hidden because its column header will not be displayed. If you hid column F, the column headers displayed at the top of the worksheet would be D, E, G, H, and so on. To unhide a hidden column, select the column to the left and the column to the right of the hidden column. Click Format, select Column, and then click Unhide.

The process for hiding and unhiding rows is the same as for columns. First select the row or rows to be hidden. Click Format, select Row, and then click Hide. The rows are then hidden. You can tell if a row is hidden because its row header will not be displayed. To unhide a hidden row, select the row above and the row below the hidden row. Click Format, select Row, and then click Unhide.

To hide a sheet, click the tab for that sheet so that it is displayed. Click Format, select Sheet, and then click Hide. The sheet is hidden and its tab is no longer displayed. To unhide a hidden sheet, click Format, select Sheet, and then click Unhide. The Unhide dialog box shown in Figure 1.20 is displayed. Select the sheet to be unhidden and click OK.

Hide a Row or Column
1. Select the column(s) or row(s) to be hidden.
2. Click Format.
3. Click either Column or Row.
4. Click Hide.

FIGURE

1.20 *The Unhide Dialog Box*

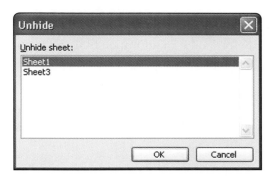

If a row or column is hidden, it will not print.

Hide a Sheet
1. Click the sheet tab.
2. Click Format, Sheet, Hide.

exercise 5

USING THE PASTE SPECIAL DIALOG BOX AND HIDING AND UNHIDING COLUMNS

1. Open **ExcelWorksheet05**.
2. Save the file using the Save As command and name it **eec1x05**.
3. Create a custom header that has your name left-aligned and the name of the file right-aligned.
4. This worksheet is for a company called Performance Threads: Theatrical Fabrics, Draperies and Supplies. Performance Threads is a company that supplies the entertainment industry (theater, film, and television) with a full line of theatrical fabrics, stage draperies, and scenic and production supplies. This worksheet lists some prices for ornate tassels the company sells. Format the numbers in this worksheet by completing the following steps:
   a. Select cells B4 through G4.
   b. Right-click one of the selected cells.
   c. Click on Format Cells from the shortcut menu.
   d. Click the Number tab if necessary. Click *Fraction* in the *Category* list box.
   e. Click *Up to one digit (1/4)* in the *Type* list box if necessary. Click OK.
   f. Select cells B5 through G5. Hold down the Ctrl key and select cells B7 through G7.
   g. Click the Currency Style button on the Formatting toolbar.
   h. Select cells B6 through G6.
   i. Click the Percent Style button on the Formatting toolbar.

5. Adjust the widths of columns E, F, and G by completing the following steps:
   a. Select columns E, F, and G.
   b. Double-click the column header border between columns E and F.
6. The data is not very easy to read as it is currently arranged on the worksheet. Transposing the columns and rows would make the data easier to understand. Transpose the columns and rows by completing the following steps:

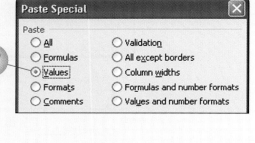

   a. Select cells A3 through G7.
   b. Click the Copy button on the Standard toolbar.
   c. Click cell A9.
   d. Click the down-pointing arrow next to the Paste Button and then click *Transpose*.
   e. Now you need to delete the old data. Select rows 3 through 7, click Edit and then click Delete.
7. Adjust the widths of the columns by completing the following steps:
   a. Select columns A through E.
   b. Double-click on any one of the selected column header borders.
8. You want to delete column D. Select cell E5 and notice that the formula in cell E5 references cell D5. If you delete column D, error messages will appear in column E. To delete column D, you must first change the formulas to values. Complete the following steps to change the formulas to values:
   a. Select cells E5 through E10.
   b. Click the Copy button on the Standard toolbar.
   c. Select cell E5.
   d. Click the Edit menu and click Paste Special.
   e. In the *Paste* section, click the *Values* option.
   f. Click OK. Notice that now there are values, not formulas, in cells E5 through E10.
   g. Press Esc to turn off the copy border.
9. Delete column D by completing the following steps:
   a. Select column D.
   b. Click Edit and then click Delete.
10. You want to do some quick calculations. Sales representatives earn 8% commission on sales they make. Complete the following steps to quickly calculate what 8% of the Price Per Dozen is.
    a. Enter **8% Commission** in cell E4.
    b. Enter .08 in cell E5.
    c. Double-click on the AutoFill fill handle in the lower right corner of cell E5.
    d. Select cells D5 through D10.
    e. Click the Copy button on the Standard toolbar.
    f. Select cell E5.
    g. Click Edit and then click Paste Special.
    h. In the *Operation* section, click the *Multiply* option.
    i. Click OK.
    j. Press Esc to turn off the copy border.

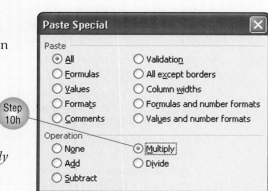

11. Someone has asked to see the prices for the tassels. You want to hide column E, the sales representatives' commission, before you show them to this person. Hide column E by completing the following steps:
    a. Select column E.
    b. Click Format, point to Column, and then click Hide.
12. Print the worksheet with the column hidden.
13. Unhide the column by completing the following steps:
    a. Select columns D and F.
    b. Click Format, point to Column, and then click Unhide.
14. Save the worksheet with the same name (**eec1x05**) and then close **eec1x05**.

Using the Page Break Preview Command

The Page Break Preview command enables you to see where page breaks are going to occur. In addition, you can edit where the page breaks are going to appear in this preview mode. If you adjust a page break so that more data is going to appear on a page, Excel automatically scales the data so that it will fit on the page. There are two ways to access the Page Break Preview command. One way is to click View and then click Page Break Preview. The second way is to click the Print Preview button on the Standard toolbar and then click the Page Break Preview button. A display similar to the one shown in Figure 1.21 appears. The blue lines indicate the current page breaks. By clicking and dragging these lines, you can adjust where the page breaks will occur. To return to the Normal view, click the Print Preview button, and then click the Normal View button.

HINT

Any rows and/or columns you may have defined as print titles to repeat on every page are not displayed in Page Break Preview. They are only displayed in Print Preview.

FIGURE

1.21 **Page Break Preview Mode**

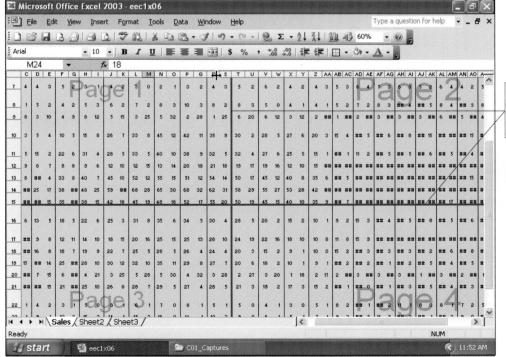

Click and drag the blue lines to adjust the page breaks.

Use Page Break Preview
1. Click View, Page Break Preview.
2. Click and drag on page break lines to adjust page breaks.
3. Click Print Preview button.
4. Click Normal View.

Changing Page Order

Change Page Order
1. Click File, Page Setup.
2. Click the Sheet tab.
3. In the *Page order* section, make the appropriate selection.
4. Click OK.

As you can see in Figure 1.21, a worksheet can be both too wide as well as too long to fit on one page. When this occurs, Excel can either print all the pages going across first and then print the pages going down, or print all the pages going down first and then print the pages going across. In Figure 1.21, the pages going down will be printed first (as indicated by the Page 1 and Page 2 labels), and then the pages going across (as indicated by the Page 3 and Page 4 labels). The default setting is to print all the pages going down first and then print all the pages going across. To change this, click File, Page Setup, and then the Sheet tab. As shown in Figure 1.22, the options for changing the order in which the pages are printed are found in the *Page order* section.

FIGURE

1.22 *Selecting the Order Worksheet Pages are Printed*

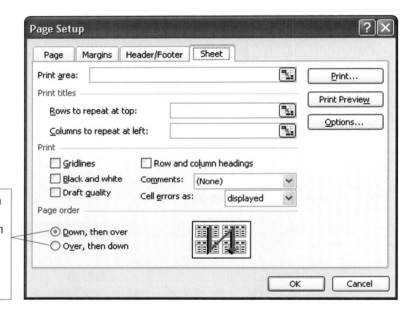

If worksheet pages are both too wide and too long to fit on one page, they either can be printed going down first and then across, or printed going across first and then going down.

Renaming Sheets and Selecting a Tab Color

Rename a Sheet
1. Right-click the sheet tab and click Rename.
2. Change the name of the sheet.

The default names on the Sheet tabs are *Sheet1, Sheet2, Sheet3*, and so on. If you want a more descriptive name for your sheets, you can click Format, point to Sheet, and then click Rename. Or you can use the shortcut menu by right-clicking the tab for the sheet and clicking Rename. The name of the currently selected sheet is highlighted. Simply type the new sheet name and press Enter to rename the sheet.

You can also organize your spreadsheets by assigning colors to the tabs. To assign a color to a tab, either click Format, point to Sheet, and then click Tab Color, or use the shortcut menu by right-clicking the tab for the sheet and clicking Tab Color. The Format Tab Color dialog box shown in Figure 1.23 is displayed. Click a color and then click OK. The edge of the tab will change to the selected color.

1.23 *Format Tab Color Dialog Box*

QUICK STEPS

Change a Sheet Tab Color
1. Right-click the sheet tab and click Tab Color.
2. Select a tab color and click OK.

exercise 6

TRANSPOSING DATA, CREATING A CUSTOM FORMAT, USING PAGE BREAK PREVIEW, CHANGING PAGE ORDER, RENAMING SHEETS, HIDING AND UNHIDING COLUMNS

1. Open **ExcelWorksheet06**.
2. Save the file using the Save As command and name it **eec1x06**.
3. Create a custom header that has your name left-aligned and the name of the file right-aligned.
4. The Whitewater Canoe and Kayak Corporation is a company that makes and sells custom-made canoes and kayaks and related sporting supplies to dealers around the country. This worksheet shows the number of canoes and kayaks Whitewater Canoe and Kayak's resellers ordered each month for the years 2004 and 2005. The data is not very easy to understand the way it is currently formatted. It would be easier to understand if the columns displayed the dates and the rows displayed the resellers. Complete the following steps to transpose the rows and columns:
   a. Click cell A3 to select it. Move the mouse pointer to the bottom edge of cell A3. When the mouse pointer turns into an arrow with a four-headed arrow attached, hold down the Shift key and double-click. Cells A3 through A51 should be selected. Move the mouse pointer to the right edge of the selected cells. When the mouse pointer turns into an arrow with a four-headed arrow attached, hold down the Shift key and double-click. Cells A3 through U51 should be selected.
   b. Click the Copy button.
   c. Select cell A53.
   d. Click Edit and then Paste Special.
   e. Click the *Transpose* check box in the Paste Special dialog box. Click OK.
   f. Now you need to delete the old data. Select rows 3 through 51, click Edit, and then click Delete.
   g. Select columns A through AW.
   h. Click Format, point to Column, and then click AutoFit Selection.
   i. Click in any cell so that the columns are no longer selected.
   j. Drag the right column heading border of column A until column A is 9.86 points wide.
   k. Select rows 6 through 24.
   l. Click Format, point to Row, and then click AutoFit.

5. You could save a considerable amount of space if all the "Canoes" and "Kayaks" labels were angled. Angle the labels by completing the following steps:
   a. Select row 4.
   b. Right-click on any one of the selected cells and click Format Cells on the shortcut menu. Click the Alignment tab.
   c. Click the red diamond in the *Orientation* section and drag it until *60* is displayed in the *Degrees* box. Click OK.
6. Use the Merge and Center button to merge cells B5 and C5, D5 and E5, F5 and G5, H5 and I5, and so on until the two cells for each date are merged.
7. Adding borders around the two columns that represent one month would make the worksheet easier to understand. Complete the following steps to add the borders:
   a. Select cells B4 through C24.
   b. Right-click on any one of the selected cells and click Format Cells from the shortcut menu. Click the Border tab.
   c. In the *Presets* section, click the Outline button, then click OK.
   d. Cells B4 through C24 should still be selected. Double-click the Format Painter button.
   e. Click cell D4. The format is applied. Click cell F4. The format is applied. Continue clicking every other cell until the cells representing each month have a border around them.
   f. Click the Format Painter button to turn it off.
8. You want to create a custom format so that the numbers are indented from the right side of the cell. Complete the following steps to create the custom format:
   a. Select cells B6 through AW24.
   b. Right-click any one of the selected cells and click Format Cells from the shortcut menu.
   c. Click the Number tab.
   d. Click *Custom* in the *Category* list box.
   e. In the *Type* box, enter 0_0, then click OK.

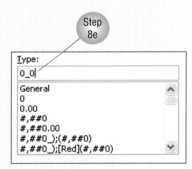

9. Complete the following steps to use the AutoFit command to reduce the widths of the columns:
   a. Select columns B through AW.
   b. Click Format, point to Column, and then click AutoFit Selection.
10. Adding shading to the numbers would also make them easier to read. Complete the following steps to add shading:
   a. Select cells B6 through AW24.
   b. Click the down-pointing arrow to the right of the Fill Color button.
   c. Click the Light Green color, the fourth color from the left in the last row.
11. Adjust the layout of the worksheet by changing the orientation to landscape and setting the left and right margins to .5 inches.
12. You need your labels to appear on each page. Complete the following steps to select rows 4 and 5 to repeat at the top of each page and column A to repeat at the left of each page:
   a. Click File and then click Page Setup.
   b. Click the Sheet tab.

c. Click the button to the right of the *Rows to repeat at top* box.
d. Select rows 4 and 5.
e. Click the button at the right side of the Page Setup - Rows to repeat at top: dialog box that appears.

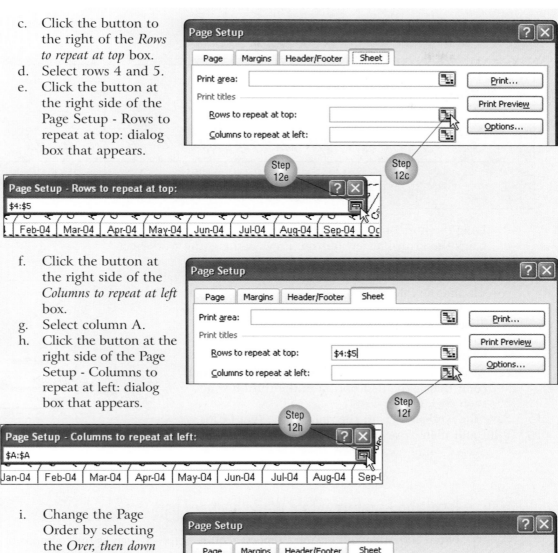

Step 12e

Step 12c

f. Click the button at the right side of the *Columns to repeat at left* box.
g. Select column A.
h. Click the button at the right side of the Page Setup - Columns to repeat at left: dialog box that appears.

Step 12h

Step 12f

i. Change the Page Order by selecting the *Over, then down* option in the *Page order* section.
j. Click OK.

13. Complete the following steps to use Page Break Preview to change the page breaks.
a. Click the Print Preview button.
b. Click the Page Break Preview button. If the Welcome to Page Break Preview dialog box is displayed, click the OK button.

Step 12i

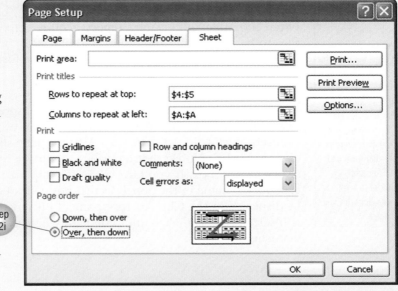

    c.   Click and drag the vertical blue dotted line until it is on the border between December 2004 and January 2005.

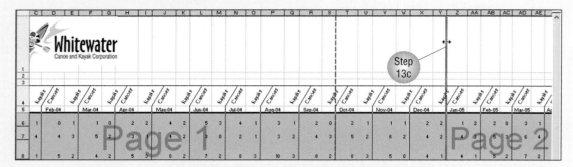

    d.   Drag the horizontal blue dotted line until it is between rows 17 and 18.

    e.   Click the Print Preview button. Preview the entire worksheet.

    f.   Click the Normal View button.

14. Rename the sheet and select a color for the worksheet tab by completing the following steps:

    a.   Click Format, point to Sheet, and then click Rename.

    b.   Type **Sales** and then press Enter.

    c.   Right-click the Sales worksheet tab.

    d.   Click Tab Color.

    e.   At the Format Tab Color dialog box, click the red color that is the first option in the third row and then click OK.

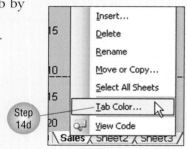

15. Save the worksheet with the same name (**eec1x06**).

16. Print and then close **eec1x06**.

Inserting Graphics into a Worksheet or Chart

Often corporate and business reports require graphics such as photographs or image files to be included in the report. Graphics can be inserted both into a worksheet as well as a graph. Once inserted, they can be formatted and resized in a number of different ways.

    To insert a graphic image into a worksheet click Insert and point to Picture. As shown in Figure 1-24, the three options for inserting a graphic image are Clip Art, From File, or From Scanner or Camera. If you want to search for a clip art image to insert, click Clip Art. The Clip Art task pane shown in Figure 1.25 is displayed. Type a word or phrase that describes the image for which you are looking in the *Search for* text box. If you have a specific clip art image that you want, you can type its file name in the *Search for* text box. Click Go. The results of your search will be displayed in the Clip Art task pane. To insert the image, simply click it. Once it is inserted, you can click and drag it to where you want it located in the worksheet.

1.24 *Inserting a Graphic Image into a Worksheet*

Click Insert and then Picture to display the three options—Clip Art, From File, and From Scanner or Camera—for inserting a graphic image into a worksheet.

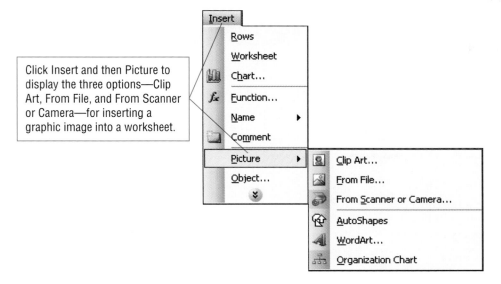

1.25 *The Clip Art Task Pane*

To search for a clip art image, enter a word or phrase describing the image you want or type in the file name of a specific clip art image.

When searching for a clip art image, you can limit the search results to a specific collection of clips or to a specific type of media file.

The results of your search will be displayed here.

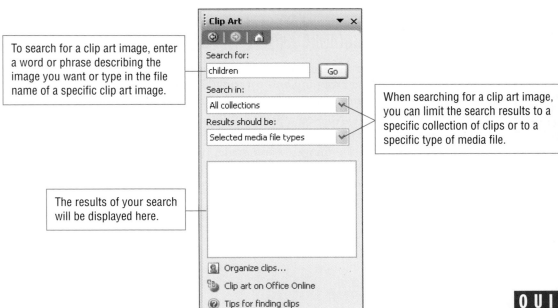

To insert a picture from a file, click Insert, point to Picture, and click From File. The Insert Picture dialog box shown in Figure 1.26 is displayed. Browse to the folder containing the picture to be inserted and then click that picture file. Click the Insert button and the picture will be embedded in the worksheet. Once the file is embedded, you can click and drag it to where you want it located in the worksheet.

QUICK STEPS

Insert a Graphic Image
1. Click Insert and point to Picture.
2. Click either Clip Art or From File.

1.26 **The Insert Picture Dialog Box**

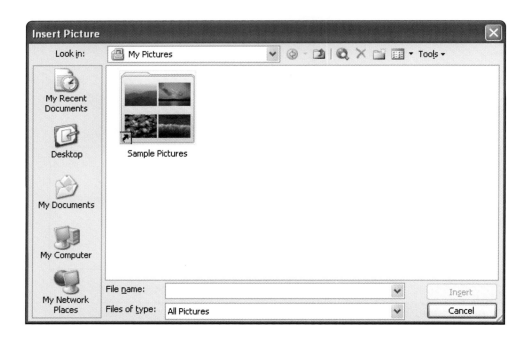

Using Cropping and Rotating Tools

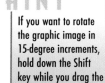

Once a graphic image is inserted into a worksheet it can be formatted in many different ways, including cropping and rotating. To crop an image means to trim it. When you crop an image, you delete the outer edges of it. Rotating an image means to revolve the image, or to turn it around its center.

There are two ways to rotate a graphic image in Excel. First, select the image to be rotated. To rotate the image to any angle, place the mouse pointer over the rotate handle. When the mouse pointer turns into a circular looking arrow, click and drag the rotate handle in the direction the image is to be rotated. Figure 1.27 illustrates how to rotate an image to any angle.

QUICK STEPS

Rotate an Image
1. Click the image to select it.
2. Place the mouse pointer over the rotate handle at the top of the image.
3. Click and drag the rotate handle.

EXCEL

1.27 *Rotating an Image*

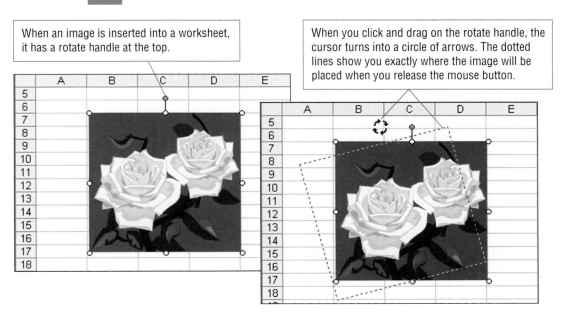

When an image is inserted into a worksheet, it has a rotate handle at the top.

When you click and drag on the rotate handle, the cursor turns into a circle of arrows. The dotted lines show you exactly where the image will be placed when you release the mouse button.

The other way to rotate a graphic image is to rotate it either 90 degrees to the left or right. You can rotate the image 90 degrees by using either the Drawing toolbar or the Picture toolbar. First the image must be selected. To use the Drawing toolbar, click Draw, point to Rotate or Flip, and then click either Rotate Left or Rotate Right, as shown in Figure 1.28. To use the Picture toolbar, click the Rotate Left 90° button shown in Figure 1.29. Each time the button is clicked, the image rotates to the left 90 degrees. If the Picture toolbar is not displayed, right-click on any toolbar that is displayed and click Picture from the drop-down menu that is displayed.

1.28 *Using the Drawing Toolbar to Rotate an Image 90 Degrees*

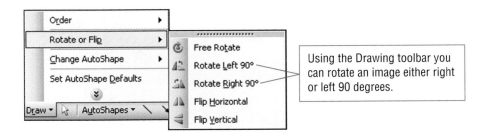

Using the Drawing toolbar you can rotate an image either right or left 90 degrees.

1.29 *Using the Picture Toolbar to Rotate an Image 90 Degrees*

Each time you click the Rotate left 90° button on the Picture toolbar, the selected image rotates 90 degrees to the left.

Crop an Image
1. Click the image to select it.
2. Click the Crop button on the Picture toolbar.
3. Place the mouse pointer over a cropping handle at the edge of the image.
4. Click and drag the cropping handle.

To crop an image, click the Crop button on the Picture tool bar after selecting the image to be cropped. As shown in Figure 1.30, the mouse pointer turns into a cropping tool and cropping handles are displayed around the edges of the image. If you want to crop one side only, drag the center handle on that side in toward the center of the image. You can crop equally on two sides at once by holding down the Ctrl key as you drag the center handle on that side in toward the center of the image. You can also crop equally on all four sides at once by holding down the Ctrl key as you drag a corner handle in. Turn off the Crop command by clicking the Crop button on the Picture toolbar.

FIGURE

1.30 *Cropping an Image*

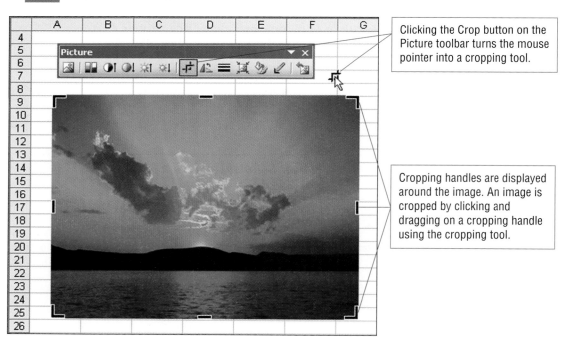

Clicking the Crop button on the Picture toolbar turns the mouse pointer into a cropping tool.

Cropping handles are displayed around the image. An image is cropped by clicking and dragging on a cropping handle using the cropping tool.

Once you are positive you will not want to undo your crop, you can press the Compress Pictures button on the Pictures toolbar. Pressing this button will delete the cropped parts of the picture from the file completely. Once you have done this, you will not be able to restore the cropped portions of the image. When you press the Compress Pictures button, the Compress pictures dialog box is displayed. You can select whether you want to compress the selected picture only or all the pictures in the document. When you click the OK button, a dialog box may appear asking if you want to apply picture optimization. If it does, click the Apply button.

Compress Pictures

Resizing a Picture

In addition to cropping, you can change the size of a picture by resizing it. Cropping changes the size of a picture by trimming it or removing parts of it. Resizing does not remove any portion of the picture; instead, it changes the dimensions of a picture by stretching or shrinking it.

Resize an Image
1. Click the image to select it.
2. Place the mouse pointer over a handle at the edge of the image.
3. Click and drag the handle.

You can resize an image either by using the mouse or by entering specific measurements. To use the mouse to resize an image, start by selecting the image. You can increase or decrease the size of the image by positioning the mouse pointer over one of the handles. When the mouse pointer turns into a resizing tool, shown in Figure 1.31, click and drag either toward or away from the center of the picture.

If you use a handle on a side of the image, the aspect ratio—the ratio of the width of the image to the height of the image of the image—will change. The result may be an image that looks stretched. To resize an image while maintaining the aspect ratio, click and drag a handle on a corner of the image. Another way to maintain the proportions of the image is to hold down the Shift key while dragging the mouse. You can keep the center of the image in the same place by holding down the Ctrl key while dragging the mouse. If you want to both maintain the proportions of the image while keeping the center in the same place, you can hold down both the Ctrl and Shift keys while dragging the mouse.

FIGURE

1.31 *Resizing an Image Using the Mouse*

If you know the exact measurements of the image, you can select the image and click Format and Picture. The Format Picture dialog box shown in Figure 1.32 is displayed. Click the Size tab and enter the measurements in the *Height* and *Width* boxes. If you want to maintain the aspect ratio of the image, select the *Lock aspect ratio* check box. If at any time you want to return to the original dimensions of the image, you can click the Reset button.

1.32 *Resizing an Image Using Measurements*

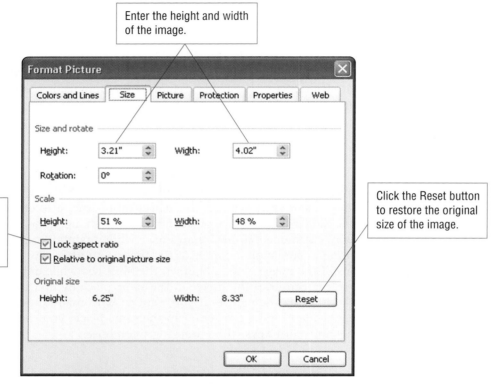

Enter the height and width of the image.

To maintain the proportions of the image, make sure the *Lock aspect ratio* option is selected.

Click the Reset button to restore the original size of the image.

More Brightness

Less Brightness

More Contrast

Less Contrast

Reset Picture

Changing the Brightness and Contrast of a Picture

Adjusting the brightness of an image can improve the appearance of a picture that is too light or too dark. You can change the brightness of an image by clicking the More Brightness or Less Brightness buttons on the Picture toolbar. Each time the button is pressed, the image becomes more, or less, bright.

Pressing the More Contrast button separates the colors to give the image a sharper appearance. Pressing the Less Contrast button makes the image colors more similar creating a hazy image. Each time the button is pressed, the contrast increases or decreases.

Resetting an Image

The Reset Picture button on the Picture toolbar will set the image back to its original size, brightness, and contrast settings. You cannot, however, reset the image back to its original size once you have pressed the Compress Pictures button after cropping an image.

exercise 7

USING CROPPING AND ROTATING TOOLS, CONTROLLING IMAGE CONTRAST AND BRIGHTNESS, AND RESIZING AN IMAGE

1. Open **ExcelWorksheet07**.
2. Save the file using the Save As command and name it **eec1x07**.
3. Create a custom header that has your name left-aligned and the name of the file right-aligned.
4. This worksheet lists the current sales figures for the sales representative Camron Davis. He would like to include his picture on the worksheet. Insert his picture onto the worksheet by completing the following steps:
   a. Click Insert, point to Picture, and click From File.
   b. Browse to the file **ReportPhoto1**. Click to select it and then click Insert.
5. The picture is too large. Complete the following steps to decrease its size:
   a. Click the photo to select it.
   b. Place the mouse pointer over the handle in the lower right corner of the photo.
   c. Click and drag until the photo is over cells A1–B12.
6. Complete the following steps to crop the upper edge of the photo:
   a. With the photo selected, click the Crop button on the Picture toolbar.
   b. Click the middle cropping handle on the top and drag until the top of the picture is at the top of the computer in the background.

   c. Click the Crop button on the Picture toolbar to exit from the cropping mode.
7. Complete the following steps to move and resize the image:
   a. Click and drag the photo to move it to the upper left corner of the worksheet. Place the photo so that its left edge is on the right edge of column A and so that it is at the top of the worksheet, but you can still see the rotate handle.

b. Click and drag the lower right handle until the bottom of the picture reaches the top of row 13.

8. Next you want to rotate the image so that his shoulder line is parallel with the top of the worksheet. Complete the following steps to rotate the image:

a. With the photo selected, place the mouse pointer over the rotate handle.

b. Click and drag the rotate handle until you think his shoulders are parallel with the top of the worksheet.

9. Crop some more off the top and bottom of the image by completing the following steps:

a. With the photo selected, click the Cropping tool on the Picture toolbar.

b Crop a bit more off the bottom and top of the photo. When you are finished, the photo should look like the following:

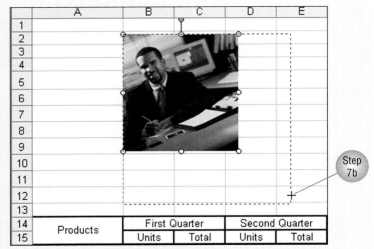

Step 7b

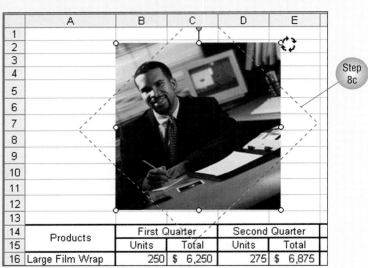

Step 8c

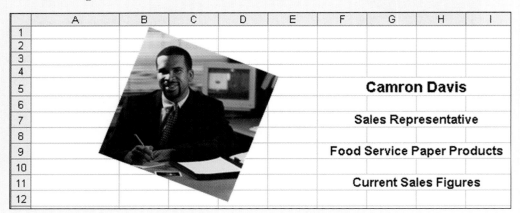

10. Complete the following steps to adjust the brightness and contrast of the image:
   a. With the photo selected, click the More Brightness button on the Picture toolbar two or three times.
   b. Click the More Contrast button two or three times.
11. Save the worksheet with the same name (**eec1x07**).
12. Print and then close **eec1x07**.

Formatting Charts and Diagrams

Creating charts is a popular feature of Excel worksheets. Charts as well as worksheets can be formatted to make them easier to read, to help emphasize specific data, and to make them more attractive.

As shown in Figure 1.33, Excel charts have standard features. Most charts include some or all of these features. Right-clicking any of these features displays a shortcut menu that enables you to format that feature.

FIGURE

1.33 Standard Features of an Excel Chart

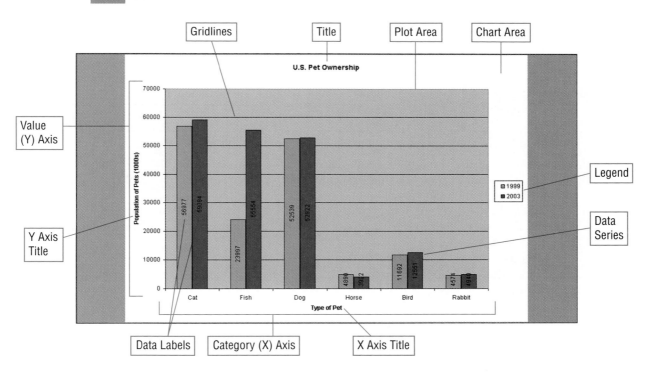

For example, if you were to right-click a data series, a shortcut menu would be displayed with the option Format Data Series. Clicking Format Data Series from the short cut menu would display the Format Data Series dialog box shown in Figure 1.34. From this dialog box you can format the appearance of how the data is displayed in the chart.

1.34 *The Format Data Series Dialog Box*

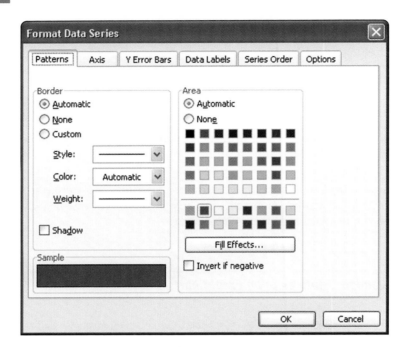

exercise 8

FORMATTING A CHART

1. Open **ExcelWorksheet08**.
2. Save the file using the Save As command and name it **eec1x08**.
3. Create a custom header that has your name left-aligned and the name of the file right-aligned.
4. This is a chart displaying the current sales figures for the sales representative Camron Davis. First you want to edit the chart so that it displays sales figures for the third and fourth quarters only.
    a. Right-click one of the bars on the bar chart.
    b. From the shortcut menu that is displayed, click Source Data.
    c. In the Sheet 1 worksheet, select A3–A11, hold the Ctrl key, and then select D3–E11.
    d. At the Source Data dialog box, click OK.
5. Next you want to make formatting changes to the data series.
    a. Right-click one of the bars representing the third quarter sales.
    b. From the shortcut menu that is displayed, click Format Data Series to display the Format Data Series dialog box.
    c. If necessary, click the Patterns tab.

d. In the *Border* section, click the *Shadow* option.

e. In the *Area* section, click the Light Blue color that is the sixth option from the left in the fourth row.

f. Click the Data Labels tab. In the *Label Contains* section, click the *Value* option.

g. Click the Series Order tab.

h. *Third Quarter* should be selected under *Series order*. Click the Move Down button. The bars for the fourth quarter will be displayed first. Click OK.

Format Data Series

Tabs: Patterns | Axis | Y Error Bars | Data Labels | Series Order | Options

Border
- ◉ Automatic
- ○ None
- ○ Custom

Style: ———
Color: Automatic
Weight: ———

☑ Shadow

Sample

Area
- ○ Automatic
- ○ None

[color palette]

Fill Effects...

☐ Invert if negative

Step 5e

Step 5d

OK | Cancel

6. Now you need to make formatting changes to the data series representing the fourth quarter data.

a. Right-click one of the bars representing the fourth quarter sales.

b. Click Format Data Series. The Format Data Series dialog box is displayed.

c. If necessary, click the Patterns tab.

d. In the *Border* section, click the *Shadow* option.

e. In the *Area* section, click the Light Yellow color that is the third option from the left in the fifth row.

f. Click the Data Labels tab. In the *Label Contains* section, click the *Value* option and then click OK.

7. The data labels now are displayed at the top of each column. Complete the following steps to change the formatting of the data labels:

a. Right-click one of the data labels that appears at the top of a column representing the fourth quarter.

b. Click Format Data Labels from the shortcut menu.

c. Click the Font tab. In the *Font Style* section, click *Bold Italic*.

d. Click the Alignment tab, enter **90** in the *Degrees* box, and then click OK.

e. Right-click one of the data labels that appears at the top of a column representing the third quarter.

f. Click Format Data Labels from the shortcut menu.

g. Click the Font tab. In the *Font Style* section, click *Bold Italic*.

h. Click the Alignment tab, enter **90** in the *Degrees* box, and then click OK.

8. Click and drag each of the data labels so that it is inside the bar. Your chart should look like this:

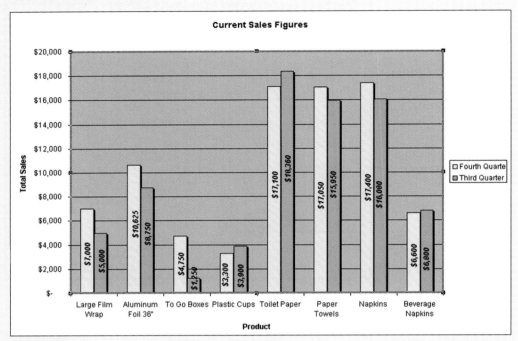

9. Complete the following steps to format the plot area:
   a. Right-click anywhere on the plot area.
   b. From the shortcut menu that is displayed, click Format Plot Area.
   c. The Format Plot Area dialog box is displayed. In the *Area* section, click the Fill Effects button. The Fill Effects dialog box is displayed.
   d. Click the Picture tab and then click the Select Picture button.
   e. Browse to the **ReportPhoto1** file. Select *ReportPhoto1* and then click Insert.
   f. Click OK to close the Fill Effects dialog box. Click OK to close the Format Plot Area dialog box.
10. Complete the following steps to clear the gridlines:
    a. Right-click one of the gridlines.
    b. From the shortcut menu that is displayed, click Clear.
11. Complete the following steps to format the chart title:
    a. Right-click the chart title.
    b. From the shortcut menu that is displayed, click Format Chart Title. The Format Chart Title dialog box is displayed.
    c. Click the Font tab and then change the font to Franklin Gothic Medium.
    d. Change the font style to Bold Italic.
    e. Change the size to 14.
    f. Click OK to close the Format Chart Title dialog box.
12. Complete the following steps to format the value axis title:
    a. Right-click *Total Sales*, the value axis title.
    b. From the shortcut menu that is displayed, click Format Axis Title. The Format Axis Title dialog box is displayed.
    c. Click the Font tab and then change the font to Franklin Gothic Medium.
    d. Change the font style to Bold Italic.
    e. Change the size to 12.
    f. Click OK to close the Format Axis Title dialog box

13. Complete the following steps to format the category axis title:
    a. Right-click *Product*, the category axis title.
    b. From the shortcut menu that is displayed, click Format Axis Title. The Format Axis Title dialog box is displayed.
    c. Click the Font tab and then change the font to Franklin Gothic Medium.
    d. Change the font style to Bold Italic.
    e. Change the size to 12.
    f. Click OK to close the Format Axis Title dialog box.
14. Complete the following steps to format the category axis:
    a. Right-click any one of the products on the category axis.
    b. Click Format Axis. The Format Axis dialog box is displayed.
    c. Click the Font tab and then change the font to Franklin Gothic Medium.
    d. Click the Alignment tab. In the *Orientation* section, enter 45 next to the *Degrees* option.
    e. Click OK to close the Format Axis dialog box.
15. Complete the following steps to format the Legend:
    a. Right-click the legend.
    b. From the shortcut menu that is displayed, click Format Legend. The Format Legend dialog box is displayed.
    d. Click the Font tab and then change the font to Franklin Gothic Medium.
    e. Change the font style to Bold Italic and then change the size to 12.
    f. Click the Placement tab. Click the *Bottom* option, then click OK.
16. Your chart should look like this:

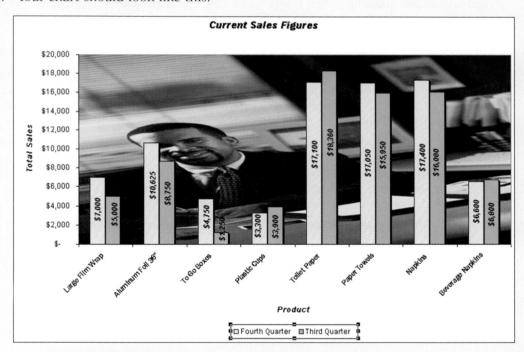

17. Save the worksheet with the same name (**eec1x08**).
18. Print and then close **eec1x08**.

CHAPTER summary

➤ Excel includes 12 categories by which numbers can be formatted. Some of Excel's more specialized number formats include Accounting, Fraction, and Scientific.

➤ The main difference between the Currency and Accounting formats is that the Accounting format aligns the currency symbols at the left side of the cell and the Currency format does not.

➤ The Scientific format is used for very large or very small numbers.

➤ When you create a custom format, the format you create is added to the bottom of the *Type* list box, where it can be selected and used as often as needed.

➤ Use the Alignment tab of the Format Cells dialog box to manage large labels by wrapping the text within a cell, shrinking the cell's entry to fit within one cell, or rotating the label a specified number of degrees.

➤ When you automatically adjust the width of a column or the height of a row, the column is displayed at its optimum width or the row is displayed at its optimum height.

➤ A style is a predefined set of formatting attributes. Each one of the check boxes on the Style dialog box corresponds to one of the tabs on the Format Cells dialog box. There are several advantages to using styles. Using styles helps to assure that the formatting from one worksheet to another is consistent, enables you to define the attributes for a particular style one time only, and simplifies editing.

➤ Excel includes 17 different predesigned formats.

➤ The layout of large worksheets often needs to be adjusted to have the worksheet print on as few pages as possible. Reduce the margins at the Page Setup dialog box with the Margins tab selected. Change the orientation to landscape and reduce the worksheet size by a percentage of its full size at the Page Setup dialog box with the Page tab selected.

➤ Graphic images inserted into a worksheet can be resized and formatted. Options for changing the size of a graphic include cropping and resizing. When an image is cropped, the edges of the image are removed. When an image is resized, the dimensions of the image are changed, but nothing is removed from the image. Options for formatting a graphic include rotating it and adjusting the image contrast and brightness.

➤ The standard features of an Excel chart include the following: title, plot area, chart area, legend, data series, x axis title, category axis (x axis), data labels, value axis (y axis), y axis title, and gridlines. There is a Format dialog box for each one of these features which can be accessed by right-clicking on the particular feature.

FEATURES summary

FEATURE	BUTTON	MENU/COMMANDS
Apply number format		Format, Cells, and select *Number*
Create a custom format		Format, Cells, and select *Custom*
Format large labels		Format, Cells, Alignment tab
Automatically adjust column widths		Format, Column, AutoFit Selection
Automatically adjust row height		Format, Row, AutoFit
Create a style		Format, Style
Apply borders	▦ ▾	Format, Cells, Border tab
Apply shading	◇ ▾	Format, Cells, Border tab
Turn off zeros		Tools, Options, View tab
Apply a predesigned format		Format, AutoFormat
Create a conditional format		Format, Conditional Formatting
Transpose columns/rows		Edit, Paste Special, *Transpose* check box
Hide columns		Format, Column, Hide
Hide rows		Format, Row, Hide
Unhide columns		Format, Column, Unhide
Unhide rows		Format, Row, Unhide
Adjust page breaks		View, Page Break Preview
Change order pages are printed		File, Page Setup, Sheet tab
Rename sheets		Format, Sheet, Rename
Select colors for worksheet tabs		Format, Sheet, Tab Color

FEATURE	BUTTON	MENU/COMMANDS
Insert a graphic image		Insert, Picture
Crop an image	[button]	Click the image. Click Format, Picture, Picture tab.
Resize an image		Click the image. Click Format, Picture, Size tab.
Adjust the brightness of an image	[buttons]	Click the image. Click Format, Picture, Picture tab.
Adjust the contrast of an image	[buttons]	Click the image. Click Format, Picture, Picture tab.

CONCEPTS check

Completion: On a blank sheet of paper, indicate the correct term, symbol, or command for each description.

1. This numbering format is used to display very large or very small numbers.
2. To create a custom format that uses text, the text must be enclosed by these characters.
3. To center a label across all the columns in a worksheet, click this button on the Formatting toolbar.
4. A label can be formatted so that it prints at an angle at the Format Cells dialog box with this tab selected.
5. Double-click on this location to automatically adjust a column so that the widest entry in the column fits in one cell.
6. These are what each one of the check boxes on the Style dialog box corresponds to.
7. To apply the formatting from one cell to another cell, click this button on the Standard toolbar.
8. Turn off zeros with an option at the Options dialog box with this tab selected.
9. This command lets you change the default settings for fonts, the number of worksheets in a workbook, and the location where files are stored.
10. Scale the size of the worksheet by a specific percentage of its full size at the Page Setup dialog box with this tab selected.
11. Use this dialog box to add the values in copied cells to the values in the cells into which they are being pasted.
12. If you are currently viewing a worksheet in the Page Break Preview mode and you want to return to the Normal view, you must click this button on the Standard toolbar.

13. Change the order in which worksheet pages are printed at the Page Setup dialog box with this tab selected.
14. List the advantages of applying formatting using styles.
15. List the steps you would complete to create a conditional format that printed all values greater than 150 as blue and italicized.
16. Column J is currently hidden. List the steps you would take to unhide it.
17. List the features of an Excel chart that can be formatted.
18. You have inserted an image into a worksheet. You want to trim an inch off the top of the image. List the steps necessary for you to remove the top inch of the image.
19. If you wanted to separate the colors in an image in order to give it a sharper appearance, which button would you press on the Picture toolbar?
20. If you want to crop an image equally on all four sides, press this key while dragging one of the corner handles on the image.

SKILLS check

Assessment 1

1. Open **ExcelWorksheet09**.
2. Save the worksheet using the Save As command and name it **eec1sc01**.
3. Create a custom header that has your name left-aligned and the file name right-aligned.
4. Center the label in cell A5 across columns A, B, and C.
5. Format the numbers in cells A8 through A12 as fractions, up to one digit.
6. Create a custom format for the numbers in cells A8 through A12. The format should read *inch(es)*. (You may need to adjust the width of Column A.)
7. Center and bold each of the labels in row 7.
8. Format the numbers in cells C8 through C12 as Accounting.
9. Add a light yellow shading to cells C8 through C12.
10. Save the worksheet again with the same name (**eec1sc01**).
11. Print and then close **eec1sc01**.

Assessment 2

1. Open **ExcelWorksheet10**.
2. Save the worksheet using the Save As command and name it **eec1sc02**.
3. Create a custom header that has your name left-aligned and the file name right-aligned.
4. Align the labels in cells B6 through G6 so that they are at a 75 degree angle.
5. Automatically adjust the widths of columns B through G.
6. Center the label in cell A5 across columns A through G.
7. Print the worksheet.
8. Copy cells A7 through A10 to cells A13 through A16.
9. Enter the label Projections in cell A12.
10. You want to know how many sections would be offered if the number of sections was increased by 2 for each semester. Enter 2 in cells B13 through G16.
11. Copy cells B7 through G10. Use the Paste Special command to add the values in these cells to the values in cells B13 through G16.
12. Print the worksheet again.
13. Save the worksheet again with the same name (**eec1sc02**).
14. Close **eec1sc02**.

Assessment 3

1. Open **ExcelWorksheet11**.
2. Save the worksheet using the Save As command and name it **eec1sc03**.
3. Create a custom header that has your name left-aligned and the file name right-aligned.
4. Center the label in A7 across columns A through F.
5. Create a custom format for cells A9 through A14 that does not display the leading zero and adds two single quotation marks to the right of the number to indicate the symbol for inches. *(Hint: You may need to refer to Table 1.1. The single quotation marks should be treated like text when creating the format.)*
6. Create a custom format for cells B9 through F14 that displays only one decimal place and adds the capital letter *A*, which is the symbol for amps, to the right of the numbers.
7. Place a border around each cell from cell A7 through cell F14. *(Hint: Use the Borders button on the Formatting toolbar and select the **All Borders** option, the second button from the left on the last row.)*
8. Add a light green shading to cell A7.
9. Automatically adjust the widths of columns B through F so that they are just wide enough to display the widest entry in each column.
10. Save the worksheet again with the same name (**eec1sc03**) and print it.
11. Close **eec1sc03**.

Assessment 4

1. Open **ExcelWorksheet12**.
2. Save the worksheet using the Save As command and name it **eec1sc04**.
3. Create a custom header that has your name left-aligned and the file name right-aligned.
4. Format the numbers in column B as fractions, up to one digit.
5. Create a custom format for cells B7 through B10 that adds *lb(s)* to the right of the numbers. Apply this custom format to cells B14 through B17 and cells B21 through B24.
6. Format the numbers in column C as Accounting with two decimal places and the dollar sign displayed.
7. Select cell A5. Create a style called Header 1. The font for the Header 1 style should be the Century Gothic font (or another sans serif font), the font style should be italic, the size should be 12, and the color should be green.
8. Apply the Header 1 style to cells A12 and A19.
9. Select cell A6. Create a style called Header 2. The horizontal alignment for the Header 2 style should be centered, the font should be Century Gothic (or another sans serif font), the font style should be bold, the size should be 11, and there should be an outside border around the cell.
10. Apply the Header 2 style to cells B6, C6, A13, B13, C13, A20, B20, and C20.
11. Print the worksheet.
12. Edit the Header 1 style so that the font style is bold italic instead of just italic.
13. Edit the Header 2 style so that it includes a light green background.
14. Print the worksheet again.
15. Save the worksheet again with the same name (**eec1sc04**).
16. Close **eec1sc04**.

Assessment 5

1. Open **ExcelWorksheet13**.
2. Save the worksheet using the Save As command and name it **eec1sc05**.
3. Create a custom header that has your name left-aligned and the file name right-aligned.

4. Apply the AutoFormat style List 1 to cells A7 through B29 as well as to cells D7 through E29.
5. Center the label in cell A6 across columns A and B. Center the label in cell D6 across cells D6 and E6. Center the label in cell A5 across cells A5 through E5.
6. Create a conditional format to apply to the numbers in cells B8 through B29 and cells E8 through E29. If a number is less than 75, it should be displayed in the bold italic font style and the color orange. If a number is greater than 250, it should be displayed in the bold italic font style and the color blue.
7. Save the worksheet again with the same name (**eec1sc05**) and print it.
8. Close **eec1sc05**.

Assessment 6

1. Open **ExcelWorksheet14**.
2. Save the worksheet using the Save As command and name it **eec1sc06**.
3. Create a custom header that has your name left-aligned and the file name right-aligned.
4. Using the Paste Special command, transpose the entries in cells A4 through K12. *(Hint: You will have to paste the cells to a clear part of the worksheet and then delete the original entries.)*
5. Apply the AutoFormat style Classic 2 to the appropriate cells in the worksheet.
6. Print the worksheet in landscape orientation.
7. Hide columns containing the Hourly Rate figures and the Gross Pay figures.
8. Print the worksheet again in landscape orientation.
9. Unhide columns that were hidden in Step 7.
10. Save the worksheet again with the same name (**eec1sc06**).
11. Close **eec1sc06**.

Assessment 7

1. Open **ExcelWorksheet15**.
2. Save the worksheet using the Save As command and name it **eec1sc07**.
3. Create a custom header that has your name left-aligned and the file name right-aligned.
4. Angle the labels in row 4 so that they are at a 60 degree angle.
5. Adjust the width of columns B through Y using the AutoFit Selection command.
6. Change the page orientation to landscape. Scale the page so that it fits to 1 page wide by 2 pages tall.
7. Set up the sheet so that rows 2 through 4 print at the top of every page. Set the left and right margins to .5 inch.
8. Use the Page Break Preview command to adjust the page breaks so that the temperatures for the state of Montana are printed at the top of page 2.
9. Create a conditional format to apply to all the temperatures. If a temperature is between 70 and 82 degrees, it should display as bold, and the cell should be shaded with pale blue.
10. Save the worksheet again with the same name (**eec1sc07**) and print it.
11. Close **eec1sc07**.

Assessment 8

1. Open **ExcelWorksheet16**.
2. Save the worksheet using the Save As command and name it **eec1sc08**.
3. Create a custom header that has your name left-aligned and the file name right-aligned.
4. Select cell A4. Create a style named Header 1. The style should use the font Tahoma (or another sans serif font), the font style bold italic, the font size 14, and the color plum.

5. Apply the Header 1 style to cells A14 and A23.
6. Select cells A5 through G5. Create a style named Header 2. The style should use the font Tahoma (or another sans serif font), the font style bold, and the font size 10. In addition, it should have a very light gray background, and the horizontal alignment should be centered.
7. Apply the Header 2 style to cells A15 through G15 and cells A24 through G24.
8. Select cells G6 through G11, G16 through G20, and G25 through G30. Create a conditional format that displays any value greater than 12 as bold and red.
9. Automatically adjust the width of the columns so that all of the labels can be read.
10. Save the worksheet again with the same name (**eec1sc08**) and print it.
11. Close **eec1sc08**.

Assessment 9

1. Open **ExcelWorksheet17**.
2. Save the worksheet using the Save As command and name it **eec1sc09**.
3. Create a custom header that has your name left-aligned and the file name right-aligned.
4. Insert the **Mexico** graphic image at the top of the worksheet.
5. Resize the image so that it fits between cells A1 through B21 without changing the aspect ratio.
6. Rotate the image so that it is right side up.
7. Resize the image so that it fits above row 21 without changing the aspect ratio.
8. Crop the photo to delete some of the extra space at the top, bottom, and left edge of the photo.
9. Adjust the brightness of the image so that it is a little less bright.
10. Add a bit more contrast to the photo.
11. Center the photo over the data in columns A, B, and C.
12. Save the worksheet again with the same name (**eec1sc09**) and print it.
13. Close **eec1sc09**.

Assessment 10

1. Open **ExcelWorksheet18**.
2. Save the worksheet using the Save As command and name it **eec1sc10**.
3. Create a custom header that has your name left-aligned and the file name right-aligned.
4. Access the Format Data Series dialog box and click the Patterns tab. In the *Border* section, create a Custom border that is red and uses the heaviest weight line possible. In the *Area* section, click *None*.
5. Click the Data labels tab from the Format Data Series dialog box. Format the data labels so that both the category name and value are displayed.
6. Access the Format Data Labels dialog box and click the Font tab. Format the font style to bold, the color to red, and the size to 11.
7. Access the Format Chart Title dialog box and click the Font tab. Format the font color to red and the size to 14.
8. Delete the legend from the chart.
9. Format the Chart Area by selecting the picture **Pyramid** as the background.
10. Access the Format Data Labels dialog box and click a pale yellow color square in the *Area* section of the Patterns tab.
11. Save the worksheet again with the same name (**eec1sc10**) and print it.
12. Close **eec1sc10**.

Assessment 11

1. Open a new Excel worksheet.
2. Change the default working folder to drive A. On a piece of paper, write down the path location currently in the *Default file location* box. At the end of the exercise you will change the path back to this current entry.
3. Change the default font setting to Bradley Hand ITC, size 12.
4. Set the default number of worksheets to 1.
5. Exit excel.
6. Restart Excel.
7. Create a custom header that has your name left-aligned and the name of the file, **eec1a11** right-aligned.
8. Enter the following data into the worksheet:

Cell	Data
A1	Greenspace Architects
A2	Perennial Plants
A4	Hyacinths
B4	1 bag/25 bulbs
C4	$25.00
A5	Tulip Mixture
B5	1 bag/25 bulbs
C5	$12.00
A6	Lily Mixture
B6	1 bag/12 bulbs
C6	$13.00

9. Widen all the columns to their optimum width.
10. Save the worksheet.
11. Print and then close **eec1sc11**.
12. Change the default settings back to what they were. The default setting for font is Arial size 10. The default number of worksheets is 3. Refer to the path name you wrote down for Step 2 for the default working folder.
13. Exit Excel.

Assessment 12

1. Use Excel's Office Assistant to learn how you can remove conditional formats. *(Hint: In the Type a question for help text box, enter the question How do I remove a conditional format? and press Enter. At the list of topics that displays, click Add, change or remove conditional formats. Read and then print the information pertaining to removing a conditional format.)*
2. Open **eec1sc08**. Save the worksheet using the Save As command and name it **eec1sc12**.
3. Select cells G6 through G11, G16 through G20, and G25 through G30. Using the help information you printed in Step 1, remove the conditional formatting from these cells.
4. Print Excel **eec1sc12**.
5. Save the worksheet using the same file name (**eec1sc12**) and close it.

CHAPTER challenge

You work in the sales department of Electronics, Etc., a store specializing in electronics such as TVs, stereos, and cameras. You have been assigned the task of creating a worksheet showing monthly sales of individual items (use at least 10 items) in the store. The worksheet should be set up to display monthly sales for each item for the entire year. Add a row containing formulas that calculate the monthly totals and a column containing formulas that calculate the yearly totals for each of the items. Create a style named Months that includes bold, 14-point, blue font and apply it to the column headings. Create another style named Items that includes 12-point, italic font and apply it to the row headings. Format the worksheet with borders and shading. Format the cells where individual sales will be typed as currency with two decimal places. Name the sheet tab *Sales* and apply a color to it. Save the workbook as **ElectronicsEtc**. Print the worksheet on one page.

You would like to protect part of a worksheet that contains labels and formulas; however, you would like some cells in the worksheet to remain unprotected so that users can enter data. Use the Help feature to learn how to protect a worksheet, except for specific cells. *(Hint: Unlock cells.)* Then using the workbook created in the first part of the Chapter Challenge, protect the worksheet except for the area where individual sales will be entered for each of the items. Save the workbook again.

After completing the worksheet, you would like your supervisor to take a look at it to see if she has any suggestions or would like to make any changes. Your supervisor is out of town for a couple of days, but is checking her e-mail. Send the **ElectronicsEtc** workbook created and used in the first two parts of the Chapter Challenge to the supervisor (your professor) for review.

WORKING WITH TEMPLATES AND WORKBOOKS

P E R F O R M A N C E   O B J E C T I V E S

Upon successful completion of Chapter 2, you will be able to:

➤ **Use an existing Excel template**
➤ **Create a new template**
➤ **Create a new workbook based upon a user-defined template**
➤ **Edit a template**
➤ **Create and use a workspace file**
➤ **Open multiple workbooks**
➤ **Copy several worksheets into a new workbook**
➤ **Consolidate data into a list**
➤ **Link workbooks**
➤ **Share workbooks**

Many people in an organization often need to share data and use the same workbooks. Excel includes several features that facilitate the sharing of data and workbooks. A template can be created that anyone in an organization could use as often as desired. A template serves as a pattern for a worksheet. The template includes data that would remain the same every time the worksheet was used. Certain labels and formulas, for example, might never change in a particular worksheet, so they could become a part of the template that anyone in the organization could then use. Being able to work with multiple workbooks at the same time is another feature that makes it easy for people to share workbooks. Several worksheets can be merged into a new workbook. Specific cells in one workbook can be linked to another workbook, making it easy to share data. Two people can even edit the same workbook at the same time. In this chapter you will learn ways to share data using Excel.

Using Excel Templates

Oftentimes worksheets are used over and over again for the same purpose. Calculating a monthly profit and loss statement is a routine task performed in most businesses. Much of the data contained in a monthly profit and loss worksheet, such as the labels and the formulas, is the same from month to month. The only things that would change from one month to the next are the actual numbers. Whenever you have a situation in which the basic format of a worksheet is going to be used repeatedly, using a template is a good idea. A template is like a form that gets filled out over and over again. You retrieve a template that has been created, fill in the relevant data, and save it. When the Save command is given, the Save As box automatically appears so that you can give the file a new name. That way, you always have the original template file to use over again.

When you create a workbook or worksheet based on a template, the workbook or worksheet will automatically include all the data and all the formatting that are included in the template. Examples of data and formatting that might be stored in a template include:

- Number and type of worksheets
- Text
- Data
- Formulas
- Functions
- Cell formatting
- Range names
- Sheet names
- Print options
- Layout options
- Graphics
- Macros
- Custom toolbars

The templates for all the Office 2003 applications are stored in the same folder. The default template folder for all the Office 2003 applications is:

C:\Documents and Settings*user_name*\Application Data\Microsoft\Templates

Access Built-in Templates
1. Click File and New.
2. In the *Templates* section of the New Workbook task pane, click the <u>On my computer</u> hyperlink.
3. On the Templates dialog box click the Spreadsheet Solutions tab.

Excel comes with templates for a Balance Sheet, an Expense Statement, a Loan Amortization, a Sales Invoice, and a Timecard. These templates are accessed by clicking the <u>On my computer</u> hyperlink in the *Templates* section of the New Workbook task pane. If the New Workbook task pane is not displayed, click File and then New to display it. Once the Templates dialog box is displayed, click the Spreadsheet Solutions tab. Excel's predesigned templates are shown in Figure 2.1.

2.1 *Excel's Predesigned Templates*

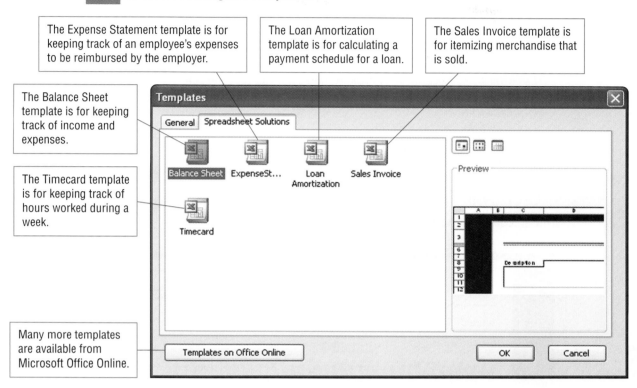

The Expense Statement template is for keeping track of an employee's expenses to be reimbursed by the employer.

The Loan Amortization template is for calculating a payment schedule for a loan.

The Sales Invoice template is for itemizing merchandise that is sold.

The Balance Sheet template is for keeping track of income and expenses.

The Timecard template is for keeping track of hours worked during a week.

Many more templates are available from Microsoft Office Online.

More templates are available from Office Online. If you are connected to the Internet, you can click the Templates on Office Online button to access many more templates for all sorts of different purposes including education, health care, marketing and travel.

exercise 1

USING AN EXISTING TEMPLATE

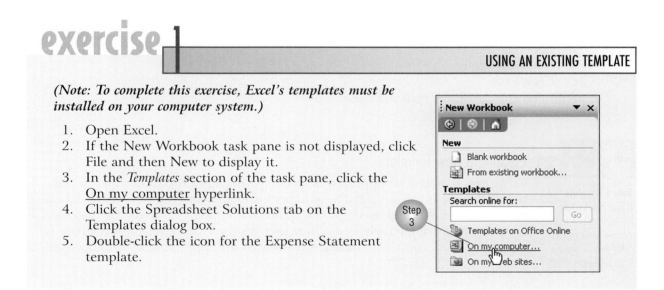

(Note: To complete this exercise, Excel's templates must be installed on your computer system.)

1. Open Excel.
2. If the New Workbook task pane is not displayed, click File and then New to display it.
3. In the *Templates* section of the task pane, click the On my computer hyperlink.
4. Click the Spreadsheet Solutions tab on the Templates dialog box.
5. Double-click the icon for the Expense Statement template.

Step 3

6. You are ready to use the template. You can move around the Expense Statement using the Tab key. In the *Employee* section, type the following data:

Name:	Lucinda Getz
Emp #:	293
SSN:	000-63-1234
Position:	Sales Representative
Department:	Sales
Manager:	Mark Wilcox
Pay Period From:	12/6
Pay Period To:	12/19

7. Type the following data into the expense statement:

Date	*Account*	*Description*	*Lodging*	*Transport*	*Fuel*	*Meals*	*Phone*
12/9	1473-96	Service Call			33.75	15.60	
12/14	2783-92	Update Orders	85.74	126.90		32.40	2.45

Your screen should look like the following illustration:

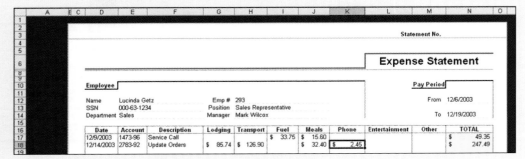

8. Create a custom header by completing the following steps:
   a. Click File and then click Page Setup.
   b. Click the Header/Footer tab.
   c. Click the Custom Header button.
   d. Type your name in the *Left section* box.
   e. Click in the *Right section* box and click the Insert File Name button.
   f. Click the OK button twice.
9. Save the worksheet by completing the following steps:
   a. Click File and then click Save.
   b. Name the file **eec2x01**.
   c. Click Save.
10. Print and then close the **eec2x01** file.

QUICK STEPS

Save a Template
1. Click File, Save As.
2. Click the down-pointing arrow to the right of the *Save as type* box.
3. Click *Template (*.xlt)*.

Creating a New Template

Creating a template is simply a matter of creating a workbook and then saving the workbook as a template. The workbook should contain the standard data that would be used over and over again each time the workbook is used. The two biggest advantages of using templates are they save you time, since much of the data is already entered, and they insure consistency in the appearance of workbooks.

Since Excel saves workbooks using the extension *.xls* and it saves templates using the extension *.xlt*, being able to see the file name extension is quite useful. If you cannot view the extensions, you cannot tell which files are templates and which files are workbooks. If the extensions are not displayed, the option to hide them must be selected. To show file name extensions, use either My Computer or Windows Explorer to find the folder containing the files with the extensions you want to see. Open the folder, and then click Tools and Folder Options. Click the View tab on the Folder Options dialog box. In the *Advanced settings* section, the check box for the *Hide file extensions for known file types* option will be selected. Click the box so that it is no longer selected and then click OK. The exercises in this book assume that the file extensions are not hidden.

If you want to be able to view the first page of a template in the *Preview* portion of the Templates dialog box, you must set this up before saving the template. Click File and then Properties. Click the Summary tab on the Properties dialog box, click the *Save preview picture* check box, then click OK.

QUICK STEPS

Display File Extensions Using Windows Explorer or My Computer
1. Open the folder in either Windows Explorer or My Computer.
2. Click Tools, then Folder Options.
3. Click the View tab.
4. The *Hide extensions for known file types* option should not be selected.

exercise 2

CREATING A TEMPLATE

(Note: Make sure to turn on your display of file extensions to complete this chapter's exercises and assessments.)

1. Open a new Excel workbook.
2. Create a custom header that has your name left-aligned and the name of the file right-aligned.
3. You are going to create a monthly income statement as a template so that it can be used over again each month. Type the following data in the cells indicated:

Cell	Data
A4	Whitewater Canoe and Kayak Corporation
A5	Income Statement
A7	For the Month Ending:
A9	Sales
A10	Less: cost of goods sold
A11	Gross margin
A13	Operating expenses:
A14	Wages expense
A15	Depreciation expense
A16	Insurance expense
A17	Operating income
A19	Other Expenses:
A20	Interest expense
A21	Net income

4. Save the file on your data disk. For now, just save it as a regular workbook file. Name the file **eec2x02**.

5. Format the worksheet by completing the following steps:
   a. Automatically adjust the width of column A so that the name of the company fits in one cell.
   b. Center the data in A4 across columns A, B, C, and D. Center the data in A5 across columns A, B, C, and D.
   c. Format cells A7, A11, A17, and A21 so that data entered into them will be right-aligned in the cell.
   d. Format the data in cells A4, A5, and A7 so that the font style is bold and the font size is 12.
   e. Format cells C9 through D21 so that numbers entered into those cells are displayed in the Accounting format with zero decimal places and the dollar sign symbol displayed.
   f. Format cell B7 so that data entered in that cell displays as the month (Mar, for example) and year only.
   g. Place a single-line border on the bottom of cells D11, C16, D16, and D20. Place a double-line border on the bottom of cell D21.
6. Enter the following formulas in the cells indicated:

Cell	Formula
D11	=D9-D10
D16	=SUM(C14:C16)
D17	=D11-D16
D21	=D17-D20

Your screen should now look like the illustration at the right. You are now ready to save the file as a template.

7. Complete the following steps to save the file as a template:
   a. Click File and Save As.
   b. When the Save As dialog box appears, click the down-pointing arrow to the right of the *Save as type* option box and then click *Template (*.xlt)*.
   c. Notice that the file name automatically changed to **eec2x02.xlt** and that the *Templates* folder is displayed in the *Save in* box. Click Save.
8. Close the **eec2x02.xlt** template. You must close the template file before you can make a new worksheet based on it.

	A	B	C	D
4	Whitewater Canoe and Kayak Corporation			
5	Income Statement			
6				
7	For the Month Ending:			
8				
9	Sales			
10	Less: cost of goods sold			
11	Gross margin			$ -
12				
13	Operating expenses:			
14	Wages expense			
15	Depreciation expense			
16	Insurance expense			$ -
17	Operating income			$ -
18				
19	Other Expenses:			
20	Interest expense			
21	Net income			$ -
22				

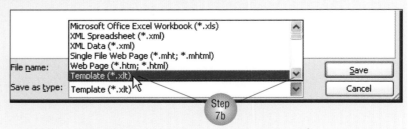

Step 7b

Editing a Template

Once a template has been created, you can easily edit it to make changes that might be needed at a later time. To edit a template, click File and then New. In the *Templates* section of the New Workbook task pane, click the <u>On my computer</u> hyperlink. Double-click the icon for the template to be edited from the General tab on the Templates dialog box. Make the necessary changes to the template and then click the Save button. When the Save As dialog box appears, click the down-pointing arrow to the right of the *Save as type* box and then click the *Template (*.xlt)* option. In the *File name* box, enter the original name of the template and click the Save button. When the warning dialog box appears asking if you want to replace the original template file, click Yes. The edited template will then be saved.

exercise 3

1. Complete the following steps to open the **eec2x02.xlt** template:
   a. If necessary, click File and then New to display the New Workbook task pane.
   b. From the New Workbook task pane under *Templates*, click <u>On my computer</u>.
   c. If necessary, click the General tab on the Templates dialog box.
   d. Double-click the **eec2x02.xlt** icon.
2. Enter the following data in the cells indicated:

Cell	Data
B7	April 2005
D9	90000
D10	50000
C14	5000
C15	1000
C16	1500
D20	800

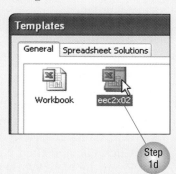

Step 1d

3. Complete the following steps to save the worksheet:
   a. Click File and then Save As.
   b. If necessary, change to the drive and/or folder where your data disk is located.
   c. Currently the name in the *File name* text box is **eec2x02.xlt**. Change the file name to **eec2x03a.xls**.
   d. Click Save.
4. Print and then close **eec2x03a.xls**.
5. You now need to edit the template. Complete the following steps to edit the **eec2x02.xlt** template:
   a. Click File and then New.
   b. From the New Workbook task pane, click the <u>On my computer</u> hyperlink.
   c. If necessary, click the General tab on the Templates dialog box.
   d. Double-click the **eec2x02.xlt** icon.
   e. Insert a new row 15.
   f. Type Rent expense in cell A15.
   g. Click File and then Save As.
   h. Make sure the *Save as type* option is *Template (*.xlt)*.
   i. Change the name in the *File name* box to **eec2x03.xlt**.

j. Click Save.

6. Close the **eec2x03.xlt** template. You must close the template file before you can make a new worksheet based on it.

7. Complete the following steps to open the **eec2x03.xlt** template:
   a. Click File and then New.
   b. From the New Workbook task pane, click the <u>On my computer</u> hyperlink.
   c. If necessary, click the General tab on the Templates dialog box.
   d. Double-click the **eec2x03.xlt** icon. Notice that the new *Rent Expense* category is now in the template.

8. Enter the following data in the cells indicated:

Cell	Data
B7	May 2005
D9	93000
D10	49500
C14	5000
C15	2200
C16	1000
C17	1500
D21	800

9. Complete the following steps to save the worksheet:
   a. Click File and then Save As.
   b. Check the *Save in* text box to make sure that the file is going to be saved on your data disk.
   c. Currently the name in the *File name* box is **eec2x03.xlt**. Change the file name to **eec2x03b.xls**.
   d. Click Save.

10. Print and then close **eec2x03b.xls**.

11. You need to delete the templates you created from the Templates folder. Complete the following steps to delete the template:
    a. Click File and then New.
    b. From the New Workbook task pane, click the <u>On my computer</u> hyperlink.
    c. If necessary, click the General tab on the Templates dialog box.
    d. Right-click the **eec2x02.xlt** and **eec2x03.xlt** icons. Click Delete.
    e. The Confirm File Delete dialog box is displayed. Click Yes.
    f. Close the Templates dialog box.

12. Close Excel.

Managing Workbook Properties

Compare Workbooks Side by Side
1. Open the workbooks.
2. Click Window.
3. Click *Compare side by side with*.
4. Click Synchronous Scrolling button.

If you are the only person using your Excel files and if you use descriptive file names, you may not need to worry about managing a workbook's properties. However, in an office where many people share files, storing document details using the Workbook Properties dialog box is a good idea. As shown in Figure 2.2, the Workbook Properties dialog box allows you to store details about the workbook such as the subject of the workbook, the name of its author, and the company. Storing details about its category and keywords provides a means for you to search for the workbook using Excel's File Search command as well as providing a means by which you can store and group the workbook files. Maintaining file properties

EXCEL

can be a lot of work at first, but in the long run it pays large benefits in terms of better file organization, especially in an office where many people share documents.

To define or modify workbook properties, click File and then click Properties. The Workbook Properties dialog box shown in Figure 2.2 is displayed. From the Summary tab you can enter information about the current workbook file such as the subject of the file, its author, the company name, a category the workbook file falls under, and keywords that describe the file. Typically, at least the author's name is entered as a default. Table 2.1 explains the types of information provided by the other tabs in this dialog box.

FIGURE

2.2 *Properties Dialog Box with Summary Tab Selected*

TABLE

2.1 *Workbook Properties Dialog Box Tab Contents*

Tab	Description
General	Information from the Windows file system on name, location, size, and so on
Statistics	Statistical information on the file such as when it was created, modified, accessed, and printed
Contents	The worksheet titles
Custom	Allows you to select from 27 built-in fields such as Date completed, Department and Purpose, or add a field of your own that can contain text, dates, numbers, or Yes/No information

You can search for a workbook file using any of the data entered into the Workbook Properties dialog box. To do so, click File and then File Search. The Basic File Search task pane is displayed. Click the Advanced Search hyperlink near the bottom of the task pane. You can select a category, such as author or company, by clicking the down-pointing arrow at the right of the *Property* box and choosing from the options in the drop-down list. You can even search on more than one category. For example, you could search by both author and keywords.

Using Multiple Workbooks

QUICK STEPS

Arrange Multiple Worksheets
1. Click Window.
2. Click Arrange.

You can easily work with data from different workbooks at the same time using Excel. One way to do this is by comparing workbooks side by side, which allows you to scroll through both workbooks at the same time. To do this, open the workbooks you want to compare. From the Window menu, click Compare Side by Side with. If only two workbooks are open, the name of the second workbook will automatically be included on the Window menu. For example, say the files First Quarter and Second Quarter are open and First Quarter is currently active. In this case the command on the Window menu will read "Compare Side by Side with Second Quarter.xls." Once the Compare Side by Side command is selected, the two workbooks are arranged side by side and the Compare Side by Side toolbar, shown in Figure 2.3, is displayed.

FIGURE

| 2.3 | *The Compare Side by Side Toolbar* |

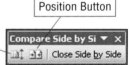

Reset Window Position Button

Synchronous Scrolling Button

HINT

After closing the Compare Side by Side toolbar, you can show it again by selecting the Tools menu and clicking Customize, clicking the Toolbars tab on the Customize dialog box, and then selecting *Compare Side by Side* in the *Toolbars* list box.

If the Synchronous Scrolling button is selected, you can scroll through the workbooks at the same time. If it is not selected, you can scroll through either one workbook or the other. Clicking the Reset Window Position button resets the workbook windows to the positions they were in when you first started comparing the workbooks. Clicking the Close Side by Side button ends the command.

Another way to work with data from different workbooks at the same time is by creating a workspace which enables you to open several workbooks at the same time with just one step. Once several workbooks are open, you can copy all the data from the open workbooks into a new workbook, and consolidate the data from several workbooks into one worksheet.

Arranging Multiple Workbooks on the Desktop

If you want to work with more than one workbook at a time, the workbooks must be arranged so that you can easily read the data contained in each one. To arrange multiple workbooks, click Window and then Arrange. As shown in Figure 2.4, there are four options for arranging windows in the desktop: Tiled, Horizontal, Vertical, and Cascade. Select one of these options and then click OK. The open workbooks will be arranged so that the data from each workbook can be viewed at the same time.

2.4 *The Arrange Windows Dialog Box*

Using a Workspace

If you frequently work with the same group of workbooks, you may want to create a customized workspace. A customized workspace allows you to open a group of workbooks in one step. Information about the open files, such as their locations, window sizes, and screen positions, is stored in a workspace file. Then, instead of opening each individual workbook, all you have to do is open the workspace file, and all the individual workbooks that are a part of the file are opened.

To create a workspace, first open the workbooks you want to be included in the workspace and then size and position them as you want them to appear each time the workspace file is opened. Click File. You may need to expand the File menu in order to click Save Workspace. Enter a name for the workspace file in the File name box. The extension for a workspace file is *.xlw*. Whenever you want to open the group of workbooks together, open the workspace file.

Create a Workspace
1. Click File.
2. Click Save Workspace.

Merging Multiple Workbooks into a Single Workbook

Once you have multiple workbooks open at the same time, you can easily copy worksheets from each workbook into a single workbook. To copy a worksheet from one workbook to another, press the Ctrl key and drag the sheet tab of the worksheet you want to copy to the sheet tabs in the workbook where you want to place the copied worksheet.

Once multiple worksheets have been copied into a single workbook, if they are not in the order you would like, you can easily change their positions. To change the position of a worksheet in a workbook, simply click on the worksheet tab and drag it to the new location.

Copy Multiple Worksheets into a Single Workbook
1. Press the Ctrl key.
2. Drag sheet tab of copied worksheet to sheet tabs in workbook into which copied worksheet is to be placed.

exercise

DEFINING WORKBOOK PROPERTIES, COMPARING WORKBOOKS SIDE BY SIDE, USING A WORKSPACE, AND MERGING WORKSHEETS INTO A WORKBOOK

1. Open Excel.
2. Greenspace Architects has a separate income workbook for each quarter of the year. Before you work with these workbooks, you want to define their workbook properties.
   a. Open the **Net Income1stQtr** workbook.
   b. Save it as **Income1st.xls**.
   c. Click File and then Properties.

d. The Workbook Properties dialog box is displayed. If necessary, click the Summary tab.

e. In the *Title* text box, enter **Net Income First Quarter**.

f. In the *Subject* text box, enter **Net Income for January, February, March**.

g. Enter your name in the *Author* text box.

h. In the *Company* text box, enter **Greenspace Architects**.

i. In the *Category* text box, enter **Income reports**.

j. In the *Keywords* text box, enter **Income, net, first quarter**.

k. In the *Comments* text box, enter **Report must be distributed to managers by April 10**.

l. Click OK.

m. Save the **Income1st** workbook and close it.

3. Now set the workbook properties for the **NetIncome2ndQuarter** workbook.

a. Open the **NetIncome2ndQtr** workbook.

b. Save it as **Income2nd.xls**.

c. Click File and then Properties.

d. The Workbook Properties dialog box is displayed. If necessary, click the Summary tab.

e. In the *Title* text box enter **Net Income Second Quarter**.

f. In the *Subject* text box enter **Net Income for April, May, June**.

g. Enter your name in the *Author* text box.

h. In the *Company* text box enter **Greenspace Architects**.

i. In the *Category* text box enter **Income reports**.

j. In the *Keywords* text box enter **Income, net, second quarter**.

k. In the *Comments* text box enter **Report must be distributed to managers by July 10**.

l. Click OK.

m. Save the **Income2nd** workbook and close it.

4. Use the Search feature to search for these two files.

a. Click File.

b. Click File Search.

c. The Basic File Search task pane is displayed. Click the <u>Advanced File Search</u> hyperlink near the bottom of the task pane.

d. The Advanced File Search task pane is displayed. Click the down-pointing arrow to the right of the *Property* box.

e. From the drop-down list, select *Keywords*.

f. Click the down-pointing arrow to the right of the *Condition* box. From the drop-down list, select *includes*.

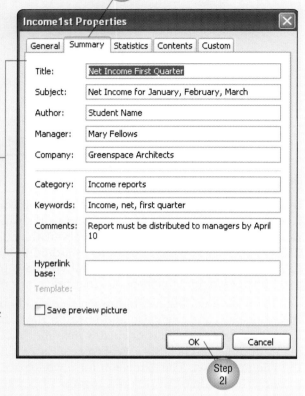

Step 2d

Steps 2e–2k

Step 2l

Step 4c

EXCEL

g. In the *Value* box, enter **net income**.

h. Click Add.

i. Click Go. It may take a few moments, but the **Income1st** and **Income2nd** files will be displayed in the Search Results task pane.

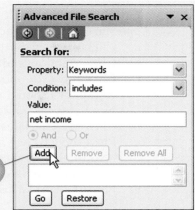

5. Next, you want to compare the net income for the first quarter with the net income for the second quarter. To do this, you will use the Compare side by side command.

a. Double-click the ***Income1st*** file in the Search Results task pane.

b. Double-click the ***Income2nd*** file in the Search Results task pane.

c. Close the Search Results task pane.

d. Click Window on the menu bar and then Compare Side by Side with.

e. At the Compare Side by Side dialog box, click ***Income1st.xls*** and then click OK.

6. The two workbooks are now displayed one on top of the other. The Compare Side by Side toolbar is also displayed. The Synchronous Scrolling button on the toolbar should be selected. Click either scroll bar to scroll through the two workbooks simultaneously. Compare the first quarter total net income after taxes with the second quarter total net income after taxes (cell E22).

7. Click the Synchronous Scrolling button so that it is no longer selected. Scroll through each workbook individually. Click the Close Side by Side button on the Compare Side by Side toolbar. Click the **Income1st** worksheet to make it active. You want to modify the workbook properties.

a. Click File and then Properties. If necessary, click the Summary tab.

b. In the *Manager* text box, enter **Mary Fellows** and then click OK.

c. Save and close the **Income1st** workbook.

d. Make sure the **Income2nd** worksheet is active.

e. Click File and then Properties. If necessary, click the Summary tab.

f. In the *Manager* text box, enter **Mary Fellows** and then click OK.

g. Save and close the **Income2nd** workbook.

8. The sales figures for individual sales representatives of Copper Clad Incorporated for the last quarter of 2004 are stored in three separate workbooks. Since these three workbooks are frequently used at the same time, you want to create a workspace for them. Open **OctSales.xls**, **NovSales.xls**, and **DecSales.xls**.

9. All three workbooks are open, but you cannot see them because they are on top of one another. Complete the following steps to adjust how the workbooks are displayed on your desktop:

a. Click Window and then Arrange.

b. Click the *Vertical* option at the Arrange Windows dialog box and then click OK. The workbooks are now arranged next to each other.

10. Create a workspace by completing the following steps:

a. Click File and then Save Workspace.

b. At the Save Workspace dialog box, enter **Last Quarter** in the *File name* box and then click Save.

11. Close the **OctSales.xls**, **NovSales.xls**, and **DecSales.xls** workbooks.

12. Open the workspace you just created by completing the following steps:

a. Click File and then Open.

b. At the Open dialog box, click ***LastQuarter.xlw*** to select it and then click Open. The workspace you created is now open.

13. Open a new workbook and copy the *October04* worksheet, the *November04* worksheet, and the *December04* worksheet into the new workbook by completing the following steps:
    a. Click the New button on the Standard toolbar to open a new workbook.
    b. Click Window and Arrange.
    c. Click the *Tiled* option at the Arrange Windows dialog box and then click OK. Four workbooks should now be displayed: the new blank workbook and **DecSales.xls**, **NovSales.xls**, and **OctSales.xls**.
    d. Click the **OctSales.xls** workbook to make it active.
    e. Press the Ctrl key and drag the *October04* sheet tab to the new workbook, placing it to the left of the *Sheet1* tab.
    f. Click the **NovSales.xls** workbook to make it active.
    g. Press the Ctrl key and drag the *November04* sheet tab to the new workbook, placing it between the *October04* tab and the *Sheet1* tab.
    h. Click the **DecSales.xls** workbook to make it active.
    i. Press the Ctrl key and drag the *December04* sheet tab to the new workbook, placing it between the *November04* tab and the *Sheet1* tab.
14. The worksheets are now all copied into the new workbook. Close the **DecSales.xls**, **NovSales.xls**, and **OctSales.xls** files. Click the Maximize button on the new workbook. Save the new workbook on your data disk using the file name **eec2x04**.
15. Close **eec2x04**.

Consolidating Data from Several Worksheets into a List

If you have several worksheets in one workbook or several worksheets from different workbooks, data from each worksheet can be consolidated on a separate worksheet. To consolidate the data, click Data and then Consolidate. The Consolidate dialog box shown in Figure 2.5 appears. You first have to decide what function you want performed on the consolidated data. Figure 2.6 shows you the options from the *Function* drop-down list. Next you have to select all the references you want consolidated. If you want the consolidated data to include labels, you can select the appropriate check boxes in the *Use labels in* section. When all the selections have been made, click OK. The data is then all consolidated onto one worksheet.

FIGURE

2.5 *The Consolidate Dialog Box*

HINT
If the data you want to consolidate is in many different workbooks, you might want to first copy the data to be consolidated into a single workbook. The consolidation process will be easier if the data is all in one workbook.

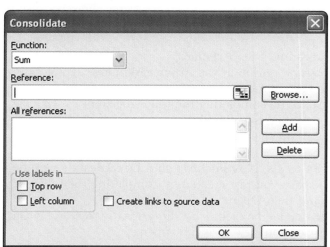

2.6 Functions That Can Be Performed on Consolidated Data

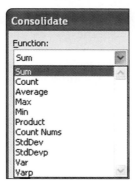

exercise 5

CONSOLIDATING DATA INTO A LIST

1. Open **eec2x04**, the file you created in Exercise 4.
2. Save the workbook with the Save As command and name it **eec2x05**.
3. You want to consolidate the figures on the three separate worksheets into one worksheet. Complete the following steps to consolidate the data:
   a. Click the *Sheet1* tab.
   b. Click Format, point to Sheet, and then click Rename. Enter the following: LastQtr04.
   c. Click cell A1 on the *LastQtr04* worksheet.
   d. Click Data and then Consolidate.
   e. Check to make sure that *Sum* is displayed in the *Function* box.
   f. If necessary, click in the *Reference* box. The insertion point must be in the *Reference* box.
   g. Click the *October04* sheet tab. You may have to scroll to the left to see it.
   h. If the Consolidate dialog box is in the way, click the title bar and drag it to the right. Select cells A1 through B17.
   i. Click the Add button.

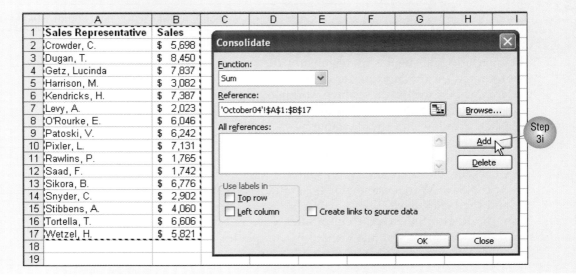

j. Click the *November04* sheet tab.

k. Cells A1 through B17 should already be selected. Click the Add button.

l. Click the *December04* sheet tab.

m. Cells A1 through B17 should already be selected. Click the Add button.

n. In the *Use labels in* section, click the *Top row* check box and the *Left column* check box.

o. Click OK.

4. The data is consolidated in the *LastQtr04* worksheet. If necessary, click the *LastQtr04* sheet tab. Widen column A to display all the names. Add a custom header that displays your name at the left margin and the file name at the right margin. Print the *LastQtr04* worksheet.

5. Save the workbook with the same name (**eec2x05**).

6. Close **eec2x05**.

Linking Workbooks

Link Workbooks

1. Click cell where linked data will be placed.
2. Type =.
3. Locate worksheet containing data to be linked.
4. Click the cell to be linked.
5. Press Enter.

In many cases, worksheets utilize data that is already located in another worksheet. For example, someone preparing a quarterly report would need the figures from the monthly reports for each month in the quarter. Instead of reentering all that data into the quarterly report, with Excel you can link the quarterly report worksheet to the monthly reports worksheets. Once a link has been established, if the data in the worksheet to which you have linked is changed, the link will automatically update itself to reflect any changes when the worksheet is opened. A link can be established between worksheets in the same workbook, between worksheets in different workbooks, and even to data found on company intranets or the Internet.

When you link worksheets, you are entering a formula that refers to another worksheet; that is why you always begin the link by keying the equal sign.

To link worksheets, click the cell where the linked data will be placed and type = to begin the link. Locate the worksheet where the data you want to link to is stored, click the cell to be linked, and then press Enter. The worksheet containing the linked data will appear with the appropriate data displayed in the linked cell. Links can even be used in formulas and functions.

exercise 6

USING A WORKSPACE AND LINKING WORKBOOKS

1. Open Excel.

2. The quarterly sales figures by regions for the sales representatives of Copper Clad Incorporated for the last quarter of 2004 are stored in three separate workbooks. Create a workspace for these three workbooks by completing the following steps:

a. Open **RegionSalesOct**, **RegionSalesNov**, and **RegionSalesDec**.

b. Click Window and then Arrange.

c. Click the *Vertical* option at the Arrange Windows dialog box and then click OK. You can now see all three workbooks.

d. Click File and then Save Workspace.

e. At the Save Workspace dialog box, enter **4thQuarterSales** in the *File name* box and then click Save.

3. Close the **RegionSalesOct**, **RegionSalesNov**, and **RegionSalesDec** workbooks.

4. Open the workspace you just created by completing the following steps:

a. Click File and then Open.

b. The Open dialog box is displayed. Double-click ***4thQuarterSales.xlw*** to open it. The workspace you created is now open.

c. Open **FourthQtrSummary**.

d. Click Window and Arrange.

e. Click the *Tiled* option on the Arrange Windows dialog box and click OK. There are now four workbooks displayed.

5. The **FourthQtrSummary** workbook is going to summarize the data found in the other three workbooks. Click cell B5 in the **FourthQtrSummary** workbook. In this cell, you want the total for the North Region's sales in October, November, and December. Complete the following steps to link the three subtotals for the North Region's sales to the **FourthQtrSummary** workbook (you may need to scroll down in each window in order to select the necessary cell):

a. In cell B5 in the **FourthQtrSummary** workbook, type =.

b. Click the **RegionSalesOct** workbook and then click cell C7 in that workbook. Notice that a reference to that cell immediately appears in the **FourthQtrSummary** workbook.

Step 5b

c. With the insertion point in cell B5 in the **FourthQtrSummary** workbook to the right of the reference to the linked cell, enter +.

d. Click the **RegionSalesNov** workbook to make it active, click cell C7 in that workbook, and then enter + in cell B5 in the **FourthQtrSummary** workbook.

e. Click the **RegionSalesDec** workbook to make it active and then click cell C7 in that workbook.

f. Press Enter. The total for the North Region's sales for the months of October, November, and December appears in cell B5 in the **FourthQuarterSummary** workbook.

6. Complete steps similar to Step 5 to link the three subtotals for the South Region's sales to the **FourthQtrSummary** workbook. Use cell B6 in the **FourthQuarterSummary** workbook and cell C13 in the monthly workbooks.

7. Complete steps similar to Step 5 to link the three subtotals for the East Region's sales to the **FourthQtrSummary** workbook. Use cell B7 in the **FourthQuarterSummary** workbook and cell C19 in the monthly workbooks.

8. Complete steps similar to Step 5 to link the three subtotals for the West Region's sales to the **FourthQtrSummary** workbook. Use cell B8 in the **FourthQuarterSummary** workbook and cell C25 in the monthly workbooks.

9. Next you want to use a link in an Excel function. In the **FourthQuarterSummary** workbook, scroll down until you can see cells A14 through B19. In this area of the

worksheet you want to calculate the average sales for each region for the fourth quarter. Complete the following steps to create the necessary links:

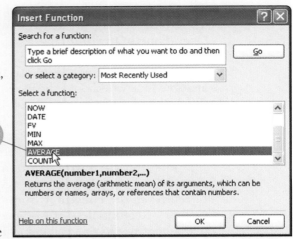

Step 9c

a. In the **FourthQtrSummary** workbook, click cell B16.
b. Click the Insert menu and then click Function.
c. In the *Select a function* list box, click *AVERAGE* and then click OK. The Function Arguments dialog box opens.
d. In the **RegionSalesOct** workbook, click cell C7. The reference to cell C7 appears in the *Number1* text box. If the Function Arguments dialog box gets in the way, you can move it by clicking it and dragging it to a new location.
f. Type , (a comma).
g. Click the **RegionSalesNov** workbook to activate it and then click cell C7.
h. Type , (a comma).
i. Click the **RegionSalesDec** workbook to activate it and then click cell C7.
j. Press Enter.

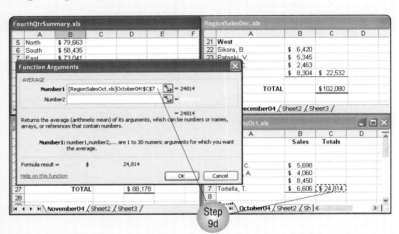

Step 9d

10. Complete steps similar to Step 9 to find the average sales for the South Region. Use cell B17 in the **FourthQtrSummary** workbook and cell C13 in the monthly workbooks.
11. Complete steps similar to Step 9 to find the average sales for the East Region. Use cell B18 in the **FourthQtrSummary** workbook and cell C19 in the monthly workbooks.
12. Complete steps similar to Step 9 to find the average sales for the West Region. Use cell B19 in the **FourthQtrSummary** workbook and cell C25 in the monthly workbooks.
13. Close the **RegionSalesOct**, **RegionSalesNov**, and **RegionSalesDec** workbooks.
14. Create a header for the workbook that displays your name at the left margin and the name of the file at the right margin. Save the **FourthQtrSummary** workbook using the file name **eec2x06**.
15. Print the **eec2x06** workbook and then close it.
16. Someone just discovered there are some mistakes on the **RegionSalesDec** workbook. Open this workbook and make the following changes:

    B7   Change *5,274* to *5,798*
    B10   Change *2,635* to *3,001*
    B24   Change *2,463* to *2,609*

17. Save and close the revised workbook.

18. Open the **eec2x06** workbook. A warning box appears asking if you want to update the links. Click Update.
19. Print the **eec2x06** workbook again. Notice how the numbers have changed.

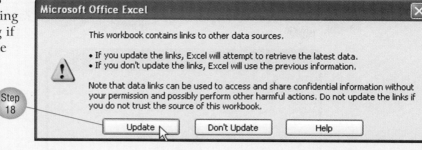

Step 18

20. Save the worksheet with the same name (**eec2x06**) and close it.

HINT

Some features are not available when you use a shared workbook. Merging cells, deleting worksheets, and defining or applying conditional formats are a few examples of things you cannot do in a shared workbook. To use these features, the workbook must be removed from shared use.

Sharing Workbooks

Excel has many workgroup features—that is, features that make it easy for people to collaborate while using Excel. For example, people can share the same workbook and even use it at the same time. More than one person can make changes to the shared file at the same time. To share a workbook, click Tools and then Share Workbook. The Share Workbook dialog box, shown in Figure 2.7, appears. On the Editing tab, click the Allow changes by more than one user at the same time option. You can tell that a workbook is shared because the word [Shared] is displayed in the title bar next to the workbook name. Once the option for sharing a workbook has been selected, additional sharing options can be selected from the Advanced Tab on the Share Workbook dialog box, as shown in Figure 2.8. Table 2.2 describes the options.

FIGURE

2.7 **The Share Workbook Dialog Box with Editing Tab Selected**

Click here to allow multiple users to edit a workbook at the same time.

Share Workbook
1. Click Tools.
2. Click Share Workbook.
3. Click the Editing tab.
4. Click the *Allow changes by more than one user at the same time* box.

2.8 *The Share Workbook Dialog Box with Advanced Tab Selected*

2.2 *Advanced Options for Sharing Workbooks*

Option	Description
Track changes	Sets the time period for how long Excel keeps the change history. The change history keeps track of how conflicting changes to the workbook were resolved.
Update changes	Sets when everyone's changes will be saved. They can be saved when the file is saved or at a regular time interval.
Conflicting changes between users	Sets how to resolve different changes made to the same data. Either your changes are saved over the other users' or Excel can prompt you to choose which change should be saved.

When you no longer want to share a workbook, you can turn the sharing option off by clicking Tools and then Share Workbook. Click the *Allow changes by more than one user at the same time* check box to remove the check mark and then click OK. A warning box will be displayed alerting you that the workbook will no longer be available for shared use. Clicking Yes removes the workbook from shared use.

exercise 7

1. Open **ExcelWorksheet01** from your data disk.
2. Save the document using the Save As command and name it **eec2x07**.
3. Create a custom header with your name displayed at the left margin and the file name displayed at the right margin.
4. Assume you are the head of personnel at Whitewater Canoe and Kayak Corporation. Changes need to be made to the employee records. You need to confer with Shirley Aultman, the office manager, regarding these changes. The easiest way to do this is for the two of you to share the worksheet. To tell which person is accessing which worksheet, you have to assign user names to the worksheets. Complete the following steps to change the user name:
    a. Click Tools and then Options.
    b. Click the General tab on the Options dialog box.
    c. Look in the *User name* box. On a piece of paper, write down the name that is currently entered. When you complete this exercise, you will change the name back.
    d. Enter your name in the *User name* box and then click OK.
5. Click the Save button on the Standard toolbar.
6. To simulate sharing workbooks, you are going to open another copy of Excel. For the simulation to work, you must open Excel from the Start button. Click the Start button, point to All Programs, and then open another copy of Excel.
7. You now have a second copy of Excel running with an unnamed worksheet on the screen. You need to change the user name for this copy of Excel. This will be the copy being run by the office manager. Complete the following steps to change the user name:
    a. Click Tools and then Options.
    b. Click the General tab on the Options dialog box.
    c. In the *User name* box, type Shirley Aultman then click OK.
    d. Right-click the Windows taskbar and click *Tile Windows Horizontally*. **(Hint: Make sure you do not right-click on a button that is on the Windows taskbar. You must right-click an empty spot on the taskbar.)**
    e. Make sure the copy of Excel that currently has the workbook **eec2x07** open is on top. If necessary, rearrange the two windows by clicking and dragging on the title bars.

8. You currently have the **eec2x07** workbook open. Complete the following steps to see what happens if Shirley tries to open the same workbook:
   a. Click in Shirley's copy of the program (the one on the bottom) to make sure it is the active program.
   b. Click the Open button on the Standard toolbar of Shirley's program and try to open the **eec2x07** file on your data disk.
   c. The File in Use dialog box is displayed. Since **eec2x07** has not been designated as a shared workbook, you cannot make any changes to it once it is open. Clicking the Read Only button will open a copy of the workbook that you can view but not modify. Clicking the Notify button will open a read-only version of the workbook and you will be notified when it is no longer being used by someone else.
   d. Click Cancel.
9. Complete the following steps to designate **eec2x07** as a shared workbook:
   a. Click in the window for **eec2x07** (the top window) to make it active.
   b. On the Menu bar of the top window, click Tools and then Share Workbook.
   c. Click the *Allow changes by more than one user at the same time* check box to select it.
   d. Click OK.
   e. At the warning box that is displayed notifying you that the workbook will be saved, click OK.

   Step 9c

   Share Workbook

   Editing | Advanced

   ☑ Allow changes by more than one user at the same time. This also allows workbook merging.

   Who has this workbook open now:

   Student Name (Exclusive) - 7/30/2003 8:44 AM

10. Complete the following steps to open a copy of the shared workbook:
    a. Click in Shirley's copy of the program (the one on the bottom) to select it.
    b. Click the Open button on the Standard toolbar of Shirley's program and open the **eec2x07** file on your data disk.
11. The workbook is now open in both program windows. Notice that the word *[Shared]* appears in the title bar of both windows. Complete the following steps to make changes to the worksheet:
    a. Access Shirley's copy of the workbook (the one on the bottom). Scroll to the bottom of the list and enter the following data for an employee that was just hired:

Cell	Data
A27	Goldman
B27	Rona
C27	000-30-8311
D27	Assistant
E27	7.50

    b. Click the Save button on the Standard toolbar of Shirley's copy of the workbook.
    c. Activate your copy of the workbook (the one on top). One of the employees was promoted, and you need to make the necessary changes. Make the following changes to the contents of the cells listed:

Cell	Data
D17	Assistant Manager
E17	8.75

    d. Adjust the width of column D so that the complete position title is displayed.
    e. Click the Save button on the Standard toolbar of your copy of the workbook.

f. An information box appears notifying you that your workbook was updated with changes made by someone else. Excel updates the workbook whenever it is saved. Click OK.

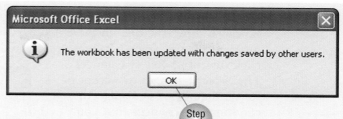

Step 11f

g. On your copy of the workbook, scroll down so that row 27 is displayed. The data on the new employee, entered by Shirley, appears in your worksheet. Notice the small triangles in the upper left corner of each cell. When you move the mouse pointer over one of those triangles, information on the change that Shirley made is displayed.

	A	B	C	D	E	F	G	H
23	Meza	Rose	777-80-5551	Manager	$ 28.75			
24	Piotrowski	Ken	999-76-8137	Manager	$ 32.00			
25	Post	Jackie	555-79-5030	Sales	$ 18.00			
26	Jackson	Elizabeth	222-60-2010	Sales	$			
27	Goldman	Rona	000-30-8311	Assistant	$			
28								
29								
30								

Shirley Aultman, 7/30/2003 8:49 AM:
Changed cell D27 from '<blank>' to 'Assistant'.

Step 11g

h. Access Shirley's copy of the workbook (the one on the bottom) and save it. When you are notified that the workbook has been updated, click OK. Look at cells D17 and E17 in Shirley's copy of the workbook to see the changes you made in your copy.

12. Complete the following steps to see what happens when users sharing a workbook enter conflicting data into the same cell:

a. In Shirley's copy of the workbook (the one on the bottom), change the data in cell E14 from *9.50* to *10.75*. Save the workbook.

b. In your copy of the workbook (the one on the top), change the data in cell E14 from *9.50* to *10.25*. Save the workbook.

c. The Resolve Conflicts dialog box appears, notifying you that conflicting changes have been made to the worksheet. The first person who saves the workbook after conflicting changes have been entered is the one who gets to resolve the conflict. Click the Accept Mine button.

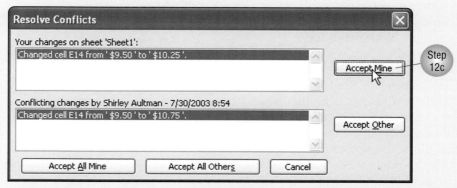

Step 12c

d. Access Shirley's copy of the workbook and save it. When the dialog box appears informing you the workbook has been updated, click OK. Notice that *10.25* is now entered in cell E14 in Shirley's workbook.

e. Shirley still has an opportunity to reject your changes. On the Menu bar in Shirley's copy (the one on the bottom), click Tools and, if necessary, wait a moment for the Track Changes option to display. Point to Track Changes and then click Accept or Reject Changes.

f. The Select Changes to Accept or Reject dialog box is displayed. You can limit the changes that you review using this dialog box. Click OK to accept the default options.

g. The Accept or Reject Changes dialog box is displayed. Click the Accept button until your dialog box displays the conflicting numbers entered in cell E14.

h. Shirley is going to reject your change to cell E14. Click the second option in the list, the option originally entered by Shirley, and then click Accept. Save the workbook.

i. Access your copy of the workbook (the one on top) and click the Save button. Click OK when the dialog box appears notifying you that changes were made by other users. Now you want to look at a history of the changes that were made. Click Tools on the Menu bar of your copy of the workbook, point to Track Changes, and click Highlight Changes.

j. The Highlight Changes dialog box is displayed. The *Since I last saved* option should be displayed in the *When* box.

k. Click the *List changes on a new sheet* check box. A check mark should be inserted in the box.

l. Click OK. A new sheet tab is added to the worksheet called *History*. On this worksheet you can see that Shirley rejected your change in cell E14.

m. Save your worksheet (the one on top). Notice that the *History* sheet tab is no longer displayed. You cannot make any changes to the *History* worksheet, and it is hidden when not needed.

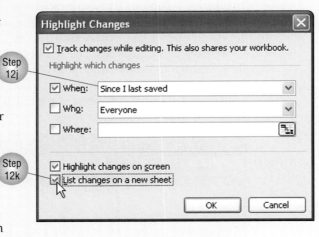

13. Print a copy of your worksheet.

14. Access Shirley's copy of the workbook (the one on the bottom). Change the user name back to the original entry and exit the workbook by completing the following steps:

a. Click Tools and then Options.

b. Click the General tab.

c. In the *User name* box, enter the name that was originally displayed when you started the exercise. Click OK. Click the Save button to save the file.

d. Click File on the menu bar in Shirley's workbook and click Exit.
15. Access your copy of the workbook. Maximize the window. Complete the following steps to designate that the workbook is no longer to be shared:
   a. Click Tools and then Share Workbook.
   b. Click the *Allow changes by more than one user at the same time* check box so that it is no longer selected. Click OK.
16. Complete the following steps to change the user name back to the original entry:
   a. Click Tools and then Options.
   b. Click the General tab.
   c. In the *User name* box, enter the name that was originally displayed when you started the exercise. Click OK.
17. Save the worksheet with the same name (**eec2x07**) and close it.

CHAPTER summary

➤ If a workbook is used repeatedly for the same purpose, a template should be created for it. A template saves the basic format of a workbook so that labels, formats, formulas—anything that would remain the same each time the workbook is used—do not have to be entered each time. Excel comes with templates for a Balance Sheet, an Expense Statement, a Loan Amortization, a Sales Invoice, and a Timecard.

➤ The default template folder for all the Office 2003 applications is:

   C:\Documents and Settings*user_name*\Application Data\Microsoft\Templates.

➤ Create a new template by entering the data that will be used repeatedly into the worksheet, clicking File and then Save As. The Save As dialog box is displayed. Save the file as a template by clicking the down-pointing arrow to the right of the *Save as type* box, selecting *Template (*.xlt)* from the drop-down list, and then clicking Save.

➤ Edit a new template by clicking File and then New. Open the template to be edited by clicking the <u>On my computer</u> hyperlink on the New Workbook task pane. When the Templates dialog box is displayed, click the General tab and then double-click the appropriate icon. Make the changes to the template and click the Save button on the Standard toolbar. When the Save As dialog box is displayed, click the down-pointing arrow to the right of the *Save as type* box, select *Template (*.xlt)* from the drop-down list, and click Save. Save the file by clicking Yes when the warning dialog box appears asking if you want to replace the original file.

➤ Using the Compare Side by Side command allows you to scroll through two workbooks at the same time.

➤ Creating a workspace allows you to open several workbooks at the same time with just one step. A workspace file uses the extension *.xlw*.

➤ Data from one worksheet can be consolidated into another worksheet. For example, data from one worksheet could be consolidated by adding it to the data in another worksheet.

➤ If a link has been established from cell A5 in *Sheet1* to cell D10 in *Sheet2*, for example, whatever data is entered in cell D10 will automatically appear in cell A5. If the data in cell D10 is changed, then the data in cell A5 will automatically be updated to reflect that change.

➤ If a workbook is shared, then more than one person can use it and make changes to it at the same time.

FEATURES summary

FEATURE	MENU/COMMANDS
Access Excel's built-in templates	Click File, New, <u>On my computer</u>, Spreadsheet Solutions tab.
Save a template	Click File, Save As, the down-pointing arrow to the right of the *Save as type* box, *Template (*.xlt)*.
Display file extensions using Windows Explorer or My Computer	Click Tools, Folder Options, View tab.
Compare workbooks side by side	Open the workbooks, click Window, Compare side by side with, Synchronous Scrolling button.
Arrange multiple worksheets	Click Window, Arrange.
Create a workspace	Click File, Save Workspace.
Copy multiple worksheets into a single workbook	Press Ctrl key, drag sheet tab of copied worksheet to sheet tabs in workbook in which copied worksheet is to be placed.
Consolidate data	Click Data, Consolidate.
Link workbooks	Click cell where linked data will be placed then type =. Locate worksheet containing data to be linked and click cell to be linked, then press Enter.
Share workbook	Click Tools, Share Workbook.

CONCEPTS check

Completion: On a blank sheet of paper, indicate the correct term, command, symbol, or explanation for each description.

1. Click this option on the New Workbook task pane to access the Templates dialog box.
2. This dialog box automatically appears whenever you try to save a template.
3. Click this tab in the Templates dialog box to access Excel's built-in templates.
4. Excel automatically adds this extension to the file name of a template.
5. Click this tab in the Templates dialog box to access the templates that you create.
6. List the information on a workbook file that you can enter from the Summary tab in the Workbook Properties dialog box.
7. This is the menu you access in order to compare workbook files side by side.
8. This is the extension given to workspace files.
9. Click this option on the Menu bar to arrange multiple windows on the desktop.

10. Press this key while dragging the sheet tab of a worksheet you want to copy to a different workbook.
11. Click this option on the Menu bar to consolidate data.
12. This is the first thing you type into a cell that is to contain linked data.
13. This is displayed in the title bar next to the workbook name of a workbook that is currently being shared.
14. To allow two or more people to make changes to a workbook at the same time, you have to access this dialog box.
15. List the advantages of using templates.
16. List the steps you would take to link cell E5 in a workbook named **QuarterlyProfits** to cell F15 in a workbook named **JanuarySales**.
17. List the steps you would take to display the file extensions to the file names of the files in a folder called **QuarterlyStatements**.

SKILLS check

Assessment 1

1. Open Excel.
2. Open Excel's built-in template named **Sales Invoice**.
3. Open the Workbook Properties dialog box, and enter Sales Invoice in the *Title* box, change the author to your name, change the company to Whitewater Canoe & Kayak, enter Forms in the *Category* box, and enter sales, invoice, form in the *Keywords* box.
4. Click *Insert Company Information Here*. Enter the following data. Press Alt + Enter to move the insertion point to the next line.

    Whitewater Canoe & Kayak
    34982 Olympia Blvd
    Seattle, WA 98101

5. At the bottom of the invoice, click where it says *Insert Fine Print Here*. Type the following: **Shipping charges included in unit price.**
6. At the bottom of the invoice, click where it says *Insert Farewell Statement Here*. Type the following: **River Adventure Specialists.**
7. Save the file as a template in the default template folder using the file name **WhitewaterInvoice**.
8. Close the **WhitewaterInvoice** template.
9. Open the **WhitewaterInvoice** template.
10. Enter the following customer information:

Name:	Rocky Mountain Outfitters
Address:	39853 Highway 50
City:	Howard
State:	CO
ZIP:	81233
Phone:	(719) 555-8032
Order No.	RT-594
Rep.	Jackson

11. Enter the following information:

Qty	Description	Unit Price
3	15' Pathfinder, vinyl trim, forest green	1149
2	14' 6" Trekker, vinyl trim, spruce	1199
4	12' Excursion, red	679

12. Toward the bottom of the invoice next to *Payment*, click *Select One*. Click the down-pointing arrow and click the *Check* option.
13. Create a custom header that prints your name at the left margin and the file name at the right margin.
14. Save the worksheet using the file name **eec2sc01**.
15. Print the file **eec2sc01** and then close it. (Change page setup options to print the invoice on one page.)
16. Delete the **WhitewaterInvoice.xlt** file from the default user template folder.

Assessment 2

1. Open **ExcelWorksheet02**.
2. You are going to create a template. Open the Workbook Properties dialog box and enter **Annual Costs by Quarter** in the *Title* box, enter your name in the *Author* box, enter **Greenspace Architects** in the *Company* box, enter **Expense form** in the *Category* box, and enter **costs, expenses, form** in the *Keywords* box.
3. Enter the following data:

Cell	Data
B12	1st Quarter
C12	2nd Quarter
D12	3rd Quarter
E12	4th Quarter
F12	TOTAL
A13	Operating Costs
A14	Selling Expenses
A15	General Administrative
A16	Total Costs and Expenses
B16	=SUM(B13:B15)
F13	=SUM(B13:E13)

4. Bold and center the labels in row 12.
5. Bold the label in cell A16.
6. Adjust the column widths so that the labels all fit in the columns.
7. Copy the function in cell B16 to cells C16 through F16.
8. Copy the function in cell F13 to cells F14 and F15.
9. Place a single-line border at the bottom of cells B15 through F15. Place a double-line border at the bottom of cells B16 through F16.
10. Save the file as a template in the default user template folder. Name the template **ExcelWorksheet02**.
11. Close the **ExcelWorksheet02.xlt** template.
12. Use the File Search feature to search for the template you just created. Search on the keywords *expense form*. When the search locates the template **ExcelWorksheet02.xlt**, open it.

13. Enter the following data:

Cell	Data
B13	21589
B14	15733
B15	7036
C13	23579
C14	21627
C15	9458
D13	26722
D14	24691
D15	10499
E13	31834
E14	25637
E15	14675

14. If necessary, adjust the column width of column F so all of the data is displayed.
15. Create a custom header that prints your name at the left margin and the file name at the right margin.
16. Save the worksheet on your student data disk using the file name **eec2sc02a.xls**.
17. Print and then close the **eec2sc02a.xls** file.
18. Open the template **ExcelWorksheet02.xlt**.
19. Edit the template by entering the following data:

Cell	Data
G12	AVERAGE
G13	=AVERAGE(B13:E13)

20. Copy the function in cell G13 to cells G14 and G15. *(Hint: Ignore the Divide by Zero error message. This message will go away as soon as data is entered into the worksheet.)*
21. Adjust the width of column G1 to fit the new label.
22. Save the file as a template in the default user template folder. Name the template **ExcelWorksheet03.xlt**. Replace the existing file.
23. Close the **ExcelWorksheet03.xlt** template.
24. Open the template **ExcelWorksheet03.xlt**.
25. Enter the following data:

Cell	Data
B13	20201
B14	14354
B15	6991
C13	24002
C14	20823
C15	9324
D13	25624
D14	23951
D15	11056
E13	30089
E14	24394
E15	13987

26. Create a custom header that prints your name at the left margin and the file name at the right margin.
27. Change the page orientation to landscape.
28. Save the worksheet using the file name **eec2sc02b.xls**.

29. Print and then close the **eec2sc02b.xls** file.
30. Delete the **ExcelWorksheet02.xlt** and **ExcelWorksheet03.xlt** file from the default user template folder.

Assessment 3

1. Open Excel.
2. Open **NetIncome1stQtr**, **NetIncome2ndQtr**, **NetIncome3rdQtr**, and **NetIncome4thQtr**. Arrange the workbooks and select the *Tiled* option. Save a workspace for the four files. Name the workspace **Income**.
3. Close the four files. Open **Income.xlw**.
4. Open a new workbook. Arrange the five workbooks and select the *Tiled* option.
5. Copy the *1stQtr* worksheet, *2ndQtr* worksheet, *3rdQtr* worksheet, and *4thQtr* worksheet into the workbook you opened in Step 4.
6. Close the **NetIncome1stQtr**, **NetIncome2ndQtr**, **NetIncome3rdQtr**, and **NetIncome4thQtr** workbooks.
7. Maximize the new workbook and save it using the file name **eec2sc03**.
8. Rename the *Sheet1* tab to *Totals*.
9. Copy the labels in cells A11 through A22 in the *1stQtr* worksheet to cells A11 through A22 in the *Totals* worksheet. Automatically adjust the width of column A so that the labels all fit in the column.
10. Click cell B10 in the *Totals* worksheet. Consolidate the data in cells E10 through E22 on the *1stQtr, 2ndQtr, 3rdQtr,* and *4thQtr* worksheets so that the totals on each worksheet are added together. Use the labels in the top row. Adjust the widths of the columns so that the consolidated data is displayed.
11. If necessary, click the *Totals* sheet tab. Add a custom header that displays your name at the left margin and the file name at the right margin. Print the *Totals* worksheet.
12. Save the workbook with the same name (**eec2sc03**).
13. Close **eec2sc03**.

Assessment 4

1. Open Excel.
2. Open **FallEnrollment**, **SpringEnrollment**, and **SummerEnrollment**. Arrange the workbooks using the *Vertical* option. Save a workspace for the three files. Name the workspace **Enrollment**.
3. Close the three files. Open **Enrollment.xlw**.
4. Open a new workbook. Arrange the four workbooks using the *Tiled* option.
5. Copy the *Fall, Spring,* and *Summer* worksheets into the workbook you opened in Step 4.
6. Close the **FallEnrollment**, **SpringEnrollment**, and **SummerEnrollment** workbooks.
7. Maximize the new workbook and save it using the file name **eec2sc04**.
8. Rename the *Sheet1* tab to *AverageEnrollment*.
9. Copy the labels in cells A13 through A18 in the *Fall* worksheet to cells A13 through A18 in the *AverageEnrollment* worksheet. Automatically adjust the width of column A so that the labels all fit in the column.
10. Click cell B14 in the *AverageEnrollment* worksheet. Consolidate the data in cells D14 through D18 on the *Fall, Spring,* and *Summer* worksheets so that the average of the data is calculated. Do not use any labels.
11. If necessary, click the *AverageEnrollment* sheet tab. Type the label Average Enrollment in cell B13. Bold the label in B13.
12. Adjust the width of column B so that the label fits in the column.
13. Format cells B14 through B18 to the Number format with no decimal places displayed.

14. Add a custom header that displays your name at the left margin and the name of the workbook at the right margin.
15. Print the *AverageEnrollment* worksheet.
16. Save the workbook with the same name (**eec2sc04**) and close it.

Assessment 5

1. Open **ExcelWorksheet03**. Save it as **eec2sc05**.
2. Open the **Income.xlw** file you created in Assessment 3. Arrange the windows vertically.
3. Link cell B13 in the **eec2sc05** worksheet to cell E11 in the **NetIncome1stQtr** worksheet.
4. Link cell B14 in the **eec2sc05** worksheet to cell E11 in the **NetIncome2ndQtr** worksheet.
5. Link cell B15 in the **eec2sc05** worksheet to cell E11 in the **NetIncome3rdQtr** worksheet.
6. Link cell B16 in the **eec2sc05** worksheet to cell E11 in the **NetIncome4thQtr** worksheet.
7. Close the **NetIncome1stQtr**, **NetIncome2ndQtr**, **NetIncome3rdQtr**, and **NetIncome4thQtr** workbooks. Maximize the window for the **eec2sc05** file.
8. Add a custom header to the **eec2sc5** worksheet that displays your name at the left margin and the file name at the right margin.
9. Save the **eec2sc05** worksheet.
10. Print the **eec2sc05** worksheet.
11. Open the **NetIncome2ndQtr** workbook. Type the following into cell C11: 69302.
12. Save and close the **NetIncome2ndQtr** workbook.
13. Notice the updated value in cell B14. Print the **eec2sc05** worksheet again.
14. Save the workbook with the same name (**eec2sc05**) and close it.

Assessment 6

1. Open **4thQuarterSales.xlw**. You created this file in Exercise 6.
2. Open **ExcelWorksheet04**. Save it as **eec2sc06**. Arrange the windows vertically.
3. Link cell B14 in the **eec2sc06** workbook to cell C27 in the **RegionSalesOct** workbook.
4. Link cell C14 in the **eec2sc06** workbook to cell C27 in the **RegionSalesNov** workbook.
5. Link cell D14 in the **eec2sc06** workbook to cell C27 in the **RegionSalesDec** workbook.
6. Close the **RegionSalesOct**, **RegionSalesNov**, and **RegionSalesDec** workbooks. Maximize the window for the **eec2sc06** file.
7. Add a custom header to the **eec2sc06** worksheet that displays your name at the left margin and the file name at the right margin.
8. Save the **eec2sc06** worksheet.
9. Print the **eec2sc06** worksheet.
10. Open the **RegionSalesOct** workbook. Type the following into cell B11: 6742.
11. Save and close the **RegionSalesOct** workbook.
12. Notice the updated value in cell B14. Print the **eec2sc06** worksheet again.
13. Save the workbook with the same name (**eec2sc06**) and close it.

Assessment 7

1. Open **ExcelWorksheet05**. Save it as **eec2sc07**.
2. Create a custom header with your name displayed at the left margin and the file name at the right margin.

3. The production manager, Ed Snyder, and the vice president of finance, Beverly Peterson, both need to make changes to Copper Clad's budget figures for January and February. They are going to do this by sharing the workbook. Click Tools and then Options. Click the General tab on the Options dialog box. Look in the *User name* box. On a piece of paper, write down the name that is currently entered. When you complete this assessment exercise, you will change the name back to what is currently entered. Assign the user name Ed Snyder to the workbook that is currently open.

4. Click Tools and Share Workbook. Click the *Allow changes by more than one user at the same time* check box to select it. Click OK. Click OK to save the workbook.

5. Start another copy of the Excel program by clicking the Start button, pointing to All Programs, and then opening another copy of Excel. Change the user name for this copy of Excel to Beverly Peterson.

6. Right-click the taskbar and click *Tile Windows Horizontally*.

7. Click in Beverly's copy of Excel to select it, and then open the **eec2sc07** file. Beverly's copy of Excel should be on the top. If it is not, rearrange the windows.

8. The workbook is now open in both program windows. Notice that the word *[Shared]* appears in the title bar of both windows. Access Beverly's copy of the workbook (on the top) and make the following changes:

B14	Change *15,250* to *16,309*
C14	Change *20,250* to *19,986*
B17	Change *8.75* to *8.50*
C17	Change *8.75* to *8.50*

9. Save the worksheet.

10. Access Ed Snyder's copy of the workbook (on the bottom) and make the following changes:

B15	Change *0.5* to *.75*
C15	Change *0.5* to *.75*

11. Save the workbook. When the information box appears telling you the workbook has been updated with changes saved by other users, click OK. Move the mouse pointer over the colored triangles to read about the changes that were made.

12. Access Beverly's copy of the workbook and save it. When the information box appears telling you the workbook has been updated with changes saved by other users, click OK. Move the mouse pointer over the colored triangles to read about the changes that were made.

13. In Beverly's copy of the workbook, enter .5 in cells B15 and C15. Save the workbook. In Ed's copy of the workbook (on the bottom), enter 1 in cells B15 and C15. Save the workbook. The Resolve Conflicts dialog box is displayed. Click the Accept All Mine button.

14. Access Beverly's copy of the workbook and save it. When the dialog box appears informing you the workbook has been updated, click OK. Click Tools on the Menu bar in Beverly's workbook and point to the Track Changes option. Click Accept or Reject Changes. Click OK to accept the default options. Click the Accept button until the dialog box displays the conflicting values entered in cell B15. Click the second option in the list, Ed Snyder's change to *0.75*, and click the Accept button. When the dialog box displays the conflicting values entered for C15, click the second option in the list, Ed Snyder's change to *0.75*, and then click the Accept button. Save the workbook.

15. Access Ed Snyder's copy of the workbook (on the bottom) and click the Save button. Click OK when the dialog box appears notifying you that changes were made by other users. Look at a history of the changes that were made by clicking Tools on the Menu bar of Ed's copy of the workbook, pointing to Track Changes, and then clicking Highlight Changes. The *Since I last saved* option should be displayed in the *When* box. Click the check box next to *List changes on a new sheet*. A check mark should be in the box. Click OK. A new sheet tab is added to the worksheet called *History*. On this worksheet you can see that Beverly accepted your changes in cells B15 and C15.
16. Save Ed's copy of the workbook (on the bottom). Print a copy of the workbook.
17. Access Beverly's copy of the workbook. Change the user name back to the original entry by clicking Tools and Options. Click the General tab. In the *User name* box, type the name that was originally displayed when you started the exercise. Click OK. Save the workbook. Click File on the Menu bar in Beverly's workbook and click Exit.
18. Access Ed's copy of the workbook. Maximize the window. Designate that the workbook should no longer be shared by clicking Tools and then Share Workbook. Click the *Allow changes by more than one user at the same time* check box so that it is no longer selected. Click OK.
19. If necessary, change the user name back to the original entry.
20. Save the worksheet with the same name (**eec2sc07**) and close it.

Assessment 8

1. When cells that supply data to a link are changed, Excel will not automatically update the link if the workbook containing the link is closed. Use Excel's Help task pane to learn how you can manually update links. **(Hint: Click Help and Microsoft Office Excel Help. In the** Search **text box, type the question** How do I update a link manually? **and click the Start Searching button. At the list of topics that displays, click Control when links are updated.)** Read all the information in the *Links to other workbooks* section. Print the information.
2. Open the **RegionSalesNov** workbook. Type the following into cell B17: 6090. Save the workbook using the same name. Close the workbook.
3. Open **eec2sc06**. When the dialog box appears asking if you want to update this workbook with changes made to another workbook, click Don't Update. Save the worksheet using the Save As command and name it **eec2sc08**.
4. Using the help information you printed in Step 1, update the linked objects in this workbook manually.
5. Print **eec2sc08**.
6. Save the worksheet using the same file name (**eec2sc08**) and close it.

CHAPTER challenge

You work in the accounting department of the corporate office for Baby Stuff and More, a store specializing in baby accessories. There are three stores throughout the country, located in St. Louis, Nashville, and Chicago. Each store maintains its own sales records in an Excel workbook. The stores are required to send the workbooks to the corporate office each month. Copy the workbooks named **St.Louis**, **Nashville**, and **Chicago** to your disk. Then create a new workbook, named **CorporateSales**, linking each of the workbooks to it. The **CorporateSales** workbook should show the total monthly sales for each of the items. Also, create a workspace named **AllStores** that includes the three workbooks: **St.Louis**, **Nashville**, and **Chicago**. (Do not include the **CorporateSales** workbook.)

You would like to quickly display items that generated sales greater than a given number. Use the Help feature to learn how to filter numbers greater than or less than another number. Then use the **CorporateSales** workbook, created in the first part of the Chapter Challenge, to display baby items with sales greater than $100,000 for each month. Print out the results for each month (identify the month filtered in the worksheet before printing).

A quarterly report in the form of a memo will be prepared for Baby Stuff and More's Board of Directors. In Word, create a memo that will be sent to the Board of Directors. Copy the data in the **CorporateSales** workbook, created in the first part of the Chapter Challenge to the memo. Provide the necessary information in the body of the memo so that the Board of Directors will have a good understanding of how the first quarter sales data was gathered and compiled. Save the memo as **BoardofDirectors**.

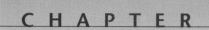

USING ADVANCED FUNCTIONS

PERFORMANCE OBJECTIVES

Upon successful completion of Chapter 3, you will be able to:

➤ **Use the PMT function**
➤ **Use the PV function**
➤ **Use the ROUND function**
➤ **Use the RAND function**
➤ **Use the SUMIF function**
➤ **Use the COUNTIF function**
➤ **Name a range**
➤ **Use a named range in a formula**
➤ **Use the VLOOKUP function**
➤ **Use the IF function**
➤ **Use array formulas**

Excel includes many functions that make the task of creating a worksheet much easier. A function is a built-in formula. Functions perform complex mathematical, financial, data-manipulation, and logical operations. Excel includes over 200 functions that are divided into the following nine categories:

> Financial
> Date and Time
> Math and Trig
> Statistical
> Lookup and Reference
> Database
> Text
> Logical
> Information

Functions include two parts. The first part is the name of the function, which always immediately follows the equal sign. The second part of the function is the argument. The argument contains the data the function needs to perform the necessary calculations or data manipulations. The argument may contain numbers, formulas, cell references, range names, or other functions, which are called nested functions. In this chapter you will learn how to use some advanced functions as well as how to work with named ranges and use them in formulas and functions.

HINT

If you select the Function category *Most Recently Used* on the Paste Function dialog box, a list of the ten most recently used function appears in the *Function name* list box. This is a quick way to select a function that was used recently.

Entering a Function

Functions can be keyed directly into a cell or entered using the Insert Function button on the formula bar. To enter a function using the Insert Function button, click the Insert Function button on the formula bar, as shown in Figure 3.1. The Insert Function dialog box shown in Figure 3.2 is displayed. One way to locate a particular function is by entering a query such as "How do I calculate the yearly interest payment for an investment?" in the *Search for a function* box. Another way is to select a category from the *Select a category* list box. All the functions for that particular category are then listed in the *Select a function* box. Select the particular function you want and then click OK.

FIGURE

3.1 **The Insert Function Button**

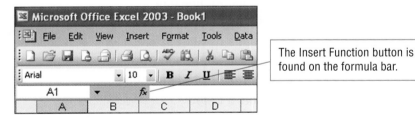

The Insert Function button is found on the formula bar.

FIGURE

3.2 **The Insert Function Dialog Box**

You can search for a function by entering a query.

If you know the function you want to use, first select the appropriate category and then select the particular function.

A description of the function name currently selected in the *Select a function* box is displayed.

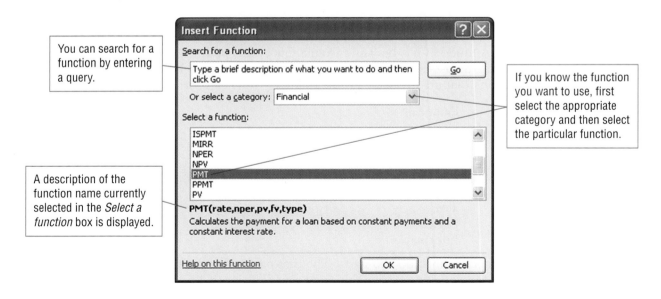

Figure 3.3 shows the Function Arguments dialog box for the PMT function. This is where you enter the data to be used in the formula. Next to each argument name is a box. If the argument name is bold, then that particular argument is required by the function and must have data assigned to it. Cell references, ranges, range names, and formulas may be entered into an argument box. You can either key the data into the argument box or select the appropriate cells from the worksheet to enter them into the argument box. Once the necessary data is entered into the argument boxes, click OK.

HINT

If the Formula Palette covers up cells on the worksheet which you want to select, you can easily move it by clicking it and dragging it to a new location.

FIGURE

3.3 **The Function Arguments Dialog Box**

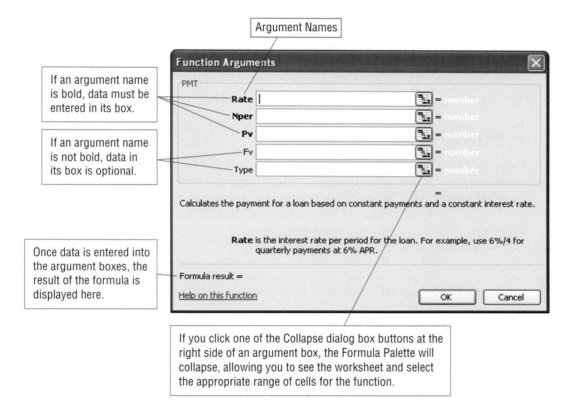

Argument Names

If an argument name is bold, data must be entered in its box.

If an argument name is not bold, data in its box is optional.

Once data is entered into the argument boxes, the result of the formula is displayed here.

If you click one of the Collapse dialog box buttons at the right side of an argument box, the Formula Palette will collapse, allowing you to see the worksheet and select the appropriate range of cells for the function.

Once an equal sign has been entered into a cell, you can click the down-pointing arrow to the right of the *Name* box to see a list of commonly used functions. The drop-down menu shown in Figure 3.4 appears. If you select one of the functions from the list, an expanded Formula Palette for that particular function is displayed. If you select the last option, *More Functions,* the Insert Function dialog box is displayed. From this dialog box you can select any function you want.

HINT

Two other ways to insert a function are to click Insert and then Function or to press Shift and F3.

When you edit a function that has more than one set of parentheses, each set of parentheses is displayed as the same color so you can tell which opening parenthesis goes with which closing parenthesis. Also when editing a function, if you place the insertion point anywhere within a reference to a range of cells (B5:B25, for example) the reference is displayed in a color and a border with a matching color is placed around that range on the worksheet.

3.4 *A Menu of Function Options*

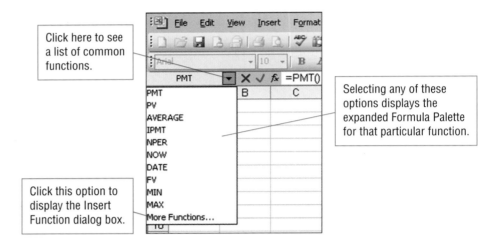

Click here to see a list of common functions.

Selecting any of these options displays the expanded Formula Palette for that particular function.

Click this option to display the Insert Function dialog box.

Financial Functions

Excel includes many financial functions that are used for calculating loan details, annuities, and investment analyses, for example. An annuity is a periodic series of equal payments. The mortgage on a house is one example of an annuity. A car loan would be another example of an annuity. Table 3.1 describes the common arguments used in Excel's financial functions.

TABLE

3.1 *Arguments Used in Excel's Financial Functions*

Argument	Argument Name	Description
Present Value	Pv	The current value of amounts to be received or paid in the future discounted at some interest rate; the amount that must be invested today at some interest rate to accumulate to some specified future value
Number of periods	Nper	The number of payments that will be made to an investment or loan, for example, 60 periods for a five-year loan with monthly payments
Payment	Pmt	The amount paid or collected for each period
Future Value	Fv	The value of a loan or investment at the end of all the periods

Argument	Argument Name	Description
Rate		The interest rate being charged or paid
Type		Payments can either be made in arrears (at the end of each period) or in advance (at the beginning of each period). The Type argument determines whether the calculation will be based on payments made in arrears or in advance. Type is the number 0 (payments in arrears) or 1 (payments in advance). If Type is omitted, it is assumed to be 0.

The PMT Function

The PMT function calculates the periodic payment of a loan based on constant payments and a constant interest rate. The format for the PMT function is:

=PMT(rate,nper,pv)

Rate is the interest rate per period. Nper is the total number of payments to be made. Pv is the present value of the amount borrowed. Look at the following PMT function:

=PMT(8%/12,60,-13000)

This formula will calculate how much each payment would be if you borrowed $13,000 at 8% interest and were going to repay the loan in 60 installments. Because the payments are made monthly, the interest rate must also be monthly; therefore, the annual rate of interest, or 8%, must be divided by 12. If the loan is for five years, that means there are 60 payments (5 × 12 = 60). The present value of the amount borrowed is -13,000, or minus 13,000, because no payments have yet been made. For all arguments, cash you pay out is represented by a negative number, and cash you receive is represented by a positive number.

exercise 1

USING THE PMT FUNCTION

1. Open **ExcelWorksheet01**.
2. Save the worksheet using the Save As command and name it **eec3x01**.
3. Create a custom header that displays your name at the left margin and the file name at the right margin.
4. Primrose Decorators is a decorating business owned and operated by Georgia and Paul Sorenson. They have outgrown their current facility and need to relocate. Their plans for relocation must include an approximation of what they can afford to pay for a mortgage. This worksheet is designed to make such an estimate. Look over the worksheet. The

interest rate per period is in cell D5. The term of the loan is in row 8, and the amount of money being borrowed is in column B. Complete the following steps to compute the loan payments:

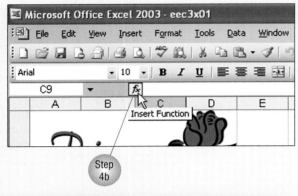

a. Select cell C9.
b. Click the Insert Function button on the formula bar.
c. When the Insert Function dialog box appears, click the down-pointing arrow to the right of the *Or select a category* box and then click *Financial*.
d. Click *PMT* in the *Select a function* list box. Click OK.
e. The Function Arguments dialog box appears. Click the title bar to the dialog box and drag it to the lower right corner of the screen. Make sure the insertion point is in the *Rate* box. Click cell D5. Press F4 to make the reference to D5 absolute. Type the following: /12.

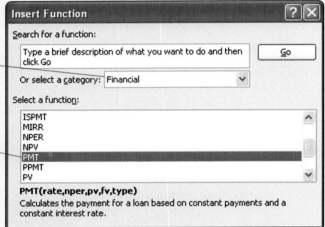

f. Place the insertion point in the *Nper* box. Click cell C8. Press F4 to make the reference to C8 absolute. Type the following: *12.
g. Place the insertion point in the *Pv* box. Press the minus sign key (or hyphen) and click cell B9.
h. Click OK.
i. Copy the function in cell C9 to cells C10 through C17.

5. Repeat Step 4 to enter the appropriate functions into cells D9, E9, F9, and G9. Copy the functions as needed. Adjust column widths as needed.

6. The Sorensons do not want to spend more than $3,000 a month on a mortgage. Format cells C9 through G17 so that any value less than or equal to 3,000 is displayed as bold and in the color green.

7. Shade cells B8 through G8 and cells B9 through B17 with a light green color.

8. Print the worksheet.

9. The Sorensons think they may be able to get a better interest rate. Enter .0675 in cell D5. Print the worksheet again.

10. Save the worksheet with the same name (**eec3x01**) and then close the worksheet.

The PV Function

The PV function calculates the present value that the total amount of a series of future payments is worth right now. The format for the PV function is

=PV(**rate,nper,pmt**,fv,type)

Rate is the interest rate per period. Nper is the total number of payment periods. Pmt is the payment made each period. Fv is the future value, and type indicates whether the payments are being made in arrears or in advance. Look at the following PV function:

=PV(5%/12,60,150)

This formula will calculate the present value of 60 payments of $150 with a 5% annual percentage rate.

exercise 2

USING THE PV FUNCTION

1. Open **ExcelWorksheet02**.
2. Save the worksheet using the Save As command and name it **eec3x02**.
3. Create a custom header that displays your name at the left margin and the file name at the right margin.
4. Copper Clad Incorporated is considering purchasing a machine that would generate significant cash savings. The machine costs $35,000. The accountant has to decide whether or not investing $35,000 in the purchase of this machine is a wise investment. Copper Clad has to make an 18% rate of return on this capital investment in order to make the investment worth it. The company expects to generate a cash savings of $6,500 for the life of the machine, which is estimated to be 15 years. Complete the following steps to use the PV function to make the necessary calculations:
   a. Type **18%** in cell B4.
   b. Type **15** in cell B5.
   c. Type **6500** in cell B6. Format the value in cell B6 as currency with no decimals displayed.
   d. Select cell B8. Click the Insert Function button.

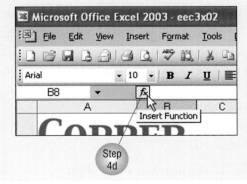

Step
4d

1) Select *Financial* from the *Or select a category* drop-down list.
2) Click *PV* in the *Select a function* list box and then click OK.

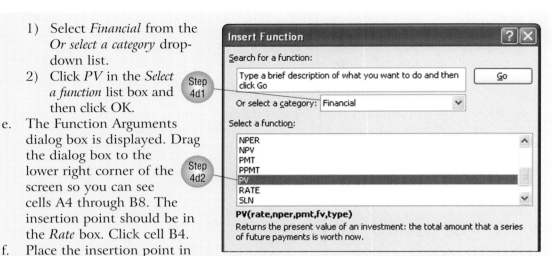

e. The Function Arguments dialog box is displayed. Drag the dialog box to the lower right corner of the screen so you can see cells A4 through B8. The insertion point should be in the *Rate* box. Click cell B4.

f. Place the insertion point in the *Nper* box. Click cell B5.

g. Place the insertion point in the *Pmt* box. Click cell B6, then click OK.

5. The present value of the money is displayed as a negative number because this represents money that would be paid out. The present value of the money is $33,095.25, which is less than the $35,000 cost of the machine. Therefore, this is not a wise investment for the Copper Clad company. The accountant advises the president of Copper Clad that unless the price of the machine can be negotiated down to $33,095, the company should not invest in the machine.

6. Save the worksheet with the same name (**eec3x02**).

7. Print and then close the worksheet.

Math and Trig Functions

Excel includes many math and trigonometric functions. These functions perform a wide variety of calculations such as sines, cosines, factorials, exponents, and logs. The following section introduces you to three of Excel's Math and Trig functions.

The ROUND Function

The ROUND function rounds a number to a specified number of digits. The format for the ROUND function is:

=ROUND(**number,num_digits**)

Number is the number that is to be rounded. Num_digits is the number of decimal places to which the number is to be rounded. If num_digits is 0, then the number is to be rounded to the nearest integer. If num_digits is 1, then the number is to be rounded to one decimal place. If num_digits is a negative number, then the number is to be rounded that many places to the left of the decimal point. For example, if the number is 2345 and num_digits is -2, the number will be rounded to 2300.

The RAND Function

The RAND function is used to calculate random numbers. The function returns a random number greater than or equal to 0 and less than 1. The result of the formula is volatile, which means it will change whenever anything on the worksheet changes. The format for the RAND function is:

HINT

Pressing F9 recalculates the RAND function.

RAND()

RAND is different from other functions in that it does not have any arguments.

The SUMIF Function

The SUMIF function calculates the total of only those cells that meet a given condition or criteria. The format for the SUMIF function is:

SUMIF(**range**,**criteria**,sum_range)

Range is the range of the cells that are to be evaluated by the function. *Criteria* is the condition or criteria the cell is to match if it is to be included in the sum. Criteria can be numbers, expressions, or text. *Sum_range* are the actual cells to sum. For example, look at the following worksheet fragment:

	A	B	C
1	Sales Rep	Sales	Commission
2	Hyde, Paul	$ 25,000	$ 3,000
3	Snyder, Holly	$ 36,000	$ 4,320
4	Jackson, Donna	$ 13,000	$ 1,560
5	Carter, Bob	$ 19,000	$ 2,280
6	Adamski, Steve	$ 23,000	$ 2,760

Using the data from this worksheet fragment, the following SUMIF function would add together only those commissions that were made on sales greater than or equal to $25,000:

SUMIF(B2:B6,">=25000",C2:C6)

The value that would be returned for this function is 7320.

exercise 3

USING THE ROUND, RAND, AND SUMIF FUNCTIONS

1. Open **ExcelWorksheet03**.
2. Save the worksheet using the Save As command and name it **eec3x03**.
3. Create a custom header that displays your name at the left margin and the file name at the right margin.
4. This is the start of a worksheet that calculates the commissions earned on sales. The sales figures are not yet available, so you need to use the RAND function to generate some figures. Complete the following steps to generate sales figures using the RAND function:

a. Click cell B5.
b. Click the Insert Function button.

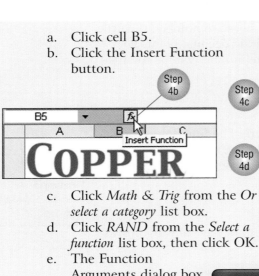

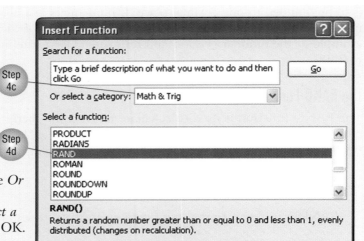

c. Click *Math & Trig* from the *Or select a category* list box.
d. Click *RAND* from the *Select a function* list box, then click OK.
e. The Function Arguments dialog box is displayed. The RAND function does not take any arguments, so click OK.
f. The RAND function generates numbers between 0 and 1. You want to generate numbers between 0 and 100,000, so you have to multiply the function by 100,000. Click in the formula bar and type *100000.

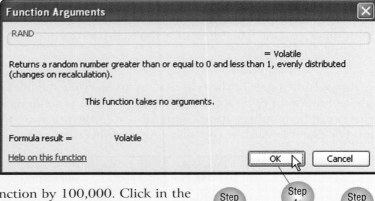

g. Click the Enter button.

5. The sales figures need to be rounded to the nearest 100. To do this, you will need to create a nested function. Complete the following steps to nest the current RAND function inside a ROUND function:
   a. If necessary, click cell B5 to select it.
   b. In the formula bar, place the insertion point between the equal sign and the letter *R*. Type the following: **ROUND(**
   c. In the formula bar, place the insertion point after the last zero in 100000. Type the following: **,-2)**. When you have finished, the nested function in the formula bar should be:

   =ROUND(RAND()*100000,-2)

   d. Click the Enter button on the formula bar.
   e. Double-click the AutoFill handle in the lower right corner of cell B5 to copy the cell to cells B6 through B16.

6. Copper Clad Incorporated pays its sales representatives a 10% commission. Complete the following steps to calculate the commissions on the sales:
   a. Click cell C5 to select it.
   b. Type the following in cell C5: =B5*.1.
   c. Click the Enter button on the formula bar.
   d. Double-click the AutoFill handle in the lower right corner of cell C5 to copy the formula.

7. You may notice that every time you change something on the worksheet, the random numbers change. That is because they are volatile. Next you want to calculate the commissions paid on sales over $40,000. Complete the following steps to use the SUMIF function to make the calculation:

a. Click cell F3 to select it.

b. Click the Insert Function button on the formula bar.

c. Click *Math & Trig* from the *Or select a category* list box.

d. Click *SUMIF* from the *Select a function* list box.

e. Click OK.

f. The Function Arguments dialog box is displayed. Click and drag the dialog box to the lower right corner of the screen.

g. The insertion point should be in the *Range* box. In the worksheet, select cells B5 through B16.

h. Place the insertion point in the *Criteria* box and then type the following: >40000.

i. Place the insertion point in the *Sum_range* box.

j. In the worksheet, select cells C5 through C16. When you have finished, your screen should look similar to the one below. Your values will be different because the RAND function is being used. Click OK.

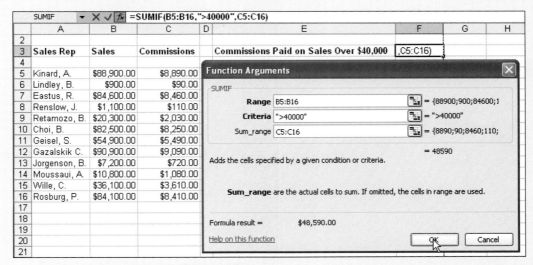

8. Repeat Step 7 to enter a SUMIF function in cell F6 that calculates the commissions paid on sales over $80,000.

9. Save the worksheet with the same name (**eec3x03**).

10. Print and then close the worksheet.

Statistical Functions

Excel's statistical functions are used on lists of data. Some of the simpler statistical functions are AVERAGE, MAX, and MIN. Excel also includes very complex statistical functions that can calculate deviations, distributions, correlations, and slopes, for example.

The COUNTIF Function

The COUNTIF function counts the number of cells in a given range that meet a specific condition. The format for the COUNTIF function is:

=COUNTIF(**range**,**criteria**)

The range is the range of cells to be counted. The criteria are the conditions that must be met in order for that cell to be counted. A condition can be a number, expression, or text. Suppose, for example, you had a worksheet that kept track of the weather for the past month. Look at the following segment from this worksheet:

	A	B
1	Day of the Month	Cloud Report
2	1	Overcast
3	2	Partly Cloudy
4	3	Overcast
5	4	Overcast
6	5	Partly Cloudy
7	6	Partly Cloudy
8	7	Partly Cloudy
9	8	Clear
10	9	Clear
11	10	Partly Cloudy
12	11	Clear
13	12	Overcast
14	13	Overcast
15	14	Overcast
16	15	Partly Cloudy
17	16	Clear
18	17	Clear
19	18	Overcast
20	19	Overcast
21	20	Overcast
22	21	Partly Cloudy
23	22	Clear
24	23	Overcast
25	24	Overcast
26	25	Overcast
27	26	Partly Cloudy
28	27	Partly Cloudy
29	28	Clear
30	29	Overcast
31	30	Overcast
32	31	Overcast

Using this worksheet segment, the COUNTIF function =COUNTIF(B2:B32,"Clear") would return 7.

exercise 4

1. Open **ExcelWorksheet04**.
2. Save the worksheet using the Save As command and name it **eec3x04**.
3. Create a custom header that displays your name at the left margin and the file name at the right margin.
4. This worksheet keeps track of grades for a CS100 class at Redwood Community College. The instructor wants to know how many students received As, how many received Bs, how many received Cs, and so on. Complete the following steps to use the COUNTIF function to find out how many students received As:

    a. Select cell O6.
    b. Click the Insert Function button on the format bar.
    c. Click *Statistical* in the *Or select a category* list box.
    d. Click *COUNTIF* in the *Select a function* list box.
    e. Click OK.
    f. The Function Arguments dialog box is displayed, and the insertion point is in the *Range* box. Type the following in the *Range* box: m6:m58.

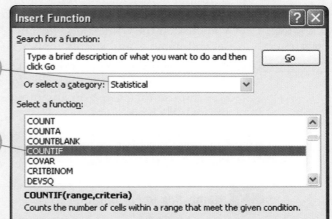

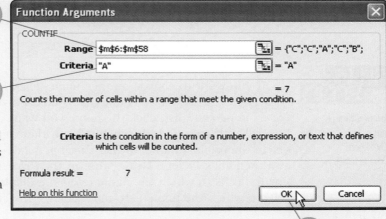

    g. Place the insertion point in the *Criteria* box and type "A".
    h. Click OK.

5. Click cell O6 if necessary. Double-click the AutoFill handle to copy the formula. Click cell O7 and edit the function to count the number of B's. Click cell O8 and edit the function to count the number of C's. Click cell O9 and edit the function to count the number of D's. Click cell O10 and edit the function to count the number of F's.
6. Change the orientation of the page to landscape.
7. Select rows 3 through 5 as a print title to repeat at the top of each page.
8. Save the worksheet with the same name (**eec3ex04**).
9. Print and then close the worksheet.

QUICK STEPS

Name a Range
1. Select the range of cells to be named.
2. Click the *Name* box.
3. Type the range name.
4. Press Enter.

HINT

Use range names whenever possible in functions.

Naming a Range

You can define a name that can be used to represent specific cells in a worksheet. The name you create should describe the range of cells. The name *January_Sales*, for example, could be defined for the range of cells containing the January sales figures. When naming a cell or range of cells, the first character of the name must be a letter or an underscore character. The other characters in the name can be letters, numbers, periods, and underscore characters. Spaces are not allowed in names, so use either the underscore character or a period to separate the words used in a name, such as *May_Sales* or *Third.Quarter*. Even though uppercase and lowercase letters can be used in a name, they are not case sensitive. That is, if you created the name *Sales_Tax* and then created a second name *sales_tax*, the second name would simply replace the first.

Any worksheet in a workbook can utilize the names you create. For example, if the name *Freight_Cost* is the name for the range of cells C5 through H25 on *Sheet1*, you can use that name on any other sheet in the workbook to refer to cells C5 through H25 on *Sheet1*.

To create a name for a cell or a range of cells, select the cell or range of cells to be named. Click the *Name* box at the left side of the formula bar, as shown in Figure 3.5. Key the name for the cell or cells and press Enter.

FIGURE

 **Name *Box in Formula Bar***

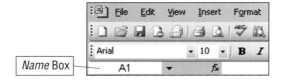

QUICK STEPS

Change a Range Name
1. Click Insert.
2. Point to Name.
3. Click Define.

If you want to change a range name, click Insert, point to Name, and then click Define. The Define Name dialog box shown in Figure 3.6 is displayed. In the *Names in workbook* list, click the name you want to change. In the *Names in workbook* box, select the name to be changed and then type the new name. Click Add. To delete the original name, in the *Names in workbook* list click the name to be deleted and then click Delete. Notice that in the *Refers to* box at the bottom of the dialog box the cells to which the name refers are displayed. If you want to change the cells to which the name is to refer, change the cell references in the Refers to box.

FIGURE

3.6 *Define Name Dialog Box*

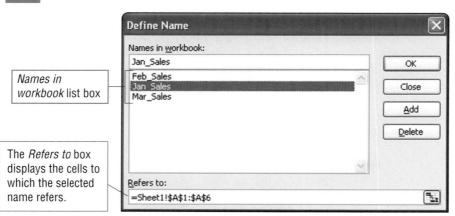

You can select a named range by clicking the down-pointing arrow to the right of the *Name* box and clicking the range to be selected from the drop-down list that appears. If you want to select two or more named ranges, click the first range from the drop-down list, hold down the Ctrl key, and then click the other ranges.

Using a Named Range in a Formula

Range names can be used in formulas in place of the references to the cells. For example, say the sales figures for January are in cells B5 through B30. To find the total of these figures you could use the function =SUM(B5:B30). If you named the range of cells B5 through B30 *Jan_Sales*, you could also use the formula =SUM(Jan_Sales). One of the advantages of using range names in formulas is that the purpose of the formula is easier to understand. Looking at the formula =SUM(B5:B30) does not provide you with any information about what is being added. But by looking at the formula =SUM(Jan_Sales), you know the sales figures for the month of January are being added.

HINT

Range names use absolute cell references by default.

Lookup and Reference Functions

When worksheets contain long lists of data, you need a way to be able to find specific information within the list. Excel's Lookup and Reference functions provide a way to extract certain information from a list. These functions can return cell references when the information is found, or they can return the actual contents of the found cell.

The VLOOKUP Function

The VLOOKUP function searches for a value in the leftmost column of a table on the worksheet and then enters a value from a specific column, in the same row as the value it found, into a different location in the worksheet. The format for the VLOOKUP function is:

=VLOOKUP(**lookup_value**,**table_array**,**col_index_num**)

The lookup_value is the value to be found in the first column of the table that is being searched. The lookup_value can be a value, text, or reference. The table_array is the table, or range, of information in which data is looked up. The col_index_num is the column number in the table from which the matching value should be returned. The first column in the table or range is column 1, the second column is column 2, and so on. For example, look at the table in figure 3.7. This table shows how much various salaries increase year by year if the increase rate is 5%. To look up how much you would be earning in four years if your starting salary was $25,000, you would use the following VLOOKUP function:

=VLOOKUP(25000,B5:G16,5)

HINT

The #N/A error often occurs when using the VLOOKUP function. It means that a required match was not available.

3.7 *A Lookup Table*

The VLOOKUP function looks up the look_up value in the first column of the table.

The table_array is the range of cells that make up the entire table. In this case, the table_array is B5:G16.

The col_index_num is the column number in the table in which the returned value should be found—in this case, the fifth column.

The return value is the same row as the look_up value and the same column as the col_index_num.

The lookup_value is 25,000, or your starting salary. The table_array, or the range of the table, is B5 through G16. The col_index_num is 5 because the fifth column lists the salaries people earn after having worked for four years. This VLOOKUP function would return the value $30,388.

In some cases, the lookup value does not exactly match a value in the first column of the VLOOKUP table. If this happens, the function looks in the first column of the table for the largest value that is less than or equal to the lookup_value. Say, for example, your starting salary was $28,000 and you wanted to use the VLOOKUP table in figure 3.7. The VLOOKUP function would look in the first column of the table for the largest value that is less than or equal to $28,000. The value it would find would be $25,000. So, using the VLOOKUP function to look up how much you would be earning in four years if your starting salary was $28,000 would return the same value: $30,388.

exercise 5

USING NAMED RANGES AND THE VLOOKUP FUNCTION

1. Open **ExcelWorksheet05**.
2. Save the worksheet using the Save As command and name it **eec3x05**.
3. Create a custom header that displays your name at the left margin and the file name at the right margin.
4. This worksheet keeps track of grades for a CS100 class at Redwood Community College. The instructor wants to use the VLOOKUP function to automatically

calculate if a student's grade is an A, B, C, D, or F. VLOOKUP tables must always be sorted in ascending order. Type the following into the cells indicated to enter the VLOOKUP table:

Cell	Data	Cell	Data
O6	50%	P6	F
O7	60%	P7	D
O8	70%	P8	C
O9	80%	P9	B
O10	90%	P10	A

5. Name the table you just entered Lookup_Grade by completing the following steps:
   a. Select cells O6 through P10.
   b. Click the *Name* box and type Lookup_Grade.

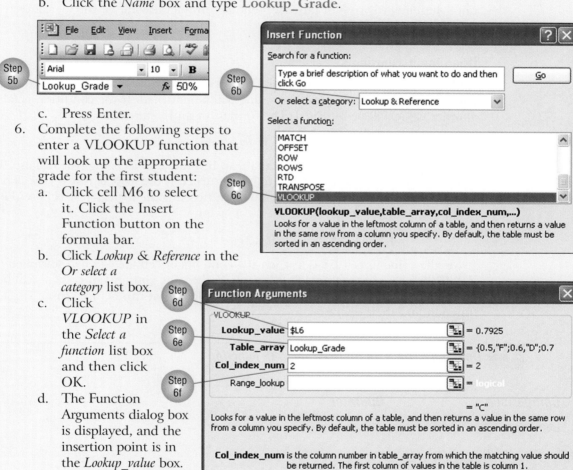

   c. Press Enter.
6. Complete the following steps to enter a VLOOKUP function that will look up the appropriate grade for the first student:
   a. Click cell M6 to select it. Click the Insert Function button on the formula bar.
   b. Click *Lookup & Reference* in the *Or select a category* list box.
   c. Click *VLOOKUP* in the *Select a function* list box and then click OK.
   d. The Function Arguments dialog box is displayed, and the insertion point is in the *Lookup_value* box. Type $L6 in the *Lookup_value* box. You are going to be copying the formula, so the reference to column L has to be absolute.
   e. Place the insertion point in the *Table_array* box. You are going to use the range name to refer to the table. Type Lookup_Grade.
   f. Place the insertion point in the *Col_index_num* box and type 2.
   g. Click OK.

7. Double-click the AutoFill handle in the lower right corner of cell M6 to copy the function to cells M7 through M58.
8. Change the orientation of the page to landscape.
9. Select rows 3 through 5 as a print title to repeat at the top of each page.
10. Save the worksheet with the same name (**eec3x05**).
11. Print and close the worksheet.

Logical Functions

Excel's logical functions are used to perform logical tests, which test whether or not a statement is true or false. Depending on the outcome of the logical test, a specific result is returned.

Using the IF Function

An IF function is a logical function that sets up a conditional statement to test data. If the condition is true, one value will be returned. If the condition is false, another value will be returned. The format for an IF statement is:

$$=IF(logical\_test,value\_if\_true,value\_if\_false)$$

The logical_test is a condition that can be evaluated as being true or false. The value_if_true is the value that should be returned if the logical_test is true. The value_if_false is the value that should be returned if the logical_test is false. Look at the following IF function:

$$=IF(B7=1,C7*.10,C7*.12)$$

If the value in cell B7 is 1, then the contents of cell C7 will be multiplied by .10. If the value entered in cell B7 is not 1, then the contents of cell C7 will be multiplied by .12. Table 3.2 shows the conditions that can be used in an IF function and their operators.

TABLE

3.2 **Operators That Can Be Used in an IF Function**

Comparison	Operator
Less than	<
Greater than	>
Less than or equal to	<=
Greater than or equal to	>=
Equal to	=
Not equal to	<>

exercise 6

1. Open **ExcelWorksheet06**.
2. Save the worksheet using the Save As command and name it **eec3x06**.
3. Create a custom header that displays your name at the left margin and the file name at the right margin.
4. Sales representatives for Whitewater Canoe and Kayak Corporation earn a commission on their sales. Sales representatives who are managers earn a 12% commission. If a sales representative earns 10%, the commission code is *1*. If a sales representative earns 12%, the commission code is *2*. Complete the following steps to use an IF function to calculate the commission amount for C. J. Kimsey:

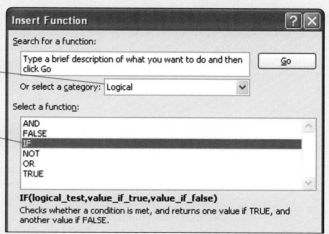

   a. Click cell D8 to select it.
   b. Click the Insert Function button on the formula bar.
   c. Click *Logical* in the *Or select a category* list box.
   d. Click *IF* in the *Select a function* list box then click OK.

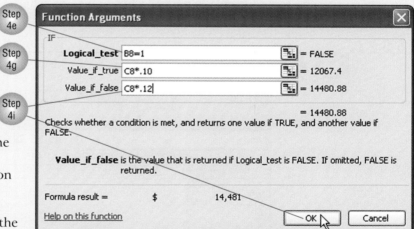

   e. The Function Arguments dialog box is displayed, and the insertion point is in the *Logical_test* box. Type **B8=1** in the *Logical_test* box.
   f. Place the insertion point in the *Value_if_true* box.
   g. Type **C8*.10** in the *Value_if_true* box.
   h. Place the insertion point in the *Value_if_false* box.
   i. Type **C8*.12** in the *Value_if_false* box, then click OK.
5. Double-click the AutoFill handle in the lower right corner of cell D8 to copy the function to cells D9 through D13.
6. Whitewater Canoe and Kayak Corporation has decided to give a bonus to sales representatives who sell more than $85,000 in merchandise. Sales representatives who sell more than $85,000 in merchandise earn a 2% bonus. Those who sell less than $85,000 in merchandise do not earn a bonus. Complete the following steps to use the IF function to calculate the sales representatives' bonuses:
   a. Click cell E6 and type **Bonus**.

b. Add a border to the bottom of cell E6 to match the border on the bottom of cell D6.

c. Click cell E8 to select it.

d. Click the Insert Function button on the formula bar.

e. Click *Logical* in the *Or select a category* list box.

f. Click *IF* in the *Select a function* list box then click OK.

h. The Function Arguments dialog box is displayed, and the insertion point is in the *Logical_test* box. Type C8>85000 in the *Logical_test* box.

i. Place the insertion point in the *Value_if_true* box.

j. Type C8*.02 in the *Value_if_true* box.

k. Place the insertion point in the *Value_if_false* box, type 0, and then click OK.

7. Double-click the AutoFill handle in the lower right corner of cell E8 to copy the function to cells E9 through E13.

8. Format the cells from E8 through E13 as currency with zero decimal places.

9. Save the worksheet with the same name (**eec3x06**).

10. Print and close the worksheet.

Using Array Formulas

An array formula is a formula in which the arguments used in the functions that make up the formula are arrays rather than individual numbers. An array is a group of elements that form a complete unit. Array formulas perform multiple calculations that can produce multiple results. The array formula does this by operating on a range of cells rather than on just one cell. With an array formula, the same formula is repeated for a range of cells.

For example, look at the worksheet fragment in Figure 3.8.

FIGURE

3.8 **An Example of an Array Formula**

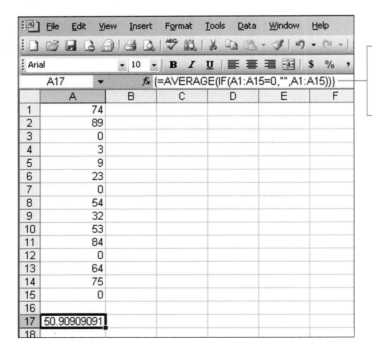

An array formula is always displayed surrounded by braces { }.

Excel's AVERAGE function includes zeros as part of the average. Suppose you wanted to be able to find the average of all non-zero values. An array formula such as the one used in Figure 3.8 enables you to do this. By entering the array formula shown in Figure 3.8, you are instructing the =AVERAGE function to go through the range A1 to A15 to compare the value in each cell to zero. If the value is zero, it is to be ignored—nothing is assigned to it. If a value is not zero, it is to become a part of the range of cells used in the AVERAGE function. In this case, the array formula operates on the range of cells A1 through A15; it "removes" all the zeros from the range, allowing the AVERAGE function to apply to what is left.

An array formula is created the same way that a regular formula is created. The only difference is that instead of pressing Enter to enter the formula, you press Ctrl + Shift + Enter. Once you press Ctrl + Shift + Enter, Excel automatically surrounds the formula with braces {}.You must press Ctrl + Shift + Enter each time you enter an array formula and each time you edit an array formula. If you try entering an array formula by just pressing Enter, a #VALUE! error is displayed.

If more than one range is used in an array formula, all the ranges must contain the same number of cells. If they do not, an error is returned.

QUICK STEPS

Enter an Array Formula
1. Type the formula.
2. Press Ctrl + Shift + Enter.

exercise 7

USING AN ARRAY FORMULA

1. Open **ExcelWorksheet07**.
2. Save the worksheet using the Save As command and name it **eec3x07**.
3. Create a custom header that displays your name at the left margin and the file name at the right margin.
4. This worksheet keeps track of how many units of each type of canoe or kayak the sales representatives for Whitewater Canoe and Kayak Corporation sold. As sales representatives made sales during the month, those sales were entered into the worksheet. Now the sales manager wants to know the total units of each type of canoe or kayak each sales representative sold. To make this calculation, you need to use an array formula. Complete the following steps to enter an array formula that calculates how many Pathfinders were sold by Claxton:
   a. Click cell G6 to select it. Type the following in cell G6:

   =SUM((A6:A38="Pathfinder")*(B6:B38="Claxton")*C6:C38).

   b. Press Ctrl + Shift + Enter.

c. Your screen should look similar to the one shown here.

Look at the array formula you entered. The formula looks at the data in the three ranges A6 through A38, B6 through B38, and C6 through C38. If the first cell looked at (A6) is Pathfinder, a 1, which represents the value True, is returned. If A6 is not Pathfinder, a 0, which represents the value False, is returned. If B6 is Claxton, a 1 is returned; if it is not, a 0 is returned. Then C6 is returned and the three values (in this case 1, 0, and 2) are multiplied together. As the array formula loops through all the rows, the results are added together.

5. Complete the following steps to enter an array formula that calculates how many Pathfinders were sold by Jackson:
   a. Click cell G7 to select it. Type the following in cell G7:

   =SUM((A6:A38="Pathfinder")*(B6:B38="Jackson")*C6:C38).

6. Complete steps similar to Steps 4 and 5 to enter an array formula in cell G8 that calculates how many Pathfinders were sold by Kimsey.

7. Complete steps similar to Steps 4 and 5 to enter an array formula in cell G9 that calculates how many Pathfinders were sold by Millington.

8. Complete steps similar to Steps 4 and 5 to enter an array formula in cell G10 that calculates how many Pathfinders were sold by Post.

9. Complete steps similar to Steps 4 and 5 to enter an array formula cell G11 that calculates how many Pathfinders were sold by Toven.

10. To calculate the units sold for Trekkers, complete the following steps:
    a. Click cell G6.
    b. Place the insertion point between the *A* and the *6* in the formula bar and press F4. The reference to A6 is now absolute ($A$6).
    c. Place the insertion point between the *A* and the *38* in the formula bar and press F4. The reference to A38 is now absolute ($A$38).
    d. Place the insertion point between the *B* and the *6* in the formula bar and press F4. The reference to B6 is now absolute ($B$6).
    e. Place the insertion point between the *B* and the *38* in the formula bar and press F4. The reference to B38 is now absolute ($B$38).

f. Place the insertion point between the *C* and the *6* in the formula bar and press F4. The reference to C6 is now absolute ($C$6).

g. Place the insertion point between the *C* and the *38* in the formula bar and press F4. The reference to C38 is now absolute ($C$38).

h. Press Ctrl + Shift + Enter.

i. Press the Copy button on the Standard toolbar.

j. Click cell G14.

k. Press the Paste button on the Standard toolbar.

l. In the Formula bar delete "Pathfinder" and replace it with "Trekker." Be sure to press Ctrl + Shift + Enter to enter the function. The function should look like this.

{=SUM(($A$6:$A$38="Trekker")*($B$6:$B$38="Claxton")*$C$6:$C$38)}.

m. Copy the function in cell G14 to cells G15 through G19.

n. Click cell G15. Delete "Claxton" and replace it with "Jackson." Be sure to press Ctrl + Shift + Enter to enter the function. The function should look like this:

{=SUM(($A$6:$A$38="Trekker")*($B$6:$B$38="Jackson")*$C$6:$C$38)}.

o. Click cell G16. Delete "Claxton" and replace it with "Kimsey." Be sure to press Ctrl + Shift + Enter to enter the function. The function should look like this:

{=SUM(($A$6:$A$38="Trekker")*($B$6:$B$38="Kimsey")*$C$6:$C$38)}.

p. Click cell G17. Delete "Claxton" and replace it with "Millington." Be sure to press Ctrl + Shift + Enter to enter the function. The function should look like this:

{=SUM(($A$6:$A$38="Trekker")*($B$6:$B$38="Millington")*$C$6:$C$38)}.

q. Click cell G18. Delete "Claxton" and replace it with "Post." Be sure to press Ctrl + Shift + Enter to enter the function. The function should look like this:

{=SUM(($A$6:$A$38="Trekker")*($B$6:$B$38="Post")*$C$6:$C$38)}.

r. Click cell G19. Delete "Claxton" and replace it with "Toven." Be sure to press Ctrl + Shift + Enter to enter the function. The function should look like this:

{=SUM(($A$6:$A$38="Trekker")*($B$6:$B$38="Toven")*$C$6:$C$38)}.

11. Complete Steps Similar to Steps 10i-10r to calculate how many Excursions were sold by each sales representative.

12. Save the worksheet with the same name (**eec3x07**).

13. Print and close the worksheet.

CHAPTER summary

➤ A function is a built-in formula. Functions include two parts: the function name and the argument. The argument, which may contain numbers, formulas, cell references, range names, or other functions, provides the data that the function needs to perform the calculation or data manipulation.

➤ A function can be entered using the Insert Function button on the formula bar.

➤ Financial functions are used for calculating financial data such as loan details, annuities, and investment analyses.

➤ An annuity is a periodic series of equal payments.

➤ The PMT function calculates the periodic payment of a loan based on constant payments and a constant interest rate. The format for the PMT function is =PMT(rate,nper,pv).

➤ The PV function calculates the present value that the total amount of a series of future payments is worth right now. The format for the PV function is =PV(rate,nper,pmt,fv,type).

➤ The ROUND function rounds a number to a specified number of digits. The format for the ROUND function is =ROUND(number,num_digits).

➤ The RAND function calculates random numbers. The format of the RAND function is =RAND().

➤ The SUMIF function calculates the total of specific cells that meet given conditions or criteria. The format for the SUMIF function is =SUMIF(range,criteria,sum_range).

➤ The COUNTIF function counts the number of cells in a given range that meet a specific condition. The format for the COUNTIF function is =COUNTIF(range,criteria).

➤ Names can be assigned to a specific cell or range of cells. The first character in a range name must be an underscore or a letter. The rest of the characters can be letters, numbers, the underscore character, or periods. You cannot use spaces in a range name.

➤ Range names can be used in formulas in place of the references to the cells. The formula =AVERAGE(Exam1_Grades) would average the values entered in the range of cells named *Exam1_Grades*. Using range names in formulas makes it easier to understand the purpose of the formula.

➤ Excel's Lookup and Reference functions provide a way to find specific information within a list of data.

➤ The VLOOKUP function searches for a value in the first column of a table. Upon finding that value, it enters into a different location in the worksheet a value from the table that is in a specific column in the same row as the value that was found in the first column. The format for the VLOOKUP function is =VLOOKUP(lookup_value,table_array,col_index_num).

➤ Logical functions perform logical tests to see whether or not a statement is true or false. Specific results are returned depending on the outcome of the logical test.

➤ The IF function sets up a conditional statement to test data. If the condition is true, one value is returned. If the condition is false, a different value is returned. The format for the IF statements is =IF(logical_test,value_if_true,value_if_false).

➤ Array formulas perform multiple calculations that can produce multiple results. To enter an array formula, press Ctrl + Shift + Enter. Array formulas are always surrounded by braces.

FEATURES summary

FEATURE	MENU/COMMANDS
Enter an array formula	Enter the formula and press Ctrl + Shift + Enter
Name a range	Select the range of cells, click the *Name* box, type the name, and press Enter
Change a range name	Click Insert, point to Name, click Define

CONCEPTS check

Completion: On a blank sheet of paper, indicate the correct term, symbol, or command for each description.

1. This term refers to the second part of a function.
2. This term refers to a periodic series of equal payments, such as the mortgage on a house.
3. A three-year loan with monthly payments would have this many periods.
4. This formula calculates what the monthly payments would be on a five-year, $15,000 loan at a 6% annual interest rate.
5. This formula rounds the number 589.345 to the nearest integer.
6. This formula will generate random numbers between 0 and 100.
7. The result of a RAND function is said to be this term because the result automatically changes whenever anything on the worksheet changes.
8. This function does not have any arguments.
9. This function would add together the values in cells B5:B25 only if the values are greater than zero.
10. This function would count the number of cells in a given range where the values are greater than 250.
11. Click here to create a name for a selected range of cells.
12. This function would look up the value in cell B5 in a table located in cells D20:G35 in the third column of the table.
13. If the value in cell C6 is less than 60, this function will add 5 to it. If the value in cell C6 is greater than or equal to 60, the value will not change.
14. Press these keys to enter an array formula.
15. Explain an advantage to using range names in formulas.
16. Explain what is wrong with the following array formula. Edit the formula so that it is correct.

    {=SUM(IF(A5:I5=B5:B10,1,0))}

17. Suppose you correctly edited the array formula from the previous question, but the #VALUE! error is displayed. Explain what you did wrong and what you must do to fix it.

SKILLS check

Assessment 1

1. Open **ExcelWorksheet08**.
2. Save the worksheet using the Save As command and name it **eec3sc01**.
3. Create a custom header with your name displayed at the left margin and the file name displayed at the right margin.
4. Georgia and Paul Sorenson, the owners of Primrose Decorators, have made a decision on the building they want to buy to expand their business. Now they want to create a loan amortization table that calculates their payments. Name cell B5 *Rate*. Name cell B6 *Term*. Name cell B7 *Principal*. Name cell B9 *Monthly_Payment*. In cell B9, enter a PMT function that will calculate their monthly payments. Be sure to use the range names in the formula.

5. Enter a formula in cell B11 that will calculate the total amount paid on the loan. This would be the monthly payment times the total number of payments being made. Be sure to use range names in the formula. Use the ROUND function so that the result is rounded to two decimal places. Format the result as currency.

6. Enter a formula in cell B12 that calculates the total interest paid for the loan. This would be the total amount paid minus the principal. Use a range name in the formula.

7. The first entry on the payment schedule, the principal owed at the beginning of the loan is already entered in cell B15. In cell C15, enter a formula that calculates one month's interest on the loan. One month's interest would be the principal times the interest rate. But remember, you have to divide the annual interest rate by 12 to get the interest for one month. Use the cell reference B15 to refer to the principal. Use the range name *Rate* to refer to the interest rate. Use the ROUND function so that the result is rounded to two decimal places. Format the result as currency.

8. In cell D15 enter a formula that will calculate how much of the payment goes toward the principal, which would be the monthly payment minus how much was paid to interest. Be sure to use the *Monthly_Payment* range name in the formula.

9. Enter a formula in cell E15 that calculates the principal owed after the payment is made, which would be the principal minus the amount paid to the principal. Use the cell reference B15 to refer to the principal.

10. Type =E15 in cell B16 to enter the new principal.

11. Click cell B16 to select it. Double-click the AutoFill handle to copy cell B16 to cells B17 through B180.

12. Click cell C15 to select it. Double-click the AutoFill handle.

13. Click cell D15 to select it. Double-click the AutoFill handle.

14. Click cell E15 to select it. Double-click the AutoFill handle.

15. Select row 14 as a print title to be repeated at the top of each page when the worksheet is printed.

16. Save the workbook with the same name (**eec3sc01**).

17. Print and close **eec3sc01**.

Assessment 2

1. Open **ExcelWorksheet09**.

2. Save the worksheet using the Save As command and name it **eec3sc02**.

3. Create a custom header with your name displayed at the left margin and the file name displayed at the right margin.

4. You recently entered a contest and won the grand prize. You can take this prize in one of two payments. With Option A you will be paid $10,000 now and $3,500 each year for the next five years. With Option B you will not be paid any cash now, but you will be paid $6,000 a year for the next five years. You need to determine which option is the better deal. In cell B3 use the PV function to calculate the present value of $3,500 paid annually for the next five years. Assume the appropriate interest rate is 12%. Remember that the result will be displayed as a negative number because the present value is assumed to be cash that will be paid out.

5. In cell B4, use the PV function to calculate the present value of the one time payment of $10,000. The appropriate interest rate would be 0% because you would be getting the money immediately.

6. In cell B6 enter a formula that adds together the present value of the installment payments and the present value of the cash you would receive now.

7. In cell B11 use the PV function to calculate the present value of $6,000 paid annually for the next five years. Assume the appropriate interest rate is 12%.

8. Save the workbook with the same name (**eec3sc02**).

9. Print and close **eec3sc02**.

Assessment 3

1. Open **ExcelWorksheet10**.
2. Save the worksheet using the Save As command and name it **eec3sc03**.
3. Create a custom header with your name displayed at the left margin and the file name displayed at the right margin.
4. The EastWest Crossroads Company sells imported and unique gifts through the mail. This worksheet helps the warehouse manager keep track of daily shipping expenses. Shipping expenses depend upon two things: the weight of the package and the zone to which it is being shipped. There are six different shipping zones. Look at cells J6 through P42. This is the table that must be used to look up how much it costs to ship a package. Now look at cells A6 through F54. This is the form the manager used to calculate the shipping expense, together with the total charge for each item shipped.
5. Name the range of cells J8 through P42 *Shipping*.
6. Click cell E7 to select it. Use the VLOOKUP function to enter a formula that finds the shipping expenses for the packages shipped to zone 1. The formula should look up the weight of the package (D7) in the range of cells named *Shipping*. (Be sure to use the range name in the formula.) The costs of shipping packages to zone 1 are found in column 2 of the table.
7. Cell E7 should still be selected. Double-click the AutoFill handle to copy the formula.
8. Enter a formula in F7 that adds together the charge and the shipping expense. Double-click the AutoFill handle to copy the formula.
9. Click cell E15 to select it. Use the VLOOKUP function to enter a formula that finds the shipping expenses for packages shipped to zone 2.
10. Cell E15 should still be selected. Double-click the AutoFill handle to copy the formula.
11. Enter a formula in cell F15 that adds together the charge and the shipping expense. Double-click the AutoFill handle to copy the formula.
12. Enter the appropriate VLOOKUP function in cell E23 to find the shipping expense for zone 3. Copy the formula. Enter the appropriate formula in cell F23 to add together the charge and the shipping expense. Copy the formula.
13. Enter the appropriate VLOOKUP function in cell E31 to find the shipping expense for zone 4. Copy the formula. Enter the appropriate formula in cell F31 to add together the charge and the shipping expense. Copy the formula.
14. Enter the appropriate VLOOKUP function in cell E39 to find the shipping expense for zone 5. Copy the formula. Enter the appropriate formula in cell F39 to add together the charge and the shipping expense. Copy the formula.
15. Enter the appropriate VLOOKUP function in cell E47 to find the shipping expense for zone 6. Copy the formula. Enter the appropriate formula in cell F47 to add together the charge and the shipping expense. Copy the formula.
16. Adjust the width of column F to automatically display the widest entry.
17. Enter today's date in cell B4.
18. Insert a page break so that zones 1, 2, and 3 print on one page and zones 4, 5, and 6 print on a second page.
19. Print the first two pages of the worksheet.
20. Save the workbook with the same name (**eec3sc03**).
21. Close **eec3sc03**.

Assessment 4

1. Open **ExcelWorksheet11**.
2. Save the worksheet using the Save As command and name it **eec3sc04**.
3. Create a custom header with your name displayed at the left margin and the file name displayed at the right margin.

4. This worksheet is used to keep track of Whitewater Canoe and Kayak's weekly payroll. Scroll horizontally and vertically to view the entire worksheet.

5. In cell I9 enter a formula that calculates the total hours that Norman Campbell worked. Copy the formula to cells I10 through I13.

6. In cell K9 use the IF function to enter a formula that calculates the regular pay. If an employee works 40 hours or less during the week, the regular pay would be the hours worked times the wage. If an employee works more than 40 hours a week, the regular pay would be the wage times 40. Enter the appropriate IF function in cell K9. Copy the formula to cells K10 through K13. Format cells K9 through K13 as currency.

7. In cell L9 use the IF function to enter a formula that calculates overtime. If an employee works more than 40 hours during the week, he or she gets paid time-and-a-half on all the hours over 40 that were worked. If the employee does not work more than 40 hours, no overtime pay is earned. *(Hint: Time-and-a-half would be 1.5 times the regular wage. Remember, time-and-a-half is paid only on the hours that are worked over the normal 40 hours.)* Copy the formula to cells L10 through L13. Format cells L9 through L13 as currency.

8. Enter a formula in M9 that calculates the gross pay (regular pay plus overtime). Copy the formula to cells M10 through M13.

9. Use the IF function to enter a formula in cell N9 that calculates the deduction for FICA. Look at the tax table in cells D17 through F21. If the gross pay is less than $600, one set of tax percentages is to be used. If the gross pay is greater than or equal to $600, a different set of tax percentages is to be used. Click cell N9 to select it and enter the following formula:

    =IF(M9<600,M9*$E$18,M9*$F$18)

    If the value in M9, which is gross pay, is less than 600, the gross pay will be multiplied by cell E18, which is the FICA tax for gross pay less than $600. If the value in M9 is not less than 600, then the gross pay will be multiplied by cell F18, which is the FICA tax for gross pay that is greater than or equal to $600. Copy the formula to cells N10 through N13. Format cells N9 through N13 as currency.

10. Use the appropriate IF function to enter a formula in cell O9 to calculate the deduction for federal tax. Be sure to reference the cells for federal tax from the tax table. Copy the formula to cells O10 through O13. Format cells O9 through O13 as currency.

11. Use the appropriate IF function to enter a formula in cell P9 to calculate the deduction for state tax. Be sure to reference the cells for state tax from the tax table. Copy the formula to cells P10 through P13. Format cells P9 through P13 as currency.

12. Use the appropriate IF function to enter a formula in cell Q9 to calculate the deduction for local tax. Be sure to reference the cells for local tax from the tax table. Copy the formula to cells Q10 through Q13. Format cells Q9 through Q13 as currency.

13. Enter a formula in cell R9 to calculate the net pay (gross pay minus FICA, federal tax, state tax, and local tax). Copy the formula to cells R10 through R13.

14. Adjust the page setup so that the orientation of the page is landscape, row 7 is printed at the top of every page, and columns A and B repeat at the left of every page. Center the worksheet on the page horizontally.

15. Save the worksheet with the same name (**eec3sc04**).

16. Print and close **eec3sc04**.

Assessment 5

1. Open **ExcelWorksheet12**.
2. Save the worksheet using the Save As command and name it **eec3sc05**.
3. Create a custom header with your name displayed at the left margin and the file name displayed at the right margin.

4. This worksheet is a running tabulation of how many Pathfinders, Trekkers, and Excursions were sold during January by Whitewater Canoe and Kayak's sales representatives. You need to calculate the total units that were sold for each product. Name the range of cells C6 through C38 *Units_Sold*. Name the range of cells A6 through A38 *Product*.

5. Click in cell F5 to select it. Using the SUMIF function, enter a formula that calculates the total number of Pathfinders that were sold in January. Use the range names *Product* and *Units_Sold* in the function.

6. Click in cell F6 to select it. Using the SUMIF function, enter a formula that calculates the total number of Trekkers that were sold in January. Use the range names *Product* and *Units_Sold* in the function.

7. Click in cell F7 to select it. Using the SUMIF function, enter a formula that calculates the total number of Excursions that were sold in January. Use the range names *Product* and *Units_Sold* in the function.

8. Save the worksheet with the same name (**eec3sc05**).

9. Print and close **eec3sc05**.

Assessment 6

1. Open **ExcelWorksheet13**.

2. Save the worksheet using the Save As command and name it **eec3sc06**.

3. Create a custom header with your name displayed at the left margin and the file name displayed at the right margin.

4. This worksheet is used by Performance Threads, a company that supplies the entertainment industry with theatrical fabrics, stage draperies, and scenic and production supplies, to keep track of its inventory of velour fabrics at both its New York and Los Angeles warehouses. You want to add a couple of functions to this worksheet, but the current inventory figures have not yet arrived, so you need to enter some dummy values to make sure your functions are going to work. You want to use the RAND function to generate numbers between 1 and 300. These numbers have to be whole numbers, so you have to use the ROUND function as well. Click cell B8 and type the following formula:

    =ROUND((RAND()*300),0)

    Multiplying the RAND function by 300 produces random numbers between 1 and 300. Copy the formula to cells B9 through B29.

5. Click cell E8. Use the RAND and ROUND functions to generate a whole number between 1 and 300. Copy the formula to cells E9 through E29.

6. Type the following label in both cell A31 and D31:

    # of Fabrics with Bolts > 200

    Automatically adjust the widths of columns A and D.

7. Name the range of cells B8 through B29 *NY_Bolts*. Name the range of cells E8 through E29 *LA_Bolts*.

8. Click cell B31. Use the COUNTIF function to count how many cells in the range B8:B29 contain values greater than 200. Use the range name *NY_Bolts* in the formula.

9. Click cell E31. Use the COUNTIF function to count how many cells in the range E8:E29 contain values greater than 200. Use the range name *LA_Bolts* in the formula.

10. Save the workbook with the same name (**eec3sc06**).

11. Print and close **eec3sc06**.

Assessment 7

1. You can use the PMT function to make payments to annuities other than loans. Say, for example, in five years you want to have saved up $10,000 for the down payment on a house. You can use the PMT function to calculate what you need to save each month to reach your goal. Use Excel's Help feature to figure out how to do this.
2. Type How do I determine payments to annuities other than loans?. Press Enter. Click the PMT worksheet function option from the list of recommended functions that is displayed.
3. Scroll through the information that is displayed until you find the example for determining payments to annuities other than loans. Follow the directions to copy the example given to a blank worksheet, and use the example to calculate the amount you would have to save if you were going to save for five years, would earn an annual interest rate of 7%, and wanted to have saved $10,000 in five years.
4. Create a custom header with your name displayed at the left margin and the file name displayed at the right margin.
5. Save the worksheet using the Save As command and name it **eec3sc07**.
6. Print and close **eec3sc07**.

CHAPTER challenge

You work as a loan officer for Mid-America Bank. One of your customers has asked you to help him determine whether to take out a loan to purchase a boat or to save for the boat and then purchase it with cash. You decide to create an Excel worksheet to show information that will help the customer with his decision. Use the PMT function to determine what the monthly payment would be for a boat that costs $15,000. The loan will be for five years at a rate of 6%. Use the FV function to determine how much money will accrue after five years with the same interest rate. Each month, the customer will invest the amount of money that would have been used for the monthly payment. Save the workbook as **Boat**.

Since interest rates fluctuate daily, you would like to show how varying interest rates affect a monthly payment. One method of displaying this information is through a one-variable data table. Use the Help feature to learn about data tables. Then create a one-variable data table based on the information in the first part of the Chapter Challenge. The table should show interest rates ranging from 3%-8% (increments of .5%) and how they affect the monthly payment. Save the workbook again. Print the worksheet.

The customer that was described in the first part of the Chapter Challenge would like you to e-mail him (your professor) the workbook named Boat as an attachment so that he can make his decision. Assume that the boat will increase in price by $2,000 after five years. In the body of the e-mail, help the customer make his decision by providing suggestions as to whether to borrow or invest and why.

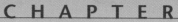

CHAPTER 4

WORKING WITH LISTS

PERFORMANCE OBJECTIVES

Upon successful completion of Chapter 4, you will be able to:

➤ Enter data using the Data Form
➤ Use data validation
➤ Sort a list
➤ Perform a multilevel sort on a list
➤ Find and display records using the Data Form
➤ Edit records using the Data Form
➤ Delete records using the Data Form
➤ Outline a worksheet
➤ Subtotal a list
➤ Filter a list using AutoFilter
➤ Create a custom AutoFilter
➤ Filter a list using advanced filtering
➤ Create and modify list ranges
➤ Create and edit database functions

In Excel, a list is a series of worksheet rows containing similar sets of data that are identified by labels in the top row. Employee names, addresses, and telephone numbers would be an example of a list. Each column in a list contains similar information based on the label for that column. Column A, for example, might be labeled "Last Name" and contain last names, column B might be labeled "First Name" and contain first names, column C might be labeled "Address" and contain street addresses, and so on. In a list, the labels have to be in the top row; they cannot be in the first column. There are no blank rows in a list.

Excel automatically recognizes a list as a database. A database is used for performing record-keeping tasks such as keeping track of all of a company's incoming orders or keeping track of inventory. As shown in Figure 4.1, each row in the list is a record, and each column in the list is a field. The labels in the first row of the list are the field names. A value found in a single cell is called a field value. The list range is the range of cells that contains all the records, fields, and field names of the list. Once you have your Excel data organized as a list, certain database operations can be performed, such as sorting data, finding specific data, and subtotaling data. The purpose of this chapter is to teach you how to create and use lists in Excel.

FIGURE

4.1 *An Excel List*

Each column is a field.

Column labels are field names.

Each row is a record.

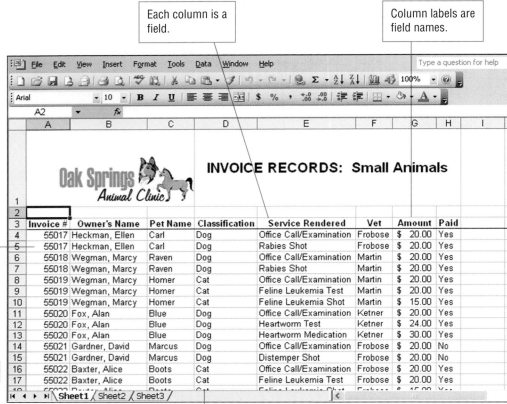

Each column contains similar information.

QUICK
STEPS

Display a Data Form
1. Click Data.
2. Click Form.

HINT

When using Data Form to enter records, the record is placed on the worksheet when you move to another record or close the Data Form.

HINT

If a field in the list is a formula, the result of the formula is displayed in the Data Form as a label and cannot be edited.

Entering Data Using the Data Form

Oftentimes data stored in an Excel database is quite extensive and therefore requires a great deal of data entry. Data can be entered either by entering it into the individual cells on the worksheet or by using the Data Form. Using the Data Form makes the data entry job a little easier. To enter data using the Data Form, select any cell in the list. Click Data. If necessary, expand the menu by clicking the down-pointing arrow at the bottom of the list. Click the Form option once it appears. The Data Form dialog box, as shown in Figure 4.2, is displayed. Each field name is displayed with a corresponding box. Click the New button. A new blank record is displayed. The appropriate data can be entered into each box. If more records are to be added, press Enter and another new blank record will be displayed. Once you have completed entering the data, click the Close button to return to the worksheet.

4.2 **The Data Form Dialog Box**

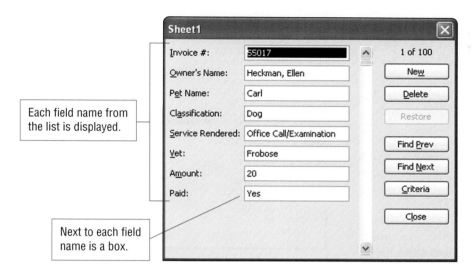

Each field name from the list is displayed.

Next to each field name is a box.

exercise 1

1. Open **ExcelWorksheet01**.
2. Save the worksheet using the Save As command and name it **eec4x01**.
3. Create a custom header that displays your name at the left margin and the file name at the right margin.
4. This worksheet stores a list of invoice records for Oak Springs Animal Clinic. Three veterinarians work at the Oak Springs Animal Clinic, and they specialize in both large and small animals. This worksheet keeps track of the invoices for their small animal business. You want to add three more records to the list. Complete the following steps to add three more records using the Data Form dialog box:
   a. Click cell A4.
   b. Click Data and then Form.
   c. The Data Form dialog box is displayed. The record that is displayed in the dialog box is the record from the row that is currently selected. Click the New button.

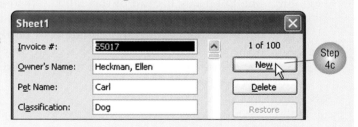

Step
4c

d. The insertion point is in the *Invoice #* box. Type the following: **55070**.

e. Press Tab. The insertion point moves to the *Owner's Name* box. Type **Henry, Irene**.

f. Press Tab. The insertion point moves to the *Pet Name* box. Type **Ralph**.

g. Press Tab. The insertion point moves to the *Classification* box. Type **Dog**.

h. Press Tab. The insertion point moves to the *Service Rendered* box. Type **Office Call/Examination**.

i. Press Tab. The insertion point moves to the *Vet* box. Type **Frobose**.

j. Press Tab. The insertion point moves to the *Amount* box. Type **20**.

k. Press Tab. The insertion point moves to the *Paid* box. Type **No**.

l. The data for the next record has now all been entered into the Data Form. Press Enter.

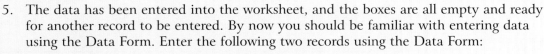

5. The data has been entered into the worksheet, and the boxes are all empty and ready for another record to be entered. By now you should be familiar with entering data using the Data Form. Enter the following two records using the Data Form:

Invoice #:	55070	*Invoice #:*	55070
Owner's Name:	Henry, Irene	*Owner's Name:*	Henry, Irene
Pet Name:	Ralph	*Pet Name:*	Ralph
Classification:	Dog	*Classification:*	Dog
Service Rendered:	Distemper Shot	*Service Rendered:*	Rabies Shot
Vet:	Frobose	*Vet:*	Frobose
Amount:	20	*Amount:*	20
Paid:	No	*Paid:*	No

When you have finished entering the data, click the Close button. If you accidentally press the Enter key instead of the Tab key before you have entered all the data in a record, you can click the Close button, scroll to the bottom of the worksheet, and then enter the data in the appropriate cells on the worksheet.

6. Adjust the page setup so that row 3 repeats as a print title at the top of each page.

7. Save the worksheet with the same name (**eec4x01**). You are going to use this worksheet in Exercise 2.

8. Print and close the worksheet.

Using Data Validation

Excel's data validation feature allows you to specify the exact data that can be entered into a cell. This feature helps to prevent errors from being made when data is entered. Using the data validation feature, entries can be limited to the options on a list. Allowing a user to enter data by selecting it from a list also eliminates having to type in the exact same entry over and over again.

To use the data validation feature, select the cells that have data you want to validate. You can select either an entire column or only specific cells within a column. Click Data and Validation. The Data Validation dialog box, as shown in Figure 4.3, is displayed. The entries on the Settings tab allow you to establish the validation criteria. As shown in Figure 4.3, clicking the down-pointing arrow to the right of the *Allow* box displays a drop-down list that shows the options for what can be allowed into the selected cells. The options available on the Settings tab change when something other than *Any value* is entered in the *Allow* box.

FIGURE

4.3   *The Data Validation Dialog Box with the Settings Tab Selected*

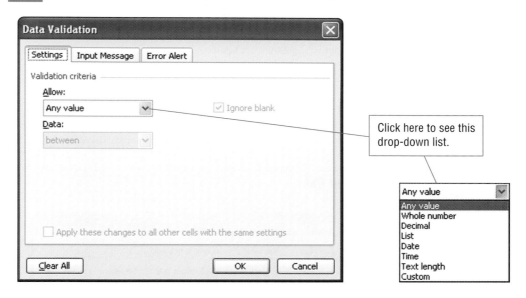

If you select *Whole number, Decimal, Date, Time,* or *Text Length* from the drop-down list for the *Allow* box, a *Data* box like the one in Figure 4.4 is activated. Clicking the down-pointing arrow to the right of the *Data* box displays a drop-down list that lists the Data operator options shown in Figure 4.4. Select one of the data operators and enter the Minimum and Maximum values.

4.4 *Validating Numeric Data*

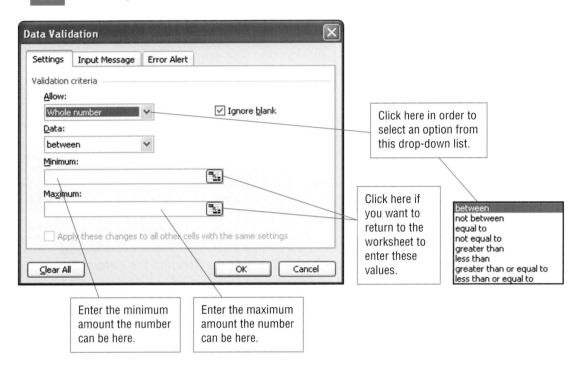

For example, you can set the data validation for a cell so that a whole number greater than or equal to 100 must be entered. If someone tries entering 98 into the cell, the error message shown in Figure 4.5 is displayed.

4.5 *Entering Invalid Data*

Validating List Data

In situations in which the same few items are to be entered into a column, you can create a drop-down list containing the options from which the user must choose. First select the entire column to be validated. Click Data and Validation. Click the down-pointing arrow to the right of the *Allow* box and select *List*. Enter the options to be included in the list in the *Source* box. To select the options from the worksheet, click the Cell Reference button to the right of the *Source* box, as shown in Figure 4.6.

4.6 *Validating List Data*

Select the *List* option for the *Allow* box.

Enter the source data for the list here.

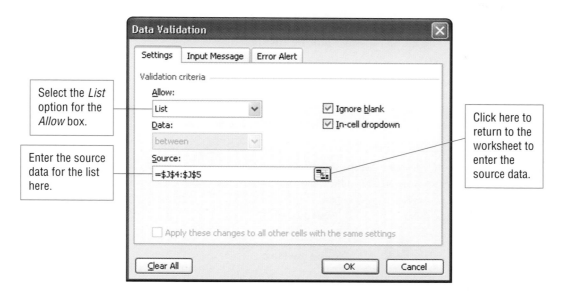

Click here to return to the worksheet to enter the source data.

Including Input and Error Messages

You can include messages that will display if a user tries to enter invalid data. To include an input message, click the Input Message tab on the Data Validation dialog box. As shown in Figure 4.7, you need to enter the title for the Title bar and the input message. Make sure the *Show input message when cell is selected* check box is selected. When a user selects the cell, the Input message will be displayed.

4.7 *Including an Input Message*

Enter the name to appear in the Title bar here.

Enter the message to be displayed here.

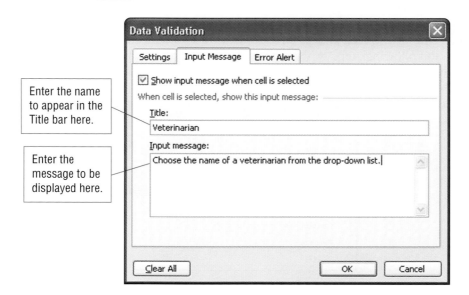

To include an error message, click the Error Alert tab. As shown in Figure 4.8, you need to select the style for the error alert, which can be either *Stop*, *Warning*, or *Information*. You also need to enter the title for the Title bar and the error message to be displayed when someone tries to enter invalid data. Make sure the *Show error alert after invalid data is entered* check box is displayed. When a user tries to enter invalid data, the error message will be displayed.

FIGURE

4.8 *Including an Error Message*

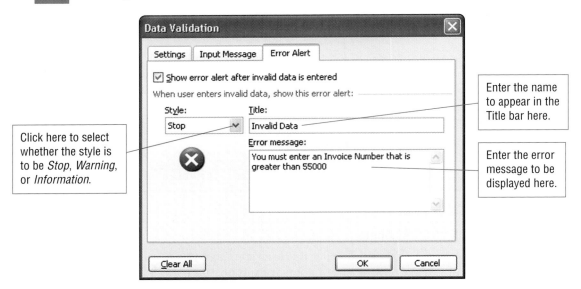

Click here to select whether the style is to be *Stop*, *Warning*, or *Information*.

Enter the name to appear in the Title bar here.

Enter the error message to be displayed here.

exercise 2

USING DATA VALIDATION

1. Open **eec4x01**. This is the worksheet that was completed in Exercise 1.
2. Save the worksheet using the Save As command and name it **eec4x02**.
3. Make sure the header displays your name at the left margin and the file name at the right margin.
4. You want to validate some of the data that is entered into this worksheet. Select column A. Complete the following steps to validate data that is entered into column A:
   a. Click Data and then click Validation. If necessary, click the Settings tab.
   b. Click the down-pointing arrow to the right of the *Allow* box. Select *Whole number*.
   c. Click the down-pointing arrow to the right of the *Data* box. Select *greater than or equal to*.
   d. Place the insertion point in the *Minimum* box. Type the following: 55000.

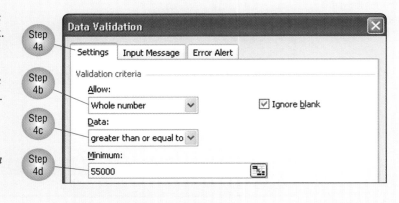

Step 4a
Step 4b
Step 4c
Step 4d

EXCEL

e. Click the Input Message tab.

f. Type the following in the *Title* box: **Invoice Number**.

g. Type the following in the *Input message* box: **Enter an invoice number. Invoice numbers start at 55000.**

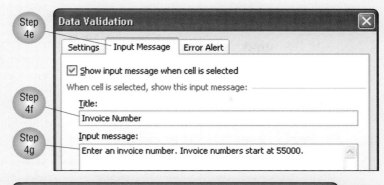

h. Click the Error Alert tab.

i. Type the following in the *Title* box: **Error**.

j. Type the following in the *Error message* box: **Invoice numbers must be 55000 or higher.**

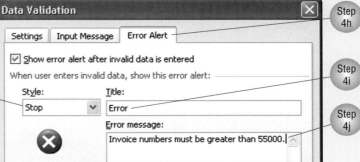

k. Make sure the *Stop* option is selected in the *Style* box.

l. Click OK.

5. The only entry made in column F is the name of one of the veterinarians. Select column F. Complete the following steps to create a drop-down list of options for column F:

a. Click Data and then click Validation. Click the Settings tab.

b. Click the down-pointing arrow to the right of the *Allow* box. Select *List*.

c. Place the insertion point in the *Source* box. Type **Frobose, Ketner, Martin**.

d. Click the Input Message tab.

e. Type the following in the *Title* box: **Veterinarian**.

f. Type the following in the *Input message* box: **Select one of the veterinarian's names from the drop-down list.**

g. Click the Error Alert tab.

h. Type the following in the *Title* box: **Error**.

i. Type the following in the *Error message* box: **You must select a name from the drop-down list.** Click OK.

6. The only entries made in column H are Yes or No. Select column H. Complete the following steps to create a drop-down list of options for column H:

a. Click Data and then click Validation. Click the Settings tab.

b. Click the down-pointing arrow to the right of the *Allow* box. Select *List*.

c. Place the insertion point in the *Source* box. Type the following: **Yes, No**.

d. Click the Input Message tab.

e. Type the following in the *Title* box: **Paid**.

f. Type the following in the *Input message* box: **Select either Yes or No from the drop-down list to indicate whether or not the invoice has been paid.**

g. Click the Error Alert tab.

h. Type the following in the *Title* box: **Error**.

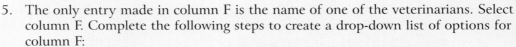

i. Type the following in the *Error message* box: **You must select either Yes or No from the drop-down list.** Click OK.

7. Use the vertical split bar at the top of the vertical scroll bar to freeze rows 1, 2, and 3 in the window. Complete the following steps to enter a new record:

   a. Select cell A107. This should be the first empty cell at the end of the list. Notice the Invoice Number input message is displayed.

   b. Type the following in cell A107: **5571**.

   c. Press Tab. An error message is displayed informing you that the invoice number you entered is not large enough.

3	Invoice #	Owner's Name	Pet Name	Classification	Service Rendered	Vet	Amount	Paid
102	55068	Keyes, Dan	Ike	Iguana	Office Call/Examination	Frobose	$ 20.00	Yes
103	55069	Harris, Victoria	Bugs	Rabbit	Office Call/Examination	Martin	$ 20.00	Yes
104	55070	Henry, Irene	Ralph	Dog	Office Call/Examination	Frobose	$ 20.00	No
105	55070	Henry, Irene	Ralph	Dog	Distemper Shot	Frobose	$ 20.00	No
106	55070	Henry, Irene	Ralph			obose	$ 20.00	No
107	5571							
108								
109								
110								
111								
112								

Step 7a

Invoice Number
Enter an invoice number. Invoice numbers start at 55000.

Error

✕ Invoice numbers must be 55000 or higher.

[Retry]   [Cancel]

Step 7c

   d. Click the Retry button. Type the following: **55071**.

   e. Press Tab. Type the following: **Mason, Anita**.

   f. Press Tab. Type the following: **Snickers**.

   g. Press Tab. Type the following: **Dog**. As soon as you type the letter *D*, Excel automatically fills in the rest of the word.

   h. Press Tab. Start to type **Office Call/Examination**. As soon as you type the letter *O*, Excel automatically fills in the rest of the entry.

   i. Press Tab. The Veterinarian input message is displayed. A down-pointing arrow automatically is displayed to the right of the cell.

3	Invoice #	Owner's Name	Pet Name	Classification	Service Rendered	Vet	Amount	Paid
102	55068	Keyes, Dan	Ike	Iguana	Office Call/Examination	Frobose	$ 20.00	Yes
103	55069	Harris, Victoria	Bugs	Rabbit	Office Call/Examination	Martin	$ 20.00	Yes
104	55070	Henry, Irene	Ralph	Dog	Office Call/Examination	Frobose	$ 20.00	No
105	55070	Henry, Irene	Ralph	Dog	Distemper Shot	Frobose	$ 20.00	No
106	55070	Henry, Irene	Ralph	Dog	Rabies Shot	Frobose	$ 20.00	No
107	55071	Mason, Anita	Snickers	Dog	Office Call/Examination	▾		
108								
109								
110								
111								
112								

Step 7i

Veterinarian
Select one of the veterinarian's names from the drop-down list.

   j. Click the down-pointing arrow to the right of the cell and select *Martin* from the drop-down list.

   k. Press Tab. Type the following: **20**.

   l. Press Tab. The Paid input message is displayed. A down-pointing arrow automatically is displayed to the right of the cell.

   m. Click the down-pointing arrow to the right of the cell and select *Yes* from the drop-down list.

EXCEL

8. By now you should be familiar with entering data using data validation. Enter the following records in rows 108 and 109:

Invoice #:	55071	Invoice #:	55071
Owner's Name:	Mason, Anita	Owner's Name:	Mason, Anita
Pet Name:	Snickers	Pet Name:	Snickers
Classification:	Dog	Classification:	Dog
Service Rendered:	Heartworm Test	Service Rendered:	Heartworm Medication
Vet:	Martin	Vet:	Martin
Amount:	24	Amount:	35
Paid:	Yes	Paid:	Yes

9. Make any necessary adjustments so that all the columns fit on one page.
10. Save the worksheet with the same name (**eec4x02**). You are going to use this worksheet in Exercise 3.
11. Print and close the worksheet.

Sorting a List

Excel's sort feature helps you organize the data in a list. Column fields can be quickly sorted in ascending or descending order. To sort the data in a column, select any cell in the column by which you want to sort. To sort in ascending order, click the Sort Ascending button on the Standard toolbar. To sort in descending order, click the Sort Descending button on the Standard toolbar.

Sort Ascending

Sort Descending

Performing a Multilevel Sort

If you want to sort a list by more than one field, you can use the Sort dialog box. Suppose, for example, you wanted to sort first by a last name field and then by a first name field. To perform such a multilevel sort, select any cell in the list to be sorted. Click Data and then click Sort. The Sort dialog box shown in Figure 4.9 is displayed.

FIGURE

4.9   *The Sort Dialog Box*

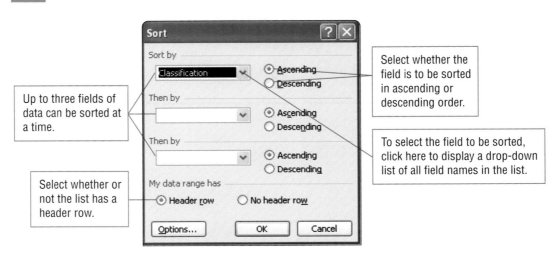

To select the first field to be sorted, click the down-pointing arrow to the right of the *Sort by* box. A list of all the field names is displayed. Select the field name of the column to be sorted first, and select whether the sort should be in ascending or descending order. If you want to sort by a second field, click the down-pointing arrow to the right of the first *Then by* box and select the field name of the column to be sorted next, and so on. At the bottom of the dialog box, select whether or not the list has a header row and then click OK.

Creating a Custom List

At times you may want to sort by an unusual order, that is, not simply ascending or descending. You can do this by creating a custom list. To create a custom list, type the list into a worksheet and select all the cells containing the list. Click Tools and then click Options. Click the Custom Lists tab on the Options dialog box. As shown in Figure 4.10, the selected cell range appears in the *Import list from cells* box. Click the Import button. The list is then displayed in the *Custom lists* box and the *List entries* box. Click the OK button.

FIGURE

4.10 *The Options Dialog Box with the Custom Lists Tab selected*

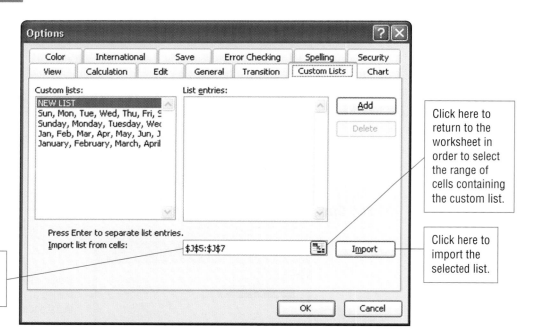

Enter the cell range containing the custom list.

Click here to return to the worksheet in order to select the range of cells containing the custom list.

Click here to import the selected list.

You can use a custom list to sort only the first or top level of the sort. Click the down-pointing arrow to the right of the *Sort by* list box and select the column for which the custom list was created. To sort that column using the custom list, click the Options button at the bottom of the Sort dialog box. The Sort Options dialog box shown in Figure 4.11 is displayed. Click the down-pointing arrow to the right of the *First key sort order* box. The custom list will be included in the drop-down list that appears. Select the custom list and click OK.

Another way to create a custom list is to click Tools, Options, and the Custom Lists tab. Click *NEW LIST* in the *Custom lists* box. Type the list into the *List entries* box starting with the first item on the list and pressing enter after each item. Click the Add button after typing the list's last item.

FIGURE

| 4.11 | **The Sort Options Dialog Box**

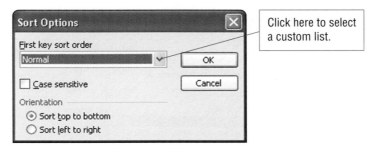

Click here to select a custom list.

Once a custom list is created, Excel saves it on the computer system so that it is always available. To delete a custom list, Click Tools and then Options. Click the Custom Lists tab on the Options dialog box. Select the custom list to be deleted from the Custom lists box and click the Delete button. Click OK. A box warning you that the list will be permanently deleted is displayed. Click OK.

exercise 3

SORTING A LIST, PERFORMING A MULTILEVEL SORT, AND SORTING BY A CUSTOM LIST

1. Open **eec4x02**. This is the worksheet that was completed in Exercise 2.
2. Save the worksheet using the Save As command and name it **eec4x03**.
3. Make sure the header displays your name at the left margin and the file name at the right margin.
4. Right now the list is sorted by invoice number. You would like to sort it by owner's name. Click cell B4. Click the Sort Ascending button. Scroll through the list to see how it is now sorted.
5. Next try sorting the list by vet. Click cell F4. Click the Sort Ascending button. Scroll through the list to see how it is now sorted.

6. Now you want to sort by the owner's name first, by the classification of animal second, and finally by the pet's name. Select any cell in the list. Complete the following steps to perform the multilevel sort.

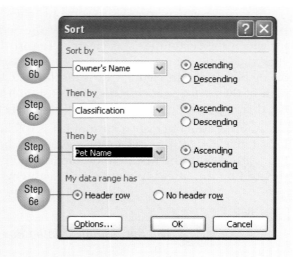

Step 6b

Step 6c

Step 6d

Step 6e

a. Click Data and then Sort.
b. Click the down-pointing arrow to the right of the *Sort by* box, and then select *Owner's Name*.
c. Click the down-pointing arrow to the right of the first *Then by* box and then select *Classification*.
d. Click the down-pointing arrow to the right of the second *Then by* box and then select *Pet Name*.
e. Be sure that *Header row* is selected at the bottom of the dialog box.
f. Click OK.
g. Scroll through the list to see how it is now sorted.
7. Make any necessary adjustments so that the columns all fit on one page. Print the sorted list.
8. The veterinarians want to be able to sort the list in order by who has worked at the clinic the longest. Dr. Ketner has worked there the longest, followed by Dr. Frobose, followed by Dr.

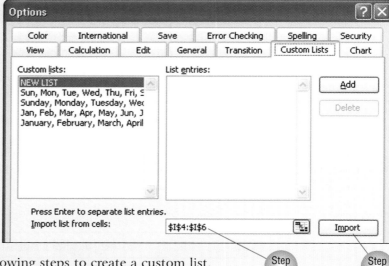

Step 8f

Step 8g

Martin. Complete the following steps to create a custom list.
a. Type **Ketner** in cell I4.
b. Type **Frobose** in cell I5.
c. Type **Martin** in cell I6.
d. Select cells I4 through I6.
e. Click Tools and then Options.
f. Click the Custom Lists tab. Check to make sure that the cell range I4:I6 is in the *Import list from cells* box.
g. Click the Import button, then click OK.
h. Delete cells I4:I6.
9. You are ready to sort using the custom list you just created. Complete the following steps to sort by the custom list:
a. Click any cell in the list.
b. Click Data and then Sort.
c. Click the down-pointing arrow to the right of the *Sort by* box and then select *Vet*.
d. Click the Options button at the bottom of the dialog box.

EXCEL

e. Click the down-pointing arrow next to the *First key sort order* box. Select *Ketner, Frobose, Martin*, then click OK.

f. Click the down-pointing arrow to the right of the first *Then by* box and then select *Owner's Name*.

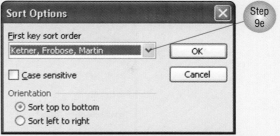

g. Click the down-pointing arrow to the right of the second *Then by* box and then select *Classification*, then click OK.

h. Scroll through the list to see how it is now sorted.

10. Make any necessary adjustments so that the columns all fit on one page. Print the sorted list.

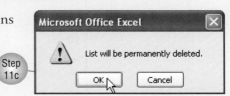

11. Complete the following steps to delete the custom list you created:

a. Click Tools and then Options.

b. Select *Ketner, Frobose, Martin* in the *Custom lists* box and click Delete.

c. A warning box is displayed letting you know that the list will be permanently deleted. Click OK.

d. Click OK.

12. Save the worksheet with the same name (**eec4x03**). You are going to use this worksheet in Exercise 4.

13. Close the worksheet.

Modifying Records

Updates usually have to be made to data lists. Records need to be deleted or edited in some way. In addition to allowing you to enter new records, the Data Form can be used to search for, display, edit, and delete specific records.

Finding Records

To find specific records, select any cell in the data list and click Data and then Form. Clicking the Find Prev button displays the previous record. Clicking the Find Next button displays the next record. Clicking the Criteria button allows you to enter specific criteria Excel will use when searching for the record. A blank record is displayed. You can enter the search criteria in the field name boxes. If you enter criteria in more than one field, the record must contain the criteria in both fields in order to be found. Using the criteria entered in Figure 4.12, Excel will find all the records containing "Heckman, Ellen" in the *Owner's Name* field and "Cat" in the *Classification* field.

FIGURE

4.12 *Finding Specific Records*

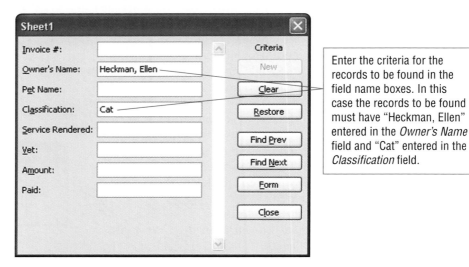

Enter the criteria for the records to be found in the field name boxes. In this case the records to be found must have "Heckman, Ellen" entered in the *Owner's Name* field and "Cat" entered in the *Classification* field.

The comparison operators listed in Table 4.1 can be used as part of the search criteria. For example, if you wanted to find all the records in which the *Amount* field was greater than 20, you would type **>20** in the *Amount* box.

TABLE

4.1 *Comparison Operators*

Operators	Description
=	Equals
>	Greater than
<	Less than
>=	Greater than or equal to
<=	Less than or equal to
<>	Not equal to

Once the search criteria have been entered in the boxes, click the Find Next button. The first record Excel finds is displayed. Click the Find Next button until you hear a beep. The beep indicates that Excel could not find any more matches. To return to the worksheet, click the Close button.

HINT

If the record you are editing contains a formula, the formula is not recalculated until you move to another record or close the dialog box.

Editing Records

Once a specific record has been located using the Data Form, you can make any changes to it right on the Data Form. Type the changes in the appropriate field name boxes. Remember to press Tab to move from field to field and press Enter to move from record to record. Once you click the Close button or move to a different record in the Data Form, whatever changes were made are entered into the worksheet. You can also edit records directly on the worksheet.

HINT

Clicking the Restore button undoes any changes you have made to the record currently displayed in the Data Form.

Deleting Records

Records can be deleted using the Data Form. Once the record to be deleted has been located using the Data Form, click the Delete button. A warning box is displayed letting you know that the record will be permanently deleted. Click OK to delete the record. You can also delete records by deleting the row containing the record from the worksheet.

exercise 4

FINDING, EDITING, AND DELETING RECORDS

1. Open **eec4x03**. This is the worksheet that was completed in Exercise 3.
2. Save the worksheet using the Save As command and name it **eec4x04**.
3. Make sure a custom header displays your name at the left margin and the file name at the right margin.
4. First you want to find all the records in which Heartworm Medication was the service rendered. Complete the following steps to use the Data Form to conduct the search:
   a. Click any cell in the data list. Click Data and then Form.
   b. Click the Criteria button.
   c. Type the following in the *Service Rendered* box: **Heartworm Medication**.
   d. Click the Find Next button. The first record found is displayed. Click the Find Next button until no more records are found. Notice how many records were found.
5. Complete the following steps to find all the records where the Heartworm Medication sold cost more than $50.00.
   a. You want to start the search beginning with record 1. To do this, record 1 must be displayed. To display record 1, click the button on the scroll bar and drag it to the top. It should say 1 of 106 in the upper right corner of the dialog box. This means the record that is displayed is the first record out of a total of 106 records.
   b. Click the Criteria button.
   c. *Heartworm Medication* should still be entered in the *Service Rendered* box. Type **>50** in the *Amount* box.

Dialog box (Step 4c / Step 4d):

Sheet1		Criteria
Invoice #:		New
Owner's Name:		Clear
Pet Name:		
Classification:		Restore
Service Rendered:	Heartworm Medication	Find Prev
Vet:		Find Next
Amount:		Form
Paid:		

Dialog box (Step 5a):

Sheet1		1 of 106
Invoice #:	55028	New
Owner's Name:	Brunell, David	Delete
Pet Name:	King	Restore
Classification:	Dog	
Service Rendered:	Office Call/Examination	Find Prev
Vet:	Ketner	Find Next
Amount:	20	Criteria
Paid:	Yes	

     d.   Click the Find Next button. The first record found is displayed. Click the Find Next button until no more records are found. Notice how many records were found this time.

6. Linda Covington has gotten married and wants her last name changed on all her records. Complete the following steps to make this change:

     a.   Use the scroll bar to move to record 1. The first record in the list should be displayed in the Data Form.

     b.   Click the Criteria button.

     c.   Delete the entries in the *Service Rendered* box and the *Amount* box.

     d.   Type the following in the *Owner's Name* box: **Covington, Linda**.

     e.   Click the Find Next button.

     f.   Type the following in the *Owner's Name* box: **Kale, Linda**.

    Be sure to press the Enter key after typing the changes. The editing changes will not be made until the Enter key is pressed. Once the Enter key is pressed, Excel automatically finds the next record with *Covington, Linda* in the *Owner's Name* field.

     g.   Edit the next record that is found so that **Kale, Linda** is in the *Owner's Name* box.

     h.   Edit all of Linda Covington's records to reflect her name change.

     i.   Click the Find Prev button to make sure there are no more records for Linda Covington. When you have finished, Excel should not be able to find any records for Linda Covington when you press either the Find Next or the Find Prev buttons.

7. A mistake was made on invoice 55070. Irene Henry was charged for a rabies shot, but her dog was not given a rabies shot. Complete the following steps to delete this record.

     a.   Use the scroll bar to move to record 1.

     b.   Click the Criteria button.

     c.   Delete the entry in the *Owner's Name* box.

     d.   Type **55070** in the *Invoice #* box.

     e.   Type **Rabies Shot** in the *Service Rendered* box. Click the Find Next button.

     f.   Click the Delete button.

     g.   A warning box is displayed informing you that the record will be permanently deleted. Click OK.

     h.   Click the Close button.

Sheet1

Invoice #:	55070		Criteria
Owner's Name:			New
Pet Name:			Clear
Classification:			Restore
Service Rendered:	Rabies Shot		
Vet:			Find Prev
Amount:			Find Next
Paid:			Form

Step 7d

Step 7e

8. Sort the list by *Owner's Name* first, *Classification* second, and *Pet Name* third.

9. Save the worksheet with the same name (**eec4x04**). You are going to use this worksheet in Exercise 7.

10. Print and close the worksheet.

Outlining a Worksheet

When working with long lists of data, quickly finding the specific information you need could be difficult. One way to make locating information in a list easier is by outlining the worksheet. Once you outline a worksheet, a single mouse click will hide or reveal levels of detail within the worksheet. With an outline you can quickly display only the rows or columns that provide summaries. In Figure 4.13, for example, the details for the East Central Region's sales are displayed. The details for the other regions—East Central, North Central, Northeast, and so on—are hidden. Figure 4.13 has three levels of detail. An outline can have up to eight levels of detail. Each inner level provides details for the preceding outer level. In Figure 4.13, level 1 is the row displaying the Grand Total, level 2 comprises the rows displaying the totals for each of the regions, and level 3 comprises the detail rows for all the regions. To see a particular level of the outline, click the outline symbol that represents the number of the level you want to see. These symbols are located in the upper left corner of Figure 4.13.

FIGURE

4.13 *A Worksheet Outline*

These outline symbols indicate there are three levels of detail in this outline.

To hide details, click the Hide Detail symbol.

To display details, click the Show Detail symbol.

		A	B	C	D
	1	Last Name	First Name	Region	Sales
	2	Bachman	John	East Central	$ 10,001.35
	3	Malone	Michael	East Central	$ 9,902.84
	4	McBride	Robert	East Central	$ 11,985.20
	5			East Central Total	$ 31,889.39
	8			North Central Total	$ 21,101.00
	12			Northeast Total	$ 29,339.21
	16			Northwest Total	$ 30,914.55
	20			South Central Total	$ 29,607.42
	24			Southeast Total	$ 32,032.49
	28			Southwest Total	$ 31,904.98
	29			Grand Total	$ 206,789.04
	30				

If you want to outline a worksheet automatically, it must contain formulas that summarize the data, such as formulas that find subtotals and a grand total. If the summary formulas are in columns, all the columns containing the summary formulas must be either to the right or to the left of the detail data. If the summary formulas are in rows, all the rows containing the summary formulas must be either below or above the detail data. That is, the summary formulas cannot be mixed in with the detail data.

Outline a Worksheet Automatically
1. Click Data.
2. Click Group and Outline.
3. Click Auto Outline.

Once you are sure the worksheet is set up correctly, select the range of cells to be outlined. If you want to outline the entire worksheet, click any cell in the worksheet. If you are outlining only a portion of the worksheet, select the range of cells to be outlined. Click Data, point to Group and Outline, and then click Auto Outline. The appropriate outline symbols are displayed. You can then hide and show levels of detail, as explained in Table 4.2.

TABLE

4.2 | *Showing and Hiding Levels of Detail in an Outline*

To Show	**Click**
The detail data for a group	The Show Detail symbol ⊞.
A specific level in an outline	The Row or Column Level symbol [1][2][3].
All detail in an outline	The Row or Column Level symbol for the lowest row or column. If there are three levels, the lowest level would be three.

To Hide	**Click**
The detail data for a group	The Hide Detail symbol ⊟.
A specific level in an outline	The preceding Row or Column Level symbol [1][2][3]. For example, if an outline has three levels, hide the third level by clicking the symbol for level 2.
All detail in an outline	The first level symbol, which would be one.

HINT

A shortcut for creating an outline manually is to select the rows or columns to be outlined and press Alt + Shift + Right Arrow.

To remove an outline, click any cell on the worksheet. Click Data, point to Group and Outline, and then click Clear Outline. The outline is removed. None of the data on the worksheet changes when an outline is removed.

Instead of having Excel automatically create an outline for you, you can create an outline manually. To create an outline manually, select the rows or columns that will be hidden when the details are not displayed. One outline area cannot be immediately adjacent to another. If you try, for example, to create one outline level that hides rows 5 through 10 and then try to create a second outline level that hides rows 11 through 15, you will end up with one outline level that hides rows 5 through 15. A row or column has to separate the two areas that you want to outline. In many cases, that row or column will contain the summarization function, such as SUM or AVERAGE.

Outline a Worksheet Manually
1. Click Data.
2. Click Group and Outline.
3. Click Group.

To create an outline level, select the rows or columns to be outlined. Click Data, point to Group and Outline, and then click Group. The outline is created. To remove an outline, select the rows or columns that make up the outline to be removed. If you want to clear an entire outline, click a single cell in the worksheet. Click Data, point to Group and Outline, and then click Ungroup. The outline is removed.

exercise 5

1. Open **ExcelWorksheet02**.
2. Save the worksheet using the Save As command and name it **eec4x05**.
3. Create a custom header that displays your name at the left margin and the file name at the right margin.
4. Scroll through the worksheet to look at the information stored in it. The records are sorted by veterinarian, and subtotals for the invoices for each veterinarian are in rows 40, 73, and 111. You would like to be able to easily see just the subtotals. Creating an outline would allow you to do this. Create an outline for the worksheet manually by completing the following steps:
   a. Select row 4. Move the mouse pointer to the bottom of row 4. When the mouse pointer turns into an arrow with a four-headed arrow attached, hold down the Shift key and double-click. Rows 4 through 39 should be selected.
   b. Click Data, point to Group and Outline, and then click Group.
   c. Select row 41. Move the mouse pointer to the bottom of row 41. When the mouse pointer turns into an arrow with a four-headed arrow attached, hold down the Shift key and double-click. Rows 41 through 72 should be selected.
   d. Click Data, point to Group and Outline, and then click Group.
   e. Select row 74. Move the mouse pointer to the bottom of row 74. When the mouse pointer turns into an arrow with a four-headed arrow attached, hold down the Shift key and double-click. Rows 74 through 110 should be selected.
   f. Click Data, point to Group and Outline, and then click Group. The outline for the worksheet now has two levels.

   Step 4f

5. Experiment with displaying different levels of the outline by completing the following steps:
   a. Click the level 1 Column Level symbol. Only the subtotals are displayed.

   Step 5a

	A	B	C	D	E	F	G	H
1					INVOICE RECORDS: Small Animals			
2								
3	Invoice #	Owner's Name	Pet Name	Classification	Service Rendered	Vet	Amount	Paid
40					Frobose Subtotal		$ 849.00	
73					Ketner Subtotal		$ 872.00	
111					Martin Subtotal		$1,023.00	
112								

   b. Change the page setup option to fit the worksheet on one page and then print the worksheet.
   c. Click the Show Detail symbol to the left of row 111. The details for Martin's invoices are now displayed. The Show Detail symbol changed to a Hide Detail symbol.
   d. Print the worksheet. (Make sure the Fit to one page option is still selected.)

e. Click the Hide Detail symbol to the left of row 111.

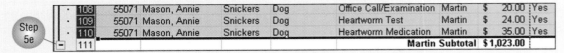

Step
5e

108	55071	Mason, Annie	Snickers	Dog	Office Call/Examination	Martin	$	20.00	Yes
109	55071	Mason, Annie	Snickers	Dog	Heartworm Test	Martin	$	24.00	Yes
110	55071	Mason, Annie	Snickers	Dog	Heartworm Medication	Martin	$	35.00	Yes
111						Martin Subtotal	$1,023.00		

6. Ungroup the records for Frobose by completing the following steps:
   a. Click the Show Detail symbol to the left of row 40. The details for Frobose's invoices are now displayed.
   b. Select row 4. Move the mouse pointer to the bottom of row 4. When the mouse pointer turns into an arrow with a four-headed arrow attached, hold down the Shift key and double-click. Rows 4 through 39 should be selected.
   c. Click Data, point to Group and Outline, and then click Ungroup. Frobose's records are no longer grouped. Deselect rows 4 through 39.
7. To clear the outline for the rest of the worksheet, click Data, point to Group and Outline, and then click Clear Outline.
8. Save and close eec4x05.

exercise 6

1. Open ExcelWorksheet03.
2. Save the worksheet using the Save As command and name it eec4x06.
3. Create a custom header that displays your name at the left margin and the file name at the right margin.
4. Scroll through the worksheet to look at the information stored in it. The records are sorted by invoice. There is a subtotal for each invoice and a grand total of all the invoices. Outlining this worksheet manually would be a lot of work. Outline the worksheet automatically by completing the following steps:
   a. Click anywhere in the worksheet.
   b. Click Data, point to Group and Outline, and then click Auto Outline. The worksheet is now outlined. The outline has three levels.
5. Experiment with displaying different levels of the outline by completing the following steps:
   a. Click the level 1 Column Level symbol. Only the grand total is displayed.

Step
5a

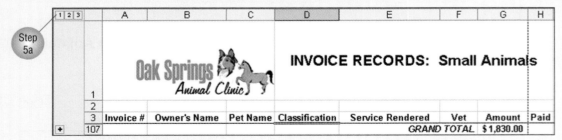

	A	B	C	D	E	F	G	H
1					INVOICE RECORDS: Small Animals			
2								
3	Invoice #	Owner's Name	Pet Name	Classification	Service Rendered	Vet	Amount	Paid
107						GRAND TOTAL	$1,830.00	

   b. Change the page setup option to fit the worksheet on one page and then print the worksheet.
   c. Click the Show Detail symbol to the left of row 107.
   d. Click the level 2 Column Level symbol. All the invoice totals are displayed.
   e. Click the Show Detail symbol to the left of row 17. The details for invoice 55020 are now displayed.
   f. Print the worksheet. (Make sure the Fit to one page option is still selected.)

g.   Click the level 3 Column Level symbol. All the details are displayed.
6.   To clear the outline for the worksheet, click Data, point to Group and Outline, and then click Clear Outline.
7.   Save and close **eec4x06**.

Subtotaling a List

Data in a list can be summarized using subtotals. To subtotal a list you must first sort the list by the field on which you want the list subtotaled. For example, suppose you want a subtotal of each veterinarian's invoices. The list would first have to be sorted by veterinarian. Once the list is sorted by the field on which the subtotals are to be based, select any cell in the list. Click Data and then click Subtotals. The Subtotal dialog box, as shown in Figure 4.14, is displayed.

Subtotal a List
1. Click Data.
2. Click Subtotals.

FIGURE

4.14 **The Subtotal Dialog Box**

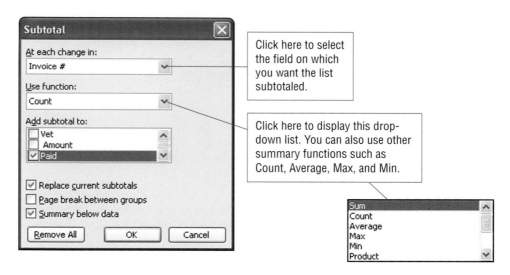

To select the field by which the list is to be subtotaled, click the down-pointing arrow to the right of the *At each change in* box. A list of all the field names is displayed. Click the appropriate field. Click the down-pointing arrow to the right of the *Use function* box. To find subtotals, click *Sum*. Other summary functions, such as *Count, Average, Max,* and *Min,* are also available. In the *Add subtotal to* box, click the check box next to the field containing the values that are to be subtotaled. Click OK. You are returned to the worksheet, and the subtotals along with a grand total are displayed.

Subtotals are displayed in outline view. The Hide Detail Level buttons, as shown in Figure 4.15, allow you to display as much or as little of the data as you want. Suppose you want to display only the data subtotal and not all the individual records. Click the Hide Detail Level button for that subtotal, and only that subtotal will be displayed. The Hide Detail Level button changes to a Show Detail Level button. To display the records, click the Show Detail Level button.

FIGURE

4.15 *Creating Subtotals*

	A	B	C	D	E	F	G	H
1				INVOICE RECORDS: Small Animals				
2								
3	Invoice #	Owner's Name	Pet Name	Classification	Service Rendered	Vet	Amount	Paid
4	55022	Baxter, Alice	Boots	Cat	Office Call/Examination	Frobose	$ 20.00	Yes
5	55022	Baxter, Alice	Boots	Cat	Feline Leukemia Test	Frobose	$ 20.00	Yes
6	55022	Baxter, Alice	Boots	Cat	Feline Leukemia Shot	Frobose	$ 15.00	Yes
7	55061	Baxter, Alice	Boots	Cat	Rabies Shot	Frobose	$ 20.00	Yes
8	55061	Baxter, Alice	Boots	Cat	Office Call/Examination	Frobose	$ 20.00	Yes
9		**Baxter, Alice Total**					$ 95.00	
10	55028	Brunell, David	King	Dog	Office Call/Examination	Ketner	$ 20.00	Yes
11	55028	Brunell, David	King	Dog	Distemper Shot	Ketner	$ 20.00	Yes
12	55066	Brunell, David	Sport	Dog	Office Call/Examination	Ketner	$ 20.00	Yes
13	55066	Brunell, David	Sport	Dog	Distemper Shot	Ketner	$ 20.00	Yes
14		**Brunell, David Total**					$ 80.00	
15	55029	Bruton, Joe	Patches	Dog	Office Call/Examination	Martin	$ 20.00	Yes
16	55029	Bruton, Joe	Patches	Dog	Distemper Shot	Martin	$ 20.00	Yes
17		**Bruton, Joe Total**					$ 40.00	
18	55030	Cavataio, Anthony	Rex	Dog	Office Call/Examination	Ketner	$ 20.00	Yes
19	55030	Cavataio, Anthony	Rex	Dog	Distemper Shot	Ketner	$ 20.00	Yes
20		**Cavataio, Anthony Total**					$ 40.00	

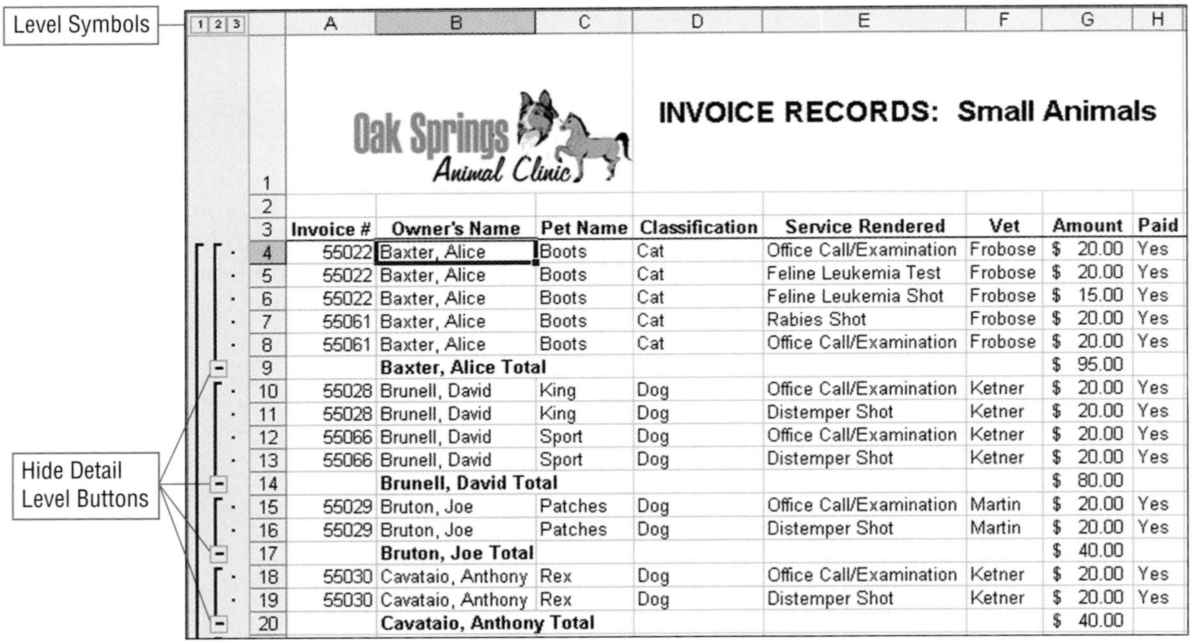

The level symbols, also shown in Figure 4.15, allow you to quickly control how much detail is displayed. Clicking the Level 1 button displays the grand total only. Clicking the Level 2 button displays all the subtotals. None of the individual records are displayed. Clicking the Level 3 button displays all the records, subtotals, and the grand total.

When you have finished working with subtotals, they can be removed by selecting any cell in the list and clicking Data and then Subtotals. Click the Remove All button and click OK.

exercise 7

SUBTOTALING A LIST

1. Open **eec4x04**. This is the worksheet that was completed in Exercise 4.
2. Save the worksheet using the Save As command and name it **eec4x07**.
3. Make sure a custom header displays your name at the left margin and the file name at the right margin.
4. Complete the following steps to subtotal the list by veterinarian:
   a. Sort the list in ascending order on the *Vet* field.
   b. Click Data and then Subtotals.

c. Click the down-pointing arrow to the right of the *At each change in* box and then select *Vet*.

d. Click the down-pointing arrow to the right of the *Use function* box and then select *Sum*.

e. Select the *Amount* check box. Deselect any other check boxes.

f. Click OK.

g. The subtotals have been created. Click the Level 2 button to display only the subtotals and the grand total.

h. Adjust the width of columns F and G.

i. To see only the records for Dr. Frobose, click the Show Details button to the left of row 40.

Step 4c
Step 4d
Step 4e
Step 4f

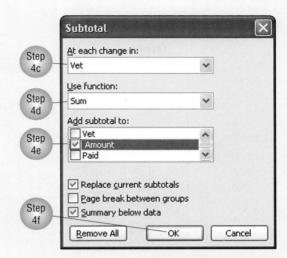

Step 4g

Step 4i

j. To see all the individual records, click the Level 3 button. All of the records, subtotals, and the grand total will be displayed.

5. Complete the following steps to remove the subtotals:
   a. If necessary, select a cell in the list.
   b. Click Data and then Subtotals.
   c. In the Subtotal dialog box, click the Remove All button.

6. Complete the following steps to subtotal the list by invoice number:
   a. Sort the list in ascending order on the *Invoice Number* field.
   b. Click Data and then Subtotals.
   c. Click the down-pointing arrow to the right of the *At each change in* box and then select *Invoice #*.
   d. If necessary, click the down-pointing arrow to the right of the *Use function* box and select *Sum*.
   e. Make sure the *Amount* check box is the only box selected and then click OK.
   f. The subtotals have been created. Click the Level 2 button.

7. You want to print the subtotals, but you want to print only the data in columns A and G. Complete the following steps to print the worksheet:

a. Select columns B through F and then press the Ctrl key and select column H. Columns B, C, D, E, F, and H should be selected.

Step 7a

1 2 3	A	B	C	D	E	F	G	H
		Oak Springs Animal Clinic			INVOICE RECORDS: Small Animals			
1								▼
2								
3		Invoice #	Owner's Name	Pet Name	Classification	Service Rendered	Amount	Paid
6	+	55017 Total					40.00	
9	+	55018 Total					40.00	
13	+	55019 Total					55.00	
17	+	55020 Total					74.00	
20	+	55021 Total					$ 40.00	
24	+	55022 Total					$ 55.00	
28	+	55023 Total					$ 64.00	
30	+	55024 Total					$ 40.00	

Paid
Select either Yes or No from the drop-down list to indicate shether or not the invoice has been paid.

b. Click Format, select Column, and then click Hide.
c. If necessary, adjust the column widths so that all the data is displayed.
d. Print the worksheet.
e. Select columns A through I.
f. Click Format, select Column, and then click Unhide.

8. Complete the following steps to remove the subtotals:
a. Click any cell in the list.
b. Click Data and then Subtotals.
c. Click the Remove All button.

9. Complete the following steps to subtotal the list by classification:
a. Sort the list in ascending order on the *Classification* field.
b. Click Data and then Subtotals.
c. Click the down-pointing arrow to the right of the *At each change in* box and then select *Classification*.
d. If necessary, click the down-pointing arrow to the right of the *Use function* box and select *Sum*.
e. Make sure the *Amount* check box is the only check box selected and then click OK.
f. The subtotals have been created. Click the Hide Detail Level button to the left of the Cat Total.

Step 9f

1 2 3	A	B	C	D	E	F	G	H
30	55061	Baxter, Alice	Boots	Cat	Office Call/Examination	Frobose	$ 20.00	Yes
31	55065	Fox, Amy	Hickory	Cat	Office Call/Examination	Frobose	$ 20.00	Yes
32	55065	Fox, Amy	Hickory	Cat	Feline Leukemia Test	Frobose	$ 20.00	Yes
33	55065	Fox, Amy	Hickory	Cat	Feline Leukemia Shot	Frobose	$ 15.00	Yes
34				Cat Total			$ 785.00	
35	55017	Heckman, Ellen	Carl	Dog	Office Call/Examination	Frobose	$ 20.00	Yes

g. Click the Hide Detail Level button to the left of the Dog Total.
h. Hide columns E, F, and H.
i. Adjust the width of column D.
j. Print the worksheet.
k. Select rows C through I.
l. Click Format, select Column, and then click Unhide.

10. Complete the following steps to remove the subtotals:
a. Click any cell in the list.

b. Click Data and then Subtotals and then click the Remove All button.

11. Save the worksheet with the same name (**eec4x07**). You are going to use this worksheet in Exercise 8.

12. Close the worksheet.

Filtering a List

Another way of displaying only certain records in a list is by applying filters to display in the worksheet only those records that meet certain criteria. The records that do not meet the criteria are temporarily hidden from view.

Filtering a List Using AutoFilter

The quickest and easiest way to filter a list is by using the AutoFilter feature. To use AutoFilter, select any cell in the list to be filtered. Click Data, point to Filter, and then click AutoFilter. As shown in Figure 4.16, drop-down lists appear next to each column heading. Click the down-pointing arrow to the right of the field name you want to filter. The drop-down list that appears allows you to display all the records in the list, display the top 10 records, create a custom filter, or select an entry that appears in one or more records on the list.

Filter a List Using AutoFilter
Click Data, point to Filter, and then click AutoFilter.

The down-pointing arrow to the right of the column heading that was used to perform an AutoFilter turns blue after the filter has been applied. The row numbers of the displayed records are also blue. This alerts you to the fact that not all the records are currently displayed and also indicates which column has to be selected in order to display all the records. As you can see in Figure 4.16, if you select one of the cell entries, then only those records containing that entry are displayed. To go back to displaying all the records, click the down-pointing arrow to the right of the field name and select *All*.

4.16   *Using AutoFilter*

When using AutoFilter, drop-down lists appear next to each column heading.

2								
3	Invoice ▾	Owner's Nam ▾	Pet Nan ▾	Classificati ▾	Service Rendered ▾	Vet ▾	Amour ▾	Pa ▾
4	55022	Baxter, Alice	Boots	Sort Ascending	Office Call/Examination	Frobose	$ 20.00	Yes
5	55022	Baxter, Alice	Boots	Sort Descending	Feline Leukemia Test	Frobose	$ 20.00	Yes
6	55022	Baxter, Alice	Boots	(All)	Feline Leukemia Shot	Frobose	$ 15.00	Yes
7	55061	Baxter, Alice	Boots	(Top 10...)	Rabies Shot	Frobose	$ 20.00	Yes
8	55061	Baxter, Alice	Boots	(Custom...) Cat	Office Call/Examination	Frobose	$ 20.00	Yes
9	55028	Brunell, David	King	Dog	Office Call/Examination	Ketner	$ 20.00	Yes
10	55028	Brunell, David	King	Guinea Pig	Distemper Shot	Ketner	$ 20.00	Yes
11	55066	Brunell, David	Sport	Hamster	Office Call/Examination	Ketner	$ 20.00	Yes
12	55066	Brunell, David	Sport	Iguana Mouse	Distemper Shot	Ketner	$ 20.00	Yes
13	55029	Bruton, Joe	Patches	Rabbit	Office Call/Examination	Martin	$ 20.00	Yes
14	55029	Bruton, Joe	Patches	Rat Turtle	Distemper Shot	Martin	$ 20.00	Yes
15	55030	Cavataio, Anthony	Rex	Dog	Office Call/Examination	Ketner	$ 20.00	Yes
16	55030	Cavataio, Anthony	Rex	Dog	Distemper Shot	Ketner	$ 20.00	Yes
17	55025	Covington, Linda	Lady	Dog	Office Call/Examination	Frobose	$ 20.00	No

By selecting one of the cell entries that appears on the list, only the records containing that entry are displayed.

2								
3	Invoice ▾	Owner's Nam ▾	Pet Nan ▾	Classificati ▾	Service Rendered ▾	Vet ▾	Amou ▾	Pa ▾
47	55023	Harford, Sid	Munch	Hamster	Office Call/Examination	Martin	$ 20.00	Yes
48	55052	Harford, Sid	Krunch	Hamster	Office Call/Examination	Martin	$ 20.00	Yes
93	55046	Taylor, Brittany	Squeeky	Hamster	Office Call/Examination	Martin	$ 20.00	Yes
107								
108								
109								
110								

The *(Top 10...)* option from the drop-down list works only if there are values (rather than text) stored in that column. When you select it, the dialog box shown in Figure 4.17 is displayed. You can choose whether you want to display the top or bottom items or percents. You can also indicate how many items (or percents) should be displayed. Click OK and the filtered records are displayed.

4.17   *The Top 10 AutoFilter Dialog Box*

Creating a Custom AutoFilter

To create a custom AutoFilter, select any cell in the list, click Data, point to Filter, and then click AutoFilter. Click the down-pointing arrow to the right of the field name you want to filter. Select *(Custom...)*. The Custom AutoFilter dialog box is

EXCEL

displayed. As shown in Figure 4.18, to select a comparison operator, click the down-pointing arrow to the right of the first box in the *Show rows where* section. Select one of the comparison operators. Either click the down-pointing arrow to the right of the next box to select the data to be compared, or type the data to be compared in the box. A second set of criteria can be entered in the bottom two boxes. If the *And* option is selected, both sets of criteria must be met by the record. If the *Or* option is selected, either one or the other set, but not necessarily both, of the criteria must be met by the record. Click OK to display the records that match the criteria. When you have finished with the filter, display all the records by clicking the down-pointing arrow to the right of the field name and selecting *All*.

HINT

You may apply more than one filter at a time.

FIGURE

4.18 *The Custom AutoFilter Dialog Box*

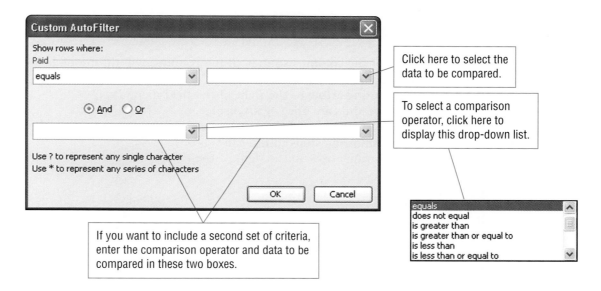

Click here to select the data to be compared.

To select a comparison operator, click here to display this drop-down list.

If you want to include a second set of criteria, enter the comparison operator and data to be compared in these two boxes.

To turn the AutoFilter feature off, click Data, point to Filter, and then click AutoFilter. The AutoFilter feature will then be turned off.

exercise

USING AUTOFILTER

1. Open **eec4x07**. This is the worksheet that was completed in Exercise 7.
2. Save the worksheet using the Save As command and name it **eec4x08**.
3. Make sure a custom header displays your name at the left margin and the file name at the right margin.
4. Sort the list in ascending order on the *Invoice* column.

5. First you want to see all the records in which the invoices have not been paid. Complete the following steps to filter the records:
   a. Click any cell in the list.
   b. Click Data, point to Filter, and then click AutoFilter. Drop-down lists appear next to all the field names.
   c. Click the down-pointing arrow to the right of the field name *Paid*.
   d. Click *No*.

Invoice #	Owner's Name	Pet Name	Classification	Service Rendered	Vet	Amount	Paid
55017	Heckman, Ellen	Carl	Dog	Office Call/Examination	Frobose	Sort Ascending	
55017	Heckman, Ellen	Carl	Dog	Rabies Shot	Frobose	Sort Descending	
55018	Wegman, Marcy	Raven	Dog	Office Call/Examination	Martin	(All)	
55018	Wegman, Marcy	Raven	Dog	Rabies Shot	Martin	(Top 10...)	
55019	Wegman, Marcy	Homer	Cat	Office Call/Examination	Martin	(Custom...)	
55019	Wegman, Marcy	Homer	Cat	Feline Leukemia Test	Martin	No	
55019	Wegman, Marcy	Homer	Cat	Feline Leukemia Shot	Martin	Yes	
55020	Fox, Alan	Blue	Dog	Office Call/Examination	Ketner	$ 15.00	Yes
55020	Fox, Alan	Blue	Dog	Heartworm Test	Ketner	$ 20.00	Yes
55020	Fox, Alan	Blue	Dog	Heartworm Medication	Ketner	$ 24.00	Yes
						$ 30.00	Yes

Step 5c

Step 5d

   e. Adjust the widths of the columns so that all the columns will fit on one page.
   f. Print the worksheet.
   g. Click the down-pointing arrow to the right of the field name *Paid*.
   h. Click *(All)*. All the records are once again displayed.
6. The veterinarians want to know which invoices contributed to the top 5% of their income. Complete the following steps to filter the records:
   a. Click the down-pointing arrow to the right of the field name *Amount*.
   b. Click *(Top 10...)*.
   c. In the middle box type 5.
   d. Click the down-pointing arrow to the right of the last box and then click *Percent*.
   e. Click OK.
   f. Print the worksheet. The worksheet should fit on one page.
   g. Click the down-pointing arrow to the right of the field name *Amount*.
   h. Click *(All)*. All the records are once again displayed.

Step 6c

Step 6d

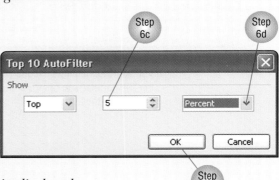

Step 6e

7. The veterinarians want to see the records of all the animals treated that were not dogs or cats. Sort the list in ascending order on the *Classification* field. Complete the following steps to create a custom filter:
   a. Click the down-pointing arrow to the right of the field name *Classification*.
   b. Click *Custom*. The Custom AutoFilter dialog box is displayed.

c. Click the down-pointing arrow to the right of the first box in the *Classification* section and then click *does not equal*.
d. Click the down-pointing arrow to the right of the second box in the first row, and then click *Dog*.
e. Make sure the *And* option is selected.
f. Click the down-pointing arrow to the right of the first box in the second row, and then click *does not equal*.
g. Click the down-pointing arrow to the right of the second box in the second row, click *Cat* and then click OK.

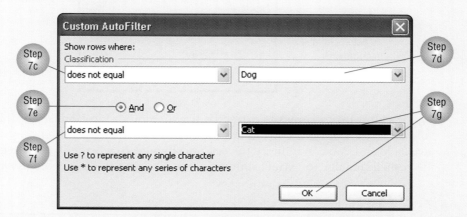

h. Adjust the column widths so that all the data can be seen but still fits on one page.
i. Print the worksheet.
j. Click the down-pointing arrow to the right of the field name *Classification*.
k. Click *(All)*. All the records are once again displayed.
8. Complete the following steps to turn the AutoFilter feature off:
a. Click any cell in the list.
b. Click Data, point to Filter, and then click AutoFilter. Drop-down lists should no longer be displayed next to the field names.
9. Save the worksheet with the same name (**eec408**). You are going to use this worksheet in Exercise 9.
10. Close the worksheet.

Filtering a List Using Advanced Filters

Using advanced filters allows you to be very precise in searching for specific records. With an advanced filter, you can denote the exact criteria to be found.

Extracting Unique Records

One task for which an advanced filter can be used is to create a list of unique values. To create a list of unique values, select the portion of the list to be extracted from. Click Data, point to Filter, and then click Advanced Filter. The Advanced Filter dialog box shown in Figure 4.19 is displayed.

QUICK STEPS

Filter a List Using Advanced Filter
Click Data, point to Filter, and then click Advanced Filter.

4.19 *The Advanced Filter Dialog Box*

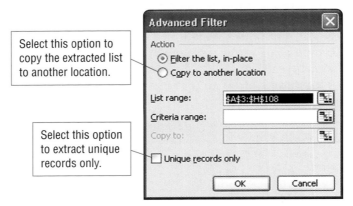

Select this option to copy the extracted list to another location.

Select this option to extract unique records only.

If you want to copy the extracted list to another location, select the *Copy to another location* option. Once that option is selected, the *Copy to* option becomes available and you can indicate the cell or cell range to where the extracted list should be copied. Finally, to extract unique records, select the *Unique records only* option.

exercise 9

EXTRACTING UNIQUE RECORDS

1. Open **eec4x08**. This is the worksheet that was completed in Exercise 8.
2. Save the worksheet using the Save As command and name it **eec4x09**.
3. Make sure a custom header displays your name at the left margin and the file name at the right margin.
4. The veterinarians want a list of each client and the names of the clients' pets. Sort the list first by *Owner's Name*, then by *Classification*, and then by *Pet Name*.
5. You need to select the portion of the list you want to extract from, which would be columns B, C, and D. Complete the following steps to select a portion of the list:
    a. Click cell B3.
    b. While holding down the Shift key, double-click the bottom of the cell. Be sure you do not double-click the AutoFill handle. All of the field values in column B should be selected.
    c. While holding down the Shift key, press the Right Arrow key twice. All of the field values in columns B, C, and D should be selected.
    d. Click Data, point to Filter, and click Advanced Filter. The Advanced Filter dialog box is displayed.
    e. Click the *Copy to another location* option to select it.
    f. Make sure that *$B$3:$D$108* is entered in the *List range* box.
    g. Click the Collapse dialog box button at the right of the *Copy to* box.
    h. Click cell J3. Click the Expand dialog box button.
    i. Click the *Unique records only* option to select it.
    j. Click OK.

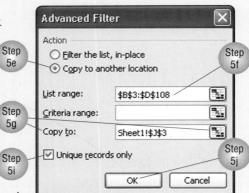

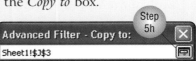

6. The unique records are copied to columns J, K, and L. Adjust the widths of these columns so that all the data can be seen.
7. Complete the following steps to print the unique records:
    a. Click cell J3. While holding down the Shift key, double-click the bottom of the cell. While still holding down the Shift key, press the Right Arrow key twice. Cells J3 through L51 should be selected.
    b. Click File, point to Print Area, and then click Set Print Area.
    c. Print the records.
8. Click File, point to Print Area, and then click Clear Print Area to clear the print area.
9. Save the worksheet with the same name (**eec4x09**).
10. Close the worksheet.

Using a Criteria Range

As shown in Figure 4.20, the middle box on the Advanced Filter dialog box provides a place to enter a criteria range. Filtering a list using a criteria range is similar to filtering a list using AutoFilter, only instead of selecting the criteria range from a drop-down list, it is typed into the worksheet in the *Criteria range* box. The criteria range is a range of cells that is set aside specifically as the place where the search conditions are entered. The criteria range is made up of one header row and one or more rows where the search condition is defined.

FIGURE

4.20 **The Criteria Range in the Advanced Filter Dialog Box**

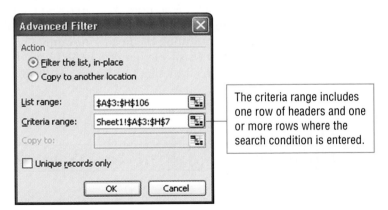

Typically the criteria range is placed in the rows above the list, so the first step is to insert four or more blank rows above the list that can be used for the criteria range. There must be at least one blank row between the criteria range and the list. Next, the header row or field names from the list have to be copied to the first blank row in the criteria range. The search criteria are entered into the rows below the header row.

Several different types of conditions can be used with advanced filters. An advanced filter criteria can include one or more conditions applied to a single column. For example, the following criteria range would display rows containing either Frobose or Ketner in the *Vet* column.

Vet
Frobose
Ketner

You can also have a condition in one column or another. For example, the following criteria range would display rows containing either values greater than 50 in the *Amount* column or *No* in the *Paid* column.

Amount	Paid
>50	
	No

When conditions are entered in different rows, either one or the other condition may be met, but not necessarily both. If both conditions must be met, then the criteria must be placed in the same row. For example, the following criteria range would display only those rows containing both values greater than 50 in the *Amount* column and *No* in the *Paid* column.

Amount	Paid
>50	No

HINT

If the range of cells entered in the *Criteria range* box includes a blank row, then none of the data will be filtered out. Make sure the criteria range contains only rows that have conditions entered into them.

Once the criteria you want to match have been entered in the criteria range, click any cell in the list. Click Data, point to Filter, and then click Advanced Filter. The Advanced Filter dialog box shown in Figure 4.20 is displayed. The range of cells for the criteria range, including the header row, must be entered in the *Criteria range* box. There must be at least one blank row between the criteria range and the list. Click OK and the records that are found are displayed.

exercise 10

USING A CRITERIA RANGE

1. Open **ExcelWorksheet04**.
2. Save the worksheet using the Save As command and name it **eec4x10**.
3. Create a custom header that displays your name at the left margin and the file name at the right margin.
4. Complete the following steps to set up a criteria range:
   a. Insert four blank rows above row 2. The header row for the list should now be in row 6.

E162 Chapter Four

EXCEL

b. Copy cells A6 through H6 to cells A1 through H1. The header row should now be in both row 6 and row 1.

	A	B	C	D	E	F	G	H	
1	Invoice #	Owner's Name	Pet Name	Classification	Service Rendered	Vet	Amount	Paid	Step 4b
2									
3									
4									
5									
6	Invoice #	Owner's Name	Pet Name	Classification	Service Rendered	Vet	Amount	Paid	
7	55017	Heckman, Ellen	Carl	Dog	Office Call/Examination	Frobose	$ 20.00	Yes	
8	55017	Heckman, Ellen	Carl	Dog	Rabies Shot	Frobose	$ 20.00	Yes	
9	55018	Wegman, Marcy	Raven	Dog	Office Call/Examination	Martin	$ 20.00	Yes	
10	55018	Wegman, Marcy	Raven	Dog	Rabies Shot	Martin	$ 20.00	Yes	

5. You want to find all the records of invoices that were for either feline leukemia shots or feline leukemia tests. Complete the following steps to enter the search criteria in the criteria range:
   a. Click cell E2 and then type Feline Leukemia Shot.
   b. Click cell E3 and then type Feline Leukemia Test.

	A	B	C	D	E	F	G	H	
1	Invoice #	Owner's Name	Pet Name	Classification	Service Rendered	Vet	Amount	Paid	Step 5a
2					Feline Leukemia Shot				
3					Feline Leukemia Test				Step 5b
4									
5									
6	Invoice #	Owner's Name	Pet Name	Classification	Service Rendered	Vet	Amount	Paid	
7	55017	Heckman, Ellen	Carl	Dog	Office Call/Examination	Frobose	$ 20.00	Yes	
8	55017	Heckman, Ellen	Carl	Dog	Rabies Shot	Frobose	$ 20.00	Yes	
9	55018	Wegman, Marcy	Raven	Dog	Office Call/Examination	Martin	$ 20.00	Yes	

6. If you name the criteria range Criteria, Excel will automatically recognize it as the criteria range. Complete the following steps to name the criteria range Criteria:
   a. Select cells A1 through H3.
   b. Click Insert, point to Name, and click Define.
   c. Type Criteria.
   d. Click OK.

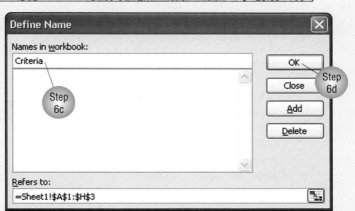

7. Complete the following steps to apply the advanced criteria:
   a. Click any cell in the data list (not in the criteria range).
   b. Click Data, point to Filter, and then click Advanced Filter. The Advanced Filter dialog box appears. Excel automatically recognizes both the list range and the criteria range.
   c. Click OK. Only the records that meet the criteria are displayed.
   d. Print the worksheet.
   e. Click Data, point to Filter, and then click Show All.

8. Next you want to find invoices that either are over $50.00 or have not been paid. Complete the following steps to apply the advanced criteria:
   a. Clear cells E2 and E3.
   b. Click cell G2 and then type **>50**.
   c. Click cell H3 and then type **No**.

	A	B	C	D	E	F	G	H
1	Invoice #	Owner's Name	Pet Name	Classification	Service Rendered	Vet	Amount	Paid
2							>50	
3								No
4								
5								
6	Invoice #	Owner's Name	Pet Name	Classification	Service Rendered	Vet	Amount	Paid
7	55017	Heckman, Ellen	Carl	Dog	Office Call/Examination	Frobose	$ 20.00	Yes
8	55017	Heckman, Ellen	Carl	Dog	Rabies Shot	Frobose	$ 20.00	Yes
9	55018	Wegman, Marcy	Raven	Dog	Office Call/Examination	Martin	$ 20.00	Yes

Step 8b
Step 8c

   d. Click any cell in the data list (not in the criteria range).
   e. Click Data, point to Filter, and then click Advanced Filter. The Advanced Filter dialog box appears. Excel automatically recognizes both the list range and the criteria range.
   f. Click OK. Only the records that meet the criteria are displayed.
   g. Print the worksheet.
   h. Click Data, point to Filter, and then click Show All.

9. Now find the invoices that are both over $50.00 and have not been paid. Complete the following steps to apply the advanced criteria:
   a. Clear cell H3.
   b. Click cell H2 and then type **No**. The entries in the criteria range are now both in row 2.
   c. Click any cell in the data list (not in the criteria range).
   d. Click Data, point to Filter, and then click Advanced Filter. The Advanced Filter dialog box appears.
   e. Check to make sure the entry in the *List range* box is *$A$6:$H$106*.
   f. The criteria range has to be changed because now it is A1 through H2, since the criteria are in row 2. Edit the entry in the *Criteria range* box so that it says *$A$1:$H$2*.

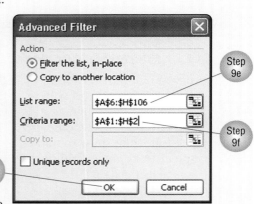

Step 9e
Step 9f
Step 9g

   g. Click OK. Only the records that meet the criteria are displayed.
   h. Print the worksheet.
   i. Click Data, point to Filter, and then click Show All.
10. Now find the invoices for when either Frobose, Martin, or Ketner spayed a cat. Complete the following steps to apply the advanced criteria:
    a. Clear cells G2 and H2.
    b. Type the following data in the cells indicated:

Cell	Data
D2	Cat
E2	Spay
F2	Frobose
D3	Cat
E3	Spay
F3	Martin
D4	Cat

EXCEL

E4	Spay
F4	Ketner

c. Click any cell in the data list (not in the criteria range).
d. Click Data, point to Filter, and then click Advanced Filter. The Advanced Filter dialog box appears.
e. Check to make sure the entry in the *List range* box is *$A$6:$H$106*.
f. The criteria range has to be changed because now it is A1 through H4, since the criteria are in rows 2, 3, and 4. Edit the entry in the *Criteria range* box so that it says *$A$1:$H$4*.
g. Click OK. Only the records that meet the criteria are displayed.
h. Print the worksheet.
i. Click Data, point to Filter, and then click Show All.
11. Save the worksheet with the same name (**eec4x10**).
12. Close the worksheet.

Create and Modify List Ranges

So far, you have worked with lists that were already created for you. Creating your own list is quite simple, but you must follow certain rules. The first row of the list must contain the labels or field names. The labels should be formatted differently from the rest of the data in the list. Use bold, italics, or cell borders (or a combination of the three) to differentiate them from the list data. There cannot be any blank rows in the list, which means there cannot be a blank row between the labels and the data.

Only one list should be stored on a worksheet. If you have several related lists, store each one on a separate worksheet. You cannot have any extraneous data stored in columns or rows adjacent to the list, or they might be considered to be a part of the list. It is best not to store any data on the worksheet other than the list itself.

Once the data for the list has been entered, highlight it. Click Data, point to List, and then click Create List. The Create List dialog box shown in Figure 4.21 is displayed. Click OK. Once a list has been created, if you modify it by adding more data to the row immediately below the last row in the list, Excel automatically recognizes that row as part of the list. You can tell what data is considered to be a part of a list because it is enclosed in a blue box.

HINT

An Excel list can be used as a flat database, which is a two-dimensional database made up of rows and columns.

HINT

File names should be brief, but descriptive enough so that anyone looking at the list knows what data goes in that particular column.

FIGURE

4.21 *Creating a List*

If the first row of your list contains labels or field names, make sure the *My list has headers* check box is selected.

The range of cells you selected before clicking Data, List, and Create list, automatically is displayed in the *Where is the data for your list?* box.

QUICK STEPS

Create a List
Click Data, point to List, and then cick Create List.

4.22 **Data that is Part of a List**

	A	B	C	D	E	F
1	**Week**	**Employee**	**Payrate**	**Hours**	**Total for Week**	
2	4	Cross, Erika				
3						
4	**Week**	**Employee**	**Payrate**	**Hours**	**Total for Week**	
5	1	Cross, Erika	$ 6.50	14	$ 91.00	
6	1	Farver, Michael	$ 7.55	10	$ 75.50	
7	1	Wilhelm, A.J.	$ 6.80	12	$ 81.60	
8	2	Cross, Erika	$ 6.50	15	$ 97.50	
9	2	Farver, Michael	$ 7.55	17	$ 128.35	
10	2	Wilhelm, A.J.	$ 6.80	10	$ 68.00	
11	3	Cross, Erika	$ 6.50	18	$ 117.00	
12	3	Farver, Michael	$ 7.55	13	$ 98.15	
13	3	Wilhelm, A.J.	$ 6.80	11	$ 74.80	
14	4	Cross, Erika	$ 6.50	12	$ 78.00	
15	4	Farver, Michael	$ 7.55	9	$ 67.95	
16	4	Wilhelm, A.J.	$ 6.80	10	$ 68.00	
17	5	Cross, Erika	$ 6.50	19	$ 123.50	
18	5	Farver, Michael	$ 7.55	15	$ 113.25	
19	5	Wilhelm, A.J.	$ 6.80	12	$ 81.60	
20						

Data that is part of a list is enclosed in a blue box.

Create and Edit Database Functions

In Chapter 3 you learned about worksheet functions, or formulas, built into Excel. Excel also includes Dfunctions, which are worksheet functions specifically for easy analysis of data stored in lists or databases.

All Dfunctions use the same format or syntax for calculations. The syntax for a Dfunction is:

=function(database, field, criteria)

The three arguments—database, field, and criteria—refer to the worksheet ranges that are used by the function. Database refers to the range of cells that make up the entire database, including the row with the field names. Field refers to the field, or column to be analyzed and used in the function. It can be entered into the Dfunction either as the field label within quotation marks or as a number that represents the position of the column within the list with 1 representing the first column, 2 the second column and so on. The criteria range is the cells that contain the conditions Excel will use to identify which records will be evaluated to complete the function.

To perform a Dfunction, place the cursor in the cell where the results of the function are to appear. Click the Insert Function button on the Formula Bar. The Insert Function Dialog Box is displayed. Select *Database* from the *Or select a category* list box. As shown in Figure 4.23, the Dfunctions are listed in the *Select a function* list box. Select the appropriate Dfunction from the *Select a function* list box and click OK. A dialog box for the selected function is displayed, as shown in Figure 4.24. Enter the appropriate arguments in the *Database*, *Field*, and *Criteria* boxes and click OK. Table 4.3 describes some of Excel's more commonly used Dfunctions.

4.23 *Inserting a Database Function*

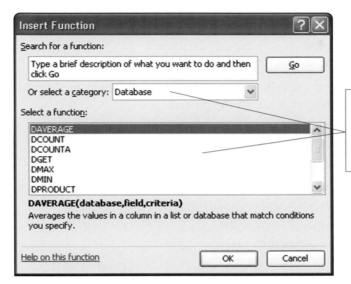

When you select Database from the *Or select a category* list box, Excel's Dfunctions are listed in the *Select a function* list box.

4.24 *Selecting Function Arguments for a Database Function*

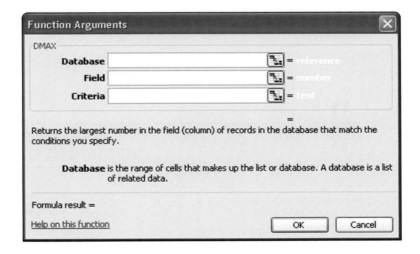

4.3 *Database Functions*

Name	Description	Syntax
DAVERAGE	Calculates the average of database entries that match the criteria	=DAVERAGE(database, field, criteria)
DCOUNT	Counts the cells that contain numbers that match the criteria	=DCOUNT(database, field, criteria)
DCOUNTA	Counts the cells that contain non-numerical data that match the criteria	=DCOUNTA(database, field, criteria)
DGET	Locates a single record that matches the specified criteria	=DGET(database, field, criteria)
DMAX	Returns the maximum value that matches the criteria	=DMAX(database, field, criteria)
DMIN	Returns the minimum value that matches the criteria	=DMIN(database, field, criteria)
DPRODUCT	Multiplies the values that match the criteria	=DPRODUCT(database, field, criteria)
DSUM	Adds the numbers in the field column of records that match the criteria	=DSUM(database, field, criteria)

exercise 11

CREATING AND MODIFYING LIST RANGES
AND CREATING AND EDITING DATABASE FUNCTIONS

1. You are responsible for managing the student employees who work in a computer lab at Redwood College. Open a new Excel Workbook. Enter the data shown at the right. Use a function to enter the values in column E. Save the workbook using the file name **eec4x11**.

2. Create a custom header that displays your name at the left margin and the file name at the right margin.

3. Complete the following steps to create a list range:
   a. Select cells A4 through E16.

	A	B	C	D	E
1	Week	Employee	Pay Rate	Hours	Total for Week
2					
3					
4	Week	Employee	Pay Rate	Hours	Total for Week
5	1	Cross, Erika	$6.50	14	$91.00
6	1	Farver, Michael	$7.55	10	$75.50
7	1	Wilhelm, A.J.	$6.80	12	$81.60
8	2	Cross, Erika	$6.50	15	$97.50
9	2	Farver, Michael	$7.55	17	$128.35
10	2	Wilhelm, A.J.	$6.80	10	$68.00
11	3	Cross, Erika	$6.50	18	$117.00
12	3	Farver, Michael	$7.55	13	$98.15
13	3	Wilhelm, A.J.	$6.80	11	$74.80
14	4	Cross, Erika	$6.50	12	$78.00
15	4	Farver, Michael	$7.55	9	$67.95
16	4	Wilhelm, A.J.	$6.80	10	$68.00

EXCEL

b. Click Data, point to List, and click Create List.

c. Check to make sure the range in the *Where is the data for your list* box is A4 through E16.

d. Make sure the *My list has headers* box is selected and then click OK.

4. You want to know the total amount Erika Cross was paid during the first four weeks of the semester.

a. Type the following in cell G4: Cross 4 Week Total.

b. Adjust the width of column G to display the entire label.

c. Type the following in cell B2: Cross, Erika.

d. Select cell H4.

e. Click the Insert Function button.

f. The Insert Function dialog box is displayed. Select *Database* from the *Or select a category* box.

g. Select *DSUM* from the *Select a function* list box and then click OK.

h. The Function Arguments dialog box is displayed. The cursor should be in the *Database* box. Select the database which is cells A4 through E16.

i. Click in the *Field* box. You want the total amount Erika earned, so click cell E4 to enter the field.

Step 4h

Step 4i

Step 4j

Function Arguments

DSUM

Database A4:E16   = {"Week","Employee"

Field E4   = "Total for Week"

Criteria B1:B2   = B1:B2

= 383.5

Adds the numbers in the field (column) of records in the database that match the conditions you specify.

Criteria is the range of cells that contains the conditions you specify. The range includes a column label and one cell below the label for a condition.

Formula result =   383.5

Help on this function   [OK] [Cancel]

Step 4k

j. Click the *Criteria* box. You want to know the total only for Erika Cross, so she is the criteria. You already entered this in cell B2. Select cells B1 and B2 to enter the criteria.

k. Click OK. The total Erika Cross earned in the first four weeks is entered in cell H4.

5. You need to know the average number of hours that the students worked during the fourth week of the semester.

a. Enter 4 in cell A2.

b. Enter Average Hours Worked in Week 4 in cell G5.

c. Adjust the width of column G to display the entire label.

d. Select cell H5.

e. Click the Insert Function button.

f. The Insert Function dialog box is displayed. If necessary, select *Database* from the *Or select a category* box.

g. Select *DAVERAGE* from the *Select a function* list box and then click OK.

h. The Function Arguments dialog box is displayed. The cursor should be in the *Database* box. Select the database which is cells A4 through E16.

i. Click in the *Field* box. You want the average hours worked, so click cell D4 to enter the field.

j. Click the *Criteria* box. You want to know the average for week 4. You already entered this criteria in cell A2. Select cells A1 and A2 to enter the criteria.

k. Click OK. The average number of hours worked in week 4 is calculated.

6. You need to enter the data for week 5. Enter the following into the worksheet:

Cell	Data
A17	5
A18	5
A19	5
B17	Cross, Erika
B18	Farver, Michael
B19	Wilhelm, A.J.
C17	6.50
C18	7.55
C19	6.80
D17	19
D18	15
D19	12

Use a function to calculate the data for cells E17, E18, and E19. The list should automatically be modified to include the new data. You can tell because the blue box should now encompass rows 17, 18, and 19.

7. You need to know the maximum number of hours worked during week 5.
   a. Enter 5 in cell A2.
   b. Enter **Maximum Hours Worked in Week 5** in cell G6.
   c. Adjust the width of column G to display the entire label.
   d. Select cell H6.
   e. Click the Insert Function button.
   f. The Insert Function dialog box is displayed. If necessary, select *Database* from the *Or select a category* box.
   g. Select *DMAX* from the *Select a function* list box and then click OK.
   h. The Function Arguments dialog box is displayed. The cursor should be in the *Database* box. Select the database which is cells A4 through E19.
   i. Click in the *Field* box. You want the maximum hours worked, so click cell D4 to enter the field.
   j. Click the *Criteria* box. You want to know the maximum for week 5. You already entered the criteria in cell A2. Select cells A1 and A2 to enter the criteria.
   k. Click OK. The maximum number of hours worked in week 5 is calculated.
8. Save the worksheet with the same name (**eec4x11**).
9. Print and close the worksheet.

CHAPTER summary

- A list is a labeled series of worksheet rows that contain similar sets of data such as student names and addresses. Each row in a list is a record. Each column in a list is a field. The labels in the first row of the list are field names. A value in a cell is a field value. The range of cells containing all the records, fields, and field names is the list range.

- The first row of a list must contain labels or field names. There cannot be any blank rows in the list. There should not be any data in the rows or columns immediately adjacent to the list. Only one list can be stored on a worksheet.

- Records in an Excel list can be entered, edited, and deleted using a Data Form. Data Forms can be used to search for and find only those records that meet specific criteria.

- You can specify the exact data that can be entered into a cell using data validation. You can specify that the data being entered must meet specific criteria or that the data must be selected from a list.

- Sorting helps to organize the data in a list. Sort the data in a column by selecting any cell in the column to be sorted and then clicking the Sort Ascending button to sort in ascending order or the Sort Descending button to sort in descending order.

- To sort in an order other than ascending or descending, a custom list must be created. A custom list can be used to sort the first or top level of a sort only. Once a custom list has been created, it is always available.

- Outlining a worksheet provides a way to quickly find specific information in a long list of data. Levels of detail can be easily displayed or hidden by clicking the Show Detail symbol and the Hide Detail symbol. Rows or columns that provide a summary of the data using functions such as AVERAGE or SUM can be displayed quickly.

- When the data in a list is subtotaled using the subtotal command, it is displayed in outline view. The list must be sorted by the field on which it is to be subtotaled before using the subtotal command. Levels of detail can be hidden or displayed in a list that has been subtotaled using the Show Detail symbol and the Hide Detail symbol.

- Filtering a list using AutoFilter temporarily displays only those records that meet certain criteria. Creating a custom AutoFilter enables the use of comparisons such as equals or is less than. An example of a custom AutoFilter search criterion might be *Salary is greater than 50,000.*

- An advanced filter extracts the unique records that meet specific criteria. The extracted data can be copied to a new location. With an advanced filter, a list is filtered using a criteria range. The criteria range is usually placed in the rows above the list. The header row (or field names) from the list has to be copied to the first row in the criteria range. The criteria used to filter the list are typed into the criteria range. If the criteria are typed into different rows, either one or the other condition may be met, but not necessarily both. If the criteria are typed into the same row, then both conditions must be met.

- The first row of a list must contain labels or field names. The first row must be formatted differently (bold, italic, borders) from the rest of the list. A list cannot contain any blank rows. Only store one list on a worksheet. Do not store any other data in columns or rows adjacent to the list.

- Database functions, or Dfunctions, help you to analyse the data in a database. Using Dfunctions such as DAVERAGE, DCOUNT, DMAX, and DSUM, you can extract information from the database that meets the specific criteria you establish.

FEATURES summary

FEATURE	MENU/COMMANDS
Display the Data Form	Click Data, Form
Use data validation	Click Data, Validation
Perform a multilevel sort	Click Data, Sort
Create/Delete a custom list	Click Tools, Options, Custom Lists tab
Outline a worksheet manually	Click Data, Group and Outline, Group
Outline a worksheet automatically	Click Data, Group and Outline, Auto Outline
Subtotal a list	Click Data, Subtotals
Filter a list using AutoFilter	Click Data, Filter, AutoFilter
Filter a list using Advanced Filter	Click Data, Filter, Advanced Filter
Create a List	Click Data, List, Create List.

CONCEPTS check

Completion: On a blank sheet of paper, indicate the correct term, symbol, or command for each description.

1. This term refers to the individual rows in a list.
2. This term refers to each column in a list.
3. Click this to display the Data Form.
4. Select this option from the drop-down list for the *Allow* box on the Data Validation dialog box if you want users to be able to enter data by selecting it from a list.
5. Click this tab on the Options dialog box to create a custom list.
6. This is the comparison operator that stands for *not equal to*.
7. Click this to subtotal a list.
8. Subtotals are displayed in this view.
9. This is what will be displayed if you click the Level 1 button after subtotaling a list.
10. Click this to turn the AutoFilter feature off.
11. Click this option on the Advanced Filters dialog box if you want to extract unique records from a list.

12. This term refers to the range of cells that is set aside as the area where the search conditions are entered when using Advanced Filters.
13. Explain the difference between using the AutoFilter command and the Criteria button on a Data Form.
14. Explain what records are going to be displayed using the following criteria range:

Sales Representative	Sales
Zimmerman	<1000
Robinson	<=1500

15. List all the rules that must be followed when creating a list.
16. This is the syntax for all Dfunctions.
17. This is the name of the Dfunction that locates a single record that matches the criteria.

SKILLS check

Assessment 1

1. Open **ExcelWorksheet05**.
2. Save the worksheet using the Save As command and name it **eec4sc01**.
3. Create a custom header with your name displayed at the left margin and the file name displayed at the right margin.
4. This worksheet keeps track of the profit the EastWest Crossroads Company makes on some of the items in its mail-order catalog. Use the Data Form to add the following three records to the list:

Item Number:	GL-10-1
Item:	Chinese Nesting Baskets
Selling Price:	35
Unit Cost:	18

Item Number:	GM-39-1
Item:	Asian Desk Set
Selling Price:	125
Unit Cost:	70

Item Number:	GT-29-1
Item:	Bird Box
Selling Price:	85
Unit Cost:	35

5. The EastWest Crossroads Company no longer sells the Antler Bookends, Item Number GH-88-2. Use the Data Form to delete this record.
6. The cost of the Stained Glass Lamp, Item Number GH-82-2, has come down. Use the Data Form to edit this record so that the *Selling Price* is $225.00 and the *Unit Cost* is $150.00.
7. Adjust the page setup so that row 3 repeats at the top of each page as a print title.
8. Save the workbook with the same name (**eec4sc01**).
9. Print and close **eec4sc01**.

Assessment 2

1. Open **ExcelWorksheet06**.
2. Save the worksheet using the Save As command and name it **eec4sc02**.
3. Create a custom header with your name displayed at the left margin and the file name displayed at the right margin.
4. The Little Music Shop, a music store, sells opera CDs, videos, and laserdiscs. This worksheet is the beginning of a list to keep track of all the opera CDs, videos, and laserdiscs that the store sells. You want to use data validation to make it easier to enter more data into the list. The order numbers are all exactly six characters long. You want to set it up so that an order number that is anything other than six characters cannot be entered. Select column A and display the Data Validation dialog box. From the *Allow* drop-down list on the Settings tab, select *Text length*. From the *Data* list box select *equal to*. Type 6 in the *Length* box.
5. Include an input message that has *Order #* for a title. The message should read, "Enter the six-character order number."
6. Include an error message that has *Error* for a title. The message should read, "The order number must be exactly six characters long."
7. The only three entries that are ever made in the *Medium* column are Video, CD, or Laserdisc. Create a drop-down list from which the user can select Video, CD, or Laserdisc in order to enter data into column C.
8. Include an input message that has *Medium* for a title. The message should read, "Select an option from the drop-down list."
9. Include an error message that has *Error* for a title. The message should read, "The medium must be selected from the drop-down list."
10. The cost for any item in the list will never be over $100.00. Set up data validation so that any decimal entered into column D is less than or equal to $100.00.
11. Include an input message that has *Cost* for a title. The message should read, "Enter the cost of the video, CD, or laserdisc."
12. Include an error message that has *Error* for a title. The message should read, "The cost cannot be over $100.00."
13. Starting in row 18, enter the following records into the list:

Order #	Opera	Medium	Cost
COS09V	Cosi Fan Tutte	Video	44.95
COS61C	Cosi Fan Tutte	CD	37.95
DON40V	Don Carlo	Video	44.95
DON40L	Don Carlo	Laserdisc	79.95
DON79C	Don Carlo	CD	47.95

14. Save the workbook with the same name (**eec4sc02**).
15. Print and close **eec4sc02**.

Assessment 3

1. Open **ExcelWorksheet07**.
2. Save the worksheet using the Save As command and name it **eec4sc03**.
3. Create a custom header with your name displayed at the left margin and the file name displayed at the right margin.
4. Use the Sort Ascending button to sort the list by *Order #*. Print the worksheet.
5. Use the Sort Descending button to sort the list by *Cost*. Print the worksheet.
6. Perform a multilevel sort, sorting first by *Cost* in descending order and then by *Opera* in ascending order. Print the list.

7. The Little Music Shop wants to be able to sort the list in order of popularity of the medium. Create the following custom list:

   CD
   Video
   Laserdisc

8. Sort the list first by the custom list created in Step 7 in ascending order and then by *Opera* in ascending order. Print the worksheet.
9. Delete the custom list created in Step 7.
10. Save the workbook with the same name (**eec4sc03**).
11. Close **eec4sc03**.

Assessment 4

1. Open **ExcelWorksheet08**.
2. Save the worksheet using the Save As command and name it **eec4sc04**.
3. Create a custom header with your name displayed at the left margin and the file name displayed at the right margin.
4. Outline the worksheet manually. Place all the records for CDs in one group, all the records for Videos in another group, and all the records for Laserdiscs in a third group.
5. Display only the average prices for the CDs, Videos, and Laserdiscs. Print the worksheet.
6. Display the details for the Videos. Print the worksheet.
7. Ungroup all the records for Videos.
8. Display the details for CDs and Laserdiscs.
9. Clear the outline for the entire worksheet.
10. Save the workbook with the same name (**eec4sc04**).
11. Close **eec4sc04**.

Assessment 5

1. Open **ExcelWorksheet09**.
2. Save the worksheet using the Save As command and name it **eec4sc05**.
3. Create a custom header with your name displayed at the left margin and the file name displayed at the right margin.
4. This worksheet keeps track of the EastWest Crossroads Company invoices. There is an error in the address of Dennis Davis, which is on invoice number 10-6119. Use the Data Form to find the record and change the address for Dennis Davis to P.O. Box 2860.
5. The invoice amount is currently incorrect on invoice 10-6118. Change the invoice amount to 82.58.
6. Sort the list in ascending order first by state, then by last name, and finally by first name.
7. Subtotal the *Invoice Totals* by State. Adjust the width of column H. Print the worksheet.
8. Collapse the list so that only the subtotals and grand total are displayed. Print the worksheet.
9. Expand the list so that all the details are displayed.
10. Remove the subtotals from the list.
11. Save the workbook with the same name (**eec4sc05**).
12. Close **eec4sc05**.

Assessment 6

1. Open **ExcelWorksheet10**.
2. Save the worksheet using the Save As command and name it **eec4sc06**.
3. Create a custom header with your name displayed at the left margin and the file name displayed at the right margin.

4. Sort the list first by state in ascending order and then by Invoice Total in descending order.
5. Create a custom AutoFilter to find all of the invoices over $1,000. Print the worksheet.
6. Display all the records.
7. Create custom AutoFilters, one for Invoice Totals and one for State, that will find all the invoices from either California or New York that are under $500. Print the worksheet.
8. Display all the records.
9. Turn the AutoFilter feature off.
10. Save the workbook with the same name (**eec4sc06**).
11. Close **eec4sc06**.

Assessment 7

1. Open **ExcelWorksheet11**.
2. Save the worksheet using the Save As command and name it **eec4sc07**.
3. Create a custom header with your name displayed at the left margin and the file name displayed at the right margin.
4. This worksheet keeps track of the salary and commissions for the sales representatives of Case 'n Crate, a company that manufactures and sells wooden products. Claire Hoag received a raise. Use the Data Form to find her record and change her salary to 1200.
5. The sales figures for Ria Munoz are incorrect. Use the Data Form to find her record and change the sales amount to 12299.76.
6. Sort the list in ascending order first by region, next by percent commission, and finally by last name.
7. Subtotal the *Total* column by *Region*. Adjust the width of column H. Print the worksheet.
8. Use the Hide Detail button to hide the details for the East Central region, the South Central region, the Southeast region, and the Southwest region. Print the worksheet.
9. Expand the list so that all the details are displayed.
10. Remove the subtotals from the list.
11. Create a custom AutoFilter command to find all of the sales over $9,000. Print the worksheet.
12. Display all the records.
13. Create custom AutoFilters, one for *Region* and one for *Sales*, to find all of the records from either the South Central region or the East Central region that have sales over $10,000. Print the worksheet.
14. Display all the records.
15. Use AutoFilter to find the records of the sales representatives whose sales are in the top 10%. Print the worksheet.
16. Turn the AutoFilter feature off.
17. Save the workbook with the same name (**eec4sc07**).
18. Close **eec4sc07**.

Assessment 8

1. Open **ExcelWorksheet12**.
2. Save the worksheet using the Save As command and name it **eec4sc08**.
3. Create a custom header with your name displayed at the left margin and the file name displayed at the right margin.
4. Sort the list in ascending order by *Opera*.
5. You want to create a unique list of the opera names. Select cells B3 through B39. Use Advanced Filter to copy the unique records only to cell F3.
6. Adjust the width of column F.

7. Print the worksheet.
8. Save the workbook with the same name (**eec4sc08**).
9. Close **eec4sc08**.

Assessment 9

1. Open **ExcelWorksheet13**.
2. Save the worksheet using the Save As command and name it **eec4sc09**.
3. Create a custom header with your name displayed at the left margin and the file name displayed at the right margin.
4. Sort the list in ascending order by *Last Name*.
5. Set up a criteria range for this worksheet. Insert four blank rows above row 2.
6. Copy the labels from row 6 to row 1.
7. Name the range of cells A1 through H3 *Criteria*.
8. Use Advanced Filter to find the records from either the East Central or the North Central region. Filter the list in place. Print the worksheet.
9. Show all the records.
10. Sort the list in ascending order, first by Region and then by Sales.
11. Use Advanced Filter to find the records that either are from the Northeast region or have sales over $12,000. Filter the list in place. Print the worksheet.
12. Show all the records.
13. Use Advanced Filter to find either the records that are from the East Central region that are over $10,000 or the records from the Southeast region that are over $10,000. Filter the list in place. Print the worksheet.
14. Show all the records.
15. Save the workbook with the same name (**eec4sc09**).
16. Close **eec4sc09**.

Assessment 10

1. Open **ExcelWorksheet14**.
2. Save the worksheet using the Save As command and name it **eec4sc10**.
3. Create a custom header with your name displayed at the left margin and the file name displayed at the right margin.
4. Lake George Kayak will offer a trade-in price on used kayaks to go toward the purchase of a new kayak. They fix the used kayaks up in any way they can and then resell them. This worksheet keeps track of their used kayak inventory, listing the model and manufacturer of each kayak, its length, age, the trade-in value they gave for it, its selling price, and the profit they will make from its sale. You want to use Dfunctions to make some calculations. First, create a list range using the cells A8 through G34.
5. You want to know the total profit that would be made by selling all the Eddyline kayaks. In cell I9 enter Total Profit Eddyline. Widen column I to display the entire label. In cells K9 and K10, enter the necessary criteria for the function. In cell J9, enter a Dfunction that calculates the total profit on all Eddyline kayaks. Format J9 as currency.
6. You want to know the average trade-in value on kayaks more than five years old. In cell I12, enter Average trade in on kayak >5 years. Widen column I to display the entire criteria text. In cells K12 and K13, enter the necessary criteria for the function. In cell J12, enter a Dfunction that calculates the average trade-in value on kayaks more than five years old. Format cell J10 as currency.

7. You want to know how may kayaks are in stock that are less than 16 feet long. In cell I15, enter **Number of kayaks <16 feet**. In cells K15 and K16, enter the necessary criteria for the function. In cell J15, enter a Dfunction that calculates the number of kayaks that are less than 16 feet long.

8. You want to know the least expensive Necky that is in stock. Enter **Minimum price Necky** in cell I18. In cells K18 and K19, enter the necessary criteria for the function. In cell J18, enter a Dfunction that calculates the minimum price for a Necky. Format cell J18 as currency.

9. Format the worksheet so that all the information prints on one page. Save and print the worksheet.

10. Some of the kayaks have been sold and some more used kayaks have come in. You need to modify the list range. The following kayaks were sold. Delete their records from the list range:

   Nimbus Seafarer
   Easyrider Eskimo 18-6
   Perception Eclipse

   The following kayaks were received as trade-ins. Add their records to the list range:

Avatar	Perception	15	3	$1,000	$1,150
Shadow	Perception	16	5	$1,200	$1,350
Whisper CL	Eddyline	18	2	$2,000	$2,300
Night Hawk	Eddyline	17	1	$1,850	$2,000

11. You want to know the maximum profit on kayaks with a price less than $600. Enter **Maximum profit kayaks <$600** in cell I21. In cells K21 and K22 enter the necessary criteria for the function. In cell J21, enter a Dfunction that calculates the maximum profit on all kayaks that have a price less than $600. Format cell J21 as currency.

12. Make sure the all the information in the worksheet will print on one page. Save and print the worksheet.

13. Close **eec4sc10**.

Assessment 11

1. You want to know if wildcard characters can be used when filtering data. Use Microsoft Office Excel Help to search for the Help topic *wildcard characters*. Read and print the Help topic on wildcard characters.

2. Open **eec4sc09** (You created this file in Assessment 9). Save the worksheet using the Save As command and name it **eec4sc11**.

3. Using the information from the Help topic, create an advanced filter using a wildcard character to find any region that ends with *west*. Make sure you use the correct criteria range for the filter. Filter the list in place. Print the worksheet.

4. Show all the records.

5. Save the workbook with the same name (**eec4sc11**) and close it.

CHAPTER challenge

You work in the sales department of Amazingly Affordable Autos, a car dealership specializing buying and selling a variety of new and used cars. You have been asked to create a data list in Excel to maintain records of customers who have purchased vehicles. The list should contain at least five different fields. There should be at least two fields that contain data validation. (Be sure to include input and error messages.) Add five records to the list. Sort the list in a logical order. Create a named range for the list, called CustomerList. Save the workbook as **AAA**. Print the list.

Management would like a list of customers who have purchased vehicles that are in the price range of $10,000–$20,000. This can be accomplished through the Advanced Filter feature. Use the Help feature to learn more about filtering with multiple conditions on one field. Then use the list created in the first part of the Chapter Challenge. If you did not create a *Price (Cost of Vehicle)* field, do so now. Add prices/costs, ranging from $5,000–$50,000, to each of the records. Then use the Advanced Filter feature to copy (to another location in the worksheet) records of customers who purchased a vehicle in the price range of $10,000–$20,000. Appropriately identify this section of the worksheet. Save the workbook again.

One of the individuals on the management team will be using the results of the filtered list created in the second part of the Chapter Challenge in a PowerPoint presentation. Begin the PowerPoint presentation for the member of the management team by creating a title slide. The second slide will consist of the filtered list. Use an appropriate title on the slide. Save the presentation as **AAA**.

WORK IN Progress

Advanced Formatting and Functions

ASSESSING proficiency

In this unit, you learned to create, apply, and edit custom formats, styles, conditional formatting, and templates. You learned how to modify Excel default settings. You also learned how to copy worksheets into a workbook, consolidate data into a list, and link workbooks. You learned how to use the PMT, PV, ROUND, RAND, SUMIF, COUNTIF, VLOOKUP, and IF functions. In addition, you learned how to use database functions such as DSUM and DAVERAGE. You learned how to enter, edit, and delete data using the Data Form; use data validation; create and modify list ranges; and filter a list.

Assessment 1

1. Open **ExcelWorksheet01**.
2. Save the workbook using the Save As command and name it **eeu1pa01**.
3. Create a custom header that has your name left-aligned and the file name right-aligned.
4. This workbook is an invoice used by the EastWest Crossroads Company, which sells imported and unique gifts through the mail. The form is used for taking orders. In the Workbook Properties dialog box enter **Standard Invoice** in the *Title* text box, enter your name in the *Author* text box, enter **EastWest Crossroads Company** in the *Company* text box, enter **Invoice form** in the *Category* text box, and enter **income, order form, invoice** in the *Keywords* text box.
5. Add a bottom border for filling in information to the following cells: C4, C5, C6, C7, C8, C9, F7, H7, K8, K9, C12, C13, C14, C15, F15, and H15.
6. Place an outline border around cells K4, K5, and K6.
7. Create a style called Header 1 that includes the following formatting:

Font:	Arial
Font style:	Bold
Font size:	10
Color:	Brown

8. Apply the Header 1 style to the following cells: A4, A5, A7, A8, A9, E7, G7, A12, A13, A15, E15, and G15.

9. Create a style that is based on Header 1 and name it Header 2. Header 2 should include the following formatting:

Font:	Arial
Font style:	Bold
Font size:	10
Color:	Brown
Horizontal alignment:	Right

10. Apply the Header 2 style to the following cells: I4, I5, I6, I8, I9, I26, I27, I28, I29, and I30.

11. Create a style that is based on Header 1 and name it Header 3. Header 3 should include the following formatting:

Font:	Arial
Font style:	Bold
Font size:	10
Color:	White
Horizontal alignment:	Center
Cell shading:	Brown

12. Apply the Header 3 style to the following cells: A18 through K18 and I31.
13. Format the worksheet so that zero values are not displayed.
14. Place an outline border around the following ranges of cells:

   A19:A25, B19:B25, C19:C25, D19:D25, E19:H25, I19:I25, J19:J25, J26:J30, J31.

15. Enter the following data in the cells indicated:

Cell	Data
C4	Jo Ellen Gammon
C5	348 West End Road
C7	Arcata
F7	CA
H7	95521
K5	X
C8	(707) 555-0922
K8	9999 8955 1221 0032
K9	09/09/07

16. Save the worksheet again with the same name (**eeu1pa01**).
17. Print and then close **eeu1pa01**.

Assessment 2

1. Open **ExcelWorksheet02**.
2. Save the workbook using the Save As command and name it **eeu1pa02**.
3. Create a custom header that has your name left-aligned and the file name right-aligned.
4. This worksheet keeps track of the number of hours of music lessons given for each instrument. Create a custom number format that will insert the text *hrs* (for *hours*) after a value. Format all the values on the worksheet using the custom format you create.
5. Use conditional formatting to display all the values in cells B4 through M20 that are under 200 in red and all the values that are greater than or equal to 450 as blue.

EXCEL

6. Set the left and right margins to .5. Change the orientation of the page to landscape.
7. Use the AutoFit Selection command to automatically adjust the width of all the columns.
8. Format the worksheet using the Classic 2 AutoFormat.
9. Save the worksheet again with the same name (**eeu1pa02**).
10. Print and then close **eeu01pa02**.

Assessment 3

1. Open **Excel Worksheet 03**.
2. Save the workbook using the Save As command and name it **eeu1pa03**.
3. Create a custom header that has your name left-aligned and the file name right-aligned.
4. Insert the **House** graphic image at the top of the worksheet.
5. Resize the image so that it fits between rows 1 and 20, without changing the aspect ratio.
6. Crop the photo to delete some of the extra space at the top and bottom of the photo. The photo should focus just on the house as much as possible.
7. Resize the image again so that it fits in rows 1 through 20.
8. Center the image within columns A through H.
9. Adjust the brightness of the photo so that it is a little brighter.
10. Add a bit more contrast to the photo.
11. Save the worksheet again with the same name (**eeu1pa03**) and print it.
12. Close **eeu1pa03**.

Assessment 4

1. Open **ExcelWorksheet04**.
2. Save the workbook using the Save As command and name it **eeu1pa04**.
3. Create a custom header that has your name left-aligned and the file name right-aligned.
4. The Oak Springs Animal Care Clinic wants to promote responsible pet ownership. They put together this bar chart showing top reasons why pet owners surrender their dogs and cats to animal shelters. You need to format the chart to make it more attractive before it is distributed.
5. First you are going to format the columns that represent cats. Right-click one of the columns that represents cats and access the Format Data Series dialog box. Click the Patterns tab. In the *Border* section, select *Automatic*. Click the Fill Effects button. Click the Picture tab in the Fill Effects dialog box. Click the Select Picture button. Locate the **Cat** file. Select it and click the Insert button. In the *Format* section, select *Stack*. Click OK to close the Fill Effects dialog box. Click the Data Labels tab. Format the data labels so that the value is displayed. Click OK to close the Format Data Series dialog box.
6. Following the procedure outlined in Step 5, insert the **Dog** file in the columns that represent dogs.
7. Format all the data labels to bold.
8. Format the plot area so that it is a very pale peach color.
9. Clear the gridlines from the plot area.
10. Add the following chart title: **Reasons Why Pet Owners Surrender Dogs and Cats**.
11. Delete the legend from the chart.
12. Save and print the chart.
13. Close **eeu1pa04**.

Assessment 5

1. Open **eeu1pa01**.
2. Save the workbook using the Save As command and name it **eeu1pa05**.
3. Delete the contents of the following cells: C4, C5, C7, C8, F7, H7, K5, K8, K9, A19, A20, B19, B20, C19, C20, E19, E20, I19, and I20.
4. Save the file as a template using the file name **EastWestInvoice.xlt**.
5. Close the template.
6. Open the **EastWest Invoice** template.
7. Enter the following data in the cells indicated:

Cell	Data
C4	Gary Simpson
C5	467 Filbert Ave.
C7	Chelsea Heights
F7	NJ
H7	08401
C8	(732) 555-0933
C9	(732) 555-0805
K4	X
K8	7777 3471 1144 0008
K9	05/01/06
A19	35
B19	1
C19	XD489Z
E19	Bamboo Tea Pot
I19	32

8. Save the invoice as an Excel workbook using the file name **eeu1pa05a**.
9. Print the **eeu1pa05a** workbook and then close it.
10. Open the **EastWestInvoice** template.
11. Change the standard delivery charge in cell J27 to $7.50.
12. Save the edited **EastWestInvoice** template. You want to replace the original template.
13. Close the template.
14. Open the **EastWestInvoice** template.
15. Enter the following data in the cells indicated:

Cell	Data
C4	Sue Clanton
C5	4402 Feather Sound Dr.
C7	Clearwater
F7	FL
H7	33515
C8	(727) 555-6688
C9	(732) 555-5832
K4	X
K8	3333 4562 4578 9977
K9	06/01/07
A19	28
B19	1
C19	XD985R
E19	Russian Enamel Egg
I19	120

16. Save the invoice as an Excel workbook using the file name **eeu1pa05b**.
17. Print the **eeu1pa05b** workbook.
18. Delete the **EastWest Invoice** template.
19. Close the **eeu1pa05b** workbook.

Assessment 6

1. Open **Excel Worksheet 05**.
2. Save the workbook using the Save As command and name it **eeu1pa06**.
3. Create a custom header that has your name left-aligned and the file name right-aligned.
4. The EastWest Crossroads Company uses this workbook to calculate, in U.S. dollars, the orders they placed in March. Since exchange rates are constantly changing, the exchange rates for the countries with which the EastWest Crossroads Company does business are kept in a separate workbook. You need to link the **eeu1pa06** workbook with the **ExchangeRates** workbook. Open the **ExchangeRates** workbook.
5. Switch back to the **eeu1pa06** workbook. Enter the following data in the cells indicated:

Cell	Data
C4	24,568
C6	48,952
C10	95,670
C16	205,678
C21	108,952
C25	3,467,890

6. Click cell D4. Enter a formula that multiplies cell C4 on the *MarchOrders* worksheet in the **eeu1pa06** workbook by cell C4 on the *CurrentExchange Rates* worksheet in the **ExchangeRates** workbook. The reference to cell C4 in the *CurrentExchangeRates* worksheet cannot be absolute. If it is, delete the dollar signs in front of the *C* and in front of the *4*.
7. Copy the formula in cell D4 on the *MarchOrders* worksheet in the **eeu1pa06** workbook to cells D5 through D25.
8. Print the *MarchOrders* worksheet.
9. The exchange rate for Indian Rupees has changed. Type 0.02387 in cell C16 on the *CurrentExchangeRates* worksheet in the **ExchangeRates** workbook. Save the workbook using the same file name.
10. Switch to the **eeu1pa06** workbook and print it again.
11. Save the workbook.
12. Close the **Exchange Rates** workbook.

Assessment 7

1. Open **ExcelWorksheet06**.
2. Save the workbook using the Save As command and name it **eeu1pa07**.
3. Create a custom header that has your name left-aligned and the file name right-aligned.
4. This worksheet contains the instruments sold at the Little Music Shop. The selling price of each instrument is based on a percentage markup. The percentage markup is found in the markup table. For example, if the cost of an instrument is between $0 and $400, the markup is 14%; if the cost of an instrument is between $400 and $500, the markup is 10%; and so on. Enter

a formula in cell C4 that uses the VLOOKUP function to calculate the selling price of a bass. The selling price is calculated by multiplying the cost by the markup percentage and then adding that total to the original cost.

5. Copy the formula in cell C4 to cells C5 through C20.
6. Print the *Instruments* worksheet.
7. Save the workbook using the same name (**eeu1pa07**).
8. Close the **eeu1pa07** workbook.

Assessment 8

1. Open **ExcelWorksheet07**.
2. Save the workbook using the Save As command and name it **eeu1pa08**.
3. Create a custom header that has your name left-aligned and the file name right-aligned.
4. Linda Taylor wants to use this worksheet to calculate what the budget for May expenses should be. Format the worksheet using conditional formatting so that any value that is less than zero is displayed as red.
5. May's budget is going to be based on the differences between what was budgeted in April and what was actually spent. If the difference between the budgeted amount and what was actually spent is greater than or equal to zero, then the budget for May is going to be the same as the budget for April. If the difference between the budgeted amount and what was actually spent is less than zero, then the budgeted amount for May is going to be 8% greater than the budgeted amount for April. Enter an IF function in cell E10 that calculates May's budget for insurance.
6. Copy the IF function in cell E10 to cells E11 through E19.
7. Linda Taylor wants to know the total amount of money that was spent in April that was over the budgeted amounts. Enter a SUMIF function in cell D21 that adds together any number in cells D10 through D19 that is less than zero.
8. Save the workbook using the same name (**eeu1pa08**) and print it.
9. Close the **eeu1pa08** workbook.

Assessment 9

1. Open **ExcelWorksheet08**.
2. Save the workbook using the Save As command and name it **eeu1pa09**.
3. Create a custom header that has your name left-aligned and the file name right-aligned.
4. The Little Music Shop uses this list to keep track of students taking music lessons. Use data validation to make it easier to enter more data into the list. The ID numbers are all exactly seven characters long. Use the Data Validation command to allow a text length equal to seven for column A. Include an input message that has *ID #* for a title. The message should read *Enter seven-character ID number*. Include an error message that has *Error* for a title. The message should read *The ID number must be exactly seven characters long*.
5. Use the Data Validation command to allow a text length equal to two for column F. Include an input message that has *State* for a title. The message should read *Enter the two-letter abbreviation for the state*. Include an error message that has *Error* for a title. The message should read *You must use the two-letter abbreviation for the state*.
6. Create a drop-down list for the data in column I. Create the list from the age groups listed in cells N4 through N8. Include an input message that

has *Age Groups* for a title. The message should read *Select the age group from the drop-down list*. Include an error message that has *Error* for a title. The message should read *The age group must be selected from the drop-down list*.

7. Create a drop-down list for the data in column J. Create the list from the instruments listed in cells O4 through O19. Include an input message that has *Instrument* for a title. The message should read *Select the instrument from the drop-down list*. Include an error message that has *Error* for a title. The message should read *Instrument must be selected from the drop-down list*.

8. Use the Data Validation command to allow any whole number between 1 and 12 for column K. Include an input message that has *Level* for a title. The message should read *Enter the student's level, from 1 to 12*. Include an error message that has *Error* for a title. The message should read *The class level must be a whole number between 1 and 12*.

9. Starting in row 7, enter the following records into the list:

ID#:	OA-3698	*ID#:*	FC-3873
Last Name:	O'Neill	*Last Name:*	Finn
First Name:	Andrew	*First Name:*	Carol
Address:	35 Ridgewood Cir.	*Address:*	1909 Park Place Blvd.
City:	Parkfairfax	*City:*	Franconia
State:	VA	*State:*	VA
Zip:	22302	*Zip:*	22310
Phone:	(703) 555-0980	*Phone:*	(703) 555-4498
Age:	5–9	*Age:*	Over 25
Instrument:	Drums	*Instrument:*	Flute
Level:	2	*Level:*	9

ID#:	CB-3698
Last Name:	Corley
First Name:	Betsy
Address:	602 Mitchell St.
City:	Wellington
State:	VA
Zip:	22308
Phone:	(703) 555-6642
Age:	15–19
Instrument:	Oboe
Level:	10

10. Change the orientation of the page to landscape.
11. Save the workbook using the same name (**eeu1pa09**) and print it.
12. Close the **eeu1pa09** workbook.

Assessment 10

1. Open **ExcelWorksheet09**.
2. Save the workbook using the Save As command and name it **eeu1pa10**.
3. Create a custom header that has your name left-aligned and the file name right-aligned.
4. A faculty member at Redwood Community College is conducting research studying the relationship between age, height, and weight. This worksheet is a collection of her data. You want to use Dfunctions to make some calculations. First, create a list range using all the data in the worksheet.

(If you receive an information box asking if you want to convert the selection to a list and remove all external connections, click Yes.)

5. Compute the average weight of the members of the database with age over 25 years. Label the output accordingly.
6. Compute the average height of the people with age below 30 years. Label the output accordingly.
7. Compute the lowest weight of the people with age below 30 years. Label the output accordingly.
8. Save the workbook using the same name (**eeu1pa10**) and print it.
9. Close the **eeu1pa10** workbook.

WRITING activities

The following activities give you the opportunity to practice your writing skills along with demonstrating an understanding of some of the important Word and Excel features you have mastered in this and previous units. Use correct grammar, appropriate word choices, and clear sentence constructions.

Activity 1

The Oak Springs Animal Care Clinic needs a form that will be used to keep the records of each animal seen at the clinic. Create a template that includes spaces for entering the following information:

- Owner's name, address, city, state, ZIP Code, and home and work telephone numbers
- Pet's name, birth date, breed, and sex

If you want, insert the clinic's logo onto the form. The **Oaksp.tif** file contains the logo. In the space below this general information, include a chart that looks similar to the following:

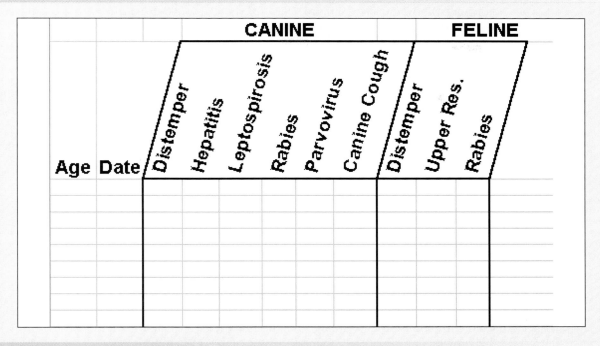

FIGURE U1.1 • Activity 1

Save the worksheet as a template using the file name **Clinic.xlt**. Use the template to complete a form for one animal. If you own a pet, use that information for completing the form. If not, use your name and address, but make up information on the pet. After the form has been filled out, save it and name it **eeu1act01**. Print and then close **eeu1act01**.

Activity 2

Georgia and Paul Sorenson, owners of the decorating business Primrose Decorators, offer discounts on large contracts they receive. Rename the *Sheet1* worksheet tab, *Contract Discounts*. Create a header that prints your name at the left margin and the file name at the right margin. On the *Contract Discounts* worksheet, include an appropriate title for the worksheet and key the following data:

Contract #	Contract Amount	Discount	Total after Discount
PD-7843	$15,000		
PD-7931	$4,000		
PD-7935	$60,000		
PD-7943	$72,000		
PD-7948	$8,000		
PD-7950	$68,000		
PD-7956	$12,000		
PD-6004	$45,000		
PD-6010	$82,000		
PD-6012	$35,000		

Rename the *Sheet2* worksheet tab, *Lookup Table*. For contracts under $10,000 there are no discounts, for contracts between $10,000 and $20,000 there is a 1% discount, for contracts between $20,000 and $40,000 there is a 2% discount, for contracts between $40,000 and $80,000 there is a 3% discount, and for contracts over $80,000, there is a 5% discount. On the *Lookup Table* worksheet, create a lookup table that reflects these discounts.

Switch to the *Contract Discounts* worksheet. In the first cell in the *Discount* column, enter a VLOOKUP function that uses the table on the *Lookup Table* worksheet to look up the contract amount. The function should return the discount given for that amount. Copy the formula to find the discount for all the contracts.

In the first cell in the *Total after Discount* column, enter a formula that subtracts the appropriate discount percentage from the contract amount. Copy the formula to find the total after discount for all the contracts.

After the *Contract Discounts* worksheet is completed, save it and name it **eeu1act02**. Print and then close **eeu1act02**.

INTERNET project

Use Excel Help to read about the existing queries in Excel. Use the Internet to research five companies whose stocks you would like to own. Be sure to write down each company's stock symbol. Use the Data, Get External Data option to run the "Microsoft Investor Stock Quotes" saved query. When asked to enter your stock symbols, separate out each one with a comma and space (i.e. PFE, MRK, CSCO). If you want the numbers to automatically adjust to the current stock quotes when the file is opened, be sure to check the boxes found in the "Enter Parameter Value" dialog box. Save the files as STOCK and print one copy.

JOB study

The owner of a large furniture company has asked you to create the following worksheet for her.

Thaxton									
Category	Dealer Name	Units Purchased	Retail Price	Cost	Volume Discount	Sell Price	Gross Profit	Commissions	Net Profit/Loss
Wall Unit	SFI Designs	5						5%	
Recliner	CJ Interiors	20						7%	
Desk	Hovey Furnishings	30						10%	
Totals									
Averages									

Insert the following lookup table to determine retail price and cost.

Dealer Name	Retail Price	Cost
CJ Interiors	1200	600
Hovey Furnishings	2100	945
SFI Designs	3300	1980

Use an =IF statement to specify who receives the volume discount. If a customer purchases 15 or more units, then place "Yes" in the cell; otherwise, place "No." Sell price is 20% off the retail price (retail price x .80). Gross profit is sell price - cost. Net profit/loss is gross profit - commissions.

Be sure to use conditional formatting to find all the net profit/loss greater than or equal to $2,500. Format the worksheet to include borders, shading, fill colors, and other formatting choices. Round your numbers to two decimal places. Copy the information to the next four worksheet tabs within the file. Rename the worksheet tabs as follows:

Worksheet Tab	Rename to
Sheet1	Qtr 1
Sheet2	Qtr2
Sheet3	Qtr 3
Sheet4	Qtr 4
Sheet5	Year-End

Click the Year-End worksheet tab. Keep the headings and cells containing totals, but delete the cells containing prices. You are going to use Year-End to consolidate the numbers for Qtr 1 - Qtr 4 worksheets. Use the Year-End worksheet to sort the net profit/loss column in descending order. Save the files as FURNITURE and print one copy of each page of the file.

EXPERT

MICROSOFT®
EXCEL

Expert Level Unit 2: Interpreting and Integrating Data

- ➤ Using Excel's Analysis Tools
- ➤ Managing and Auditing Worksheets
- ➤ Collaborating with Workgroups
- ➤ Using Data from the Internet and Other Sources

BENCHMARK MICROSOFT® EXCEL 2003

MICROSOFT OFFICE SPECIALIST
EXPERT SKILLS—UNIT 2

Reference No.	Skill	Pages
XL03E-1 Organizing and Analyzing Data		
XL03E-1-6	Add, show, close, edit, merge and summarize scenarios	
	Managing scenarios	E232-E235
XL03E-1-7	Perform data analysis using automated tools	
	Projecting values using analysis tools	E235-E241
	Performing What-If analysis	E225-E226
	Using the Solver add-in	E227-E231
XL03E-1-8	Create PivotTable and PivotChart reports	
	Creating PivotTable Reports and PivotChart Reports	E197-E225
XL03E-1-11	Trace formula precedents, dependents and errors	
	Tracing formula precedents	E269
	Tracing formula dependents	E269
	Tracing formula errors	E269
XL03E-1-12	Locate invalid data and formulas	
	Using Error Checking	E269, E271-E276
	Circling invalid data	E269-E270, E273-E276
XL03E-1-13	Watch and evaluate formulas	
	Using Evaluate formulas	E271, E275-E276
	Using cell watch	E271, E275-E276
XL03E-1-15	Structure workbooks using XML	
	Adding, modifying, and deleting maps	E338-E344
	Managing elements and attributes in XML workbooks	E343-E348
	Defining XML options	E345-E347
XL03E-3 Collaborating		
XL03E-3-1	Protect cells, worksheets, and workbooks	
	Adding protection to cells, worksheets and workbooks	E286-E291
XL03E-3-2	Apply workbook security settings	
	Using digital signatures to authenticate workbooks	E292-E294
	Setting passwords	E284-E286, E289-E291
	Setting macro settings	E293-E294
XL03E-3-4	Merge workbooks	
	Merging multiple versions of the same workbook	E300-E302
XL03E-3-5 T	rack, accept, and reject changes to workbooks	
	Tracking changes	E294-E299
	Accepting and rejecting changes	E295-E299
XL03E-4 Managing Data and Workbooks		
XL03E-4-1	Import data to Excel	
	Bringing information into Excel	E312-E317, E324-E326
	Linking Web page data	E325-E327
XL03E-4-2	Export data from Excel	
	Exporting structured data from Excel	E317-E318
XL03E-4-3	Publish and edit Web worksheets and workbooks	
	Publishing Web based worksheets	E319-E323
XL03E-5 Customizing Excel		
XL03E-5-1	Customize toolbars and menus	
	Adding and removing buttons from toolbars	E261-E267
	Adding custom menus	E261-E267
XL03E-5-2	Create, edit, and run macros	
	Creating macros	E250-E251, E253-E254
	Editing macros using the Visual Basic Editor	E254-E259

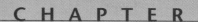

CHAPTER 5

USING EXCEL'S ANALYSIS TOOLS

PERFORMANCE OBJECTIVES

Upon successful completion of Chapter 5, you will be able to:
- ➤ Create a PivotTable report using the PivotTable Wizard
- ➤ Format a PivotTable report using AutoFormat
- ➤ Sort and filter a PivotTable report
- ➤ Hide and show detail in a PivotTable report
- ➤ Analyze data using a PivotTable report
- ➤ Create a PivotChart report
- ➤ Create an interactive PivotTable for the Web
- ➤ Analyze data using Goal Seek
- ➤ Analyze data using Solver
- ➤ Create scenarios
- ➤ Create a trendline

When worksheets become large and complex, the ability to summarize and analyze the data stored in them becomes increasingly important. Excel includes a number of features to help you analyze data, such as PivotTable reports, PivotChart reports, Goal Seek, Scenario Manager, trendlines, and Solver. The purpose of this chapter is to show you how to analyze data using Excel's analysis tools.

Introduction to Pivot Tables

Several layers of complexity are involved when analyzing data in an Excel worksheet. Chapter 4 introduced you to some of the simpler ways to analyze data. The Data Form allows you to look up and retrieve specific records one record at a time. AutoFilter allows you to extract particular records from a list based on specific criteria. Advanced Filter allows you to create more complex search criteria for extracting records. PivotTables add another level of complexity for analyzing data. With PivotTables, you can compare several facts about one element in a data list.

A PivotTable is an interactive table that quickly summarizes and analyzes large amounts of data. A PivotTable is interactive because you can easily rotate, or "pivot," its rows and columns to summarize the data in a different way. The interactive PivotTable allows you to easily change the view of the data so that you can see more or less detail. PivotTable reports are useful when you have a long list of figures that you want to summarize in a variety of ways. A PivotTable report summarizes the data in one field by breaking it down according to the data in another field. Figure 5.1 illustrates an example of a PivotTable. The data list in columns A through D lists the first and second quarter sales by sales representative for all the sales regions. This data list is the source data for the PivotTable report in cells F1 through I10. The PivotTable report summarizes the data in the *Sales* field by breaking it down according to the data in the *Region* field and the *Qtr* field. This PivotTable report allows you to easily compare the first and second quarter sales for each sales region. As shown in Figure 5.2, you can easily pivot the table and have the column field become the row field and vice versa.

HINT

Creating a PivotTable enables you to have Excel sort, subtotal, and total data for you.

FIGURE

5.1   *A PivotTable*

	A	B	C	D	E	F	G	H	I
1	**Last Name**	**Qtr**	**Region**	**Sales**		Sum of Sales	Qtr		
2	Levinson, C.	1st	Northeast	$12,378.09		Region	1st	2nd	Grand Total
3	Harden, J.	1st	Southeast	$ 9,990.22		East Central	$ 31,889.39	$ 29,852.92	$ 61,742.31
4	Ferguson, M.	1st	South Central	$11,852.60		North Central	$ 21,101.00	$ 20,387.77	$ 41,488.77
5	Orsini, B.	1st	Southwest	$ 9,762.54		Northeast	$ 29,339.21	$ 27,856.02	$ 57,195.23
6	Bachman, J.	1st	East Central	$10,001.35		Northwest	$ 30,914.55	$ 31,033.72	$ 61,948.27
7	Malone, M.	1st	East Central	$ 9,902.84		South Central	$ 29,607.42	$ 29,947.13	$ 59,554.55
8	Munoz, R.	1st	Northwest	$12,022.65		Southeast	$ 32,032.49	$ 32,192.17	$ 64,224.66
9	Rainwater, D.	1st	Northeast	$ 8,968.32		Southwest	$ 31,904.98	$ 31,600.59	$ 63,505.57
10	Santiago, R.	1st	Northeast	$ 7,992.80		Grand Total	$206,789.04	$202,870.32	$409,659.36
11	Rusowicz, C.	1st	South Central	$ 9,135.39					
12	Eiseman, J.	1st	Southeast	$12,205.76					
13	McBride, R.	1st	East Central	$11,985.20					
14	Sparks, J.	1st	Southeast	$ 9,836.51					
15	Landis, G.	1st	North Central	$11,875.98					
16	Langdon, G.	1st	South Central	$ 8,619.43					
17	Lalonde, M.	1st	North Central	$ 9,225.02					
18	Vance, A.	1st	Northwest	$ 9,900.46					
19	Peruzzi, T.	1st	Southwest	$12,300.51					
20	Turner, L.	1st	Northwest	$ 8,991.44					
21	Hoag, C.	1st	Southwest	$ 9,841.93					
22	Levinson, C.	2nd	Northeast	$12,981.34					
23	Harden, J.	2nd	Southeast	$10,234.52					
24	Ferguson, M.	2nd	South Central	$12,000.54					
25	Orsini, B.	2nd	Southwest	$ 9,804.34					
26	Bachman, J.	2nd	East Central	$ 9,874.34					
27	Malone, M.	2nd	East Central	$ 7,894.23					
28	Munoz, R.	2nd	Northwest	$12,945.35					
29	Rainwater, D.	2nd	Northeast	$ 7,984.34					
30	Santiago, R.	2nd	Northeast	$ 6,890.34					
31	Rusowicz, C.	2nd	South Central	$ 8,904.25					
32	Eiseman, J.	2nd	Southeast	$12,984.25					

Row Field — Column Field — Data Area

Source Data / Sheet2 / Sheet3

5.2 Pivoting a PivotTable

The *QTR* field is now the row field.

The *Region* field is now the column field.

	A	B	C	D	E	F	G	H	I	J	K	L	
1	Last Name	Qtr	Region	Sales		Sum of Sales	Region						
2	Levinson, C.	1st	Northeast	$12,378.09		Qtr	East Central	North Central	Northeast	Northwest	South Central	Southeast	South
3	Harden, J.	1st	Southeast	$ 9,990.22		1st	$ 31,889.39	$ 21,101.00	$ 29,339.21	$ 30,914.55	$ 29,607.42	$ 32,032.49	$ 31
4	Ferguson, M.	1st	South Central	$11,852.60		2nd	$ 29,852.92	$ 20,387.77	$ 27,856.02	$ 31,033.72	$ 29,947.13	$ 32,192.17	$ 31
5	Orsini, B.	1st	Southwest	$ 9,762.54		Grand Total	$ 61,742.31	$ 41,488.77	$ 57,195.23	$ 61,948.27	$ 59,554.55	$ 64,224.66	$ 63
6	Bachman, J.	1st	East Central	$10,001.35									
7	Malone, M.	1st	East Central	$ 9,902.84									
8	Munoz, R.	1st	Northwest	$12,022.65									
9	Rainwater, D.	1st	Northeast	$ 8,968.32									
10	Santiago, R.	1st	Northeast	$ 7,992.80									
11	Rusowicz, C.	1st	South Central	$ 9,135.39									
12	Eiseman, J.	1st	Southeast	$12,205.76									
13	McBride, R.	1st	East Central	$11,985.20									
14	Sparks, J.	1st	Southeast	$ 9,836.51									
15	Landis, G.	1st	North Central	$11,875.98									
16	Langdon, G.	1st	South Central	$ 8,619.43									
17	Lalonde, M.	1st	North Central	$ 9,225.02									
18	Vance, A.	1st	Northwest	$ 9,900.46									
19	Peruzzi, T.	1st	Southwest	$12,300.51									
20	Turner, L.	1st	Northwest	$ 8,991.44		PivotTable							
21	Hoag, C.	1st	Southwest	$ 9,841.93		PivotTable							
22	Levinson, C.	2nd	Northeast	$12,981.34									
23	Harden, J.	2nd	Southeast	$10,234.52									
24	Ferguson, M.	2nd	South Central	$12,000.54									
25	Orsini, B.	2nd	Southwest	$ 9,804.34									
26	Bachman, J.	2nd	East Central	$ 9,874.34									
27	Malone, M.	2nd	East Central	$ 7,894.23									
28	Munoz, R.	2nd	Northeast	$12,945.35									
29	Rainwater, D.	2nd	Northeast	$ 7,984.34									
30	Santiago, R.	2nd	Northeast	$ 6,890.34									
31	Rusowicz, C.	2nd	South Central	$ 8,904.25									
32	Eiseman, J.	2nd	Southeast	$12,084.25									

H ◀ ▶ H \ Source Data / Sheet2 / Sheet3 /

Creating a PivotTable

A PivotTable report is based on its source data. The source data for a PivotTable can be created from a list, a database, multiple Excel worksheets, or another PivotTable. Chapter 4 covered how to set up a list in Excel. The rules for setting up a list in Excel that were covered in Chapter 4 must be followed when using a list as the source data for a PivotTable report.

Instead of working with columns and rows, a PivotTable report works with fields and items. Each field in a PivotTable report corresponds to a column in the source data. The name of the field in the PivotTable report is the column header for that column in the list. Look at Figure 5.3, for example. *Region* is a field in the PivotTable report, and it corresponds to the *Region* column in the source data. An item in a PivotTable report is a unique value in a field. In Figure 5.3, *1st* and *2nd* are items. The *Qtr* field contains the items *1st* and *2nd*. *Sum of Sales* is a data field. A data field is a field from the source list that contains data that is summarized in a PivotTable report. Data field values can be summarized in the PivotTable report using summary functions such as SUM, COUNT, or AVERAGE.

HINT

If you do not see the PivotTable and PivotChart Report button on the Standard toolbar, click the down-pointing arrow at the right edge of the toolbar, point to Add or Remove button, and then point to Standard. Click PivotTable and PivotChart Report.

FIGURE 5.3

How Data is Organized in a PivotTable Report

"Sum of Sales" is a data field. The data that is summarized comes from the data field.

"Qtr" is a field in this PivotTable report. It corresponds to the Qtr column in the source data.

"Region" is a field in the PivotTable report. It corresponds to the Region column in the source data.

Sum of Sales	Qtr		
Region	1st	2nd	Grand Total
East Central	$ 31,889.39	$ 29,852.92	$ 61,742.31
North Central	$ 21,101.00	$ 20,387.77	$ 41,488.77
Northeast	$ 29,339.21	$ 27,856.02	$ 57,195.23
Northwest	$ 30,914.55	$ 31,033.72	$ 61,948.27
South Central	$ 29,607.42	$ 29,947.13	$ 59,554.55
Southeast	$ 32,032.49	$ 32,192.17	$ 64,224.66
Southwest	$ 31,904.98	$ 31,600.59	$ 63,505.57
Grand Total	$206,789.04	$202,870.32	$409,659.36

"1st" and "2nd" are items. The Qtr field contains the items 1st and 2nd.

QUICK STEPS

Create a PivotTable
Click Data and then click PivotTable and PivotChart Report.

PivotTable and PivotChart Report

When you are creating a PivotTable from an Excel list, the first step is to name the range of cells that make up the list *Database*. Excel will then automatically recognize the list as the data source. Excel's PivotTable Wizard takes you step-by-step through the process of creating a PivotTable. Figure 5.4 illustrates the three dialog boxes that make up the PivotTable Wizard. Once you have named your list *Database*, click Data and then click PivotTable and PivotChart Report. Step 1 of the PivotTable and PivotChart Wizard is displayed. You can also access the PivotTable Wizard by clicking the PivotTable and PivotChart Report button on the Standard toolbar. As shown in Figure 5.4, you first have to identify where the data source to be used is located and whether you want to create a PivotTable or a PivotChart. In Step 2 you have to identify the range of cells that make up the data source. If you named the list *Database*, then Excel will automatically enter the correct range. In Step 3 you have to identify whether you want the PivotTable placed on a new worksheet or on the same worksheet as the list. When you have made all the necessary selections, click the Finish button.

If you do not name the list to be used as a data source database, another way to have Excel automatically recognize the list as the data source is to position the cell pointer in the list before activating the PivotTable Wizard.

FIGURE 5.4

The PivotTable and PivotChart Wizard

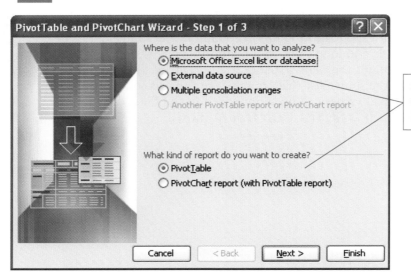

Step 1: Identify the location of the data source and the kind of report to be created.

5.4 *The PivotTable and PivotChart Wizard (continued)*

Step 2: Identify the range of cells that make up the data source. If this range was previously named *Database*, Excel will automatically recognize it. Otherwise, enter the appropriate range of cells.

Identify where to place the PivotTable. If the PivotTable is to be placed on the existing worksheet, enter the cell range of cells where it should be placed.

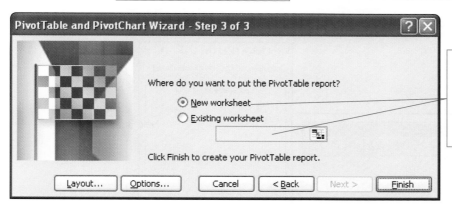

Once you click the Finish button, the PivotTable diagram, PivotTable toolbar, and PivotTable Field List are displayed, as shown in Figure 5.5. If the Pivot Table toolbar is not displayed, click View, point to Toolbars, and then click PivotTable. In order for the PivotTable field list to be displayed, the Show Field List button on the PivotTable toolbar must be selected. In the PivotTable Field List is a group of field buttons. Drag the fields with data to be displayed in rows from the PivotTable Field List to the *Drop Row Fields Here* area of the diagram. Drag the fields with data to be displayed in columns from the PivotTable Field List to the *Drop Column Fields Here* area of the diagram. More than one field can be dragged to each area. Drag fields to be used as page fields from the PivotTable Field List to the *Drop Page Fields Here* area. The order in which you should drag fields to the PivotTable diagram is fields in the row, column, and page areas first. Drag fields to the data area last. Using this order helps prevent delays when dropping fields from the PivotTable toolbar to the PivotTable diagram. To remove a field from the PivotTable, simply drag it off the diagram. To rearrange the fields in the PivotTable, simply drag them from one area to another.

5.5 *The PivotTable Diagram and PivotTable Toolbar*

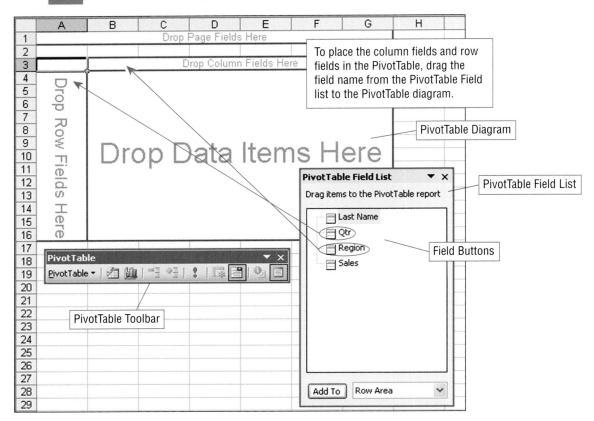

exercise 1

CREATING A PIVOTTABLE AND FILTERING A PIVOTTABLE REPORT

1. Open **ExcelWorksheet01**.
2. Save the worksheet using the Save As command and name it **eec5x01**.
3. This worksheet contains a list of orders made to the Whitewater Canoe and Kayak Corporation by various stores. You are going to use this list to create a PivotTable. Complete the following steps to name the range of cells that make up the list:
   a. Select cells A3 through F68.
   b. Click in the name box at the left side of the formula bar and then type **Database**.
   c. Press Enter.
4. Complete the following steps to create the PivotTable:
   a. Click Data and then click PivotTable and PivotChart Report.
   b. The PivotTable and PivotChart Wizard - Step 1 of 3 dialog box is displayed. To accept the default selections to analyze the data in a Microsoft Office Excel list or database and to create a PivotTable, click Next.
   c. The PivotTable and PivotChart Wizard - Step 2 of 3 is displayed. With *Database* already entered in the *Range* box, click Next.
   d. The PivotTable and PivotChart Wizard - Step 3 of 3 dialog box is displayed. The default option is to put the PivotTable on a new worksheet, which is fine. Click Finish.

e. The PivotTable diagram and PivotTable toolbar are displayed. Double-click the *Sheet1* tab, type **PivotTable**, and then press Enter.

f. Create a custom header for the *PivotTable* worksheet that displays your name at the left margin and the file name at the right margin.

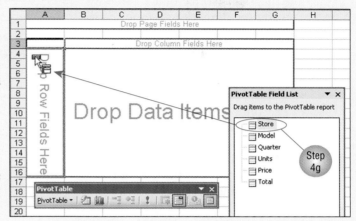

g. Drag the Store field button from the PivotTable Field List box to the *Drop Row Fields Here* area of the PivotTable diagram.

h. Drag the Model field button from the PivotTable Field List box to the *Drop Column Fields Here* area of the PivotTable diagram.

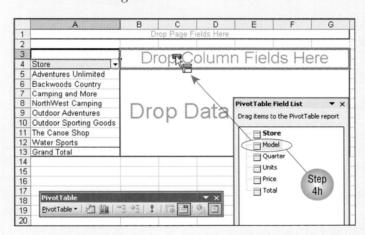

i. Drag the Units field button from the PivotTable Field List box to the *Drop Data Items Here* area of the PivotTable diagram.

5. The PivotTable is displayed on the worksheet. The PivotTable summarizes how many units of each model were ordered by each store. Grand totals for the total number of units that were ordered by each store and the total number units that were sold of each model are also displayed. Print the worksheet.

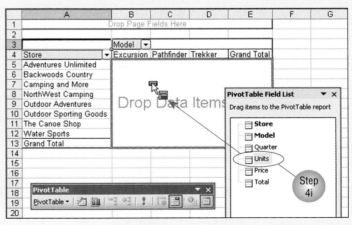

6. You want to rearrange the PivotTable so that you see the data as a summarized list. Complete the following steps to rearrange the PivotTable:

a. Move the mouse pointer over the Model field button in the PivotTable diagram. Notice that the mouse pointer changes to a four-headed arrow.

b. Click and drag the Model field button until it is under the Store field button. The models are summarized in the first column, the stores in the second, and the totals in the third. Print the worksheet.

c. Click the Store field button on the PivotTable diagram and drag it over the Model field button on the PivotTable diagram. Now the stores are summarized in the first column and the models in the second. Print the worksheet.

d. Now you want to display only the units sold of the Excursion model. Click the down-pointing arrow to the right of the Model field button.

e. Click the *Pathfinder* and *Trekker* check boxes so that they are no longer selected.

f. Click OK. The figure displayed now represents only the units sold of the Excursion model.

g. Click the down-pointing arrow to the right of the Model field button.

h. Click the *Pathfinder* check box and the *Trekker* check box so that they are selected. Click OK.

7. You can filter data in the PivotTable by dragging a field button to the *Drop Page Fields Here* area of the PivotTable diagram. Using a page field allows you to display the data for a single item at a time. Complete the following steps to use a page field:

a. Drag the Model button from the PivotTable diagram to the *Drop Page Fields Here* area of the PivotTable diagram.

b. Now the PivotTable is displaying the total for all the models. Click the down-pointing arrow to the right of the cell that has *(All)* entered in it and then click *Pathfinder*.

c. Click OK. Now the PivotTable is displaying the total number of Pathfinders ordered by each store.

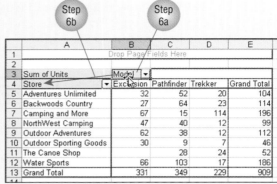

Step 6b   Step 6a

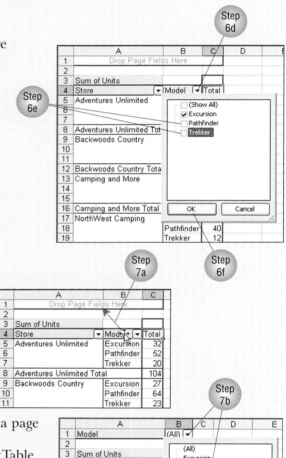

Step 6d

Step 6e

Step 7a   Step 6f

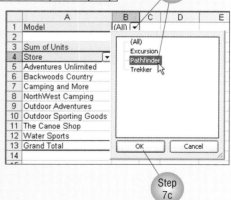

Step 7b

Step 7c

EXCEL

d. Click the down-pointing arrow to the right of the cell that now has *Pathfinder* entered in it and select *Excursion*. Click OK. Now the PivotTable is displaying the total number of Excursions ordered by each store.

e. Click the down-pointing arrow to the right of the cell that now has *Excursion* entered in it, select *(All)*, and then click OK.

8. The PivotTable you have worked with so far has summarized the number of units sold. More than one field can be summarized at a time. Complete the following steps to add a second field to be summarized:

a. The Data Items area of the PivotTable now lists the total number of units ordered by each store. Click and drag the Total field button from the PivotTable Field List box to the cell under the *Total* column heading.

b. A summary for both the total number of units each store ordered and the total cost for all the units is now displayed. Print the worksheet.

c. Drag the Data field button on the PivotTable so that it is under the Store field button on the PivotTable.

d. Print the worksheet.

9. Save the worksheet with the same name (**eec5x01**). You are going to use this worksheet in Exercise 2.

10. Close the worksheet.

Step 8a

	A	B	C	D	E	F
1	Model	(All)				
2						
3	Sum of Units					
4	Store	Total				
5	Adventures Unlimited	104				
6	Backwoods Country	114				
7	Camping and More	196				
8	NorthWest Camping	99				
9	Outdoor Adventures	112				
10	Outdoor Sporting Goods	46				
11	The Canoe Shop	52				
12	Water Sports	186				
13	Grand Total	909				

PivotTable Field List
Drag items to the PivotTable report
- Store
- Model
- Quarter
- Units
- Price
- Total

Add To   Row Area

Step 8c

	A	B	C
1	Model	(All)	
2			
3	Store	Data	Total
4	Adventures Unlimited	Sum of Units	104
5		Sum of Total	105456
6	Backwoods Country	Sum of Units	114
7		Sum of Total	119446
8	Camping and More	Sum of Units	196
9		Sum of Total	199414
10	NorthWest Camping	Sum of Units	99
11		Sum of Total	92261
12	Outdoor Adventures	Sum of Units	112
13		Sum of Total	100148
14	Outdoor Sporting Goods	Sum of Units	46
15		Sum of Total	39104
16	The Canoe Shop	Sum of Units	52
17		Sum of Total	60948
18	Water Sports	Sum of Units	186
19		Sum of Total	183544
20	Total Sum of Units		909
21	Total Sum of Total		900321

Formatting and Sorting a PivotTable

A PivotTable report can be formatted much the same way as the cells on a worksheet can be formatted. If the data is in columns, you can select all the cells belonging to a field by moving the mouse pointer to the top of the data field label. The pointer turns into a down-pointing arrow. If the data is in rows, move the mouse pointer to the left of the data field label, and the mouse pointer turns into an arrow pointing to the right. Once the mouse pointer turns into an arrow, click. All the items related to the particular data field are selected. When the items are selected, they can be formatted as you would format any other cell on the worksheet. You can also select and format a single data item.

The entire report can be formatted using the Format Report button on the PivotTable toolbar. When you click the Format Report button, the AutoFormat dialog box shown in Figure 5.6 is displayed. Click one of the report styles and then click OK.

HINT

You can use conditional formatting in a PivotTable Report, but you cannot use data validation.

Format Report

FIGURE

5.6 **The AutoFormat Dialog Box**

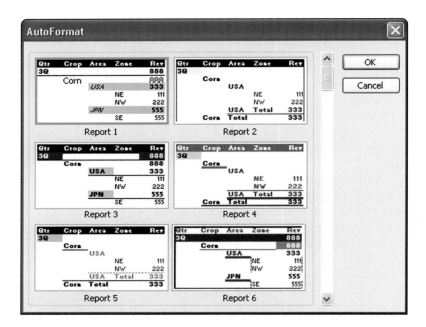

If you need to sort or change the order of items, you can manually move them. To move an item, drag the border of the item. As you drag, an I-shaped marker shows you the location of the item you are dragging. When you reach the location you want, release the mouse button and the item will appear in its new location.

Sort the Items in a Field in a PivotTable Report
1. Double-click a field button on the PivotTable.
2. Click Advanced.

You can also control how the items in a field are sorted. To sort items in a field in ascending or descending order, first click the field on the PivotTable report to be sorted and then click the down-pointing arrow to the right of the PivotTable button on the PivotTable toolbar. *The Sort and Top 10* option is on the PivotTable drop-down menu, as shown in Figure 5.7. Click this option and the PivotTable Sort and Top 10 dialog box, shown in Figure 5.8, is displayed. If the *Sort and Top 10* option is not displayed on the PivotTable toolbar, click the Toolbar Options drop-down list button at the right end of the toolbar, click Add or Remove Buttons and then point to PivotTable. Click *Sort and Top 10*. When *Manual* is selected in the *AutoSort options* section, you can manually move the items to the desired order. The *Ascending* option sorts the items in ascending order, and the *Descending* option sorts the items in descending order.

5.7 *The PivotTable Drop-Down Menu*

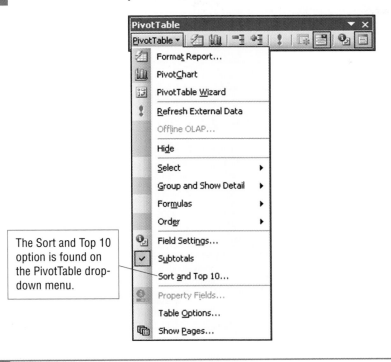

The Sort and Top 10 option is found on the PivotTable drop-down menu.

5.8 *PivotTable Sort and Top 10 Dialog Box*

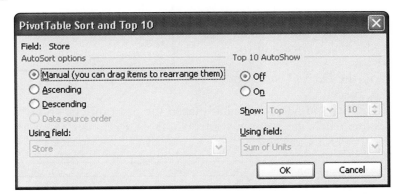

exercise 2

FORMATTING A PIVOTTABLE REPORT

1. Open **eec5x01**. You created this worksheet in Exercise 1.
2. Save the worksheet using the Save As command and name it **eec5x02**. If necessary, edit the custom header so that the file name is displayed at the right margin.
3. If necessary, click the *PivotTable* worksheet tab.
4. Numbers from the *Total* field need to be formatted as currency. First you want to arrange the PivotTable report so that those numbers are displayed in columns by themselves. Complete the following steps to arrange the layout of the PivotTable report so the numbers that need to be formatted as currency are displayed in individual columns:

a. Drag the Data field button in cell A3 to cell C3.
b. Drag the Model page field button in cell A1 to the Data field button in cell B3.

Step 4a table:

	A	B	C
1	Model	(All) ▼	
2			
3	Data ✛ ▼	Store ▼	Total
4	Sum of Units	Adventures Unlimited	104
5		Backwoods Country	114
6		Camping and More	196
		NorthWest Camping	99
		Outdoor Adventures	112
		Outdoor Sporting Goods	46
		The Canoe Shop	52
		Water Sports	186
		Adventures Unlimited	105456
		Backwoods Country	119446
		Camping and More	199414
		NorthWest Camping	92261
		Outdoor Adventures	100148
		Outdoor Sporting Goods	39104
		The Canoe Shop	60948
		Water Sports	183544
	n of Units		909
21	Total Sum of Total		900321

Step 4b table:

	A	B	C
1	Model ✛	(All) ▼	
2			
3		Data ▼	
4	Store ▼	Sum of Units	Sum of Total
5	Adventures Unlimited	104	105456
6	Backwoods Country	114	119446
7	Camping and More	196	199414
8	NorthWest Camping	99	92261
9	Outdoor Adventures	112	100148
10	Outdoor Sporting Goods	46	39104
11	The Canoe Shop	52	60948
12	Water Sports	186	183544
13	Grand Total	909	900321

5. Complete the following steps to format the numbers from the *Total* field as currency:
   a. Click the *Sum of Total* field in cell C5.
   b. Right-click the Sum of Total field in cell C5 and then click Field Settings at the shortcut menu.
   c. At the PivotTable Field dialog box, click the Number button.
   d. The Format Cells dialog box is displayed. Click *Currency* in the *Category* list.
   e. Enter 0 in the *Decimal places* box.
   f. Click OK twice.

PivotTable Field dialog box:
Source field: Total
Name: Sum of Total
Summarize by: Sum / Count / Average / Max / Min / Product / Count Nums
Buttons: OK, Cancel, Hide, Number..., Options >> (Step 5c)

6. Since the Camping and More store has placed the most orders, you would like to keep track of this one particular store in your PivotTable. Complete the following steps to format the entries for Camping and More:
   a. Select row 8 in the PivotTable report.
   b. Click the down-pointing arrow to the right of the Fill Color button. Click the pale blue color, the sixth option from the left in the fifth row.

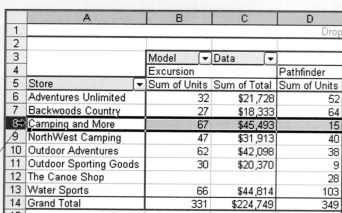

	A	B	C	D
1				Drop
2				
3		Model ▼	Data ▼	
4		Excursion		Pathfinder
5	Store ▼	Sum of Units	Sum of Total	Sum of Units
6	Adventures Unlimited	32	$21,728	52
7	Backwoods Country	27	$18,333	64
8	Camping and More	67	$45,493	15
9	NorthWest Camping	47	$31,913	40
10	Outdoor Adventures	62	$42,098	38
11	Outdoor Sporting Goods	30	$20,370	9
12	The Canoe Shop			28
13	Water Sports	66	$44,814	103
14	Grand Total	331	$224,749	349

Step 6a

c. Drag the Data field button in cell C3 to the Store field button in cell A5. The gray I-shaped pointer showing where the field will be inserted should be to the left of column A. Notice that each instance of Camping and More is highlighted in blue and that all the dollar amounts are still formatted as currency.

	A	B	C	D	E	F
1				Drop Page Fields Here		
2						
3		Model ▼	Data ▼			
4		Excursion		Pathfinder		Trekker
5	Store ▼	Sum of Units	Sum of Total	Sum of Units	Sum of Total	Sum of Unit
6	Adventure Unlimited	32	$21,728	52	$59,748	2
7	Backwoods Country	27	$18,333	64	$73,536	2
8	Camping and More	67	$45,493	15	$17,235	11
9	NorthWest Camping	47	$31,913	40	$45,960	1
10	Outdoor Adventures	62	$42,098	38	$43,662	1
11	Outdoor Sporting Goods	30	$20,370	9	$10,341	
12	The Canoe Shop			28	$32,172	2
13	Water Sports	66	$44,814	103	$118,347	1
14	Grand Total	331	$224,749	349	$401,001	22

Step 6c

d. Print the *PivotTable* worksheet.
7. Save the worksheet with the same name (**eec5x02**). You are going to use this worksheet in Exercise 3.
8. Close the worksheet.

exercise 3

SORTING A PIVOTTABLE REPORT AND FILTERING A PIVOTTABLE REPORT

1. Open **eec5x02**. You created this worksheet in Exercise 2.
2. Save the worksheet using the Save As command and name it **eec5x03**. If necessary, edit the custom header so that the file name is displayed at the right margin.
3. If necessary, click the *PivotTable* worksheet tab.
4. You want the models displayed in order from the model that sold the most number of units to the model that sold the least number of units. That order would be Pathfinder, Excursion, and Trekker. Complete the following steps to change the order in which the models are displayed:
   a. Click cell C4.

b. Drag the right border of cell C4 until the gray border line is between the *Pathfinder* and *Trekker* columns.

5. Now you want to sort the report so that the stores are listed in descending order according to their grand totals. Complete the following steps to sort the entire table:

a. Right-click cell B4, the Store field button, and then click Field Settings at the shortcut menu.

b. At the Pivot Table Field dialog box, click the Advanced button.

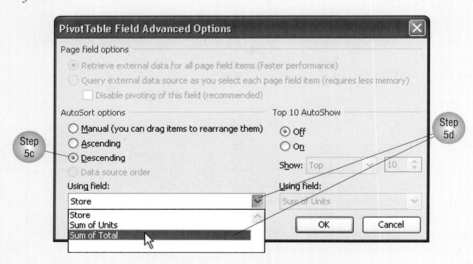

	C	D	E	F
rop Page Fields Here				
		Model ▼	D4:D22	
▼	Excursion	Pathfinder	Trekker	Grand Total
nlimited	32	52	20	104
country	27	64	23	114
More	67	15	114	196
amping	47	40	12	99
ntures	62	38	12	112
ting Goods	30	9	7	46
hop		28	24	52
	66	103	17	186

c. The PivotTable Field Advanced Options dialog box appears. In the *AutoSort options* section, click *Descending*.

d. Click the down-pointing arrow to the right of the *Using field* box and then click *Sum of Total*.

e. Click OK twice to close both dialog boxes.

6. Now you want to display the top four stores according to the units ordered. Complete the following steps to filter the report:

a. Click cell B4, the Store field button.

b. Click the Field Settings button on the PivotTable toolbar and then click the Advanced button.

EXCEL

c. The PivotTable Field Advanced Options dialog box appears. In the *Top 10 AutoShow* section, click *On*.

d. Make sure *Top* is selected in the first *Show* box. In the second *Show* box, enter 4.

e. Make sure *Sum of Units* is selected in the *Using field* box in the *Top 10 AutoShow* section.

PivotTable Field Advanced Options

Page field options
- ◉ Retrieve external data for all page field items (faster performance)
- ◯ Query external data source as you select each page field item (requires less memory)
  - ☐ Disable pivoting of this field (recommended)

AutoSort options
- ◯ Manual (you can drag items to rearrange them)
- ◯ Ascending
- ◉ Descending
- ◯ Data source order

Using field:
| Sum of Total ▾ |

Top 10 AutoShow
- ◯ Off
- ◉ On

Show: | Top ▾ | 4 ▴▾ |

Using field:
| Sum of Units ▾ |

[OK] [Cancel]

Step 6c

Step 6d

Step 6e

Step 6f

f. Click OK twice to close both dialog boxes.

g. Only the top four stores are displayed. Notice that the Total Sum of Units, Total Sum of Total, and Grand Total reflect only the orders from these top four stores.

7. Print the *PivotTable* worksheet.

8. Turn the filter off by double-clicking cell B4, the Store field button, clicking the Advanced button, and in the AutoSort *options* section, clicking *Manual*. In the *Top 10 AutoShow* section, click *Off*. Click OK twice to close both dialog boxes.

9. Save the worksheet with the same name (**eec3x03**). You are going to use this worksheet in Exercise 4.

10. Close the worksheet.

Managing a PivotTable Report

If PivotTable reports contain long lists of items, reading the information in them may become difficult. On the PivotTable toolbar there is a Hide Detail button and a Show Detail button. If the Hide Detail button or the Show Detail button is not displayed on the PivotTable toolbar, click the Toolbar Options drop-down list button at the right end of the toolbar, click Add or Remove Buttons, and then point to PivotTable. Click Hide Detail or Show Detail. Hiding details for items in a PivotTable report can make the report easier to read. To hide details, click the appropriate field button on the PivotTable report and then click the Hide Detail button on the PivotTable toolbar. To show the detail, click the field button again and then click the Show Detail button on the PivotTable toolbar.

Hiding details for items is not the same as filtering items. There are two ways to filter items: by clicking the down-pointing arrow to the right of the field button on the PivotTable report and selecting the fields to be displayed, and by using a page field. When a list is filtered, the report assumes the items that are not displayed are not a part of the report. Therefore, they are not included in any of the totals. When you hide details, the report assumes the items that are hidden are still a part of the report, so even though the individual items are not displayed in the report, their numbers are still included in the totals.

At times it may be useful to see exactly which cells from the original list went into making a particular value in the report. To see the cells from the list that go

Hide Detail   Show Detail

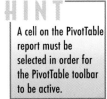

HINT

A cell on the PivotTable report must be selected in order for the PivotTable toolbar to be active.

into making a value in the report, double-click the cell containing the value you want to check. The appropriate rows from the original list are displayed.

You can remove subtotals and grand totals from a PivotTable report. To remove a subtotal, double-click the appropriate field button. The PivotTable Field dialog box shown in Figure 5.9 is displayed. Select *None* if the subtotals are not to be displayed. To remove grand totals from a report, right-click any cell in the PivotTable report and then click Table Options on the shortcut menu. The PivotTable Options dialog box shown in Figure 5.10 is displayed. On this dialog box there is a selection for *Grand totals for columns* and one for *Grand totals for rows*. If the grand totals are displayed in columns, make sure the check box for the *Grand totals for columns* option is not selected. If the grand totals are displayed in rows, make sure the check box for the *Grand totals for rows* option is not selected. Click OK.

If formatting is lost when you change the layout of a PivotTable report, right-click any cell in the report and then click Table Options from the shortcut menu. Make sure the *Preserve formatting* check box is selected. Changes to cell borders are not retained when you change the layout of a PivotTable report.

QUICK STEPS

Remove Subtotals from a PivotTable Report
1. Double-click a field button on the PivotTable.
2. Click *None* in the *Subtotals* section.

FIGURE

5.9 *The PivotTable Field Dialog Box*

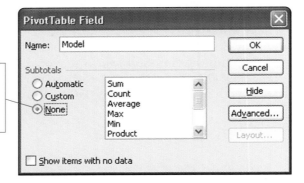

If the subtotals are not to be displayed in a PivotTable report, select *None*.

FIGURE

5.10 *The PivotTable Options Dialog Box*

If the grand totals are not to be displayed in a PivotTable report, the *Grand totals* check boxes should not be selected.

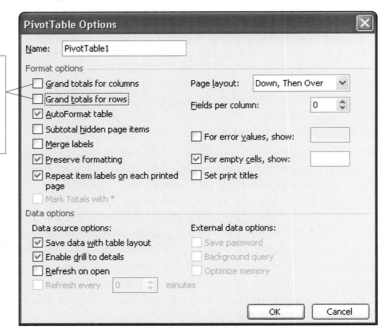

QUICK STEPS

Remove Grand Totals from a PivotTable Report
1. Right-click a cell in the PivotTable report.
2. Click Table Options.
3. Deselect the Grand totals check boxes.

You can manage the layout of the PivotTable report using the PivotTable Wizard. To do so, click the PivotTable and PivotChart Report button on the PivotTable toolbar. The PivotTable and PivotChart Wizard - Step 3 of 3 dialog box is displayed, as in Figure 5.4. Click the Layout button. The PivotTable and PivotChart Wizard - Layout dialog box as shown in Figure 5.11 is displayed. You can rearrange the layout of the PivotTable report by dragging the field buttons on the right side of the dialog box to the PivotTable diagram in the middle of the dialog box. To remove a field from the PivotTable, drag the field button off the PivotTable diagram. When you have finished rearranging the report, click OK. The PivotTable and PivotChart Wizard - Step 3 of 3 dialog box is displayed again. Click Finish.

FIGURE

5.11 *The PivotTable and Pivot Chart Wizard – Layout Dialog Box*

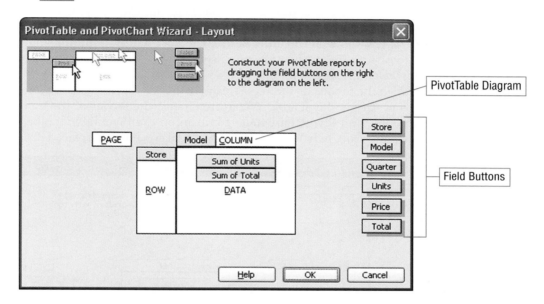

exercise 4

HIDING DETAIL IN A PIVOTTABLE REPORT, CHANGING THE LAYOUT, AND REMOVING SUBTOTALS AND GRAND TOTALS

1. Open **eec5x03**. You created this worksheet in Exercise 3.
2. Save the worksheet using the Save As command and name it **eec5x04**.
3. If necessary, click the *PivotTable* worksheet tab.
4. If necessary, edit the custom header so that the file name is displayed at the right margin.
5. Rearrange the layout of the PivotTable report by dragging the Model field button in cell C3 to the Data field button in cell A4. The gray border line should be to the left of column A.

Step 5

	A	B	C	D	E	F
1		Drop Page Fields Here				
2						
3			Model ▾			
4	Data ▾	Store ▾	Excursion	Pathfinder	Trekker	Grand Total
5	Sum of Units	Adventures Unlimited	32	52	20	104
6		Backwoods Country	27	64	23	114
7		Camping and More	67	15	114	196
8		NorthWest Camping	47	40	12	99
9		Outdoor Adventures	62	38	12	112
10		Outdoor Sporting Goods	30	9	7	46

6. You want to compare the orders for each model, but it is difficult to do that with all the stores listed. Complete the following steps to hide the detail:
   a. Click the Model field button in cell A3.
   b. Click the Hide Detail button on the PivotTable toolbar. Only the figures for the three models are displayed.
   c. Print the *PivotTable* worksheet.
   d. Next you want to show the details for the Excursion model only. Click cell A6.
   e. Click the Show Detail button on the PivotTable toolbar. The details for the Excursion model only are displayed.
   f. Display all the detail by clicking the Model field button in cell A3 and then clicking the Show Detail button on the PivotTable toolbar.
7. Find the cell that displays the total number of units of the Trekker model ordered by the store Camping and More. The number is considerably higher than all the other orders, and you want to see the cells in the source data that make up this value. Complete the following steps to see the values from the source data that this number summarizes:
   a. Double-click the cell showing the units of Trekkers ordered by Camping and More. The values from the data source are displayed.
   b. Click the *PivotTable* worksheet tab to return to the PivotTable report.
8. You want to rearrange the layout of the report using the PivotTable Wizard. Complete the following steps to use the PivotTable Wizard to change the layout of the report:
   a. Click the PivotTable and PivotChart Report button on the PivotTable toolbar.
   b. The PivotTable and PivotChart Wizard - Step 3 of 3 dialog box is displayed. Click the Layout button.
   c. The PivotTable and PivotChart Wizard - Layout dialog box is displayed. Drag the Quarter button to the COLUMN area on the PivotTable diagram.

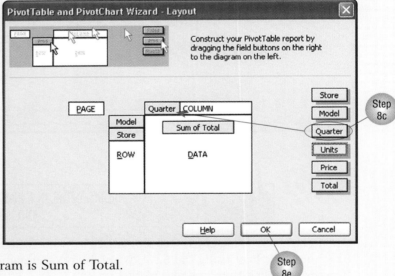

   d. Drag the Sum of Units field button off the PivotTable. The only button that should be in the DATA area on the PivotTable diagram is Sum of Total.
   e. Click OK.
   f. Click Finish.
9. Complete the following steps to remove the subtotals and the grand totals from the report:
   a. Double-click the Model field button in cell A4.
   b. The PivotTable Field dialog box is displayed. In the *Subtotals* area, click the *None* option.
   c. Click OK.

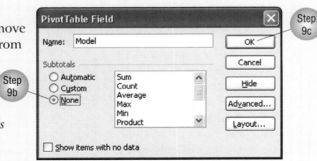

d. Right-click any cell in the PivotTable report.
e. Click Table Options on the shortcut menu.
f. The PivotTable Options dialog box is displayed. Click the check box next to *Grand totals for columns* and the check box next to *Grand totals for rows* to remove the check marks.
g. Click OK.

10. Print the *PivotTable* worksheet.

11. Complete the following steps to display the subtotals and grand totals:
    a. Double-click the Model field button in cell A4.
    b. In the *Subtotals* section, click the *Automatic* option and then click OK.
    c. Right-click any cell in the PivotTable report and then click Table Options on the shortcut menu.
    d. Click the check box next to *Grand totals for columns* and the check box next to *Grand totals for rows* to insert checkmarks and then click OK.

12. Save the worksheet with the same name (**eec5x04**). You are going to use this worksheet in Exercise 5.

13. Close the worksheet.

exercise 5

FORMATTING A PIVOTTABLE REPORT USING AUTOFORMAT

1. Open **eec5x04**. You created this worksheet in Exercise 4.
2. Save the worksheet using the Save As command and name it **eec5x05**. If necessary, edit the custom header so that the file name is displayed at the right margin.
3. If necessary, click the *PivotTable* worksheet tab.
4. To format the entire PivotTable report using AutoFormat, complete the following steps:
   a. Click the Format Report button on the PivotTable toolbar.
   b. At the AutoFormat dialog box, click the option for Report 4 and then click OK.

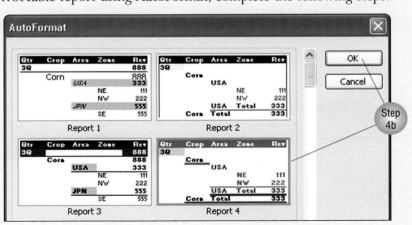

d. Use the Page Break Preview command to adjust the layout so that the first and second quarter figures print on the first page and the third quarter figures, fourth quarter figures, and grand totals print on the second page.
   e. Return to Normal view.
5. Print the *PivotTable* worksheet.
6. Complete the following steps to change the layout of the PivotTable report and to select a different formatting style:
   a. Click the PivotTable and PivotChart Report button on the PivotTable toolbar.
   b. Click the Layout button.
   c. Drag the Model field button from the ROW area of the PivotTable diagram to the COLUMN area of the PivotTable diagram.
   d. Click OK.
   e. Click Finish.
   f. Click the Format Report button on the PivotTable toolbar.
   g. Scroll down to find the Table 6 option and then click the Table 6 option.
   h. Click OK.
7. Print the *PivotTable* worksheet.
8. Save the worksheet with the same name (**eec5x05**), then close the worksheet.

[AutoFormat dialog box showing Table 3, Table 4, Table 5, and Table 6 layouts, with Step 6h pointing to OK button and Step 6g pointing to Table 6]

Creating PivotChart Reports

Chart Wizard

A PivotChart report is created from a PivotTable report. You can create the PivotChart report from scratch using the PivotTable and PivotChart Report Wizard. A PivotTable report will be created when you create the PivotChart report. Or you can create a PivotChart report based on an existing PivotTable report by clicking the Chart Wizard button on the Standard toolbar. Row fields in the PivotTable report become category fields in the PivotChart report. Column fields in the PivotTable report become series fields in the PivotChart report. Since a PivotChart report is associated with a PivotTable report, changes made to the PivotTable report are reflected in the PivotChart report and vice versa.

QUICK STEPS

Create a PivotChart Report
1. Click Data.
2. Click PivotTable. and PivotChart Report.

To create a PivotChart report from scratch, name the Excel list that is going to be used as the data source *Database*. Click Data and then click PivotTable and PivotChart Report. The PivotTable and PivotChart Wizard - Step 1 of 3 dialog box is displayed. As shown in Figure 5.12, you need to select *PivotChart (with PivotTable)* to create a PivotChart report. Click Next. The PivotTable and PivotChart Wizard - Step 2 of 3 dialog box will be displayed. Excel will automatically enter the *Database* range as the data source. Click Next. The PivotTable and PivotChart Wizard - Step 3 of 3 dialog box is displayed. Since PivotCharts must be linked to a PivotTable, Excel is going to automatically create a PivotTable. Specify whether you want the PivotTable on a new worksheet or on the existing worksheet. The PivotChart will be created on a new worksheet. Click Finish.

5.12 *Creating a PivotChart Report Using the PivotTable and PivotChart Wizard*

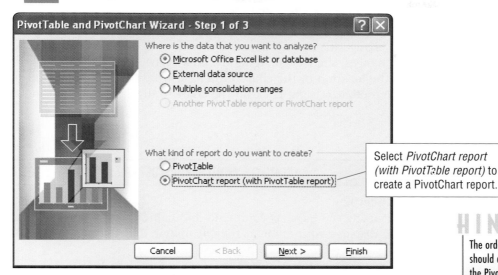

Select *PivotChart report (with PivotTable report)* to create a PivotChart report.

The PivotChart diagram shown in Figure 5.13 is displayed. From the PivotTable toolbar, drag the field buttons for the fields you want to display in categories to the Drop Category Fields Here area of the diagram. From the PivotTable toolbar, drag the fields to be displayed in series to the Drop Series Fields Here area of the PivotChart diagram. From the PivotTable toolbar, drag the fields containing the data to be compared or measured to the Drop Data Items Here area of the PivotTable diagram. You can rearrange the fields by dragging them from one area to another. Remove a field by dragging it off the PivotTable diagram.

HINT

The order in which you should drag fields to the PivotChart diagram is fields in the series, category, and page areas first. Drag fields to the data area last. Using this order helps to prevent delays when dropping fields from the PivotTable toolbar to the PivotChart diagram.

5.13 *A PivotChart Diagram*

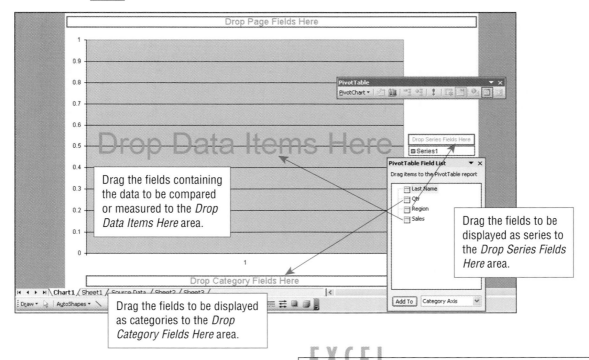

Drag the fields containing the data to be compared or measured to the *Drop Data Items Here* area.

Drag the fields to be displayed as series to the *Drop Series Fields Here* area.

Drag the fields to be displayed as categories to the *Drop Category Fields Here* area.

To create a PivotChart report from an existing PivotTable report, click any cell in the PivotTable report. Click the Chart Wizard button on the Standard toolbar. Excel automatically creates a stacked column chart on a new worksheet named Chart. Row fields in the PivotTable report are the category fields in the PivotChart report. Column fields in the PivotTable report are the series fields in the PivotChart report. To change the chart type, click the Chart Type button on the Chart toolbar. To make changes, such as changing the chart type, adding or editing titles, or changing the location of the chart, either click the Chart Wizard button on the PivotTable toolbar or right-click on the chart to display a shortcut menu.

exercise 6

CREATING A PIVOTCHART REPORT FOR AN EXISTING PIVOTTABLE REPORT

1. Open **ExcelWorksheet02**.
2. Save the worksheet using the Save As command and name it **eec5x06**. Create a custom header that displays your name at the left margin and the file name at the right margin.
3. Click the *PivotTable* worksheet tab, if necessary.
4. You want to make a chart representing the total sales amount of each model of canoe for all the stores in each quarter. Complete the following steps to edit the PivotTable Report so that it displays the figures as you need them:
   a. Click the PivotTable and PivotChart Report button.
   b. Click the Layout button.
   c. Drag the Sum of Units button off the DATA area. The only button that should be in the DATA area is Sum of Total.
   d. Drag the Store button from the ROW area to the PAGE area.
   e. Drag the Quarter button to the ROW area.
   f. Click OK.
   g. Click Finish.
5. Complete the following steps to create a chart from this PivotTable report:
   a. Click any cell in the PivotTable report.

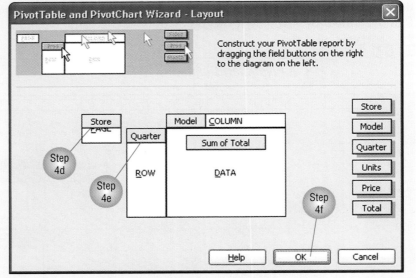

   b. Click the Chart Wizard button on the PivotTable toolbar. Excel automatically creates a stacked column chart on a chart sheet.
   c. Double-click the *Chart1* worksheet tab.
   d. Type **PivotChart** and then press Enter.
6. Create a custom header for the *PivotChart* worksheet that displays your name at the left margin and the file name at the right margin.

EXCEL

7. You want to make some changes to the PivotChart report. Complete the following steps to edit the chart:

a. Click the Chart Wizard button on the PivotTable toolbar. The Chart Wizard - Step 1 of 4 - Chart Type dialog box is displayed.

b. In the *Chart type* section, click *Line*.

c. In the *Chart sub-type* section, click the second option from the left in the second row.

d. Click Next.

e. Click in the *Chart title* box. Type **Sales by Quarter**.

f. Click in the *Category (X) axis* box. Type **Quarter**.

g. Click in the *Value (Y) axis* box. Type **Sales**.

h. Click Next.

i. Accept the default entries for the Chart Wizard - Step 4 of 4 - Chart Location dialog box. Click Finish.

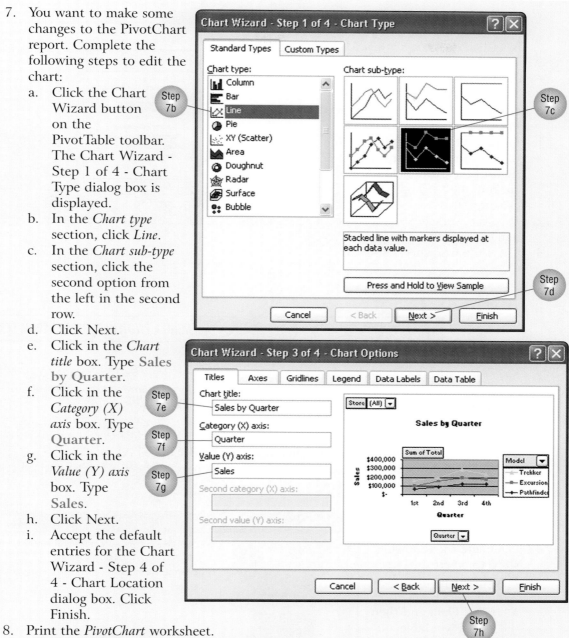

8. Print the *PivotChart* worksheet.

9. The *PivotChart* worksheet should still be displayed. Now you want to create a PivotChart report that shows the figures for the Camping and More store only. Complete the following steps to change the PivotChart report:

a. Click the down-pointing arrow to the right of the Store field button.
b. Click the *Camping and More* option.
c. Click OK.

10. Now only the figures for the store Camping and More are displayed. Print the *PivotChart* worksheet.
11. Display all the stores by clicking the down-pointing arrow to the right of the Store field button, clicking the *(All)* option, and then clicking OK.
12. Save the worksheet with the same name (**eec5x06**).
13. Close the worksheet.

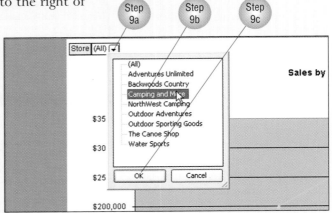

exercise 7

CREATING A PIVOTCHART REPORT FROM SCRATCH

1. Open **ExcelWorksheet03**.
2. Save the worksheet using the Save As command and name it **eec5x07**. Create a custom header that displays your name at the left margin and the file name at the right margin.
3. Complete the following steps to name the data source *Database*:
   a. Click the *Source Data* worksheet tab.
   b. Click cell A1.
   c. Hold the Shift key and double-click the right border of cell A1.
   d. Hold the Shift key and double-click the bottom border of cell A1. The entire list (A1:D81) should be selected.
   e. Click the name box.
   f. Type **Database**, then press Enter.
4. Complete the following steps to create a PivotChart report from scratch:
   a. Click Data and then click PivotTable and PivotChart Report.
   b. The PivotTable and PivotChart Wizard - Step 1 of 3 dialog box is displayed. In the *What kind of report do you want to create?* section, click the *PivotChart report (with PivotTable report)* option.
   c. Click Next.

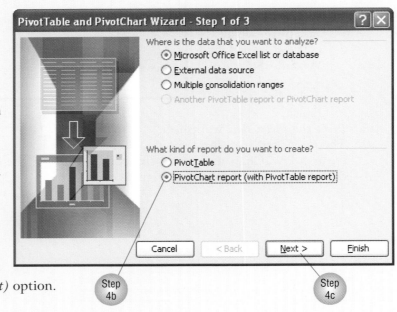

d. Excel should automatically recognize the *Database* range. Click Next.
e. Click Finish.
f. Double-click the Chart 1 sheet tab and type **PivotChart** and then press Enter.
g. Drag the Last Name button from the PivotTable Field List box to the *Drop Page Fields Here* area of the PivotChart diagram.
h. Drag the Qtr button from the PivotTable Field List box to the *Drop Series Fields Here* area of the PivotChart diagram.
i. Drag the Region button from the PivotTable Field List box to the *Drop Category Fields Here* area of the PivotChart diagram.
j. Drag the Sales button from the Field List box to the *Drop Data Items Here* area of the PivotChart diagram.

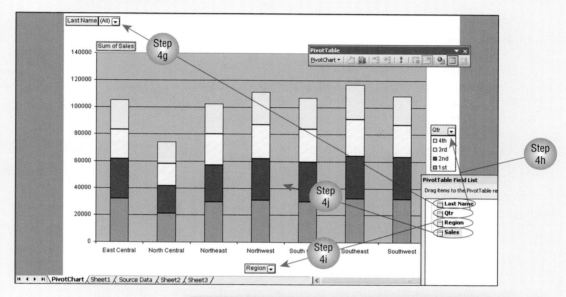

k. Create a custom header for the PivotChart worksheet that displays your name at the left margin and the file name at the right margin.

5. Complete the following steps to edit the PivotChart report:
a. Click the Chart Wizard button on the PivotTable toolbar.
b. Select the first option in the *Chart sub-type* area.
c. Click Next.

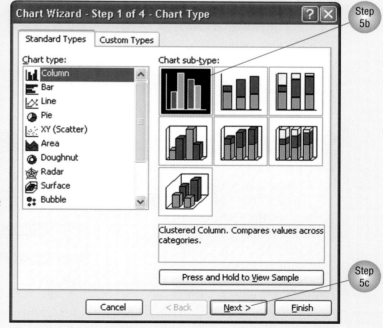

d. Click in the *Chart title* box and type **Sales by Region**.

e. Click in the *Category (X) axis* box and type **Region**.

f. Click in the *Value (Y) axis* box and type **Sales**.

g. Click Next.

h. Accept the default entries on the Chart Wizard - Step 4 of 4 Chart Location dialog box by clicking Finish.

6. If the Chart toolbar is not automatically displayed, right-click any toolbar. Click Chart on the drop-down menu that is displayed. Complete the following steps to format the PivotChart report:

a. Click the down-pointing arrow to the right of the Chart Area box, the first box on the Chart toolbar.

b. Click *Value Axis*.

c. The value axis is now selected. You want to format the numbers on the value axis as currency. Click the Format Chart Area button on the Chart toolbar.

d. The Format Axis dialog box is displayed. Click the Number tab.

e. In the *Category* list box, click *Currency*.

f. Enter **0** in the *Decimal places* box.

g. Click OK.

h. Click the down-pointing arrow to the right of the first box on the Chart toolbar.

i. Click *Category Axis*.

j. Click the Angle Counterclockwise button on the Chart toolbar.

7. Print the *PivotChart* worksheet.

8. Now you want to see just the sales figures for Levinson. Complete the following steps to display the sales figures for one sales representative:

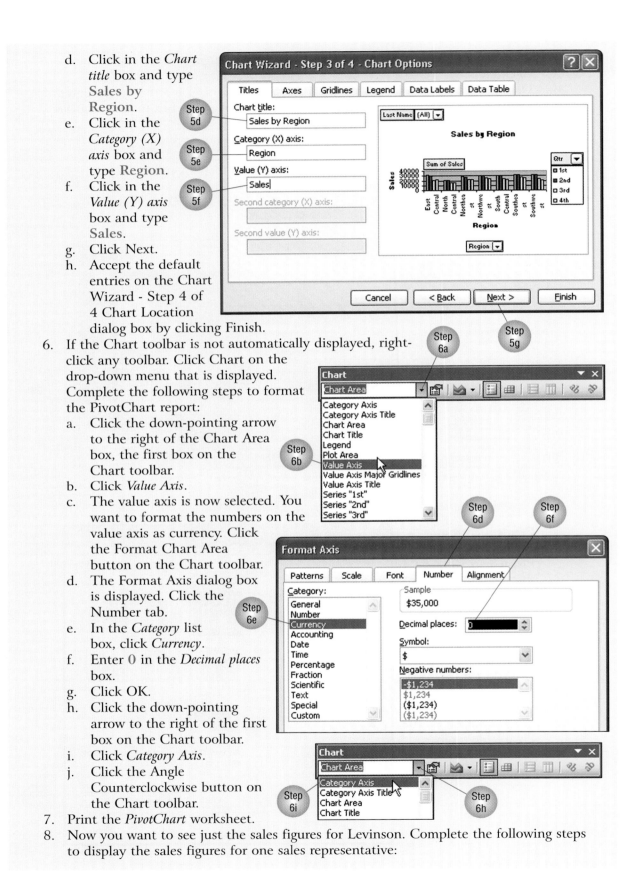

EXCEL

a.   Click the down-pointing arrow to the right of the Last Name field button.
b.   Click *Levinson, C.*
c.   Click OK.
d.   Print the *PivotChart* worksheet.
e.   Display all the sales representatives by clicking the down-pointing arrow to the right of the Last Name field button, clicking *(All)*, and clicking OK.

9.   Complete the following steps to create a pie chart that illustrates the sales for the fourth quarter:

a.   Click the down-pointing arrow to the right of the Qtr field button.
b.   Click the *1st*, *2nd*, and *3rd* check boxes so that they are no longer selected.
c.   Click OK.
d.   Click the down-pointing arrow to the right of the Chart Type button on the Chart toolbar.
e.   Click the 3-D Pie Chart option, the second option from the left in the fifth row.
f.   Click the down-pointing arrow to the right of the Chart Objects box, the first box on the Chart toolbar.
g.   Click *Series "4th."*
h.   Click the Format Data Series button on the Chart toolbar.
i.   Click the Data Labels tab on the Format Data Series dialog box.
j.   In the *Label Contains* section, click the *Category name* option.
k.   In the *Labels Contains* section, click the *Percentage* option.
l.   Click OK.
m.   Click the chart title *Sales by Region* to select it. Once the chart title is selected, place the insertion point after the *n* in *Region*. Press the spacebar once and then type **4th Quarter**.
n.   If the data label *Southwest 14%* is covered by the Sum of Sales field button, click the label to select it. When handles appear around that one data label only, click one of the borders around the label and drag it so that it is not being covered by the Sum of Sales field.

10.   Print the *PivotChart* worksheet and save it with the same name (**eec5x07**).
11.   Close the worksheet.

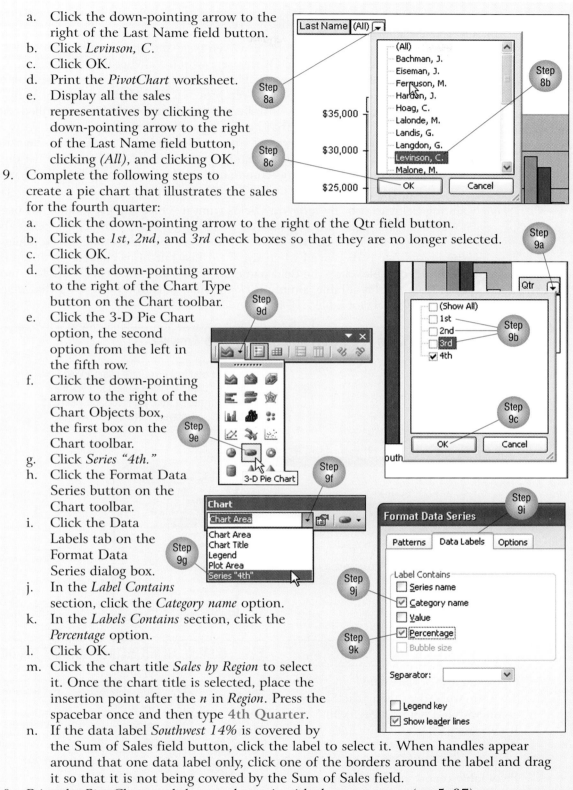

Creating Interactive PivotTables for the Web

A PivotTable report can be saved as a Web page and then published to a public location such as a Web server. Other users who have Microsoft Office Web Components installed can view the PivotTable report using version 4.01 or later of the Microsoft Internet Explorer Web browser. The Microsoft Office Web components are automatically installed when Microsoft Office is installed. An interactive PivotTable report that has been published in a public location is called a PivotTable list. Users can interact with a PivotTable list in many of the same ways as PivotTable reports can be manipulated in Excel. A PivotTable list on a Web page includes features and commands similar to an Excel PivotTable report.

HINT

When you place a PivotTable report on the Web it is called a PivotTable list.

One of the ways you can interact with a PivotTable list on a Web page is by adding fields to it or by removing fields from it. Once the PivotTable has been saved as a Web page and is displayed in a Web browser, a toolbar appears above it. As shown in Figure 5.14, a list of all the available fields that can be added to the PivotTable is displayed when the Field List button is clicked. To add a field to the PivotTable, click the field name in the list and then click OK. To remove a field from the PivotTable, simply click the field button representing that field and drag it off the PivotTable.

FIGURE

5.14 *Adding Fields to a PivotTable Using a Web Browser*

To add a field to a PivotTable using a Web browser, click the Field List button, click the field to be added from the PivotTable Field List box that is displayed, and then click Add to.

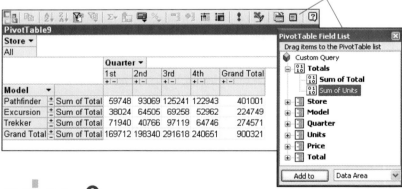

exercise 8

CREATING AN INTERACTIVE PIVOTTABLE FOR THE WEB

1. Open **ExcelWorksheet04**.
2. Save the worksheet using the Save As command and name it **eec5x08**.
3. If necessary, click the *PivotTable* worksheet tab.
4. Complete the following steps to save the PivotTable report as a Web page:
   a. Click File and then click Save as Web Page.

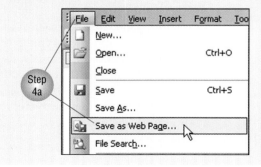

b. At the Save As dialog box, make sure *Entire Workbook* is selected.
c. Click Publish.

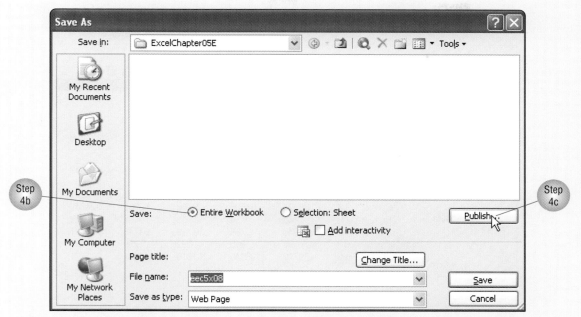

d. The Publish as Web Page dialog box is displayed. If necessary, select *Items on PivotTable* from the drop-down list for the *Choose* box.
e. Select *PivotTable* from the list box under the *Choose* box.
f. In the *Viewing options* section, click the *Add interactivity with* check box to select it.
g. If necessary, choose *PivotTable functionality* from the drop-down list for the *Add interactivity with* box.
h. Make sure the *File name* is **eec5x08.htm**.
i. Click the *Open published web page in browser* check box to select it.
j. Click Publish.

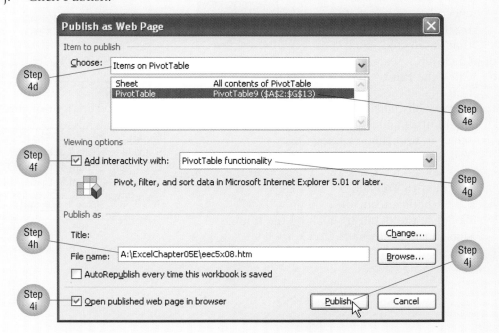

5. The PivotTable is displayed in Microsoft Internet Explorer. Complete the following steps to interact with the PivotTable as a Web page:

   a. You do not want to see the figures for the Sum of Units. Click one of the Sum of Units field buttons and drag it off the PivotTable.

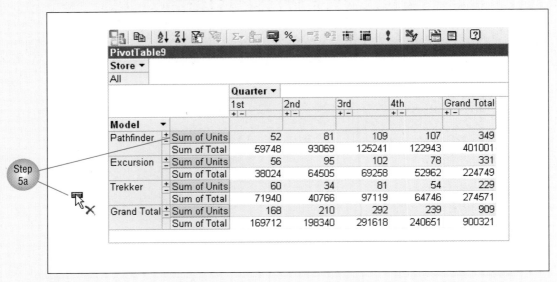

   b. You want to see the figures for the NorthWest Camping store only. Click the down-pointing arrow to the right of the Store field button.

   c. Click the *(All)* box so that it is no longer selected. Click the *NorthWest Camping* check box to select it. It should be the only box that is selected.

   d. Click OK.

   e. Click the Print button.

   f. Display all the stores by clicking the down-pointing arrow to the right of the Store field button, clicking the *(All)* check box to select it, and then clicking OK.

   g. You want to display the detail for the Trekker model. Click the plus sign in the box next to Trekker.

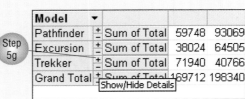

   h. Click the Print button.

   i. Collapse the detail by clicking the minus sign in the box next to Trekker.

   j. You want to put the Units back into the PivotTable list. Click the Field List button.

k. The PivotTable Field List box is displayed. Click Sum of Units and drag the item to below the first Sum of Total field button.

l. Close the PivotTable Field List box.

6. Close Microsoft Internet Explorer.

7. Save the worksheet with the same name (**eec5x08**) and close it.

PivotTable9				
Store ▾				
All				
			Quarter ▾	
			1st	2nd
			+ -	+ -
Model ▾				
Pathfinder	+	Sum of Total	59748	93
Excursion	+	Sum of Total	38024	64
Trekker	+	Sum of Total	71940	40
Grand Total	+	Sum of Total	169712	198

PivotTable Field List

Drag items to the PivotTable list

Custom Query
Totals
Sum of Total
Sum of Units
Store
Model
Quarter
Units
Price

Step 5k

Performing What-If Analysis

Excel includes a suite of commands that are sometimes called what-if analysis tools. What-if analysis is a process whereby you change the values in cells in order to see how those changes affect the outcome of formulas on the worksheet. For example, say you wanted to save $100 a month. You know what your total income is for a month and you know all the categories on which you spend money in a month—food, rent, gas, entertainment, and so on. By varying the amounts in the various categories, you can determine what it would take to have $100 left at the end of the month. What if I spent $25 dollars a month less on food? How would that affect the amount of money I have left at the end of the month? Goal Seek, Solver, and Scenario Manager are all what-if analysis tools.

Analyzing Data Using Goal Seek

Excel's Goal Seek is used to calculate a specified result by changing the value of another cell. Goal Seek adjusts the value in a specified cell until a formula dependent on that cell reaches the desired result. For example, suppose a company wanted to buy a machine costing $70,000. The company knows the interest that must be paid on the loan, and they know their payments cannot exceed $4,000. What they need to know is the period of the loan or how many payments it will take to pay off the loan. They know the goal they are seeking—paying off a $70,000 loan at a specific interest rate with monthly payments of $4,000. Goal Seek can tell them what they need to do to reach that goal—that is, how many payments they will need to make.

To use the Goal Seek command, enter the formula and corresponding values in the worksheet. Click Tools and then either wait a few seconds or click the down-pointing arrow at the bottom of the menu for the Goal Seek option to be displayed. Click Goal Seek. The Goal Seek dialog box is displayed. Enter the cell reference to the cell containing the formula in the *Set cell* box. Enter the goal you are seeking in the *To value* box. Enter the cell reference to the cell containing the value that can change in the *By changing cell* box. The Goal Seek Status dialog box is displayed. The value on the worksheet has changed to display the goal being sought after. To enter the goal into the worksheet, click OK. To cancel Goal Seek and return the original value to the worksheet, click Cancel. Practice using this feature in the following exercise.

QUICK STEPS

Use Goal Seek
Click Tools and then Goal Seek.

1. Open **ExcelWorksheet05**.
2. Save the worksheet using the Save As command and name it **eec5x09**.
3. Create a custom header that displays your name at the left margin and the file name at the right margin.
4. This worksheet keeps track of the profit the EastWest Crossroads Company makes on each item it sells through its mail-order catalog. View the item in row 16. Right now, item GG-47-1 is making only a $5.00 profit. Complete the following steps to use Goal Seek to find out how much the selling price of the Mosaic Glass Bracelet would have to be to make an $8.00 profit.
   a. Click Tools and then click Goal Seek.
   b. The Goal Seek dialog box appears. The current entry in the *Set cell* box is already selected. Type **F16**.
   c. Click the *To value* box and type **8.00**.
   d. Click the *By changing cell* box and type **C16**.
   e. Click OK.
   f. The Goal Seek Status dialog box is displayed. Click OK.

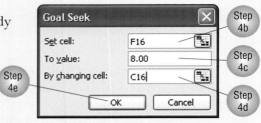

5. Scroll down to view the item in row 43. Right now item GH-82-2, the Stained Glass Lamp, has a 30% markup. Complete the following steps to use Goal Seek to find out how much the selling price would have to be if the markup is 40%:
   a. Click Tools and then click Goal Seek.
   b. The Goal Seek dialog box appears. The current entry in the *Set cell* box is already selected. Type **E43**.
   c. Click the *To value* box and type **40%**.
   d. Click the *By changing cell* box and type **C43**.
   e. Click OK.
   f. The Goal Seek Status dialog box is displayed. Click OK.

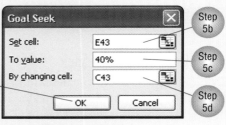

6. View the item in row 11. The unit cost of the Jakarta Drum is $65.00. Complete the following steps to use Goal Seek to find out how much that unit cost would have to decrease in order for the EastWest Crossroads Company to realize a 40% profit on the drum:
   a. Click Tools and then click Goal Seek.
   b. The Goal Seek dialog box appears. The current entry in the *Set cell* box is already selected. Type **E11**.
   c. Click the *To value* box and type **40%**.
   d. Click the *By changing cell* box and type **D11**.
   e. Click OK.
   f. The Goal Seek Status dialog box is displayed. Click OK.
7. Save the worksheet with the same name (**eec5x09**) and print it.
8. Close the worksheet.

Analyzing Data Using Solver

Businesses can always meet their objectives in a number of different ways. What businesses must determine is which way is the most efficient way, or the way that will generate the maximum profit, or the way that will optimize the use of plant facilities. The variables involved in meeting the specific objective are subject to restrictions or constraints. For example, a constraint involved in determining the optimal use of plant facilities is that the plant cannot operate more than 24 hours a day. By using Excel's Solver, you can solve problems that have multiple, interdependent variables. Excel's Goal Seek can arrive at a specific result in problems with only one changing variable. With Solver, you can arrive at a specific result in problems that have many changing variables.

Suppose a factory makes two different products using the same machine. The goal is to maximize the total net profit from these two products. The profit for each product is different. The time it takes the machine to produce each product is different. The machine can run only a certain number of hours a week. The products are shipped out at the end of each week, so the products produced in one week cannot exceed the space available for storing them in the warehouse. There is a limit on the weekly demand for one of the products. As you can see, several variables are involved: the net profit for each product, the machine time, the warehouse space, and the demand for one of the products. Each one of these variables has a constraint. The machine can run only a certain number of hours a week. The warehouse is a specific size. There is a limit to the number of one of the products that can be sold in a week. By taking into consideration all the variables and their constraints, Solver finds the optimal solution: the number of each product that should be produced in a week in order to maximize the total net profit.

To use Solver, click Tools and then click Solver. If the Solver command is not on the Tools menu, the Solver add-in needs to be installed. The Solver Parameters dialog box shown in Figure 5.15 is displayed. In the *Set Target Cell* box, enter the cell reference or name for the target cell. The target cell must contain a formula. If the target cell is to be as large as possible, click *Max*. If it is to be as small as possible, click *Min*. If it is to be a specific value, click *Value of* and enter the value in the *Value of* box. Enter a name or reference for each cell that can be adjusted to meet the target in the *By Changing Cells* box. Separate nonadjacent references using commas. If you want Solver to automatically propose the cells to be adjusted based on the target cell, click Guess. The cells to be adjusted must not contain formulas, and the target cell must be dependent on them. An adjustment to the value in a cell listed in the *By Changing Cells* box must affect the value in the target cell. Any constraints to be applied are entered in the *Subject to the Constraints* box. Once you have defined the problem in the Solver Parameters dialog box, click Solve.

QUICK STEPS

Use Solver
Click Tools and then Solver.

HINT

The target cell must be a single cell. Only one cell is optimized when using Solver.

5.15 *The Solver Parameters Dialog Box*

Solver will optimize the result of the target cell.

Solver arrives at the optimal result for the target cell by modifying the cells entered in the *By Changing Cells* box.

Solver optimizes the result of the target cell by finding a maximum value, minimum value, or a specific value.

Clicking *Guess* has Solver automatically select the cells to be changed.

The rules that Solver must follow in order to find the optimal result for the target cell are entered in the *Subject to the Constraints* box.

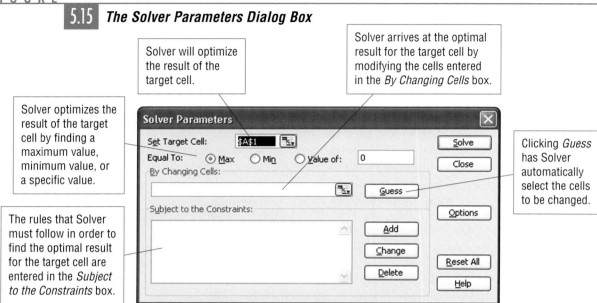

Once you click Solve, the Solver Results dialog box shown in Figure 5.16 is displayed. Click *Keep Solver Solution* to keep the solution values on the worksheet. Click *Restore Original Values* to restore the original data. The *Reports* list box allows you to select the type of report you would like to see and places each report on a separate sheet in the workbook. The Answer Report displays the target cell, the changing cells, and the constraints. The Sensitivity Report presents the detailed sensitivity information about the target cell. The Limits Report displays how much the values of the changing cells can be increased or decreased without violating the constraints of the problem.

5.16 *The Solver Results Dialog Box*

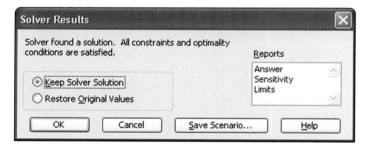

In the exercise that follows, use Problem Solver to solve a production issue for a manufacturer. Copper Clad Incorporated makes modem circuit boards for three different modem manufacturers off a single production line. The production line runs 60 hours a week. A weekly production schedule is run where the week is spent producing the three different modem circuit boards and the output is stored in a warehouse during the week. At the end of each week, the modem boards are shipped to each modem manufacturer. It takes three hours to produce 100 boxes of Board A, four hours to produce 100 boxes of Board B, and five hours to produce

100 boxes of Board C. It takes 1.5 cubic feet to store one box of Board A, 2.5 cubic feet to store one box of Board B, and 3 cubic feet to store one box of Board C. The warehouse holds, at most, 2,000 cubic feet. The net profit per box of Board A is $75. The net profit per box of Board B is $100, and the net profit per box of Board C is $150. You can sell as many boxes as you can produce in a week to the companies that buy Board A and Board B. But the company that buys Board C will never purchase more than 250 boxes a week. You want to use Solver to determine a production plan that abides by all the constraints and maximizes the total net profit.

exercise 10

DEFINING AND SOLVING A PROBLEM USING SOLVER

(Note: If Solver is not included on the Tools menu, click Tools and then Add-ins. At the Add-ins dialog box, click the Solver Add-in *check box and then click OK.)*

1. Open **ExcelWorksheet06**.
2. Save the worksheet using the Save As command and name it **eec5x10**.
3. Create a custom header that displays your name at the left margin and the file name at the right margin.
4. Look at the worksheet. The target cell, or the total net profit, is surrounded by a blue border. The changing cells, or the number of boxes produced for each modem board, are surrounded by a green border. The constraints on the variables are surrounded by a violet border. First, you are going to name some of the cells in order to make using Solver a little easier to understand. Complete the following steps to name the cells:
   a. Name cell F7 Total_Profit.
   b. Name cell G7 Total_Space.
   c. Name cell H7 Total_Hours.
   d. Name cell C11 Available_Space.
   e. Name cell C12 Max_Boxes_Board_C.
   f. Name cell C13 Available_Hours.
5. Complete the following steps to define the problem using Solver:
   a. Click Tools and then click Solver.
   b. Type Total_Profit in the *Set Target Cell* box.
   c. Make sure *Max* is selected in the *Equal To* section.
   d. Type $E$3:$E$5 in the *By Changing Cells* box.
   e. Next you must add the constraints. Click Add.

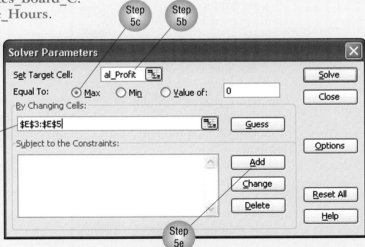

f. The Add Constraint dialog box is displayed. The first
    constraint you are going to add is that the total space
    cannot exceed the space available.
    1) Type **Total_Space** in the *Cell Reference* box.
    2) Make sure the comparison operator <= is displayed in the middle box.
    3) Type **Available_Space** in the *Constraint* box.
    4) Click Add.

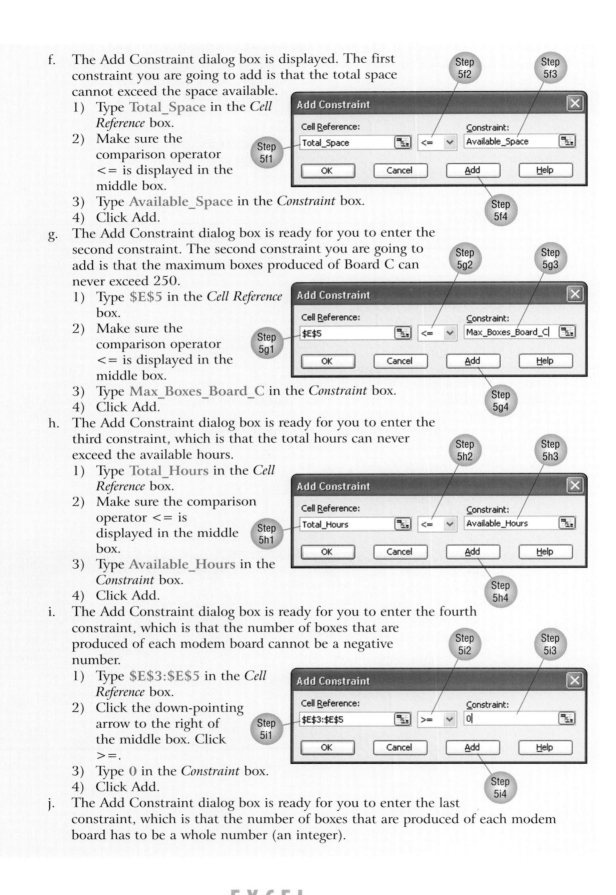

g. The Add Constraint dialog box is ready for you to enter the
    second constraint. The second constraint you are going to
    add is that the maximum boxes produced of Board C can
    never exceed 250.
    1) Type **$E$5** in the *Cell Reference* box.
    2) Make sure the comparison operator <= is displayed in the middle box.
    3) Type **Max_Boxes_Board_C** in the *Constraint* box.
    4) Click Add.

h. The Add Constraint dialog box is ready for you to enter the
    third constraint, which is that the total hours can never
    exceed the available hours.
    1) Type **Total_Hours** in the *Cell Reference* box.
    2) Make sure the comparison operator <= is displayed in the middle box.
    3) Type **Available_Hours** in the *Constraint* box.
    4) Click Add.

i. The Add Constraint dialog box is ready for you to enter the fourth
    constraint, which is that the number of boxes that are
    produced of each modem board cannot be a negative
    number.
    1) Type **$E$3:$E$5** in the *Cell Reference* box.
    2) Click the down-pointing arrow to the right of the middle box. Click >=.
    3) Type **0** in the *Constraint* box.
    4) Click Add.

j. The Add Constraint dialog box is ready for you to enter the last
    constraint, which is that the number of boxes that are produced of each modem
    board has to be a whole number (an integer).

EXCEL

1) Type $E$3:$E$5 in the *Cell Reference* box.
2) Click the down-pointing arrow to the right of the middle box. Click *int*.
3) Click OK.

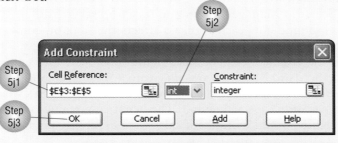

Step 5j2
Step 5j1
Step 5j3

k. The Solver Parameters dialog box is displayed again. The problem has now been defined. Click Solve.

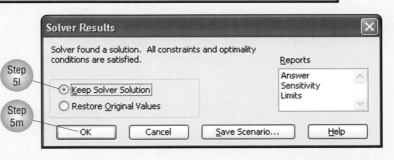

Step 5k

l. The Solver Results dialog box is displayed. Make sure *Keep Solver Solution* is selected.
m. Click OK.

6. The solution is displayed in the worksheet. The number of boxes that should be produced in order to obtain the maximum profit is displayed in cells E3, E4, and E5. Print the *ProductionPlan* worksheet.

Step 5l
Step 5m

7. Complete the following steps to generate an Answer Report:
   a. Click Tools and then click Solver.
   b. Click Solve.
   c. Click *Answer* in the *Reports* list.
   d. Click OK.
   e. Click the *Answer Report 1* worksheet tab.
   f. Create a custom header that displays your name at the left margin and the file name at the right margin.
   g. Print the *Answer Report 1* worksheet.

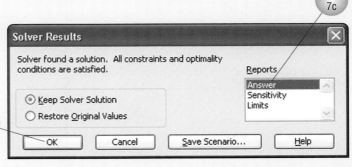

Step 7c
Step 7d

8. Save the workbook with the same name (**eec5x10**) and close it.

Creating Scenarios

Goal Seek and Solver provide one specific answer to a specific question. There are times, however, when examining several different answers to a question would be useful. Scenario Manager allows you to set up several different scenarios. Then you can examine how each scenario affects the final outcome. A company trying to establish a budget for the upcoming year does not know, for example, what the sales for the year will be. The sales figures obviously affect the rest of the budget. With the Scenario Manager you can create a "best case" and a "worst case" scenario. The best case scenario would show what the budget figures would look like if sales for the year were especially good. The worst case scenario would show what the budget figures would look like if sales were especially poor.

To create a scenario, click Tools and then either wait for a few seconds or click the down-pointing arrow at the bottom of the menu and click Scenarios. The Scenario Manager dialog box is displayed. Click the Add button. The Add Scenario dialog box is displayed.

exercise 11

CREATING SCENARIOS

1. Open **ExcelWorksheet07**.
2. Save the worksheet using the Save As command and name it **eec5x11**.
3. Create a custom header that displays your name at the left margin and the file name at the right margin.
4. Case 'N Crate, a company that manufactures wooden boxes and crates, is working on a budget for the upcoming year. Expenses for the year—rent, utilities, and general administrative—are known. What is not known is how much the company will earn in gross revenues and how much the company will spend on the cost of goods sold. Complete the following steps to name the cells with which you will be working:
   a. Name cell B5 **Revenue**.
   b. Name cell B6 **Goods**.
5. Complete the following steps to create a scenario that calculates an outcome for the worst case, which is a low gross revenue and a high cost of goods sold:
   a. Click Tools and then click Scenarios.
   b. At the Scenario Manager dialog box, click Add.

c. The Add Scenario dialog box is displayed. Type **Worst Case** in the *Scenario name* box.

d. Type **B5:B6** in the *Changing cells* box.

e. Click OK.

f. The Scenario Values dialog box is displayed. Type **2399128** in the *Revenue* box.

g. Type **1963610** in the *Goods* box.

h. Click Add.

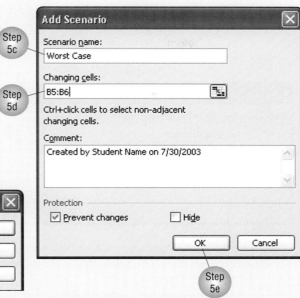

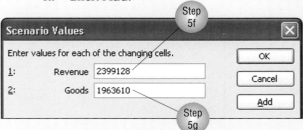

6. The Add Scenario dialog box is displayed again. Complete the following steps to create a second scenario that calculates a probable case:

a. Type **Probable Case** in the *Scenario name* box.

b. Make sure *B5:B6* is still entered in the *Changing cells* box.

c. Click OK.

d. The Scenario Values dialog box is displayed. Type **3427325** in the *Revenue* box.

e. Type **1785100** in the *Goods* box.

f. Click Add.

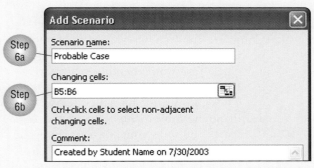

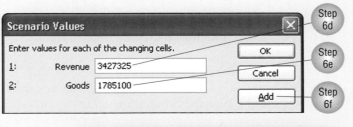

7. The Add Scenario dialog box is displayed again. Complete the following steps to create a third scenario that calculates the best case:

a. Type **Best Case** in the *Scenario name* box.

b. Make sure *B5:B6* is still entered in the *Changing cells* box.

c. Click OK.

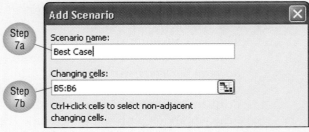

d. The Scenario Values dialog box is displayed. Type 4284156 in the *Revenue* box.

e. Type 1428080 in the *Goods* box and then click OK.

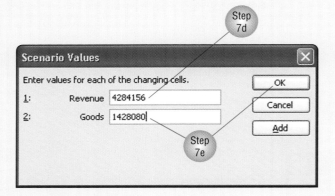

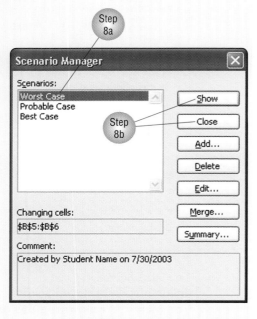

8. The Scenario Manager dialog box is displayed again. Complete the following steps to show the worst case scenario:

a. In the *Scenarios* list box, click *Worst Case*.

b. Click Show and then click Close.

c. Print the *ProjectedBudget* worksheet.

9. Complete the following steps to show the probable case scenario:

a. Click Tools and then click Scenarios.

b. In the *Scenarios* list box, click *Probable Case*.

c. Click Show and then click Close.

d. Print the *ProjectedBudget* worksheet.

10. Complete the following steps to show the best case scenario:

a. Click Tools and then click Scenarios.

b. In the *Scenarios* list box, click *Best Case*.

c. Click Show and then click Close.

d. Print the *ProjectedBudget* worksheet.

11. Complete the following steps to create a scenario summary:

a. Click Tools and then click Scenarios.

b. Click the Summary button.

c. The Scenario Summary dialog box appears. Make sure the *Scenario summary* option is selected.

d. Make sure *B15* is entered in the *Result cells* box and then click OK.

e. The scenario summary is created on a new worksheet. Create a custom header for the *Scenario Summary* worksheet that prints your name at the left margin and the file name at the right margin.

f. Print the *Scenario Summary* worksheet.

12. Save the workbook with the same name (**eec5x11**) and close it.

Projecting Values

In many fields such as business, economics, and science, there often is the need to project values or to ask the question, "Given the way data has performed in the past, how will the same data perform in the future?" You might want to be able to project, for example, the sales volume for the next six months based upon the sales volume for the last six months. Excel includes many tools that enable you to project values. Two of these tools are trendlines and regression analysis.

Creating a Trendline on a Chart

Creating a trendline in a chart enables you to make a forecast. A trendline graphically displays trends in data. Based on the given data, a trendline predicts what will happen in the future. A trendline allows you to forecast, for example, what the next five years' population growth will be, based on the past five years' population growth.

Create a Trendline
Click Chart and then Add Trendline.

HINT

Trendlines can be added to data series in unstacked 2-D area, bar, column, line, stock, xy (scatter), and bubble charts.

To add a trendline to a chart, you must first select the appropriate data series in the chart. Next, click the Chart menu and then click the Add Trendline option from the Chart menu. The Add Trendline dialog box shown in Figure 5.17 is displayed. This dialog box allows you to select the type of trendline you want. Table 5.1 explains the different types of trendlines. The *Order* box is used for entering the highest power for the independent variable. The *Period* box is used for entering the number of periods to be used to calculate the moving average. All of the data series in the chart that support trendlines are listed in the *Based on series* box. To add a trendline to another series, click the name in the box and then select the options you want.

TABLE

5.1 Types of Trendlines

Type of Trendline	Description
Linear	A linear trendline is used with linear data sets to represent something that is increasing or decreasing at a steady rate.
Logarithmic	A logarithmic trendline is a curved line that is used to represent data that rises or falls quickly and then levels off.
Polynomial	A polynomial trendline is a curved line that is used to represent data that fluctuates. When *Polynomial* is selected, enter the highest power for the independent variable in the Order box.
Power	A power trendline is a curved line that is used to represent data that increases at a specific rate.
Exponential	An exponential trendline is a curved line that represents data values that rise or fall at increasingly higher rates.
Moving Average	A moving average trendline is used to smooth out fluctuations in data in order to show a trend more clearly. When *Moving Average* is selected, enter the number of periods to be used for calculating the moving average in the *Period* box.

The Add Trendline Dialog Box with the Type Tab Selected

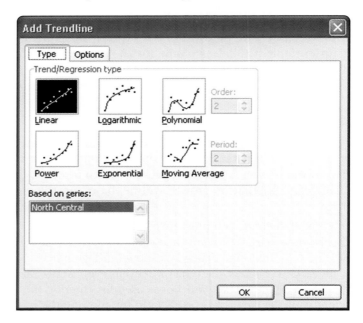

Clicking the Options tab displays the options available for a trendline, as shown in Figure 5.18. You can either accept the name given to the trendline automatically or create your own custom name. In the Forecast section you can indicate how many periods you want the trendline to predict into the future or the past.

The Add Trendline Dialog Box with the Options Tab Selected

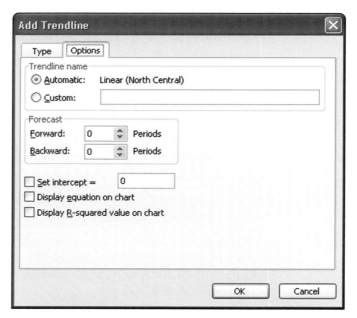

1. Open **ExcelWorksheet08**.
2. Save the worksheet using the Save As command and name it **eec5x12**.
3. Create a custom header that displays your name at the left margin and the file name at the right margin.
4. This workbook contains sales figures by quarters. You want to create a PivotChart report using this data. Name the list *Database*.
5. First you need to create a PivotTable report to summarize the data.
   a. Click Data and then click PivotTable and PivotChart Report.
   b. When the PivotTable and PivotChart Wizard – Step 1 of 3 dialog box is displayed, click Next.
   c. The PivotTable and PivotChart Wizard – Step 2 of 3 dialog box is displayed. *Database* should already be entered in the range box. Click Next.
   d. The PivotTable and PivotChart Wizard – Step 3 of 3 dialog box is displayed. Click the Layout button.

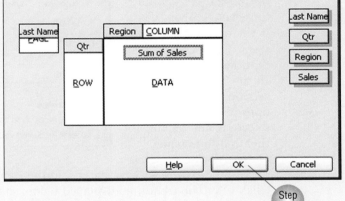

Step 5i

   e. Drag the Last Name button to the PAGE area.
   f. Drag the Qtr button to the ROW area.
   g. Drag the Region button to the COLUMN area.
   h. Drag the Sum of Sales button to the DATA area.
   i. Click OK.
   j. Click Finish.
6. Complete the following steps to remove the grand total from the report:
   a. Right-click in any cell in the PivotTable report.
   b. Click the Table Options on the shortcut menu.
   c. Click the check box next to *Grand totals for columns* and the check box next to *Grand totals for rows* so that they are not selected. Click OK.
7. Complete the following steps to create a PivotChart report:
   a. Click the Chart Wizard button on the PivotTable toolbar.
   b. Excel automatically creates a stacked column chart. Click the Chart Wizard button on the PivotTable toolbar.
   c. In the *Chart type* section, click *Line*.
   d. In the *Chart sub-type* section, click the first option in the second row and then click Next.
   e. Enter **Sales by Quarter** in the *Chart title* box.
   f. Enter **Quarter** in the *Category (X) axis* box, enter **Sales** in the *Value (Y) axis* box, and then click Next.
   g. Click Finish.
   h. Click the down-pointing arrow to the right of the Chart Objects box on the Chart toolbar and then click the *Value Axis* option.
   i. Click the Format Axis button.
   j. When the Format Axis dialog box is displayed, click the Number tab.
   k. In the *Category* section, click *Currency*.
   l. Enter **0** in the *Decimal places* box and then click OK.

8. You are now ready to create a trendline. You want to forecast North Central's sales for the next four quarters.

   a. Click the down-pointing arrow to the right of the Region button. Click *(Show All)* and then click *North Central*. The *North Central* check box should be the only box that is selected. Click OK.

   b. Click anywhere on the line that is displayed. The North Central data series is now selected.

   c. Right-click on the line and select Add Trendline from the shortcut menu that displays.

   d. The Add Trendline dialog box is displayed with the Type tab selected. The first option, *Linear*, should be selected. This is the option you want. Click the Options tab.

   e. In the *Trendline name* section, the *Automatic* option should be selected. The default for the Trendline name, *Linear (North Central)*, is fine. In the *Forecast* section, enter 4 in the *Forward* box.

   f. Click OK. The trendline displayed below shows what North Central's sales will drop to in another year if they continue their current trend.

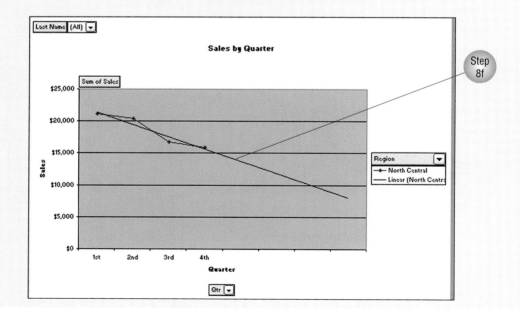

9. Enter a custom header that displays your name at the left margin and the name of the file at the right margin.
10. Print the PivotChart report.
11. Save the workbook with the same name (**eec5x12**) and close it.

Performing Regression Analysis

Excel comes with an add-in called the Analysis ToolPak. The Analysis ToolPak includes a large number of built-in tools that perform complex data analysis tasks. The Analysis ToolPak is not installed by default. In order to install it, click Tools, point to Add-Ins, and then check the *Analysis ToolPak* option. Click OK. Excel will then go through the installation process for the Analysis ToolPak.

One of the tools included in the Analysis ToolPak is regression analysis. Regression analysis is a statistical technique used to find relationships between variables for the purpose of predicting future values. Regression analysis analyzes the relation between two or more quantitative variables so that one variable can be predicted from the other. The first variable is called dependent variable (Y) and the other is called independent variable (X). For example, if you wanted to analyze the relationship between height and weight in a human beings. Performing regression analysis on a sample of actual weights and heights of a number of people would allow you to answer such questions as: is there a relation between weight and height; is this relation due just to chance or can the conclusion we make based on our sample of human beings be extended to all human beings; if we know just the height of a person, can we predict his or her weight?

To use regression analysis, click Tools and Data Analysis. The Data Analysis dialog box shown in Figure 5.19 is displayed. Scroll down the *Analysis Tool* list, select *Regression*, and click OK. The Regression dialog box is displayed. As shown in Figure 5.20, you enter the dependent variable (Y) and the independent variable (X) in this dialog box.

QUICK STEPS

Perform Regression Analysis
Click Tool, Data Analysis, and then Regression.

FIGURE

5.19 *The Data Analysis Dialog Box*

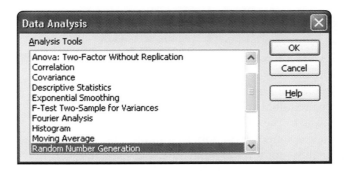

5.20 **The Regression Dialog Box**

The dependent variable is entered here.

The independent variable is entered here.

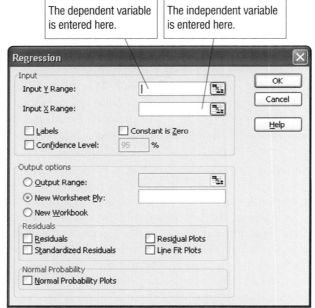

exercise 13

USING REGRESSION ANALYSIS

(Note: If Data Analysis is not included on the Tools menu, install it by clicking Tools and then Add-ins. At the Add-ins dialog box, check the boxes next to Analysis ToolPak *and* Analysis ToolPak-VBA *and then click OK.)*

1. Open **ExcelWorksheet09**.
2. Save the worksheet using the Save As command and name it **eec5x13**.
3. Create a custom header that displays your name at the left margin and the file name at the right margin.
4. The controller for Copper Clad Incorporated wants to set the salary amount for employees. She has researched the market salary data for each job and has come up with a figure for each job based upon that data. In addition, she has developed job evaluation points for each job based on the knowledge required to do the job, how crucial the job is to the business, the responsibilities assigned to the job, and so on. She wants to use Excel's regression analysis to develop a pay line. The pay line will show the relationship between the market salaries and the job evaluation points, thus indicating if any jobs depart significantly from that pay line. Complete the following steps to conduct a linear regression analysis to develop a pay line:

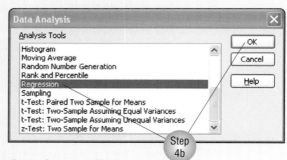

   a. Click Tools and Data Analysis.
   b. The Data Analysis dialog box is displayed. Scroll down to *Regression* in the *Analysis Tools* list. Select *Regression* and then click OK.

c. The Regression dialog box is displayed. Click the *Input Y Range* box. Select cells B2 through B7, the Salary data.

d. Click the *Input X Range* box. Select cells C2 through C7, the Job Points data.

e. Make sure *New Worksheet Ply* is checked in the *Output options* section.

f. Click *Line Fits Plots* in the *Residuals* section.

g. Click OK.

5. Sheet 4 is added to the workbook. If necessary, click the *Sheet4* tab. You will see a set of statistical results and a graph of the pay line. Complete the following steps to make a copy of the graph so that you can look at it more closely:

a. Right-click the graph.

b. Click Copy.

c. Click the *Sheet2* tab.

d. Click the Paste button.

e. Click the handle in the lower right corner of the graph. Drag it to make the graph larger. Your screen should look like the image at the right:

6. Examine the Line Fit Plot closely. The blue diamonds represents *Y* or the salary for each job based on the market salary data you entered. The pink square represents what the projected salary for that job is based on the

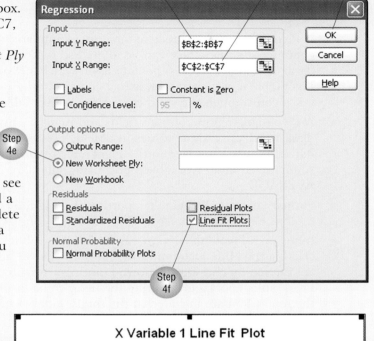

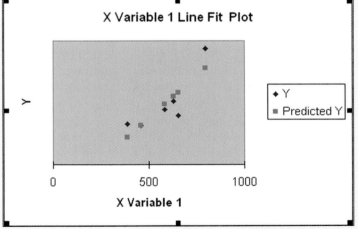

relationship between salary and job evaluation points. Place the mouse pointer over the first blue diamond in the series. A box is displayed that says *Series "Y" Point "388" (388, 32000)*. This represents the data for the internal sales job. Place the mouse pointer over the first pink square. A box is displayed that says *Series "Predicted Y" Point "388" (388, 21564.938)*. Excel's regression analysis projected that the salary for a job with 388 evaluation points would rate a salary of $21,565. Continue to move the mouse pointer over the rest of the triangles and squares in the chart to examine the discrepancies from the pay line. These discrepancies could be handled in one of two ways. Either the job evaluation system could change or the salary amount could change.

7. Enter a custom header that displays your name at the left margin and the name of the file at the right margin.

8. Print the Line Fit Plot.

9. Save the workbook with the same name (**eec5x13**) and close it.

CHAPTER summary

➤ A PivotTable is an interactive table that summarizes large amounts of data. The rows and columns of a PivotTable can be rotated so that you can see various summaries of the data. The source data is the data upon which a PivotTable report is based. Each field in a PivotTable report corresponds to a column in the source data. The PivotTable Wizard takes you through the steps of creating a PivotTable report.

➤ A PivotTable report contains fields and items. Fields correspond to columns in the source data. Items are unique values in a field. The fields from the source list containing the data that is summarized in the PivotTable report are the data fields. Data fields can be summarized in a PivotTable report using summary functions such as SUM, COUNT, and AVERAGE.

➤ Format an entire PivotTable report by clicking the Format Report button on the PivotTable toolbar.

➤ Items on a PivotTable report can be hidden or filtered. Items are hidden and displayed by clicking the Hide Detail button and Show Detail button on the PivotTable toolbar. Items are filtered by clicking the down-pointing arrow to the right of the field button on the PivotTable report and selecting the fields to be displayed. Hidden items are still a part of the report and are included in the totals. Filtered items are not a part of the report and are not included in the totals.

➤ The layout of a PivotTable report can be changed by clicking the PivotTable Wizard button on the PivotTable toolbar and then clicking the Layout button on the PivotTable and PivotChart Wizard – Step 3 of 3 dialog box. The PivotTable and PivotChart Wizard – Layout dialog box containing the PivotTable diagram is displayed. Field buttons can be dragged onto and off the dialog box in order to rearrange the report.

➤ A PivotChart report is created from a PivotTable report. Row fields in a PivotTable report become category fields in a PivotChart report, and column fields in a PivotTable report become series fields in a PivotChart report. Changes made to the PivotTable report are reflected in the PivotChart report and vice versa.

➤ An interactive PivotTable that has been saved as a Web page and published to a public location such as a Web server is called a PivotTable list. Users can access a PivotTable list and interact with it in many of the same ways as PivotTable reports can be manipulated in Excel.

➤ Excel includes many tools that allow the user to perform what-if analysis. What-if analysis looks at what changes will take place to the results of formulas if a specific variable or variables are changed. A typical what-if analysis would be, what would happen to my loan payments if the interest rate is increased? Goal Seek, Solver, and Scenarios are some of Excel's what-if analysis tools.

➤ The Goal Seek command calculates a specified result by changing the value of another cell until a formula dependent on that cell reaches the result specified.

➤ The Solver command calculates a specified result that is based on many changing variables. Solver is used to determine the "best" solution to a problem—that is, the solution that generates the most profit or utilizes resources in the most efficient way, for example. The variables that go into determining the solution can be subject to restrictions or constraints, such as that an employee cannot work more than 40 hours a week. By analyzing the variables and their constraints, Solver finds the optimal solution.

EXCEL

➤ Several different answers, or scenarios, to a specific question can be set up using Excel's Scenario Manager. Each scenario can be examined to see how it affects the final outcome. For example, you can set up one scenario where sales are high and costs are low and a second scenario where sales are low and costs are high and then examine how the two scenarios affect profits.

➤ Excel includes many tools to project values. By analyzing the data that is known, Excel can project what the future data might look like. This type of analysis is sometimes referred to as "what-if" analysis. A company could project next summer's sales based upon the sales of the current summer. Trendlines and regression analysis are two Excel tools that can be used to project values.

➤ A trendline can be added to data series in a chart to display trends in data and to make predictions based on those trends. Trendlines in a chart can be extended beyond the actual data to predict future values based on the data in the selected data series.

FEATURES summary

FEATURE	BUTTON	MENU/COMMANDS
Create a PivotTable	🔲	Click Data, PivotTable, and PivotChart Report
Sort the items in a field in a PivotTable report		Double-click a field button on the PivotTable and click Advanced button
Remove subtotals from a PivotTable report		Double-click a field button on the PivotTable, click *None*
Remove grand totals from a PivotTable report		Right-click a cell in the PivotTable report, click Table Options
Create a PivotChart report	🔲	Click Data, PivotTable and PivotChart Report
Use Goal Seek		Click Tools, Goal Seek
Use Solver		Click Tools, Solver
Create a Scenario		Click Tools, Scenarios
Create a trendline		Click Chart, Add Trendline
Perform regression analysis		Click Tools, Data Analysis, Regression

CONCEPTS check

Completion: On a blank sheet of paper, indicate the correct term, symbol, or command for each description.

1. This term refers to a report that is used to quickly summarize and analyze large amounts of data.
2. This term refers to the list upon which a PivotTable report is based.
3. If you name the list this term, Excel will automatically recognize it as the data upon which to base a PivotTable report.
4. To select all the cells belonging to a field in a PivotTable report, the mouse pointer must turn into this symbol when you move it to the top of the data field label in a column.
5. To sort the fields in a PivotTable report, double-click a field button on the PivotTable and click this button.
6. To remove grand totals from a PivotTable report, right-click a cell in the report and click this option from the shortcut menu.
7. To manage the layout of a PivotTable report using the PivotTable Wizard, click the PivotTable and PivotChart Wizard button on the PivotTable toolbar and click this button.
8. This term refers to what you must have in order to create a PivotChart report.
9. This term refers to the process where values in cells are changed in order to see how those changes affect the outcome of formulas on the worksheet.
10. This term refers to Excel's analysis tool that calculates a specified result by changing the value of one cell.
11. This term refers to Excel's analysis tool that calculates a specified result by changing several variables.
12. This term refers to Excel's analysis tool that allows you to examine how several different projected plans will affect the final outcome.
13. List the two ways you can filter items on a PivotTable report.
14. List the steps for creating a PivotChart report from scratch and for creating a PivotChart report based on an existing PivotTable.
15. List the steps for saving a PivotTable report as a Web page.

SKILLS check

Assessment 1

1. Open **ExcelWorksheet10**.
2. Save the worksheet using the Save As command and name it **eec5sc01**.
3. Case 'N Crate is a company that manufactures wooden boxes, crates, and trays. They sell their products to businesses that use them for packaging fresh fruit and other specialty items. This worksheet keeps track of orders made the first quarter of the year. Name the list *Database*.
4. Create a PivotTable from the list. Place the PivotTable on a new worksheet. Rename the new worksheet *PivotTable*. **(Hint: Remember to press Enter after typing in the new worksheet name.)**

5. Create a custom header for the *PivotTable* worksheet with your name displayed at the left margin and the file name displayed at the right margin.
6. Drag the Region button to the *Drop Page Fields Here* area of the PivotTable diagram. Drag the Month and Sales Representative buttons to the *Drop Row Fields Here* area. Drag the Product button to the *Drop Column Fields Here* area. Drag the Total Order button to the *Drop Data Items Here* area.
7. Format the entire PivotTable report using the Table 8 format from the AutoFormat dialog box.
8. Format all the values for boxes, crates, trays, all the subtotals, and the grand totals as currency with no decimal places.
9. Automatically adjust the width of columns A through F so that each column is at its optimal width.
10. Filter the PivotTable report so that only the orders for the South region are displayed. Print the *PivotTable* worksheet.
11. Display all the orders. Filter the PivotTable report so that only the orders for March are displayed. Print the *PivotTable* worksheet.
12. Display all the months. Change the layout of the PivotTable report so that *Product* is displayed as a row field and *Month* is displayed as a column field. Make any necessary adjustments so that the PivotTable report prints on one page. Print the *PivotTable* worksheet.
13. Adjust the layout of the PivotTable so that both the month and product are displayed as column fields. Hide the detail for the *Month* field. Make sure all the values are formatted as currency with no decimal places. Adjust column width if necessary. Print the *PivotTable* worksheet.
14. Show the detail for the *Month* field.
15. Edit the layout of the PivotTable by removing the Sales Representative button from the ROW area. Move the *Month* field to the ROW area and the *Product* field to the COLUMN area.
16. Remove the grand totals for columns and the grand totals for rows.
17. Create a PivotChart report. The *Chart type* should be *Line* and the *Chart sub-type* should be the first option in the second row.
18. You want to create a trendline. Select the crates data series and create a logarithmic trendline. Forecast ahead for three periods.
19. Print the chart.
20. Save the workbook with the same name (**eec5sc01**) and close it.

Assessment 2

1. **Open ExcelWorksheet11**.
2. Save the worksheet using the Save As command and name it **eec5sc02**.
3. Nichols Dairy Ice Cream is a company that makes and sells its own ice cream. This list keeps track of ice cream orders. Name the list *Database*.
4. Create a PivotTable from the list. Place the PivotTable on a new worksheet. Rename the new worksheet *PivotTable*.
5. Create a custom header for the *PivotTable* worksheet with your name displayed at the left margin and the file name displayed at the right margin.
6. Drag the Month button to the *Drop Page Fields Here* area of the PivotTable diagram. Drag the Flavor and Customer buttons to the *Drop Row Fields Here* area. Drag the Type button to the *Drop Column Fields Here* area. Drag the Amount button to the *Drop Data Items Here* area.
7. Format the entire PivotTable report using the Table 4 format from the AutoFormat dialog box.
8. Format the values in the PivotTable report as currency with two decimal places.

9. Display the top two customers according to the total amount of their orders.
10. Adjust the page setup so that rows 1 through 4 repeat at the top as a print title.
11. Print the *PivotTable* worksheet.
12. Display all the customers.
13. Filter the report by selecting only *Low Fat* from the *Type* drop-down list.
14. Remove the grand totals from the report.
15. Print the PivotTable report.
16. Remove the filter from the *Type* field and display the grand totals in the PivotTable report. Print the *PivotTable* worksheet.
17. Save the workbook with the same name (**eec5sc02**) and close it.

Assessment 3

1. Open **ExcelWorksheet12**.
2. Save the worksheet using the Save As command and name it **eec5sc03**.
3. Name the list *Database*.
4. Create a PivotChart using the PivotTable and PivotChart Wizard. Place the PivotTable on a new worksheet.
5. Drag the Paid button to the *Drop Page Fields Here* area of the PivotChart diagram. Drag the Vet button to the *Drop Series Fields Here* area. Drag the Service Rendered button to the *Drop Category Fields Here* area. Drag the Amount button to the *Drop Data Items Here* area.
6. Click the Chart Wizard button on the PivotTable toolbar. Select the first option in the first row in the *Chart sub-type* section.
7. The chart title should be Income from Services Rendered. The title for the Category (*X*) axis should be Veterinarian. The title for the Value (*Y*) axis should be Dollars.
8. Place the chart on a new sheet. Rename the *Chart1* worksheet tab *PivotChart*.
9. Create a custom header for the *PivotChart* worksheet with your name displayed at the left margin and the name of the file displayed at the right margin.
10. Format the numbers on the value axis as currency with no decimal places.
11. Angle the text on the category axis counterclockwise.
12. Print the PivotChart.
13. Filter the PivotChart so that in the *Paid* field only the No records are displayed and in the *Veterinarian* field only Martin's records are displayed.
14. Click the Chart Wizard button on the PivotTable toolbar. Select the *Pie* option in the *Chart type* section. Select the second option in the second row in the *Chart sub-type* section.
15. The chart title should be Dr. Martin's Unpaid Invoices.
16. The Data labels should show the percent.
17. Place the chart on a new sheet named *PivotChart*.
18. Print the PivotChart.
19. Save the workbook with the same name (**eec5sc03**) and close it.

Assessment 4

1. Open **ExcelWorksheet13**.
2. Save the worksheet using the Save As command and name it **eec5sc04**.
3. If necessary, click the *PivotTable* worksheet tab.
4. Save the PivotTable as a Web page. Use the same file name (**eec5sc04**). Click the Publish button. Click *PivotTable* from the list under the *Choose* box. The items you want to publish are the *Items on PivotTable*. Click the *Add interactivity with* check box and choose *PivotTable functionality* from the drop-down list. Make sure the *Open published web page in browser* check box is selected and then click Publish.

5. You do not want to see the Sum of Amount figures. Drag one of the Sum of Amount field buttons off the PivotTable.
6. Display the figures for the Second Street Market only. Print the PivotTable.
7. Display all the stores.
8. Display the detail for Triple Mocha Madness ice cream by clicking the plus sign next to it. Print the PivotTable.
9. Collapse the detail for Triple Mocha Madness by clicking the minus sign.
10. Put the Sum of Amount button back on the PivotTable as a row field. Print the PivotTable.
11. Close Microsoft Internet Explorer.
12. Save the workbook with the same name (**eec5sc04**) and close it.

Assessment 5

1. Open **ExcelWorksheet14**.
2. Save the worksheet using the Save As command and name it **eec5sc05**.
3. Create a custom header for the *Salary & Commissions* worksheet with your name displayed at the left margin and the file name displayed at the right margin.
4. Using Goal Seek, find the total amount Michael Malone's sales would have to be in order for him to earn a total of $2,500. Enter that value into the worksheet.
5. Using Goal Seek, find what percentage commission Robert McBride would have to earn in order for his total income to be $3,500. Enter that value into the worksheet.
6. Using Goal Seek, find what Charles Levinson's salary would have to be in order for his total income to be $3,200.
7. Print the *Salary and Commissions* worksheet.
8. Save the workbook with the same name (**eec5sc05**) and close it.

Assessment 6

1. Open **ExcelWorksheet15**.
2. Save the worksheet using the Save As command and name it **eec5sc06**.
3. Create a custom header for the worksheet with your name displayed at the left margin and the file name displayed at the right margin.
4. The production manager at Case 'N Crate has to figure out how many gross each of boxes and crates to produce in order to generate the most profit. Look over the worksheet carefully. The worksheet shows how many hours it takes to build and varnish a gross of boxes and a gross of crates. Because of the number of employees available, there is a limit on how many hours a week can be devoted to building and varnishing the boxes and crates.
5. Define the problem using Solver. The target cell is cell E8 and you are trying to find the maximum profit. The cells that can be changed are the number of gross of each product to produce (B9 and C9). Add the two constraints: the resources used for carpentry cannot exceed 240 hours; the resources used for varnishing cannot exceed 100 hours.
6. Keep the Solver solution. Print the worksheet.
7. Save the workbook with the same name (**eec5sc06**) and close it.

Assessment 7

1. Open **ExcelWorksheet16**.
2. Save the worksheet using the Save As command and name it **eec5sc07**.
3. Create a custom header for the *Bad Debts* worksheet with your name displayed at the left margin and the file name displayed at the right margin.

4. This worksheet is going to be used to project three scenarios. The veterinarians want to know how much money they are going to lose on uncollected accounts and how much this will affect the overall revenue of the company. The total bad debt is a percentage of the total uncollected accounts. Click cell B8. Type =(B7*B6)+B5.
5. The anticipated revenue is the gross revenue minus the total bad debt. Click cell B11. Type =B10-B8.
6. Name cell B6 *Uncollected*. Name cell B7 *BD_Allowance*.
7. Create a scenario named *Worst Case*. The changing cells should be B6 and B7. Enter 15500 as the uncollected amount. Enter .3 as the bad debt allowance.
8. Create a scenario named *Probable Case*. The changing cells should be B6 and B7. Enter 8500 as the uncollected amount. Enter .2 as the bad debt allowance.
9. Create a scenario named *Best Case*. The changing cells should be B6 and B7. Enter 3200 as the uncollected amount. Enter .1 as the bad debt allowance.
10. Show the Worst Case scenario. Print the *BadDebts* worksheet.
11. Show the Probable Case scenario. Print the *BadDebts* worksheet.
12. Show the Best Case scenario. Print the *BadDebts* worksheet.
13. Save the workbook with the same name (**eec5sc07**) and close it.

CHAPTER challenge

As the sales analyst for Patty's Pretzels, you have been asked to summarize and analyze data gathered throughout the year. Use the source data found in the *Annual Sales* worksheet of the workbook named **PattysPretzels** to create a PivotTable and Chart (in new worksheets) that summarize the pretzel sales by quarter for each of the mall locations. AutoFormat the PivotTable. Using the Goal Seek feature, determine how much East region's annual sales would have to increase to earn $10,000 in net income. Assume expenses are $55,000. Place the results in a separate sheet of the workbook. Name all of the sheet tabs appropriately. Save the workbook as **PattysPretzelsSalesAnalysis**.

In the chart created in the first part of the Chapter Challenge, you would like to draw attention to the region with the highest sales. Use the Help feature to learn about text boxes and arrows. Then use a text box to add the text "Highest Sales" to the chart. Using an arrow, point (from the text box) to the region with the highest sales. Save the workbook again.

The chart created and modified in the first two parts of the Chapter Challenge will be used by you in a PowerPoint presentation given at the Annual Meeting of the Board of Directors. Begin the presentation by placing the chart on a slide in PowerPoint. Format it. Save the PowerPoint presentation as **AnnualMeetingPresentation**.

MANAGING AND AUDITING WORKSHEETS

PERFORMANCE OBJECTIVES

Upon successful completion of Chapter 6, you will be able to:

- ➤ **Record a macro**
- ➤ **Run a macro**
- ➤ **Edit a macro using the Microsoft Visual Basic editor**
- ➤ **Assign a macro to a command button**
- ➤ **Hide and display toolbars**
- ➤ **Create a custom toolbar**
- ➤ **Create a custom menu**
- ➤ **Use the Auditing toolbar**
- ➤ **Trace precedents**
- ➤ **Trace dependents**
- ➤ **Trace errors**
- ➤ **Locate and resolve errors in formulas**
- ➤ **Identify dependencies in formulas**

Chapter06E

EXCEL

Excel includes a number of features that help you manage worksheets. Macros are useful for automating many tasks typically performed on a worksheet. They can save you time by automatically performing tasks that you do repeatedly, or tasks that involve the same sequence of steps. When you assign a macro to a command button, the macro is placed right on the worksheet to give you quick and easy access to it. You can also manage your worksheets by creating custom menus and by creating custom toolbars containing buttons for the commands you routinely use or the macros you have created. Making sure that your worksheet is functioning properly is also a part of worksheet management. The auditing features that come with Excel help you trace the cells to which a formula refers and help you trace formulas that refer to a specific cell. If there is an error in the worksheet, Excel's auditing feature will track down the source of the error. The purpose of this chapter is to introduce you to these features in Excel so that you can successfully manage and audit your worksheets.

Introduction to Macros

Macros are used to increase productivity by automating tasks that perform the same sequence of steps or by automating tasks that are performed repeatedly. Instead of performing this same sequence of steps over and over every time you need to perform the task, you can record the steps in a macro. Then by pressing a key or two, the macro automatically performs the task for you. Once a macro has been created, it can be executed in a number of ways. A macro can be executed by selecting a menu item or by pressing a particular key combination. You can also assign the macro to a toolbar button or to a graphic object on a worksheet.

HINT

The macro recorder does not record any uncompleted tasks. For example, if you open a dialog box, make some changes, and then click Cancel, the macro recorder will not record any of those actions.

Excel's macro recorder makes it easy to record a macro. The macro recorder works much like a tape recorder in that once it is turned on, it records every keystroke and mouse click you make until it is turned off. Macros can be used for very simple tasks such as formatting a worksheet and printing reports. They can also be used for very complex tasks such as automating entire worksheets so that all the user has to do is retrieve the worksheet file and follow the on-screen instructions. Planning each step the macro is to perform before actually recording the macro is very important, as the macro recorder will record every step you perform, including the steps you take to correct any mistakes you make. In order for the macro to run as efficiently as possible, any unnecessary keystrokes, such as those taken to fix a mistake, should not be a part of the macro.

Recording a Macro

Macros recorded in Excel are created automatically in the Visual Basic for Applications programming language, also known as VBA. Excel's Visual Basic toolbar can be quite useful when you are recording a macro. To display the Visual Basic toolbar shown in Figure 6.1, right-click a toolbar that is currently displayed and then click Visual Basic.

FIGURE

6.1 *The Visual Basic Toolbar*

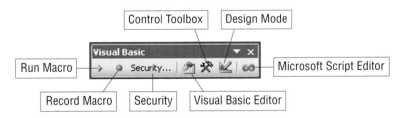

You can display the Record Macro dialog box shown in Figure 6.2 by clicking the Record Macro button on the Visual Basic toolbar. You can also display this dialog box using the menus by clicking Tools and then either waiting a couple of seconds or clicking the down-pointing arrow at the bottom of the menu to display the Macro option. Select Macro and then click Record New Macro. A macro name that describes the purpose of the macro is entered in the *Macro name* box. The first letter of the macro name must be a letter. The other characters in the name can be numbers, letters, or the underscore character. A macro name cannot contain any spaces. A letter that will be pressed together with the Ctrl key to run the macro is entered in the *Shortcut key* box next to Ctrl. You can use lowercase or uppercase letters. You must use the same case when executing the macro. That is, if you enter a capital *T* in the *Shortcut key* box, pressing Ctrl and a lowercase *t* will not execute the macro. You can also select where the macro is to be stored. Figure 6.2 shows the drop-down list that is displayed when the down-pointing arrow to the right of the *Store macro in* box is clicked. If *Personal Macro Workbook* is selected, the macro will be available whenever you use Excel. If either the *New Workbook* or *This Workbook* option is selected, the macro will be available to that workbook only. A description of the macro can be entered in the *Description* box. When you have finished filling out the dialog box, click OK.

FIGURE

6.2 **The Record Macro Dialog box (left); The Store Macro in Drop-Down Menu (right)**

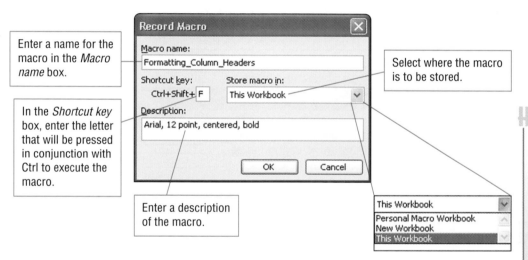

Enter a name for the macro in the *Macro name* box.

In the *Shortcut key* box, enter the letter that will be pressed in conjunction with Ctrl to execute the macro.

Enter a description of the macro.

Select where the macro is to be stored.

HINT

When designing a macro, you need to be careful about where the cell pointer is located when the macro starts. If the first step in the macro is to select a specific cell, then the macro starts executing in that cell. If the first step in the macro is not selecting a specific cell, then the macro is going to start executing in whatever cell happens to be selected when the macro was invoked. If that cell contains data, the data is going to be overwritten by any input that is part of the macro.

Once you click OK, the Stop Recording toolbar shown in Figure 6.3 is displayed. There are two buttons on the toolbar. If part of your macro includes selecting cells, Excel will always select the same cells that were selected when the macro was created because the macro records absolute cell references. If the macro is to select cells no matter where the active cell is located when the macro is run, click the Relative Reference button. Relative references will be recorded until you either click the Stop button or click the Relative Reference button to turn the feature off. When you have finished entering the macro, click the Stop Recording button, which will stop the recording of the macro.

FIGURE

6.3 **The Stop Recording Toolbar**

Stop Recording

Relative Reference

Running a Macro

QUICK STEPS

Run a Macro
1. Click Tools, point to Macro, and then click Macros.
2. At Macro dialog box, select *Macro* from list.
3. Click Run.

There are several ways to run a macro. One way is to click Tools, select Macro, and then click Macros. The Macro Dialog box shown in Figure 6.4 is displayed. You can also display this dialog box by clicking the Run Macro button on the Visual Basic toolbar. Select the name of the macro you want to run from the list box and then click Run. The macro you selected is run. If you need to delete a macro, select the name of the macro you want to delete from the list box and then click Delete. Clicking Options displays the Macro Options dialog box, shown in Figure 6.5, where you can change the letter assigned to the shortcut key command and the description.

You should always save your workbook before running a macro. If the macro does not execute exactly as you expected, it could cause serious problems for your workbook. If the macro does cause problems, you can close the workbook without saving it and go back to the version you saved right before running the macro.

FIGURE

6.4 *The Macro Dialog Box*

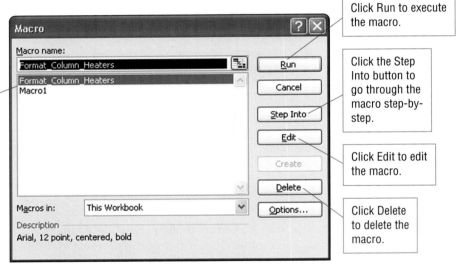

Select a macro from the *Macro name* list box.

Click Run to execute the macro.

Click the Step Into button to go through the macro step-by-step.

Click Edit to edit the macro.

Click Delete to delete the macro.

QUICK STEPS

Delete a Macro
1. Click Tools, point to Macro, and then click Macros.
2. At the Macro dialog box, select the macro from list.
3. Click Delete.

FIGURE

6.5 *The Macro Options Dialog Box*

QUICK STEPS

Edit a Macro's Shortcut Key Command
1. Click Tools, point to Macro, and then click Macros.
2. At the Macro dialog box, select Macro.
3. Click Options.

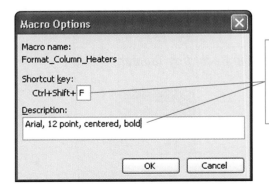

The Macro Options dialog box allows you to edit the shortcut key used to run the macro and the description of the macro.

If a keyboard shortcut key has been assigned to the macro either in the Record Macro dialog box when the macro was first recorded or in the Macro Options dialog box after the macro was recorded, the macro can be run by simply pressing the keyboard shortcut key. For example, pressing Ctrl + F might run a macro that formats column headers.

exercise 1

1. Open Excel.
2. Open **ExcelWorksheet01**.
3. Save the worksheet using the Save As command and name it **eec6x01**.
4. Create a custom header that displays your name at the left margin and the file name at the right margin.
5. Chris Robinson is a freelance PC technician. His company is called Bits Unlimited, and he specializes in offering his PC consulting services to doctors' offices. This worksheet has been created to project his earnings for next year. You are going to create a macro that takes a figure from a cell in the current year and increases it by 5%. Complete the following steps to create the macro:
   a. Click cell H5.
   b. Click View, point to Toolbars, and then click Visual Basic. The Visual Basic toolbar is displayed.
   c. Click the Record Macro button. The Record Macro dialog box is displayed.
   d. Type **Increase** in the *Macro name* box.
   e. You want to create a shortcut key. Press the Shift key and enter **I** in the *Shortcut key* box. Notice that it now says *Ctrl+Shift+I* for the shortcut key. Pressing the Ctrl, Shift, and I keys together will execute the macro.
   f. Click OK. The Stop Recording toolbar is displayed.
   g. Type **=B5*1.05** in the formula bar.
   h. Click the Enter button next to the formula bar.
   i. Click the Stop Recording button on the Stop Recording toolbar.

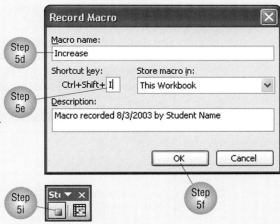

6. The macro is created. Complete the following steps to execute the macro:
   a. Click cell H6.
   b. Press Ctrl + Shift + I. The correct formula is automatically entered in cell H6.
   c. Click cell I5.
   d. Click the Run Macro button on the Visual Basic toolbar. The Macro dialog box is displayed.
   e. Make sure the *Increase* macro is selected.
   f. Click Run. The correct formula is automatically entered in cell I5.

7. Change the orientation of the page to landscape. Print the worksheet.
8. Save the worksheet with the same name (**eec6x01**). You will use this worksheet in the next exercise.
9. Close the worksheet.

QUICK
STEPS

Assign a Macro to a Command Button
1. Right-click the button.
2. Assign Macro.

Button

QUICK
STEPS

Change the Format of a Command Button
1. Right-click the button.
2. Click Format Control.

Assigning a Macro to a Command Button

You can run an existing macro from a command button placed on the worksheet. To assign a macro to a command button, display the Forms toolbar and then click the Button button. The mouse pointer turns into a crosshair, and you can drag the control to the size you want. The default name of the button is Button 1, Button 2, and so on. To change the name of the button, select the default name and then type a new one. To change the format of the button, such as the size of the button or the font and font color used on the button, right-click the button and then click Format Control on the shortcut menu. To assign a macro to the button, right-click the button and then click Assign Macro. The Assign Macro dialog box shown in Figure 6.6 is displayed. To assign the button to a macro that has already been created, select the macro name from the list and then click OK. To record a macro to be assigned to the button, click Record.

FIGURE

6.6 **The Assign Macro Dialog Box**

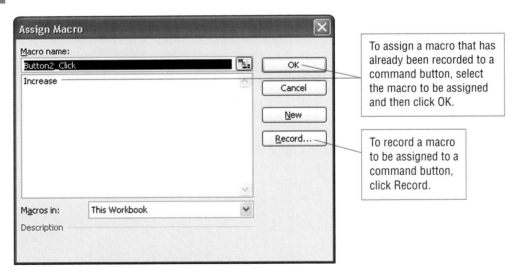

To assign a macro that has already been recorded to a command button, select the macro to be assigned and then click OK.

To record a macro to be assigned to a command button, click Record.

HINT
In order to be able to edit macros, you need to be familiar with the Visual Basic Editor.

Editing a Macro

To edit a macro, first click the Run Macro button on the Visual Basic toolbar. When the Macro dialog box appears, select the macro to be edited and then click Edit, as shown in Figure 6.7. The Visual Basic editor appears as a new application. Macros are edited using the Visual Basic editor.

EXCEL

6.7 *Editing a Macro*

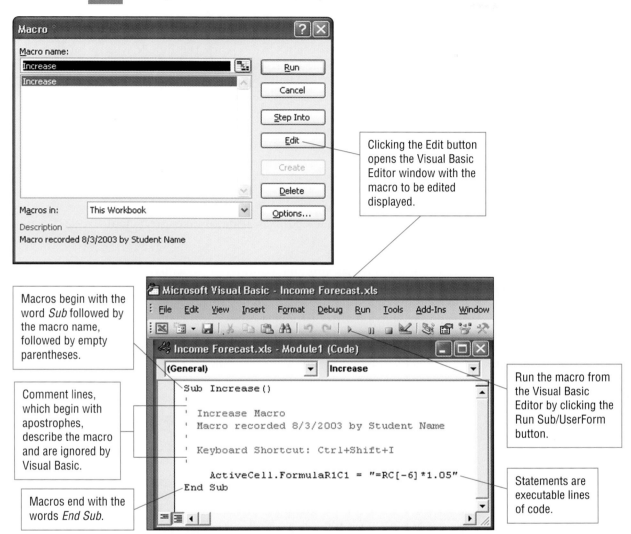

Clicking the Edit button opens the Visual Basic Editor window with the macro to be edited displayed.

Macros begin with the word *Sub* followed by the macro name, followed by empty parentheses.

Comment lines, which begin with apostrophes, describe the macro and are ignored by Visual Basic.

Macros end with the words *End Sub*.

Run the macro from the Visual Basic Editor by clicking the Run Sub/UserForm button.

Statements are executable lines of code.

As you can see in Figure 6.7, macros begin with the word *Sub,* followed by the macro name, followed by empty parentheses. The next few lines, which begin with apostrophes, are the comment lines. Comment lines describe the macro and are ignored by Visual Basic. After the comment lines is the macro. The executable lines of code in the macro are called statements. In the example in Figure 6.8, the statement is made up of two parts that are separated by a period. Everything to the left of the period is the object. The object identifies the part of Excel that is to be affected. In Figure 6.7, *ActiveCell* is the object. That is, the currently active cell is the cell that is going to be affected. Everything to the right of the period indicates how the object is to be affected. Edit the statements however necessary. You can run the edited macro right from the Visual Basic editor by clicking the Run Sub/UserForm button.

1. Open worksheet **eec6x01**, which you created in Exercise 1. When the dialog box appears warning you that macros may contain viruses, click the Enable Macros button. Click OK if you receive a Microsoft Office Excel message box indicating macros are disabled because the security level is set to High and a digitally signed Trusted Certificate is not attached to the macros. Complete the following steps to lower the security level on the computer you are using:
   a. Click Tools and then click Options.
   b. At the Options dialog box click the Security tab and then click the Macro Security button in the *Macro security* section.
   c. At the Security dialog box with the Security level tab selected, click *Medium* and then click OK.
   d. Click OK to close the Options dialog box.
   e. Excel has to be restarted for the new security setting to take effect. Exit Excel. Click Yes if prompted to save changes.
   f. Start Excel and then open **eec6x01**.
2. Save the worksheet using the Save As command and name it **eec6x02**.
3. If necessary, create a custom header that displays your name at the left margin and the file name at the right margin.
4. Click cell H6. Instead of having a macro that increases the income by 5%, you want it to increase the income by 6%. Complete the following steps to edit and execute the macro:
   a. If necessary, display the Visual Basic toolbar.
   b. Click the Run Macro button on the Visual Basic toolbar.
   c. Make sure the *Increase* macro is selected.
   d. Click the Edit button. The Visual Basic editor appears as a new application.
   e. There is one statement line, *ActiveCell.FormulaR1C1 = "=RC[-6]*1.05"*. Edit this line so that the formula is **1.06* instead of **1.05*.
   f. Click the Run Sub/UserForm button.
   g. Close the Microsoft Visual Basic window.
   h. Click cell I5.
   i. Click the Run Macro button on the Visual Basic toolbar.
   j. The Macro dialog box appears with the macro name *Increase* selected. Click Run.
   k. Click cell H5.
   l. Press Ctrl + Shift + I.
5. Complete the following steps to create and execute two more macros:
   a. Click cell J5.
   b. Click the Record Macro button on the Visual Basic toolbar. The Record Macro dialog box is displayed. Enter Same in the *Macro name* box.
   c. You want to create a shortcut key. Click the *Shortcut key* box to select it. Press the Shift key and enter S. Notice that it now says *Ctrl+Shift+S* for the shortcut key. Pressing the Ctrl, Shift, and S keys together will execute the macro.
   d. Click OK. The Stop Recording toolbar is displayed.

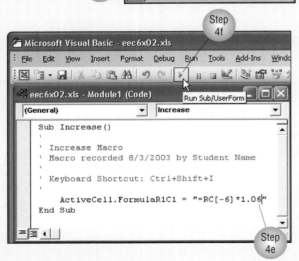

Step 4b

Step 4f

Step 4e

e. Enter =D5 in cell J5.

f. Click the Enter button next to the formula bar.

g. Click the Stop Recording button on the Stop Recording toolbar.

h. Click cell J6. Press Ctrl + Shift + S.

i. Click cell I6.

j. Click the Record Macro button. The Record Macro dialog box is displayed. Type **Decrease** in the *Macro name* box.

k. You want to create a shortcut key. Click in the *Shortcut key* box and then press the Shift key and enter **D**.

l. Click OK. The Stop Recording toolbar is displayed.

m. Enter =C6-(C6*.04) in cell I6.

n. Click the Enter button next to the formula bar.

o. Click the Stop Recording button on the Stop Recording toolbar.

p. Click cell K5, then press Ctrl + Shift + D.

6. Next you want to assign the Increase macro to a command button. Complete the following steps to assign the macro to a command button:

a. Click View, point to Toolbars, and then click Forms. The Forms toolbar is displayed.

b. Click the Button button.

c. The mouse pointer changes to crosshairs. Underneath and a little to the left of the INCOME FORECAST header, click and drag a rectangle that is approximately .25 inch high and .75 inch wide. You will set the exact size in a later step.

d. The button appears along with the Assign Macro dialog box. Select the macro name *Increase*.

e. Click OK.

f. Drag across the text currently on the button to select it and then type Increase.

g. Right-click one of the button's edges and click Format Control on the shortcut menu. The Format Control dialog box is displayed.

h. If necessary, click the Font tab.

i. Click *Bold* from the *Font style* list box.

j. Click the down-pointing arrow to the right of the *Color* box and then click the red button, the first button from the left in the third row.

k. Click the Size tab. Enter 0.25" in the *Height* box.

l. Enter 0.75" in the *Width* box and click OK.

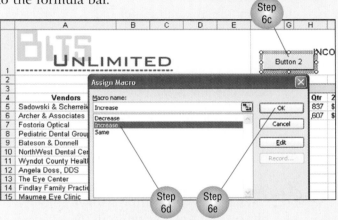

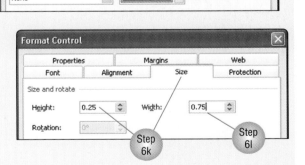

7. Complete the following steps to assign the Same macro to a command button:
   a. The Forms toolbar should still be displayed. Click the Button button.
   b. The mouse pointer changes to crosshairs. To the right of the Increase button, click and drag a rectangle that is approximately .25 inch high and .75 inch wide.
   c. The button appears along with the Assign Macro dialog box. Select the macro name *Same*. Click OK.
   d. Drag across the text currently on the button to select it and then type **Same**.
   e. Right-click one of the button's edges and then click Format Control on the shortcut menu. The Format Control dialog box is displayed.
   f. Click the Font tab, then click Bold from the *Font style* list box.
   g. Click the down-pointing arrow to the right of the *Color* box and then click the red button, the first button from the left in the third row.
   h. Click the Size tab. Enter **0.25"** in the *Height* box; enter **0.75"** in the *Width* box.
   i. Click OK.
8. Complete the following steps to assign the Decrease macro to a command button:
   a. Click the Button button.
   b. The mouse pointer changes to crosshairs. To the right of the Same button, click and drag a rectangle that is approximately .25 inch high and .75 inch wide.
   c. The button appears along with the Assign Macro dialog box. Select the macro name *Decrease*. Click OK.
   d. Drag across the text currently on the button to select it and then type **Decrease**.
   e. Right-click one of the button's edges and click Format Control on the shortcut menu. The Format Control dialog box is displayed.
   f. Click the Font tab, then click *Bold* from the *Font style* list box.
   g. Click the down-pointing arrow to the right of the *Color* box and then click the red button, the first button from the left in the third row.
   h. Click the Size button. Enter **0.25"** in the *Height* box; enter **0.75"** in the *Width* box.
   i. Click OK and close the Forms toolbar.
9. Complete the following steps to enter Macros from the command buttons:
   a. Click cell K6 and then click the Decrease button.
   b. Click cell H7 and then click the Same button.
10. To finish filling in the forecast, click the listed command button for each cell in the following list:

Cell	Command Button	Cell	Command Button
H8	Increase	J7	Same
H9	Increase	J8	Same
H10	Same	J9	Increase
H11	Increase	J10	Same
H12	Increase	J11	Increase
H13	Same	J12	Increase
H14	Increase	J13	Decrease
H15	Decrease	J14	Increase
H16	Decrease	J15	Same
H17	Decrease	J16	Increase
H18	Decrease	J17	Increase
H19	Decrease	J18	Increase
I7	Increase	J19	Same
I8	Decrease	K7	Increase
I9	Increase	K8	Decrease
I10	Decrease	K9	Increase

Cell	Command Button	Cell	Command Button
I11	Increase	K10	Same
I12	Increase	K11	Increase
I13	Increase	K12	Increase
I14	Same	K13	Same
I15	Decrease	K14	Increase
I16	Increase	K15	Increase
I17	Same	K16	Same
I18	Same	K17	Increase
I19	Decrease	K18	Increase
		K19	Same

11. Create another macro that uses conditional formatting to display the cells in the *Total* column that have values under $4,000 as red and those that have values over $6,000 as blue. Complete the following steps to create and execute the macro:
    a. Click cell F5.
    b. Click the Record Macro button on the Visual Basic toolbar.
    c. Enter **Format** in the *Macro name* box.
    d. Click the *Shortcut key* box. Press the Shift key and then enter **F**.
    e. Click OK. The Stop Recording toolbar is displayed.
    f. You are going to select some cells for the macro, but you want their reference to be relative. Click the Relative Reference button on the Stop Recording toolbar. The button should be outlined.  Step 11f
    g. Select cells F5 through F19.
    h. Click Format and then click Conditional Formatting. The Conditional Formatting dialog box appears.
    i. Add a condition that displays any value less than 4000 as bold and in the color red.
    j. Add a second condition that displays any value greater than 6000 as bold and in the color blue.
    k. Click OK.

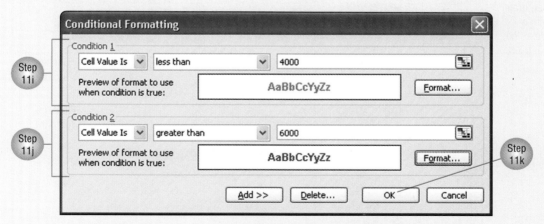

    l. Click the Stop Recording button on the Stop Recording toolbar.
    m. Click cell L5.
    n. Press Ctrl + Shift + F.
12. Close the Visual Basic toolbar.
13. Print the worksheet.
14. Save the worksheet using the same name (**eec6x02**). Close the worksheet.

Working with Toolbars and Menus

The toolbars and menus used in Office are quite flexible and adaptable. Toolbars can be docked or floating. They can be hidden or displayed. They can be reshaped. You can even make your own customized toolbar by adding and removing buttons and menus.

Floating and Docked Toolbars

Figure 6.8 shows examples of both docked and floating toolbars. A docked toolbar is attached to one of the program window's borders. A docked toolbar can be attached below the program title bar or to the left, right, or bottom border of the program window. A floating toolbar is not attached to the edge of the programming window. Toolbars can be moved to any location on the screen. To move a toolbar that is docked, drag the move handle located at the left side of the docked toolbar. To move a floating toolbar, drag the toolbar's title bar. When a toolbar is dragged to the border of the programming window or close to the edge of another docked toolbar, it becomes a docked toolbar. To undock a toolbar, drag the move handle at that toolbar's left side.

FIGURE

6.8 *Docked and Floating Toolbars*

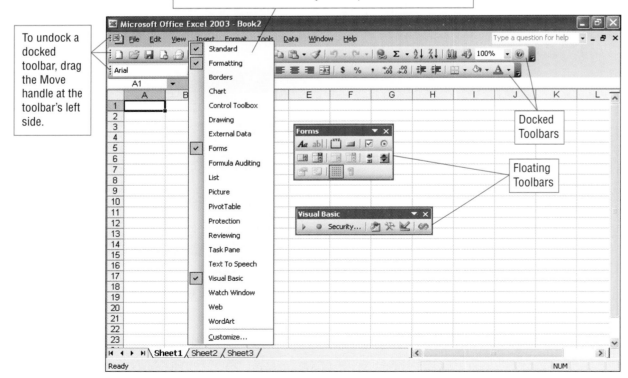

To display or hide a toolbar, right-click any displayed toolbar to see a complete menu of toolbars. Selecting a toolbar that has a check by it will close that toolbar. Selecting a toolbar that does not have a check by it will open that toolbar.

To undock a docked toolbar, drag the Move handle at the toolbar's left side.

Docked Toolbars

Floating Toolbars

Hiding and Displaying Toolbars

As shown in Figure 6.8, you can hide and display toolbars by right-clicking on any displayed toolbar. A menu pops up, listing all the toolbars. Toolbars with a check mark next to them are currently displayed. Those without check marks are currently hidden. Clicking on a hidden toolbar displays it, and clicking on a displayed toolbar hides it. You can also hide and display toolbars by clicking View and then Toolbars. The same menu appears that is displayed when you right-click a toolbar.

HINT

Unlike other toolbars, the Menu bar cannot be hidden.

Customizing Toolbars and Menus

Microsoft Office automatically formats toolbars and menus based on their use. When an Office program is first started, only basic commands are displayed on the menus. As you work in a program, the toolbars and menus are automatically modified to display the menu commands and toolbar buttons that you most often use. You can override these automatic changes by customizing the toolbars and menus yourself.

Toolbars and menus can be customized in a number of ways. The default setting for Excel 2003 is to have the Standard and Formatting toolbars share one row. With the two toolbars on one row, there might not be enough room for all the buttons to be displayed. The buttons that are displayed are the ones you have most recently used. To change this default setting so that the Standard and Formatting toolbars appear on two rows, click Tools and then click Customize. The Customize dialog box appears. Click the Options tab. The dialog box will look like Figure 6.9. Click the *Standard and Formatting toolbars on two rows* check box so that it is selected.

QUICK STEPS

Change the Default Setting for Toolbars
Click Tools, Customize, and then click the Options tab.

FIGURE

6.9 *The Customize Dialog Box with the Options Tab Selected*

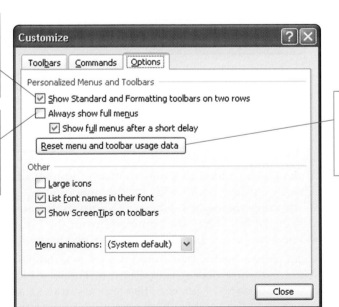

If you want the Standard and Formatting toolbars displayed on two rows, this option should be selected.

If you want the full menus always displayed rather than only the most recently used commands, this option should be selected.

Click this button to display the default set of visible commands on the menus and buttons on the toolbars.

The default setting for menus is for them to display at first only the most basic commands and then to display those commands you use most often. If after using an application for a while you want to go back to displaying the default set of visible commands on the menus and buttons on the toolbars, click the Reset my usage data button. If instead of displaying only the commands you use most often, you want the full menus to be displayed, click the Always show full menus check box.

As shown in Figure 6.10, another way to hide or display toolbars is to click the Toolbars tab on the Customize dialog box. To display a toolbar, click the check box next to it. To hide a toolbar, clear the check box next to it. By clicking the New button, you can create a new toolbar. The New Toolbar dialog box is displayed. Enter a name for the toolbar in the *Toolbar name* box and then click OK. The new toolbar is displayed on the worksheet.

FIGURE

6.10 *The Customize Dialog Box with the Toolbars Tab Selected*

QUICK STEPS

Create a New Toolbar
1. Click Tools, and then click Customize.
2. Click the Toolbars tab.
3. Click the New button.

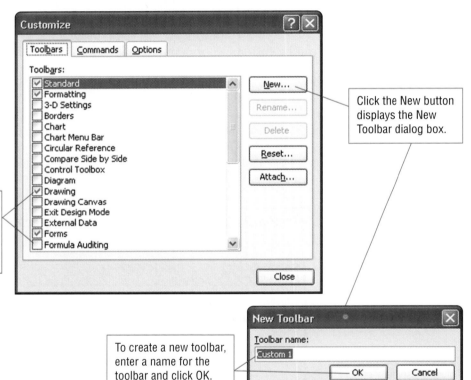

Click the check box next to those toolbars you want displayed. Clear the check box next to those toolbars you want hidden.

Click the New button displays the New Toolbar dialog box.

To create a new toolbar, enter a name for the toolbar and click OK.

QUICK STEPS

Place a Button that Runs an Excel Command on a Toolbar
1. Click Tools and then Customize.
2. Click the Commands tab.

Buttons can be added to a new toolbar a number of different ways. To place one of Excel's existing commands on the new toolbar, click the Commands tab on the Customize dialog box. Click the appropriate category of the command in the *Categories* list box. Drag the command from the *Commands* list box to the new toolbar. The appropriate button will appear on the toolbar.

You can place a button that runs a macro on a toolbar by clicking the Commands tab on the Customize dialog box (shown in Figure 6.11) and selecting *Macros* in the *Categories* list box. A *Custom Button* appears in the *Commands* list box. Drag this custom button to the toolbar. To change the name of the button, as well as the image that appears on the button, and to assign the macro to the button, right-click the button on the toolbar.

6.11 *The Customize Dialog Box with the Commands Tab Selected*

Place a Menu on a Toolbar
1. Click Tools and then Customize.
2. Click the Commands tab.
3. In the *Categories* list box, scroll down and then click *New Menu*.

Delete a Custom Toolbar
1. Click Tools and then Customize.
2. Click the Toolbars tab.
3. Click Delete.

You can also place a menu on a toolbar. Again, click the Commands tab on the Customize dialog box (shown in Figure 6.11) and select New Menu in the *Categories* list box. Drag the *Custom Button* that appear in the *Commands* list box to the toolbar. You can make changes to the button by right-clicking the button on the toolbar.

You can delete a custom toolbar that you have created by clicking the Toolbars tab on the Customize dialog box (shown in Figure 6.10). Select the toolbar you want to delete from the *Toolbars* list box and then click Delete.

exercise 3

CREATING MACROS AND CUSTOMIZING A TOOLBAR AND MENU

1. Open **ExcelWorksheet02**.
2. Save the worksheet using the Save As command and name it **eec6x03**.
3. Click the *7 Percent* worksheet tab. Press Shift and click the *8 Percent* worksheet tab. All three worksheets should be selected. Create a custom header that displays your name at the left margin and the file name at the right margin.
4. When students come into the financial advisor's office at Redwood Community College, they often want to know what kind of payments they can expect on student loans. This worksheet helps students determine what the monthly payments on a student loan would be (depending on how much money they borrow), the interest rate, and the length of the loan. Complete the following steps for creating a macro that will enter the loan amounts:
   a. Click cell A7.
   b. Display the Visual Basic toolbar by right-clicking on a toolbar and then clicking Visual Basic.

c. Click the Record Macro button on the Visual Basic toolbar. The Record Macro dialog box is displayed.

d. Enter **Amounts** in the *Macro name* box.

e. Click the *Shortcut key* box. Press the Shift key and enter **A**.

f. Click OK. The Stop Recording toolbar is displayed.

g. You do not want the cell references to be relative. Make sure the Relative References button on the Stop Recording toolbar is *not* selected. Type the following in the cells indicated:

Cell	Value	Cell	Value
A7	10000	A13	40000
A8	15000	A14	45000
A9	20000	A15	50000
A10	25000	A16	55000
A11	30000	A17	60000
A12	35000		

h. You are going to select some cells, and you want the cell references to be relative. Click the Relative Reference button on the Stop Recording toolbar so that it is selected.

i. Select cells A7 through A17. Format these cells as currency with no decimal places.

j. Click the Stop Recording button on the Stop Recording toolbar.

5. Complete the following steps to create a macro for entering the PMT function:

a. Click cell B7.

b. Click the Record Macro button on the Visual Basic toolbar.

c. Enter **Payment** in the *Macro name* box.

d. Press the Shift key and enter **P** in the *Shortcut key* box. Notice that it now says *Ctrl+Shift+P* for the shortcut key.

e. Click OK. The Stop Recording toolbar is displayed.

f. Make sure the Relative Reference button on the Stop Recording toolbar is selected.

g. Type =PMT($B$4/12,B$5,-$A7) in cell B7.

h. Click the Enter button next to the formula bar.

i. Copy the formula in cell B7 down to cell B17 and then across to column F.

j. Click the Stop Recording button on the Stop Recording toolbar.

6. Complete the following steps to create a custom toolbar that will include a button for the Amounts macro and a button for the Payment macro:

a. Click Tools and then click Customize.

b. If necessary, click the Toolbars tab. Click New.

c. Enter **Macros** in the *Toolbar name* box, then click OK.

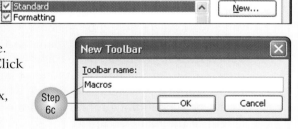

d. Click the Commands tab.
e. Select *Macros* from the *Categories* list box.
f. Drag the *Custom Button* from the *Commands* list box to the Macros toolbar twice.

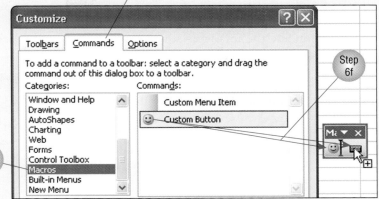

7. Since students often ask for the worksheet to be printed, having the Print and Page Setup options available on a custom menu would be convenient. Complete the following steps to add a custom menu to the Macros toolbar:
a. The Customize dialog box should still be displayed with the Commands tab selected. From the *Categories* list box, select *New Menu*.
b. Drag the *New Menu* button from the *Commands* list box to the Macros toolbar.

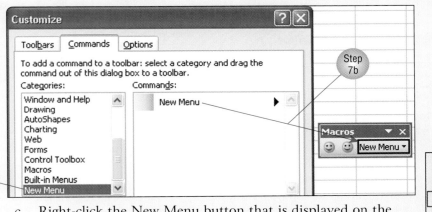

c. Right-click the New Menu button that is displayed on the Macros toolbar. In the *Name* box on the shortcut menu, enter Print.
d. Next you want to add the Print command and the Page Setup command to your new Print menu. Click *File* in the *Categories* list box.
e. Click the *Page Setup* button from the *Commands* list box and then drag it to

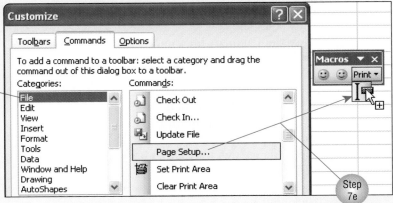

the Print menu on the Macros toolbar. When it is resting over the menu, the drop-down list box under Print is displayed. Point to the drop-down list box and release the mouse.

f. Click the Print button from the *Commands* list box and then drag it to the drop-down list box under the Print menu on the Macros toolbar. Place it under the Page Setup command. Release the mouse.

Step 7f

8. Complete the following steps to assign a macro to each of the custom buttons on the Macros toolbar:

a. The Customize dialog box should still be open. Right-click the first custom button on the Macros toolbar.
b. Enter **Amounts** in the *Name* box.
c. Select Change Button Image.
d. Click the pencil image, the fourth option from the left in the fourth row.
e. Right-click the first custom button.
f. Click Assign Macro.
g. Select *Amounts* from the *Macro name* list box.

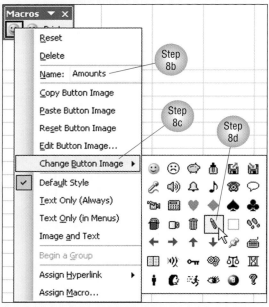

Step 8b

Step 8c

Step 8d

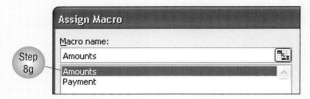

Step 8g

h. Click OK.
i. Right-click the second custom button on the Macros toolbar. Enter **Payment** in the *Name* box.
j. Select Change Button Image. Click the piggy bank button, the third option in row 1.
k. Right-click the second custom button on the Macros toolbar, then click Assign Macro.
l. Select *Payment* from the *Macro name* list box and then click OK.
m. Close the Customize dialog box and then close the Visual Basic toolbar.

9. Complete the following steps to use the Amounts and Payment macros on the *7.5 Percent* worksheet:

a. Click the *7.5 Percent* worksheet tab.
b. Click cell A7.
c. Click the Amounts button on the Macros toolbar.
d. Click cell B7.
e. Click the Payment button on the Macros toolbar.
f. Click the Page Setup option on the Print menu.
g. In the Page Setup dialog box, click the Margins tab. Click the *Horizontally* check box in the *Center on page* section, then click OK.
h. Click the Print option on the Print menu, then click OK.

Step 9c

Step 9e

Step 9f

10. Complete the following steps to use the Amounts and Payment macros on the *8 Percent* worksheet:

a. Click the *8 Percent* worksheet tab.
b. Click cell A7.
c. Click the Amounts button on the Macros toolbar.
d. Click cell B7.

e. Click the Payment button on the Macros toolbar.
f. Click the Page Setup option on the Print menu.
g. In the Page Setup dialog box, click the Margins tab. Click the *Horizontally* check box in the *Center on page* section, then click OK.
11. Complete the following steps to delete the Macros toolbar:
a. Right-click the Macros toolbar.
b. Click Customize, the last option in the menu.
c. Click the Toolbars tab.
d. Select *Macros* from the *Toolbars* list box.
e. Click Delete, then click OK and close the Customize dialog box.
12. Save the workbook using the same name (**eec6x03**) and close it.

Step 11d

Auditing Workbooks

Making sure a large and complex worksheet is functioning accurately could be a difficult chore. Excel's built-in auditing features help simplify that task. By using the Formula Auditing toolbar you can check the active worksheet for errors, locate dependencies in formulas (cells on which the formula is dependent or cells that are dependent on the formula), display tracer arrows to find precedents (the cells on which the formula is dependent because they provide data for the formula) and dependents (cells that depend on the value provided by the formula), trace errors, circle invalid data, and evaluate formulas. The following section introduces you to the tools available on the Formula Auditing Toolbar.

Displaying the Auditing Toolbar

To display the Auditing toolbar, right-click a toolbar and then click Customize. Click the Toolbars tab and then select *Formula Auditing* from the *Toolbars* list box. The Formula Auditing toolbar shown in Figure 6.12 is displayed. You can also display the Formula Auditing toolbar by clicking Tools, selecting Formula Auditing, and then clicking Show Formula Auditing Toolbar. Table 6.1 describes the buttons found on the Formula Auditing toolbar.

QUICK STEPS

Display the Auditing Toolbar
1. Click Tools and then Customize.
2. Click the Toolbars tab.

6.12 *Displaying the Auditing Toolbar*

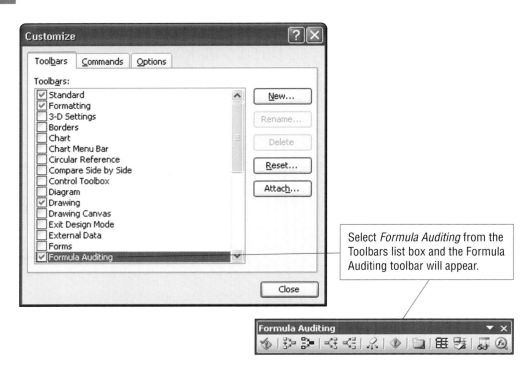

Select *Formula Auditing* from the Toolbars list box and the Formula Auditing toolbar will appear.

TABLE

6.1 *The Formula Auditing Toolbar*

Button	Button Name	Function
	Error Checking	Checks the active worksheet for errors
	Trace Precedents	Displays tracer arrows that indicate the cells on which the formula in the active cell is dependent
	Remove Precedent Arrows	Removes tracer arrows generated by the Trace Precedents button
	Trace Dependents	Displays tracer arrows that indicate cells containing formulas that depend on the value in the active cell
	Remove Dependent Arrows	Removes tracer arrows generated by the Trace Dependents button
	Remove All Arrows	Removes all precedent tracer arrows and dependent tracer arrows
	Trace Error	Finds cells contributing to an error in a cell
	The New Comment	Allows you to write a comment that is attached to a cell

	Circle Invalid Data	Circles cells containing data outside the valid range defined with the Validation feature
	Clear Validation Circles	Removes circles generated by the Circle Invalid Data button
	Show Watch Window	Displays or hides a watch window to keep track of the results of cells in the spreadsheet when it recalculates
	Evaluate Formula	Evaluates the formula one step at a time

Tracing Dependents and Precedents

A precedent cell is a cell that is referred to by a formula in another cell. For example, if cell G5 contains the formula =F5*1.05, F5 is a precedent to G5. A dependent cell is a cell containing a formula that refers to another cell. In the preceding example, G5 is a dependent of F5. To trace the precedents or dependents of a cell, select the appropriate cell and then click either the Trace Precedents or Trace Dependents button. Blue tracer arrows are displayed indicating cells with a direct relationship to the selected cell's result. If you click the button again, additional arrows that indicate the next level of cells with a relationship to the selected cell's result are drawn. You can keep clicking the button until Excel beeps, which means there are no more relationships to be found. The tracer arrows can be removed by clicking the Remove Precedent button, Remove Dependent button, or the Remove All Arrows button.

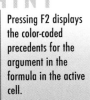

HINT

Pressing F2 displays the color-coded precedents for the argument in the formula in the active cell.

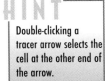

HINT

Double-clicking a tracer arrow selects the cell at the other end of the arrow.

Tracing Errors

If an error result such as #DIV/0! is being displayed in a cell, clicking the cell containing the error and then clicking the Trace Error button draws red tracer arrows to the cells that are causing the error. To remove the tracer arrows, click the Remove All Arrows button.

Locating Invalid Data and Formulas

You can locate invalid data and formulas by using the Error Checking button and the Circle Invalid Data button on the Formula Auditing toolbar. The Error Checking button will search through the worksheet for formulas. Excel uses certain rules to check for problems in formulas, much like it does with the grammar checker. If a problem is found a dialog box is displayed with options for correcting the formula. Using error checking does not guarantee that all the formulas in a workbook will be problem-free, but it is a big help in finding common mistakes. Table 6.2 lists some of the error messages you may encounter in a worksheet.

6.2 *Excel Error Messages*

Message	Problem
#DIV/0!	A formula has been divided by 0.
#NAME?	A formula has unrecognized text.
#NA	A value is not available to a function or formula.
#NULL!	A problem occurs with a number in a formula or function.
#NUM!	A problem occurs with a number in a formula or function.
#REF!	A cell reference is not valid.
#VALUE!	The wrong type of argument or operand is used.

HINT

The circles drawn around invalid data are not printed when you print the worksheet.

The Circle Invalid Data button draws a red circle around all cells that contain values that are outside the limits you set by using the Validation command on the Data menu. Figure 6.13 shows the data validation criteria you can select. Table 6.3 describes the types of criteria you can use for your validation.

If you use a copy or move command to place data in a cell, you can destroy the data validation rule for that cell. If this occurs, the Circle Invalid Data option will not locate errors in that cell.

FIGURE

6.13 *The Data Validation Dialog Box*

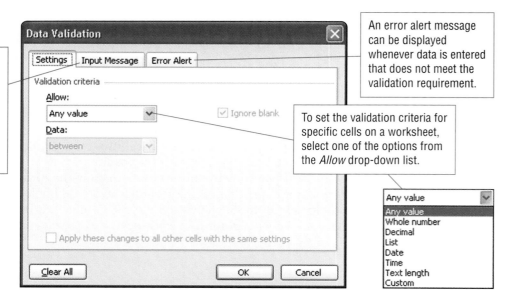

You can enter an input message that will display whenever a cell with data validation criteria is selected. The message can indicate what type of data must be entered into that cell.

An error alert message can be displayed whenever data is entered that does not meet the validation requirement.

To set the validation criteria for specific cells on a worksheet, select one of the options from the *Allow* drop-down list.

6.3 *Data Validation Criteria*

Critera	Description
Any value	Allows anything to be entered
Whole Number	Allows only whole numbers to be entered
Decimal	Allows only decimals in a specific range to be entered
List	Allows only the options from a list to be entered
Date	Allows only dates to be entered
Time	Allows only time to be entered
Text Length	Allows only so many characters to be entered
Custom	Allows only a custom formula to be entered

Watching and Evaluating Formulas

You can watch cells and their formulas even when those cells are out of view using the Watch Window toolbar. Click the Show Watch Window button on the Formula Auditing toolbar to display the Watch Window toolbar. The Watch Window toolbar displays at all times the value and formula residing in the cells you selected to watch.

With a complex formula, knowing whether or not it is returning the correct value can be difficult. If a formula is not returning the correct value, determining what part of the formula needs to be changed may also be difficult. The Evaluate Formula button helps overcome these problems. The Evaluate Formula dialog box takes you through the different parts of a nested formula and evaluates each part of the formula in the order it is calculated.

exercise 4

AUDITING A WORKSHEET USING ERROR CHECKING, TRACING PRECEDENTS, TRACING DEPENDENTS, AND ADDING COMMENTS

1. Open **ExcelWorksheet03**.
2. Save the worksheet using the Save As command and name it **eec6x04**.
3. Create a custom header that displays your name at the left margin and the file name at the right margin.
4. There are cells divided by zero error messages in this worksheet. Complete the following steps to find the cells causing this error:
   a. Right-click the Formatting toolbar and then click Customize.
   b. Click the Toolbars tab.

c. Click the *Formula Auditing* check box in the *Toolbars* list box to select it. The Formula Auditing toolbar is displayed.
d. Click the Close button.
e. Click the Error Checking button, the first button on the Formula Auditing toolbar. The Error Checking dialog box identifies the first error as a divide by zero error. Click the Help on this error button and read about a divide by zero error. When you have finished reading it, close the Microsoft Office Excel Help window.

Step 4c

f. For now you want to find just the other errors on the worksheet. Click the Resume button and then click the Next button. Click the Next button several times and you will see that the worksheet is filled with divide by zero errors. Close the Error Checking dialog box.

Step 4d

Step 4e

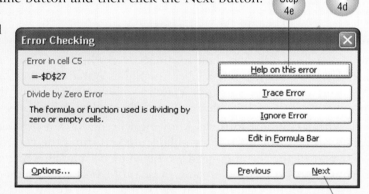

Step 4f

g. You now want to try to locate the error using the Trace Error button. Click cell C5.
h. Click the Trace Error button on the Formula Auditing toolbar. A red tracer arrow is drawn to cell D27.
i. Look at the formula in D27, which is =D25/D26. Now look at cell D26. It contains a zero. Click cell D26 and then type 5 and then press Enter.
j. The red tracer line changes to a blue tracer line because the error was fixed. All of the divide by zero error messages are replaced with data.

5. Click in cell D11. This is the net income for year 2. You want to know what the precedents are for this formula. Complete the following steps to trace the precedents for the net income formula:
   a. Click the Trace Precedents button on the Formula Auditing toolbar.
   b. Click the Trace Precedents button a second time. You can now see that cells D4, D5, D7, D9, and D10 are all precedents to the contents of cell D11. The first level precedents are cells D9 and D10. The next level precedents are cells D4, D5, and D7.
   c. You can follow a trace by double-clicking one of the dots on the tracer line. The active cell immediately becomes the cell at the other end of the arrow. Double-click the blue dot in cell D4. Cell D9 is now the active cell.
   d. Double-click the blue dot in cell D4 again to move the active cell back to cell D4.
   e. Click cell G11. This is the net income for year 5. You want to know what formulas reference this cell.

EXCEL

f.   Click the Trace Dependents button. The tracer arrow that is drawn shows you that cell G16 contains a formula that refers to cell G11.
6.   Print the worksheet.
7.   Click the Remove All Arrows button on the Formula Auditing toolbar.
8.   Complete the following steps to enter a new comment for cell A5:
    a.   Click cell A5.
    b.   Click the New Comment button on the Formula Auditing toolbar.
    c.   Type the following: **Figures for calculating the depreciation on new machines are found in cells C21 through D27.**
9.   Close the Formula Auditing toolbar.
10. Save the workbook using the same name (**eec6x04**) and close it.

exercise 5

| AUDITING A WORKSHEET BY USING ERROR CHECKING, EVALUATING FORMULAS, CIRCLING INVALID DATA AND USING CELL WATCH. |

1.   Open **ExcelWorksheet04**.
2.   Save the worksheet using the Save As command and name it **eec6x05**.
3.   Create a custom header that displays your name at the left margin and the file name at the right margin.
4.   This worksheet is a grade book used by an instructor at Redwood Community College. Each student's final grade is made up of a variety of percentages from quizzes, projects, and exams. The grades are weighted so that each quiz grade is worth 10% of the final grade, attendance is worth 10 percent of the final grade and exams are worth 20% of the final grade. First you want to check for errors in the worksheet.
    a.   Display the Formula Auditing toolbar.
    b.   Click the Error Checking button on the Formula Auditing toolbar. A division by zero error is found. This formula is finding the average of cells G6 through G34. Nothing has been entered into those cells yet, which is why the error message is being returned.
    c.   Click the Next button. At the Microsoft Office Excel message saying that no more errors were found, click OK.
5.   None of the final grades should be over 100%, so you want to use data validation criteria to make sure the grades are all 100% or lower.
    a.   Select cells I6 through I34.
    b.   Click Data and then click Validation. The Data Validation dialog box is displayed.
    c.   Click the down-pointing arrow next to the right of the *Allow* box and then click *Decimal*.
    d.   Click the down-pointing arrow to the right of the *Data* box and then click *less than*.
    e.   Enter **100** in the *Maximum* box.
    f.   Click OK.

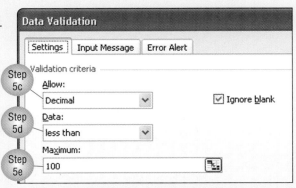

6.   The instructor needs to add the grades for attendance and participation. But first she wants to include data validation criteria. On her syllabus she included her policy that no one can get below a D for an attendance and participation grade. She wants to make sure she does not forget about her policy when she enters the grades.

a. Select cells G6 through G34.
b. Click Data and then click Validation.
c. Click the down-pointing arrow to the right of the *Allow* box and select *Decimal*.
d. Click the down-pointing arrow to the right of the *Data* box and select *between*.
e. Enter **60** in the *Minimum* box.
f. Enter **100** in the *Maximum* box.
g. Click the Input Message tab.
h. Enter **Grade Criteria** in the *Title* box.
i. Enter **Attendance/Participation grades must be between 60% and 100%** in the *Input message* box.

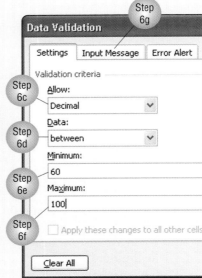

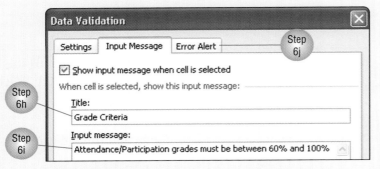

j. Click the Error Alert tab.
k. Enter **Grade Error** in the *Title* box.
l. Enter **Grades cannot be lower than 60% or higher than 100%** in the *Error message* box.
m. Click OK.

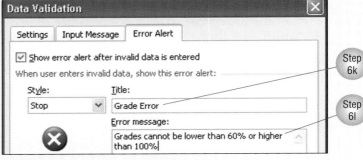

7. Enter the following Attendance/Participation grades. Notice when you select cell G6, the validation message you entered is displayed.

Cell	Value
G6	100
G7	82
G8	55

The *Error message* box is displayed indicating the grade values have to be between 60% and 100%. Click Retry.

Cell	Value	Cell	Value	Cell	Value	Cell	Value
G8	60	G15	100	G22	79	G29	89
G9	88	G16	95	G23	98	G30	76
G10	70	G17	69	G24	90	G31	71
G11	93	G18	86	G25	94	G32	98
G12	95	G19	76	G26	92	G33	95
G13	65	G20	97	G27	82	G34	69
G14	70	G21	74	G28	100		

8. You want to use the Circle Invalid data option on the Formula Auditing toolbar to check for mistakes in the worksheet. Click the Circle Invalid Data button. Two cells in column I are circled. You set a validation rule for column I that no value could be greater than 100% but these two values are greater. Somewhere on the worksheet there is a mistake since the grades cannot be over 100%.

9. Complete the following steps to use the Evaluate Formula button to try to find the mistake:
   a. Click cell I6, the first cell that is circled.
   b. Click the Evaluate Formula button on the Formula Auditing toolbar.
   c. The Evaluate Formula dialog box is displayed. Place it so that you can see all the entries in row 6. The formula entered in cell I6 is displayed in the *Evaluation* box. Notice that the first underlined expression is B6. Click the Evaluate button.
   d. The result of the underlined expression is displayed. The value 88 is entered in cell B6. Now 88*.01 is underlined. Click the Evaluate button.
   e. The result of the underlined expression, or 8.8, is displayed. The quiz is worth 10% of the final grade and the quiz score was 88, so 8.8 is correct. Click the Evaluate button.
   f. Click the Evaluate button three times to evaluate the next portion of the formula. Again the quiz is worth 10% of the final grade and the quiz score was 92, so 9.2 is correct. Click Evaluate.
   g. The next portion of the formula is to add the first two scores together. Click Evaluate.
   h. Click Step In. The Evaluate Formula dialog box now shows you specifically where on the worksheet cell D6 is and what data is entered in D6. Click Step Out.

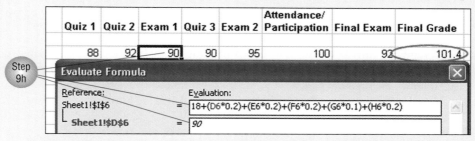

   i. Click Evaluate three times to move to the next part of the formula. The underline should be under E6. Click the Step In button. E6 is the grade for Quiz 3. Click Step Out. The underlined expression is now 90*0.2. But quiz grades are only worth 10% of the final grade, not 20%, so this is an error. Click Close.

10. In order to fix the error you have to change the validation rules for cells I6 through I34.
   a. Select cells I6 through I34.
   b. Click Data and Validation, then click the Settings tab.
   c. Click the down-pointing arrow to the right of the *Allow* box and click *Any value*.
   d. Click OK.
   e. Click cell I6 and edit the formula so that it says (D6*0.1) rather than (D6*0.2).
   f. Copy the formula in cell I6 to cells I7 through I34.

11. Look at cell I36. The overall class average is 80, which is a little high. On reexamining the final exam grades, the instructor for CS100 has decided she was too lenient and some of the grades are too high. You want to be able to watch what happens to the class average while you change the Final Exam grades.
   a. Click the Show Watch Window button on the Formula Auditing toolbar.
   b. The Watch Window toolbar is displayed. Click Add Watch.
   c. The Add Watch dialog box is displayed. Click cell I36 and then click Add.

d. Scroll to the top of the window. Arrange the watch window so that it is right next to column H as shown below. This way you can easily see how cell I36 changes while you change the data in column H.

4	Student		Quiz 1	Quiz 2	Exam 1	Quiz 3	Exam 2	Attendance/ Participation	Final Exam
5									
6	Alston								92
7	Anik, D								85
8	Barnes								70
9	Beckm								88
10	Belzer								72
11	Bogus								96
12	Browne								84
13	Currie,								73
14	Dauer,								75
15	Dunn, Stacey		88	92	88	92	96	100	95

Watch Window — Add Watch... — Delete Watch

Book	Sheet	Name	Cell	Value	Formula
eec6x...	Sheet1		I36	80.20689655	=AVERAGE(I6:I34)

Step 11d

e. Enter **86** in cell H6. The class average went down slightly.
f. Make the following changes to the final exam grades and watch what happens to the class average in the watch window.

Cell	Value	Cell	Value
H7	79	H12	80
H8	65	H13	68
H9	80	H14	70
H10	67	H15	90
H11	91	H16	85

The class average has now been brought down to a high C, which is better. The instructor could finish entering the rest of the updated final exam scores and watch the effect on the classes overall average.

12. Close the Watch Window window and the Formula Auditing toolbar.
13. Print the worksheet.
14. Save the workbook using the same name (**eec6x05**) and close it.

CHAPTER summary

➤ Macros automate tasks that perform the same sequence of steps or tasks that are performed repeatedly. Excel's macro recorder records every keystroke and mouse click so that they can be played back at a later time.

➤ Excel macros are automatically created in the Visual Basic for Applications programming language.

➤ Record a macro by clicking Tools, selecting Macro, and then clicking Record New Macro. In the Record Macro dialog box, enter a macro name and, if desired, a shortcut key and description. A macro name must begin with a letter but can contain numbers, letters, and the underscore character. A shortcut key is a letter that is pressed together with Ctrl or Ctrl + Shift in order to execute the macro.

➤ Planning the exact steps of a macro before recording it is important because everything that is entered, including mistakes and the keystrokes taken to fix the mistakes, is recorded and executed every time the macro is run.

E276 Chapter Six

EXCEL

➤ When selecting cells is a step to be included in a macro, you must know whether the selected cells should have an absolute cell reference or a relative cell reference. The default is for cells to have an absolute cell reference, which means the same cells will be selected each time the macro is executed. If the cells should have a relative cell reference, click the Relative Reference button on the Stop Recording toolbar. If the Relative Reference button appears to be pressed in when the cells are selected, the selected cells will have a relative reference. If the button is not pressed in, then the cells will have an absolute reference.

➤ Run a macro by pressing the shortcut key, pressing the Run Macro button on the Visual Basic toolbar, or clicking Tools, selecting Macro, and then clicking Macros.

➤ Macros can be run from a command button placed on the worksheet. Assign a macro to a command button by clicking the Button button on the Forms toolbar. The mouse pointer turns into a crosshair, and you can click and drag to make the command button the size you want. Once the button has been placed on the worksheet, you can change its name and format and assign a macro to it.

➤ Edit a macro by accessing the Macro dialog box, selecting the macro to be edited, and then clicking Edit. The macro is displayed in the Microsoft Visual Basic editor.

➤ Docked toolbars are attached to one of the program window's borders or to another toolbar. Floating toolbars are not attached to anything. Move a docked toolbar by dragging the move handle located at the left side of the docked toolbar. Move a floating toolbar by dragging the toolbar's title bar.

➤ Change the default setting so that Excel's Standard and Formatting toolbars are on two rows instead of one by clicking Tools and then Customize. Click the Options tab on the Customize dialog box. The *Standard and Formatting toolbars share one row* check box should not be selected.

➤ Precedents are cells that provide data to a formula. Dependents are cells containing formulas that refer to other cells.

FEATURES summary

FEATURE	BUTTON	MENU/COMMANDS
Display or hide toolbars		Click View, Toolbars
Record a macro	⬤	Click Tools, Macro, Record New Macro
Run a macro	▶	Click Tools, Macro, Macros, Run
Delete a macro		Click Tools, Macro, Macros, Delete
Edit a macro's shortcut key command		Click Tools, Macro, Macros, Options
Change the format of a command button		Right-click the Format Control button

FEATURE	BUTTON	MENU/COMMANDS
Assign a macro to a command button		Right-click the Assign Macro button
Change the default setting for toolbars		Click Tools, Customize, Options tab
Create a new toolbar		Click Tools, Customize, Toolbars tab, New
Place a button that runs an Excel command on a toolbar		Click Tools, Customize, Commands
Place a menu on a toolbar		Click Tools, Customize, Commands, *New Menu*
Delete a custom toolbar		Click Tools, Customize, Toolbars tab, Delete
Display the Formula Auditing toolbar		Click Tools, Customize, Toolbars tab

CONCEPTS check

Completion: On a blank sheet of paper, indicate the correct term, symbol, or command for each description.

1. This term refers to the programming language in which Excel macros are created.
2. This is the toolbar that needs to be displayed in order to place a command button on a worksheet.
3. This term refers to the editor used to edit Excel macros.
4. Display this box to edit a macro.
5. This is the term used to refer to the executable lines in a macro.
6. This is the button you click on the Forms toolbar if you want to place a command button on a worksheet.
7. When editing a macro, the comment lines describing the macro begin with this character.
8. This term describes a toolbar that is attached to the border of a program window.
9. If you right-click a toolbar, this is what appears.
10. This term refers to a cell that is referred to by a formula in another cell.
11. When using Error Checking, this is the message that appears if a cell reference is not valid.
12. This is the term that refers to a cell containing a formula that refers to another cell.
13. If red tracer arrows appear on a worksheet, you know that this button was pressed.
14. Clicking this button on the Formula Auditing toolbar enables you to always see the value and formula in selected cells.
15. Explain why it is so important to carefully plan the steps of a macro before recording it.
16. Explain the rules that must be followed for naming a macro.
17. List the steps you would take to place a button that runs a macro on a toolbar.
18. List the types of criteria you can set using the Validation command on the Data menu.

EXCEL

SKILLS check

Assessment 1

1. Open **ExcelWorksheet05**.
2. Save the worksheet using the Save As command and name it **eec6sc01**.
3. This workbook is used by Chris Robinson to keep track of the software installed at all the offices where he works as a freelance PC technician. There are 10 worksheets in the workbook. Each worksheet contains the records for a different office. Scroll through the worksheet tabs at the bottom of the window to see the 10 tabs that are there.
4. Click on the *Archer* worksheet tab. Scroll to the end of the worksheet tabs. Press the Shift key. Click the *River Road* worksheet tab. All the worksheet tabs should be selected. Create a custom header that displays your name at the left margin and the file name at the right margin. The header will now appear on all the selected worksheets.
5. The applications installed on the various PCs and the NT server at each office can be either served or local. If an application is local, it resides on the hard drive of that computer. If an application is served, it resides on a different computer on the network. A served application can be either an image or a copy. A served image is a unique installation. A served copy is a copy of a served image. Chris needs to keep track of the number of each kind of installation there is at each office. Click the *Archer* worksheet tab. Record a macro called Count. You should be able to execute the macro with the shortcut key combination Ctrl + Shift + C. The macro should use absolute cell referencing and should include these steps:

   - In cell H4, enter a COUNTIF function that counts the number of times the letter *I* occurs in cells B4 through G4. *(Hint: Since the macro uses absolute cell referencing, make sure that selecting cell H4 is part of the macro.)*
   - Copy the function in cell H4 down through cell H8.
   - In cell I4, enter a COUNTIF function that counts the number of times the letter *S* occurs in cells B4 through G4.
   - Copy the function in cell I4 down through cell I8.
   - In cell J4, enter a COUNTIF function that counts the number of times the letter *L* appears in cells B4 through G4.
   - Copy the function in cell J4 down through cell J8.
   - Enter a SUM function in cell H9 that totals cells H4 through H8.
   - Copy the function in cell H9 to cells I9 and J9.
   - Enter a formula in cell H11 that adds together the values in cells H9 and J9.

6. Once the Count macro has been recorded, click on the *Bateson* worksheet tab.
7. Run the macro using the shortcut key combination Ctrl + Shift + C.
8. Print the *Archer* and *Bateson* worksheets.
9. Save the workbook using the same name (**eec6sc01**). This worksheet is used in Assessment 2. Close the workbook.

Assessment 2

1. Open workbook **eec6sc01**. You created this workbook in Assessment 1.
2. Save the worksheet using the Save As command and name it **eec6sc02**.
3. Click the *Central* worksheet tab.
4. Create a custom toolbar. Name the toolbar My Commands.

5. Place a button on the My Commands toolbar for the Count macro. The name of the button for the Count macro should be Count. Choose a different graphic image for the button other than the default. Assign the Count macro to the button.
6. Place a button for the Print command on the My Commands toolbar.
7. Add a custom menu to the My Commands toolbar. Name the menu Locate. Place the Find and the Go To options found in the Edit menu on the new Locate menu.
8. Run the Count macro using the Count button on the My Commands toolbar.
9. Print the *Central* worksheet using the Print button on the My Commands toolbar.
10. Click the *Doss* worksheet tab.
11. Run the Count macro using the Count button on the My Commands toolbar.
12. Print the *Doss* worksheet using the Print button on the My Commands toolbar.
13. Click the *Findlay* worksheet tab.
14. Run the Count macro using the Count button on the My Commands toolbar.
15. Print the *Findlay* worksheet using the Print button on the My Commands toolbar.
16. Delete the My Commands toolbar.
17. Save the workbook using the same name (**eec6sc02**). Close the workbook.

Assessment 3

1. Open **ExcelWorksheet06**.
2. Save the worksheet using the Save As command and name it **eec6sc03**.
3. Create a custom header for the worksheet that displays your name at the left margin and the file name at the right margin.
4. Create a macro that uses AutoFilter to display only the shade plants. Name the macro Shade.
5. Create a macro that uses AutoFilter to display all the plants. Name the macro All.
6. Create a macro that uses AutoFilter to display all the sun plants. Name the macro Sun.
7. Create a custom button on the worksheet. The button should be toward the top and to the right of the list. Assign the Shade macro to the button. Rename the button Shade. The letters on the button should be bold and the color sea green. The size of the button should be .25 inch high and .75 inch wide. On the Properties tab in the Format Control dialog box, the option *Don't move or size with cells* should be selected.
8. Create another custom button that is underneath the Shade custom button. Assign the Sun macro to the button. Rename the button Sun. The letters on the button should be bold and the color sea green. The size of the button should be .25 inch high and .75 inch wide. On the Properties tab in the Format Control dialog box, the option *Don't move or size with cells* should be selected.
9. Create another custom button that is underneath the Sun custom button. Assign the All macro to the button. Rename the button All. The letters on the button should be bold and the color sea green. The size of the button should be .25 inch high and .75 inch wide. On the Properties tab in the Format Control dialog box, the option *Don't move or size with cells* should be selected.
10. Click the Shade button. Print the worksheet.
11. Click the All button. *(Hint: You must click the All button before clicking either the Shade button or the Sun button.)* Print the worksheet.
12. Click the Sun button. Print the worksheet.
13. Click the All button.
14. Save the worksheet using the same name (**eec6sc03**) and close it.

Assessment 4

1. Open **ExcelWorksheet07**.
2. Save the worksheet using the Save As command and name it **eec6sc04**.
3. Create a custom header for the worksheet that displays your name at the left margin and the file name at the right margin.
4. Display the Formula Auditing toolbar.
5. There is an error somewhere in this worksheet. Click cell F12. Click the Trace Error button. The tracer arrows indicate that the formula in cell E12 references cells J13 through K16, which are empty. Remove the tracer arrows. In the VLOOKUP function, the references to the cells that make up the lookup table should be absolute. Click cell E3. Edit the formula so that the references to the lookup table are absolute. Copy the formula to cells E4 through E22.
6. Click cell E3. Click the Trace Precedents button.
7. Click cell E6. Click the Trace Dependents button. Click the Trace Dependents button again.
8. Print the worksheet.
9. Remove all the tracer arrows.
10. Close the Formula Auditing toolbar.
11. Save the worksheet using the same name (**eec6sc04**) and close it.

Assessment 5

1. Open **ExcelWorksheet08**.
2. Save the worksheet using the Save As command and name it **eec6sc05**.
3. Create a custom header for the worksheet that displays your name at the left margin and the file name at the right margin.
4. This worksheet contains census data for the United States. Display the Formula Auditing toolbar. Click the Error Checking button on the Formula Auditing toolbar. A division by zero error is found in cell E2. This formula is dividing cell D2 by cell B2 to find the percentage of the females in the United States. Nothing has been entered into those cells yet, which is why the error message is being returned. Keep clicking Next until the error check is complete. Look at each error carefully.
5. All the census data should be whole numbers only. Use data validation criteria to make sure that each entry for all the population data in columns B, C, and D is a whole number greater than 350,000. Include an appropriate input message and error message.
6. Use the Circle Invalid Data command to see if there are any problems with this validation rule. As you will notice there are states with fewer than 350,000 males and/or females. Change the validation rule so that each entry for all the population data in columns B, C, and D is a whole number greater than 250,000. Clear the validation circles.
7. Enter the following population data.

State	Males	Females
Vermont	298,337	310,490
Virginia	3,471,895	3,606,620
Washington	2,924,300	2,959,821
West Virginia	879,170	929,174
Wisconsin	2,649,041	2,714,634
Wyoming	248,374	

When the error message is displayed, click Cancel. Change the validation rule so that each entry for all the population data in columns B, C, and D is a whole number greater than 200,000. Enter the following data for Wyoming:

State	Males	Females
Wyoming	248,374	245,408

8. There is still a division by zero error message in cell E2. Use the Evaluate Formula button on the Formula Auditing toolbar to find the error. Based on the information in the Evaluate Formula dialog box, fix the error. **(Hint: Row 2 is intended to calculate totals.)**

9. You are going to make some changes to the population figures, but you want to be able to watch what happens to the total population of the United States as you make the changes. Use the Show Watch Window command so that the contents of cell B2 are always displayed. Watch what happens to the total population when you make the following changes:

Cell	Data
C48	298,300
D51	929,168
C53	255,129

10. Close the Watch Window.
11. Close the Formula Auditing toolbar.
12. Save and print the worksheet on one page.

CHAPTER challenge

You work in the accounting department of Patty's Pretzels. Part of your job responsibilities include maintaining the workbook named **PattysPretzels**. Over the last year, you were asked (several times a week) to print specific sections of the worksheet. To quickly provide this information, you decide to create macros that print quarterly sales for each of the regions. Begin the process by creating three of the six macros necessary to complete this task. (Choose any three regions.) Then assign each of the macros to a command button. Name the macros and command buttons appropriately. Save the workbook as **PattysPretzelsWithMacros**.

When printing worksheets, controls/objects created with the Forms toolbar may not print automatically. In the workbook created in the first part of the Chapter Challenge, you would like to print the worksheet with the command buttons. Use the Help feature to learn about control properties and printing objects. Then print the worksheet in the **PattysPretzelsWithMacros** workbook with the command buttons. Save the workbook again.

A memo will be sent to the Board of Directors each quarter, updating them with the current sales for each of the regions. Create a memo in Word and link the information from the *Annual Sales* worksheet to it. (Do not include the command buttons.) Be sure to include the all of the necessary parts of a memo. Add a brief paragraph describing the information being sent to them. Save the memo as **AnnualSales–BOD** (Board of Directors).

EXCEL

COLLABORATING WITH WORKGROUPS

PERFORMANCE OBJECTIVES

Upon successful completion of Chapter 7, you will be able to:

➤ Apply and remove passwords
➤ Apply and remove workbook protection
➤ Apply and remove worksheet protection
➤ Add cell protection
➤ Set macro settings
➤ Use digital signatures
➤ Track changes in a shared workbook
➤ Accept and reject tracked changes
➤ Create, edit, and remove a comment
➤ Merge workbooks
➤ View multiple worksheets
➤ Print multiple worksheets

In Chapter 2 you were introduced to sharing workbooks. In this chapter, you will learn more about sharing workbooks and the concept of workgroup computing. One of the goals of computer networks is to make it easy and efficient for people to work together in groups. The term *workgroup computing* refers to a group of people working on a common project using computer resources to share ideas, software, and data. Typically, a workgroup is made up of a small number of people who work at the same location.

Excel includes two groups of features that help promote workgroup computing: workgroup sharing features and workgroup security features. As you already know, several users, or members of a workgroup, can share a workbook. Each workgroup member can edit the workbook simultaneously. These workgroup sharing features help stimulate workgroup collaboration. Excel's security features allow you to prevent certain types of access to a shared workbook. All the features that help facilitate workgroup collaboration will be discussed in this chapter.

Benefits and Limitations of Sharing Workbooks

Typically, in any kind of a business project, several people are involved. Those people directly involved in the project make up a workgroup. Often each individual in the workgroup is responsible for a certain aspect of the project. The manager of the project has to gather information from the workgroup members and consolidate that information in one place. One way for the manager to do this would be to collect hard copies of the data from individual workgroup members and then type all of the collected data into one workbook. But this method would be extremely inefficient. Instead, the workgroup members could all share the workbook, and each member could enter his or her own data. Sharing workbooks increases productivity, saves time, and increases the likelihood that the data will be accurate.

Some limitations are involved when you work with shared workbooks. Security is an issue, because anyone who has access to the network location where the shared workbook is stored has access to that shared workbook. You have to use workbook or worksheet protection (or both) to ensure the information in the workbook is available only to those who should have access to it. In addition, some features are not available in shared workbooks. These features include deleting worksheets; merging cells; using conditional formatting; using drawing tools; inserting or deleting blocks of cells; inserting or editing charts, pictures, objects, or hyperlinks; using the drawing tools, creating or editing PivotTables; creating or editing macros; and assigning passwords to individual worksheets or to the whole workbook.

Protecting Workbooks

Workbooks often contain sensitive information. Sometimes a workbook should be accessible only to certain people within the organization. At other times, people within an organization should be able to access a workbook but not make any changes to it. Or perhaps only specific users are allowed to make changes to certain cells. You may want to prohibit users from removing a workbook from shared use. Several different levels of protection can be placed on a worksheet or workbook. Setting passwords, using digital signatures, and setting macro settings are three ways in which you can help to insure the security of an Excel workbook.

Applying and Removing Passwords

Password protection for an entire workbook is the highest level of protection a workbook can have. If a password has been assigned to a workbook, the workbook cannot be opened by anyone who does not know the password. When a password has been assigned to a workbook, that workbook cannot be shared.

To apply a password to a workbook, click File and then click Save As. Click the Tools button on the Save As dialog box and click General Options. The Save Options dialog box is displayed. Enter the password in the *Password to open* box. If a workbook is to be generally accessible but only certain people should be able to make changes to it, enter a password in the *Password to modify* box. Anyone will be able to open the workbook, but only those who know the password will be able to make changes.

As can be seen in Figure 7.1, when the password is entered, bullets are displayed in the box. Passwords can be up to 15 characters long. They are case-sensitive,

QUICK STEPS

Apply or Remove a Password to a Workbook
1. Click File and then Save As.
2. Click Tools button.
3. Click General Options.

which means that uppercase and lowercase does matter. If a password contains a capital letter, that letter must be capitalized when entering the password or the workbook will not open. The same is true with lowercase letters.

FIGURE 7.1 *The Save Options Dialog Box*

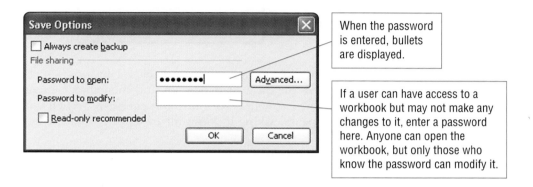

When the password is entered, bullets are displayed.

If a user can have access to a workbook but may not make any changes to it, enter a password here. Anyone can open the workbook, but only those who know the password can modify it.

Once the password has been entered, click OK. The Confirm Password dialog box shown in Figure 7.2 is displayed. Enter the password again in the *Reenter password to proceed* box. Again, the password is displayed in bullets. A message appears in this dialog box, warning you that if the password is lost or forgotten, there is no way to recover it and the workbook cannot be opened. If the warning box appears, asking if you want to replace the existing workbook with the open workbook, click Yes.

FIGURE 7.2 *Confirm Password Dialog Box*

When you try to open a password-protected workbook, the dialog box shown in Figure 7.3 is displayed. As you enter the password, bullets are once again displayed. After entering the password, click OK. If the password was entered correctly, the workbook is opened.

HINT

If you think you have entered the password correctly but Excel will not open the workbook, make sure the Caps Lock key is not on.

7.3 *The Password Dialog Box*

QUICK STEPS

Hide a Worksheet
Click Format, point to Sheet and then click Hide.

To remove a password from a workbook, click File and then click Save As. Click the Tools button on the Save As dialog box and then click General Options. Delete the bullets from the *Password to open* box and click OK. When you click Save and a warning box appears, asking if you want to replace the existing file, click Yes.

Applying and Removing Cell, Worksheet, and Workbook Protection

HINT

Shared workbooks also can be protected. To protect a shared workbook, click Tools, point to Protection, and click Protect and Share Workbook. The Protect Shared Workbook dialog box is displayed. Click the *Sharing with track changes* check box to select it. Enter a password if desired and click OK.

You can protect a worksheet by hiding it from view or by locking its cells so that changes cannot be made to them. To hide an entire worksheet from view, click the worksheet to be hidden and then click Format, select Sheet, and click Hide. The worksheet that was selected is no longer displayed.

Once a worksheet is hidden, the workbook must be protected in order to prevent other users from redisplaying it. When a workbook is protected, other users cannot insert, delete, hide, move, or rename worksheets unless they know the password. To protect the workbook, click Tools, point to Protection, and then click Protect Workbook. The Protect Workbook dialog box shown in Figure 7.4 is displayed. The *Structure* check box should be selected in order for the underlying structure of the worksheet to be protected. Enter a password in the *Password* box and then click OK. The password is case-sensitive. Once you click OK, the Confirm Password dialog box shown in Figure 7.2 is displayed. Enter the password again and then click OK.

7.4 *The Protect Workbook Dialog Box*

QUICK STEPS

Protect a Workbook
Click Tools, point to Protection, and then click Protect Workbook.

QUICK STEPS

Remove Workbook Protection
Click Tools, point to Protection, and then click Unprotect Workbook.

If you want to display a worksheet that has been hidden, you must first remove the workbook protection. To remove workbook protection, click Tools, point to Protection, and then click Unprotect Workbook. The Unprotect Workbook dialog box is displayed. Enter the password in the *Password* box and then click OK. You can then unhide the worksheet by clicking Format, pointing to Sheet, and then

clicking Unhide. The Unhide dialog box is displayed. Click the worksheet to be unhidden and then click OK. The worksheet is once again displayed.

Unhide a Worksheet
Click Format, point to Sheet, and then click Unhide.

You also can protect individual cells from being changed. This feature is useful for protecting formulas that you want to make sure do not get overwritten with other data. When you use this feature to protect cells, all the cells on the worksheet are protected. You then have to indicate those cells that can be changed. Select the cells in the worksheet that can be changed, click Format, and then click Cells. Click the Protection tab on the Format Cells dialog box. As shown in Figure 7.5, there are two options in the dialog box: *Locked* and *Hidden*.

FIGURE

7.5   *Format Cells Dialog Box with Protection Tab Selected*

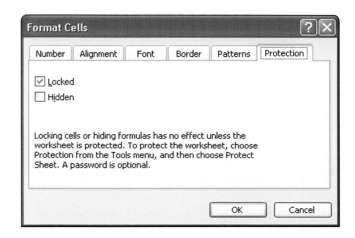

Click the *Locked* check box so that it is no longer selected. This will unlock the selected cells so that changes can be made to them. Click OK to close the Format Cells dialog box. Click Tools, select Protection, and then click Protect Sheet. The Protect Sheet dialog box shown in Figure 7.6 is displayed. The default is for Excel to protect everything in the worksheet except for the cells that you unlocked. An optional password can be entered in the *Password* box. The password is case-sensitive. If you enter a password, you will have to reenter it in the Confirm Password dialog box. The *Allow all users of this worksheet to* list box enables you to select specific formatting commands that users will be able to perform even on a protected worksheet. The password to protect a sheet is optional. However, if you do not provide a password, anyone will be able to unprotect the sheet and change the protected elements. The password to protect a sheet is optional. However, if you do not provide a password, anyone will be able to unprotect the sheet and change the protected elements.

Protect Individual Cells
1 Click Format and then Cells.
2 Click Protection tab.

7.6 The Protect Sheet Dialog Box

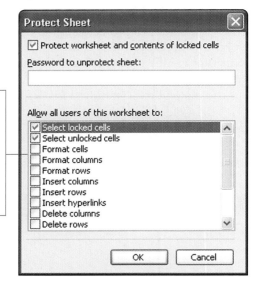

The Protect Sheet dialog box enables you to protect cell values and formulas while allowing cells to be formatted. Users will be able to perform any of the formatting commands that are selected.

Once the cells have been protected, the warning box shown in Figure 7.7 is displayed. To remove cell protection, click Tools, point to Protection, and then click Unprotect Sheet. If the worksheet is password protected, you will have to enter the password in the *Password* box on the Unprotect Sheet dialog box and then click OK.

7.7 Protect Sheet Warning Box

You can give specific users access to cells that have been protected by clicking Tools, pointing to Protection, and then clicking Allow Users to Edit Ranges. In order to use this command, the worksheet cannot be protected. The Allow Users to Edit Ranges dialog box is displayed. Click the New button. As shown in the dialog box in Figure 7.8, you need to enter a title for the range to which you are granting access in the *Title* box. In the *Refers to cells* box, enter or select the range of cells to which you are granting access. This entry must always begin with an equal sign (=). In the *Range password* box, enter the password needed to access the range. If you do not enter a password, any user will be able to edit the cells. Click OK. The Allow Users to Edit Ranges dialog box shown in Figure 7.9 is displayed. Click the Protect Sheet button. The Protect Sheet Dialog Box, shown in Figure 7.6 is displayed. Make the necessary selections and click OK. If you entered a password for the worksheet, you will need to reenter the password to confirm it.

7.8   *The New Range Dialog Box*

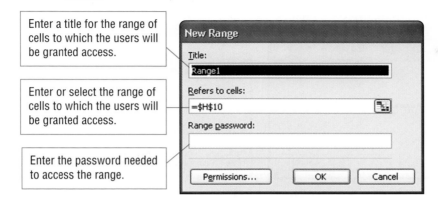

Enter a title for the range of cells to which the users will be granted access.

Enter or select the range of cells to which the users will be granted access.

Enter the password needed to access the range.

New Range

Title:
Range1

Refers to cells:
=$H$10

Range password:

Permissions...   OK   Cancel

7.9   *The Allow Users to Edit Ranges Dialog Box*

Allow Users to Edit Ranges

Ranges unlocked by a password when sheet is protected:

Title	Refers to cells
Range1	$H$10

New...
Modify...
Delete

Specify who may edit the range without a password:

Permissions...

☐ Paste permissions information into a new workbook

Protect Sheet...   OK   Cancel   Apply

QUICK STEPS

Give Specific Users Access to Protected Cells
Click Tools, point to Protection, and then click Allow Users to Edit Ranges.

exercise 1

ASSIGNING A WORKBOOK PASSWORD AND PROTECTING CELLS, WORKSHEETS, AND WORKBOOKS

1. Open Excel.
2. Open **ExcelWorksheet01**.
3. Save the workbook using the Save As command and name it **eec7x01**.
4. Create a custom header for the *IncomeStatement* worksheet that displays your name at the left margin and the file name at the right margin.
5. Complete the following steps to assign a password to the workbook:
   a. Click File and then click Save As.
   b. Click the Tools button on the Save As dialog box and click General Options.

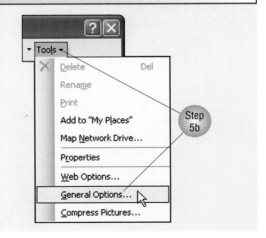

Tools

Delete   Del
Rename
Print
Add to "My Places"
Map Network Drive...
Properties
Web Options...
General Options...
Compress Pictures...

Step 5b

c. Type **C1401C** in the *Password to open* box at the Save Options dialog box. (Bullets display in place of typed text.) Click OK.

d. Type **C1401C** in the *Reenter password to proceed* box at the Confirm Password dialog box.

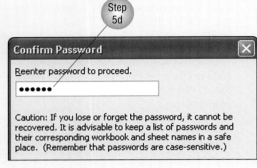

e. Click OK and then click Save.

f. At the warning asking if you want to replace the existing file, click Yes.

6. Close the **eec7x01** workbook.

7. Complete the following steps to open the password-protected workbook:

a. Click File and then click Open.

b. Double-click **eec7x01**.

c. Type **C1401C** in the *Password* box at the Password dialog box and then click OK.

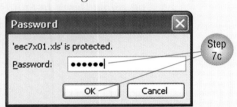

8. Make sure the *IncomeStatement* worksheet is selected. Click cell C8. This cell is linked to a cell on the *CostofGoodsSold* worksheet. The figures on this worksheet are confidential, so you want to hide this worksheet. Complete the following steps to hide the *CostofGoodsSold* worksheet:

a. Click the *CostofGoodsSold* worksheet tab.

b. Click Format, point to Sheet, and then click Hide.

c. Click Tools, point to Protection, and then click Protect Workbook. The Protect Workbook dialog box is displayed.

d. Make sure the *Structure* option is selected. Type **cg0128** in the *Password* box and then click OK.

e. Type **cg0128** in the *Reenter password to proceed* box at the Confirm Password dialog box and then click OK.

9. Click the *IncomeStatement* worksheet tab. Cells C7, C8, C9, C12, C16, C18, and C20 on the worksheet contain formulas. You want to make sure these formulas cannot be changed. Complete the following steps to protect the cells containing formulas:

a. Click cell B4. Press Ctrl and then click the following cells in order to select them all:

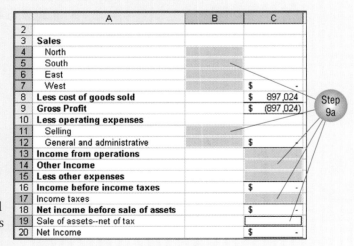

B5, B6, B7, B11, B12, C13, C14, C15, C17, and C19.

EXCEL

b. Click Format and then click Cells.

c. Click the Protection tab on the Format Cells dialog box.

d. Click the *Locked* check box so that it is no longer selected.

e. Click OK.

f. Click Tools, point to Protection, and then click Protect Sheet.

g. Type **IFY05ws** in the *Password* box at the Protect Sheet dialog box.

h. Click the *Format cells* check box to select it and then click OK.

i. Type **IFY05ws** in the *Reenter password to proceed* box on the Confirm Password dialog box and then click OK.

j. Click cell C12 and try to delete it. At the warning box that appears saying that the cell is protected, click OK. If a warning box does not appear, click Edit and Undo. Repeat Steps 9a through 9j to protect the cells on the worksheet.

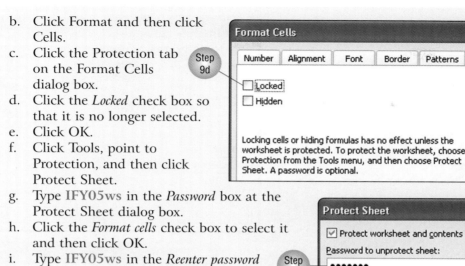

Step 9d

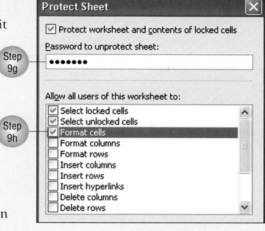

Step 9g

Step 9h

10. Save the workbook using the same name (**eec7x01**). You will be using this workbook in Exercise 4. Close the workbook.

exercise 2

GIVING SPECIFIC USERS ACCESS TO PROTECTED RANGES

1. Open **ExcelWorksheet02**.
2. Save the workbook using the Save As command and name it **eec7x02**.
3. Create a custom header for the *LoanPayments* worksheet that displays your name at the left margin and the file name at the right margin.
4. The owners of the company Bits Unlimited are considering purchasing some vans for their business. This worksheet allows them to compare different loan payment options. You are going to password-protect a range of cells in this worksheet.

a. Click Tools, point to Protection, and then click Allow Users to Edit Ranges.

b. At the Allow Users to Edit Ranges dialog box click New.

c. The New Range dialog box is displayed. In the *Title* box, type **Loan Variables**.

d. Click in the *Refers to cells* box. Select cells B5 through B9.

e. In the *Range password* box, type **02lpBU** and then click OK.

f. At the *Confirm Password* dialog box, enter **02lpBU** and then click OK.

Step 4c

Step 4d

Step 4e

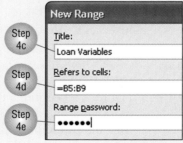

5. The Allow Users to Edit Ranges dialog box is displayed.
   a. Click the Protect Sheet button.
   b. The Protect Sheet dialog box is displayed. In the *Password to unprotect sheet* box, enter **lB*Upv01** and then click OK.
   c. At the Confirm Password dialog box, enter **lB*Upv01**, and then click OK.
6. Only those who know the password can now make changes to cells B5 through B9.
   a. Click cell B7. Type **2**.
   b. At the Unlock Range dialog box, enter **02lpBU**.
   c. Click OK.
   d. Enter **20** in cell B7.
   e. Enter **3** in cell B9.
7. Save the worksheet using the same file name and print it.
8. Save the workbook using the same name (**eec7x02**).
9. Close the workbook.

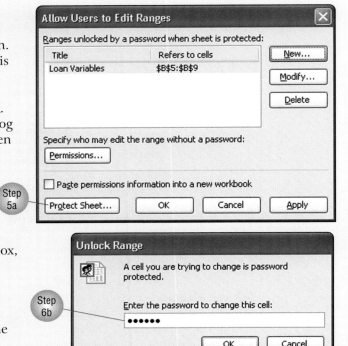

Using Digital Signatures to Authenticate Workbooks

If you send or receive workbooks through e-mail, a good security measure to employ is the use of digital signatures. A digital signature can be used as a way of identifying the source of a workbook. The signature confirms that first, the workbook actually came from the signer, and second, that the workbook has not been changed in any way.

You digitally sign a workbook by using a digital certificate. There are several sources from which you can receive a digital certificate. One source is a commercial certification authority. An example of such a company is VeriSign, Inc. Another source is a company's internal security administrator or the Information Technology department within the company. In addition, you can create a digital signature yourself using the Selfcert.exe tool. However, digital signatures you create yourself obviously are not considered to be as secure as a digital certificate that has been issued to you.

Use a Digital Signature
1. Click Tools and then click Options.
2. Click the Security tab.
3. Click the Digital Signatures button.

You can tell if you receive a workbook that has been digitally signed by looking in Excel's title bar. If a workbook has been signed, the word *[Signed]* appears next to the name of the workbook file in the title bar.

To digitally sign a workbook, click Tools. From the Tools menu, click Options. Click the Security tab on the Options dialog box. The Options dialog box shown in Figure 7.10 contains the Digital Signatures button. Clicking this button allows you to either add a digital signature to a workbook or to view the certificate and get more information about the digital signature added to it. Remember that in order to be able to sign the workbook, you must have obtained and installed a digital certificate.

EXCEL

7.10 *The Options Dialog Box with Security Tab Selected*

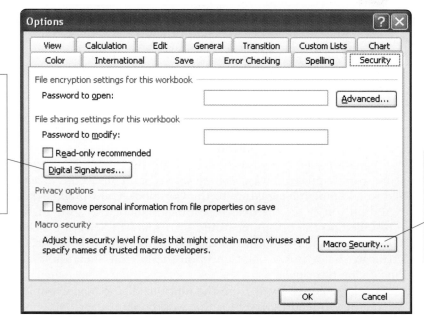

Clicking the Digital Signature button allows you to apply a digital signature to a workbook in order to identify the workbook's originator.

Clicking the Macro Security button allows you to set the security level for the macros in a workbook.

Setting Macro Security

Macros can pose a security threat as they sometimes are used as a way to spread computer viruses. You can set the security level for the macros used in any given workbook. To set the macro security level, click Tools. From the Tools menu, click Options. Refer to Figure 7.10 to see the Macro Security button on the Options dialog box. Clicking the Macro Security button displays the dialog box shown in Figure 7.11. Here you can select whether you want a High, Medium, or Low level of security for the macros used in a workbook.

QUICK STEPS

Set Macro Security Level
1. Click Tools and then click Options.
2. Click the Security tab.
3. Click the Macro Security button.

7.11 *Setting Macro Security Levels*

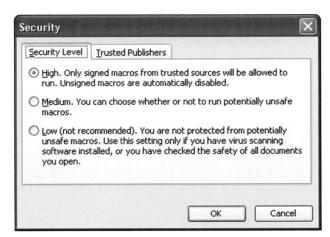

exercise 3

VIEWING THE DIGITAL SIGNATURE OPTION AND SELECTING A MACRO SECURITY LEVEL

1. Open Excel **eec7x02**. You created this workbook in Exercise 2.
2. Save the workbook using the Save As command and name it **eec7x03**.
3. If you wanted to e-mail this workbook to a colleague, it might be a good idea to attach a digital signature so that your colleague is assured that the workbook came from a reliable source. Complete the following steps to see how to attach a digital signature to a workbook.
   a. Click Tools and then click Options.
   b. At the Options dialog box, click the Security tab.
   c. Click the Digital Signatures button.
4. The Digital Signature dialog box is displayed. If this workbook had been digitally signed, the signature would appear in *The following have digitally signed this document* list box. If you wanted to add a digital signature to the workbook you would click the Add button. Click the Add button to see the Select Certificate dialog box. Any digital certificates that were installed on the computer would be displayed. Selecting a certificate and clicking OK adds a digital signature to the workbook. Click the Cancel button on the Select Certificate dialog box. Click Cancel on the Digital Signature dialog box. Leave the Options dialog box open.
5. You also set macro security levels from the Options dialog box. Complete the following steps to set the macro security level for this workbook:
   a. Click the Macro Security button.
   b. The Macro Security dialog box is displayed. Read the descriptions for the three levels of security. Click the Medium option and then click OK.
   c. Click OK to close the Options dialog box.
6. Save and close the **eec7x03** workbook.

Tracking Changes

Excel can make it easy to track changes made to the contents of a cell by highlighting those changes. If a workbook is not already set up to be shared, when you use the Highlight Changes command, the workbook sharing feature is automatically turned on. Each user's changes are highlighted in a different color.

> **QUICK STEPS**
>
> **Track Changes in a Shared Workbook**
> Click Tools, point to Track Changes, and then click Highlight Changes.

To track the changes, click Tools and then either wait for a few moments or click the down-pointing arrow at the bottom of the menu to display more options. Point to Track changes and then click Highlight Changes. Click the *Track changes while editing* check box, as shown in Figure 7.12. If you want to make specific limitations on the tracking feature, you can do so in the *Highlight which changes* area in the dialog box. You can select what to track according to when the changes were made, by whom they were made, or specifically where on the worksheet they were made. If none of these options are selected, Excel tracks changes made anywhere in the worksheet, by any user, at any time. Excel can track the changes either by highlighting them on the screen or by listing them on a new worksheet.

FIGURE

7.12 **Highlight Changes Dialog Box**

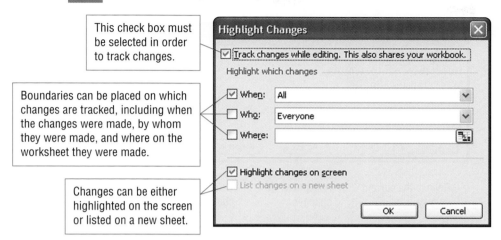

This check box must be selected in order to track changes.

Boundaries can be placed on which changes are tracked, including when the changes were made, by whom they were made, and where on the worksheet they were made.

Changes can be either highlighted on the screen or listed on a new sheet.

When any changes are made to the contents of a cell, a border appears around the cell and a revision triangle appears in the upper left corner of the cell. When the mouse pointer is moved over the revision triangle, a box is displayed that lists who made the change, when the change was made, and what the change was.

Accepting and Rejecting Tracked Changes

Tracked changes can either be accepted or rejected. They can be accepted or rejected all at one time, or you can go through each change individually and decide whether to accept or reject it. To accept or reject tracked changes, click Tools, point to Track Changes, and then click Accept or Reject Changes. The Select Changes to Accept or Reject dialog box, shown in Figure 7.13 is displayed. The changes to be viewed can be limited by when they were made, by whom they were made, or where on the worksheet they were made. Click OK and the Accept or Reject Changes dialog box shown in Figure 7.14 is displayed. To accept just the one change that is displayed, click Accept. To reject just the one change that is displayed, click Reject. To accept all of the changes that were made, click Accept All. To reject all the changes that were made, click Reject All.

Accept or Reject Tracked Changes
Click Tools, point to Track Changes, and then click Accept or Reject Changes.

FIGURE

7.13 **Select Changes to Accept or Reject Dialog Box**

7.14 *Accept or Reject Changes Dialog Box*

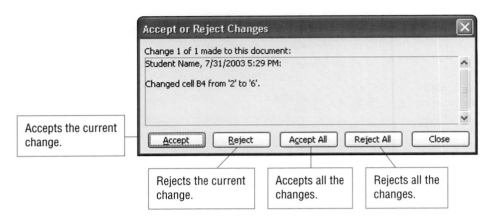

Accepts the current change.

Rejects the current change.

Accepts all the changes.

Rejects all the changes.

exercise 4

TRACKING CHANGES AND ACCEPTING OR REJECTING CHANGES TO A WORKBOOK

1. Open **eec7x01**. You created this worksheet in Exercise 1. The password to open the workbook is C1401C.
2. Save the workbook using the Save As command and name it **eec7x04**.
3. If necessary, edit the custom header for the *IncomeStatement* worksheet so that the current file name is displayed at the right margin.
4. You are going to be sharing this workbook, and you cannot share a workbook that is password protected. Complete the following steps to remove the password protection from the workbook:
   a. Click Tools, point to Protection, and then click Unprotect Workbook. The Unprotect Workbook dialog box is displayed.
   b. Type **cg0128** in the *Password* box and then click OK.
   c. Click File and then click Save As.
   d. Click the Tools button on the Save As dialog box and then click General Options.
   e. Delete all the bullets from the *Password to open* box.
   f. Click OK and then click Save.
   g. When the warning appears, asking if you want to replace the existing file, click Yes.
5. Since you are going to be sharing the workbook, you need to change the user name so that you can keep track of who is using the shared workbook. Complete the following steps to change the user name:
   a. Click Tools and then Options.
   b. Click the General tab on the Options dialog box.
   c. Look in the *User name* box. Write down on a piece of paper the name that is currently entered. When you complete this exercise, you will change the name back to what is currently entered.
   d. Enter your name in the *User name* box and then click OK.
   e. Click the Save button on the Standard toolbar.
6. Complete the following steps to turn on the tracking feature:
   a. Click Tools, point to Track Changes, and then click Highlight Changes.

EXCEL

b. At the Highlight Changes dialog box, click the *Track changes while editing* check box to select it and then click OK.

c. Click OK to save the workbook.

7. Look in the title bar. The word *[Shared]* should now be in the title bar after the workbook name. Complete the following steps to set up a second copy of the workbook in a second Excel window:

Step 6b

a. Click the Start button.

b. Select All Programs, point to Microsoft Office, and then open another copy of Excel.

c. Make sure no windows other than the two copies of Excel are open on the taskbar. Right-click the taskbar and then click Tile Windows Vertically. If necessary, rearrange the two Excel windows so your copy is on the left and the blank Excel worksheet you opened in Step 7b is on the right.

d. Click Tools on the Menu bar in the Excel window on the right and then click Options.

e. Click the General tab on the Options dialog box.

f. In the *User name* box, type **Larry Ford** and then click OK.

g. Open **eec7x04** in the Excel window on the right.

8. Larry Ford is the vice president of finance, and he has some estimates you need to complete this income statement. Type the following values in the cells indicated in Larry's copy of Excel (the copy on the right):

Cell	Value
B4	333,300
B5	250,996
B6	345,023
B7	242,024
B11	94,039
B12	124,178

Save the workbook.

9. Click your copy of Excel (the one on the left). Click the Save button to save the workbook so that Excel updates your copy with the changes made by Larry Ford. Click OK at the information box that appears, notifying you that the workbook has been updated.

10. Enter the remaining values into the worksheet and then save the workbook.

Cell	Value
C13	86,101
C14	22,828
C15	21,765
C17	23,369
C19	24,349

11. Select Larry's copy of Excel (the one on the right) and save the workbook so that the changes you just made are displayed. Click OK when the information box is displayed, notifying you that the workbook has been updated.

12. Notice that the changes you made are highlighted in one color on Larry Ford's copy of the worksheet and Larry's changes are highlighted in a different color on your copy. Click cell B4 on your copy of Excel (the one on the left). Position the mouse pointer on top of the revision triangle in the upper left corner of cell B4. The box explaining the change that was made should be displayed.

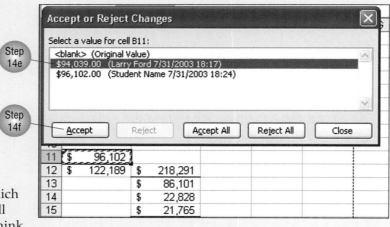

Step 12

	B	C	D	E	F
2					
3		Larry Ford, 7/31/2003 6:17 PM:			
4	$ 333,3	Changed cell B4 from '<blank>' to '			
5	$ 250,996	$333,300.00 '.			
6	$ 345,023				
7	$ 242,024	$			
8		$ 897,024			
9		$ 274,319			
10					

13. As you and Larry look over the figures each other entered, you agree that some of the figures the other person entered are incorrect. Complete the following steps to make some changes to each worksheet:
    a. Click Larry's copy of Excel (the one on the right) to select it.
    b. Click cell C17 and type 24,287.
    c. Click cell C19 and type 26,024.
    d. Save the workbook.
    e. Click your copy of Excel (the one on the left) to select it.
    f. Click cell B11 and type 96,102.
    g. Click cell B12 and type 122,189.
    h. Save the workbook.
    i. Click OK when the box displays telling you the workbook has been updated.
    j. Click Larry's copy of Excel (the one on the right) to select it.
    k. Save the workbook.
    l. Click OK when the box displays telling you the workbook has been updated.
14. Complete the following steps to accept or reject the tracked changes:
    a. Click your copy of Excel (the one on the left) to select it.
    b. Click Tools, point to Track Changes, and then click Accept or Reject Changes. The Select Changes to Accept or Reject dialog box is displayed.
    c. Click OK. The Accept or Reject Changes dialog box is displayed.
    d. The first change made is for cell B4. Notice that cell B4 has a moving border to indicate which cell is currently under consideration. Click Accept.
    e. Accept all the changes until you get to the change for cell B11. After further investigation, you have decided Larry Ford's figure is correct. Click the option for $94,039, the figure Larry entered, to select it.
    f. Click Accept.
    g. You need to select which value to accept for cell B12. This time you think your figure is the correct one. Click the option for $122,189 to select it.
    h. Click Accept.
    i. You want to accept all the rest of the changes, so click Accept All.

Step 14e

Step 14f

Accept or Reject Changes

Select a value for cell B11:

<blank> (Original Value)
$94,039.00 (Larry Ford 7/31/2003 18:17)
$96,102.00 (Student Name 7/31/2003 18:24)

| Accept | Reject | Accept All | Reject All | Close |

11	$ 96,102		
12	$ 122,189	$ 218,291	
13		$ 86,101	
14		$ 22,828	
15		$ 21,765	

EXCEL

j.   Print a copy of the worksheet.
15. Click Larry's copy of Excel (the one on the right). Complete the following steps to change the user name back to the original entry and exit Larry's copy of Excel:
    a. Click Tools and then click Options.
    b. Click the General tab.
    c. In the *User name* box, type the name that was originally displayed when you started the exercise. Click OK.
    d. Save the file. Click File and then click Exit.
16. Maximize the window of your copy of Excel. Complete the following steps to turn off the Track Changes option:
    a. Click Tools, point to Track Changes, and then click Highlight Changes. The Highlight Changes dialog box is displayed.
    b. Click the *Track changes while editing* check box so that it is no longer selected.
    c. Click OK.
17. Complete the following steps to change the user name back to the original entry:
    a. Click Tools and then click Options.
    b. Click the General tab.
    c. In the *User name* box, type the name that was originally displayed when you started the exercise. Click OK.
18. Complete the following steps to unhide the hidden worksheet:
    a. Click Format, point to Sheet, and then click Unhide.
    b. At the Unhide dialog box, with *CostofGoodsSold* already selected in the *Unhide sheet* list box, click OK.
19. Save the workbook with the same name (**eec7x04**) and close it.

Creating, Editing, and Removing a Comment

Comments can be added to any cell on a worksheet. Comments can be used to explain or clarify the contents of a cell. Comments are not printed when the worksheet is printed. If a cell has a comment attached to it, a small red triangle appears in the upper right corner of the cell. Passing the mouse pointer over this triangle displays the comment. To add a comment, right-click the cell to which the comment is to be added. Click Insert Comment from the shortcut menu. As shown in Figure 7.15, the comment box appears with the name of the user who is entered on the General tab of the Options menu. Enter the comment and then click anywhere outside the comment box. To edit a comment, right-click the cell containing the comment to be edited and then click Edit Comment from the shortcut menu. Make the necessary changes and click anywhere outside the comment. To delete a comment, right-click the cell containing the comment to be deleted and then click Delete Comment.

HINT
You can review the comments in a workbook by clicking View and Comments. The Reviewing toolbar is displayed. Click the Next Comments button or the Previous Comments button.

QUICK STEPS

Add a Comment
1. Right-click the cell.
2. Click Insert Comment.

FIGURE

7.15 *Creating Comments*

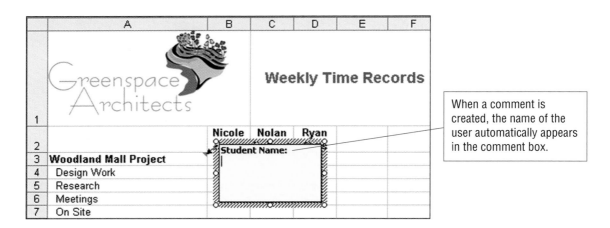

> When a comment is created, the name of the user automatically appears in the comment box.

Merging Workbooks

Merge Shared Workbooks
Click Tools and then Compare and Merge Workbooks.

Another way to share workbooks is to send a copy of the shared workbook to different users. Each user can then make his or her own changes to the workbook. All those changes can then be merged into one workbook. The first step in merging workbooks is to open the shared workbook that will be used as the copy into which all the other copies will be merged. Next, click Tools and Compare and Merge Workbooks. If you are prompted to save the workbook, click OK. The Select Files to Merge Into Current Workbook dialog box is displayed. Choose the workbooks to be merged and click OK. As many workbooks as needed can be merged.

exercise 5

CREATING, EDITING, AND REMOVING COMMENTS, AND MERGING WORKBOOKS

1. Open **ExcelWorksheet03**.
2. Save the workbook using the Save As command and name it **eec7x05**.
3. Create a custom header for the *TimeSheet* worksheet that displays your name at the left margin and the file name at the right margin.
4. This worksheet is used to keep track of the weekly project time spent by three of the employees at Greenspace Architects, a company that provides landscaping services.
5. Complete the following steps to add a comment to cell A3:
   a. Right-click cell A3.
   b. Click Insert Comment on the shortcut menu.

c. Type the following in the comment box:

> This project is nearing completion and therefore very few hours need to be devoted to it.

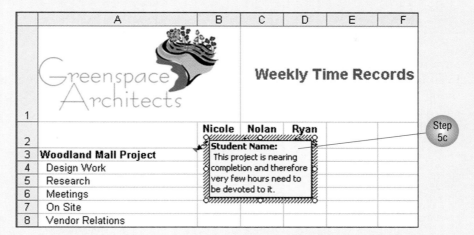

Step 5c

d. Click anywhere outside the comment box.
6. Nicole, Nolan, and Ryan each need to enter their hours in this worksheet. Before they can do that, you need to set up the workbook as a shared workbook. Complete the following steps to designate **eec7x05** as a shared workbook:
   a. Click Tools and then click Share Workbook.
   b. If necessary, click the Editing tab.
   c. Click the *Allow changes by more than one user at the same time* check box to select it, then click OK.
   d. Click OK to save the workbook.
   e. Close the **eec7x05** workbook.
7. In order to simulate this shared workbook being sent to three different employees, you will have to open the file three times. Each employee would open up his or her copy of the shared workbook to enter the requested figures. Nicole is now ready to enter her hours in the weekly time sheet. Open **eec7x05**. It should say *[Shared]* in the title bar. Save the workbook using the Save As command and name it **Nicole9-18**.
8. Type the following values in the cells indicated:

Cell	Value	Cell	Value	Cell	Value
B7	1	B16	10	B23	2
B9	2	B17	4	B25	4
B14	3	B18	8		
B15	5	B19	4.5		

9. Save the workbook using the same name (**Nicole9-18**) and close it.
10. Nolan is now ready to enter his hours in the weekly time sheet. Open **eec7x05**. It should say *[Shared]* in the title bar. Save the workbook using the Save As command and name it **Nolan9-18**.

11. Type the following values in the cells indicated:

Cell	Value	Cell	Value	Cell	Value
C6	1	C14	2	C23	3
C8	2	C16	5	C24	2
C9	1	C18	1	C25	6
C13	10	C22	15		

12. Save the workbook using the same name (**Nolan9-18**) and close it.
13. Ryan is now ready to enter his hours in the weekly time sheet. Open **eec7x05**. It should say *[Shared]* in the title bar. Save the workbook using the Save As command and name it **Ryan9-18**.
14. Type the following values in the cells indicated:

Cell	Value	Cell	Value	Cell	Value
D13	4	D18	2	D25	6
D14	2	D19	2	D26	3
D15	3	D22	3	D27	2
D16	5	D23	2	D28	3
D17	1	D24	4		

15. Save the workbook using the same name (**Ryan9-18**) and close it.
16. You are now ready to merge the three workbooks into one workbook. Open **eec7x05**. Complete the following steps to merge the workbooks:
    a. Click Tools and then click Compare and Merge Workbooks.
    b. Click OK to save the workbook. The Select Files to Merge Into Current Workbook dialog box is displayed.
    c. Select the **Nicole 9-18**, **Nolan 9-18**, and **Ryan 9-18** files.
    d. Click OK. The values from the three workbooks are merged into the one workbook.

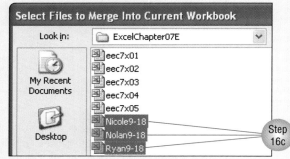

Step 16c

17. You no longer want this to be a shared workbook. Click Tools and Share Workbook. Click the *Allow changes by more than one user at the same time* check box so that it is no longer selected and then click OK.
18. Complete the following steps to edit the comment box:
    a. Right-click cell A3.
    b. Click Edit Comment from the shortcut menu.
    c. In the comment box delete the phrase *is nearing completion* and type the following to take its place: **will be completed on 9/25**.
19. Save the workbook using the same name (**eec7x05**) and print it.
20. Close the workbook.

Working with Multiple Worksheets

When there is more than one worksheet in a workbook, you often want to perform the same command on two or more, or perhaps even on all, of the worksheets in the workbook. For example, you might want to place the same header on all the worksheets. Or you might want to print two of the four worksheets. In order to perform a command on more than one worksheet at a time, you first need to select the worksheets. If more than one worksheet is selected, the command executed on the active worksheet will be made on all the selected worksheets.

To select two or more adjacent worksheets in a workbook, click the worksheet tab for the first worksheet, hold down the Shift key, and then click the worksheet tab for the last worksheet you want selected. To select two or more worksheets that are not adjacent, click the worksheet tab for the first worksheet, hold down the Ctrl key, and then click the worksheet tab for each worksheet you want selected. To select all the worksheets in a workbook, right-click a worksheet tab and then click Select All Sheets on the shortcut menu.

If you wanted to view more than one worksheet at a time, for example, you would select all the worksheets to be viewed and then click the Print Preview button on the Standard toolbar. The first worksheet would be displayed. Clicking the Next button would display the next worksheet and so on. If you want to print more than one worksheet at a time, select the worksheets to be printed before issuing the Print command. All of the selected worksheets will print.

	WORKING WITH MULTIPLE WORKSHEETS

1. Open **ExcelWorksheet04**.
2. Save the workbook using the Save As command and name it **eec7x06**.
3. You want the custom header you create to appear on all the worksheets in this workbook. Complete the following steps to create a header that appears on all the worksheets:
   a. Right-click the *North* worksheet tab.
   b. Click Select All Sheets from the shortcut menu. Notice that the word *[Group]* now appears in the title bar to the right of the file name.
   c. Create a custom header that displays your name at the left margin and the file name at the right margin.
4. You want to preview all the worksheets to make sure the header appears on all of them. All the worksheets should still be selected. Click the Print Preview button on the Standard toolbar. The first worksheet is displayed. Click the Next button. The next worksheet is displayed and the header appears at the top of it. Keep clicking Next until you have viewed all the worksheets. Click Close.
5. Click the *North* worksheet tab. Only the *North* worksheet is selected.
6. You want to print the *South* and *West* worksheet. Click the *South* worksheet tab. Press the Ctrl key and then click the *West* worksheet tab. The two worksheets are now selected. Click the Print button on the Standard toolbar. The two worksheets should print.
7. Click the *North* worksheet tab. Only the *North* worksheet is selected.
8. Save the workbook using the same name (**eec7ex06**) and close it.

CHAPTER summary

➤ A workgroup is made up of individuals who are working together on the same project.

➤ Being able to share a workbook enables workgroup members to work together more efficiently.

➤ Security is an issue when sharing a workbook because whoever has access to the network location where the shared workbook is located has access to that shared workbook.

➤ A workbook can be completely protected by assigning a password to it. Only those who know the password are able to open it. A workbook can also be protected so that anyone can view the workbook but only those who know the password can make changes to it.

➤ Worksheets can be hidden from view. Hidden worksheets can be assigned a password so that only those knowing the password can unhide the worksheet.

➤ Individual cells on a worksheet can be protected. If a cell is protected, the contents of the cell cannot be changed or deleted. This feature is useful for protecting formulas.

➤ A security measure that can be taken to ensure the reliability and safety of an Excel workbook is to attach a digital signature to it. The purpose of a digital signature is to ensure that a workbook is from a reputable source and that no alterations have been made to the workbook.

➤ As a security measure to help reduce the problems associated with macro viruses, you can set the macro security level for macros used in a workbook. With a high security level, only macros from a trusted source, those that have been signed with a digital signature, will be run. With a medium security level, the user chooses whether or not to run macros. A low security level does not offer any protection from potentially unsafe macros.

➤ Use the Highlight Changes command to track the changes made by each person using a shared workbook. A cell that has been changed is displayed with a border around it and a revision triangle in the upper left corner. When the mouse pointer is passed over the revision triangle, a box is displayed that lists who made the change, when the change was made, and what the change was.

➤ Tracked changes can be accepted or rejected all at one time, or each change can be accepted or rejected individually.

➤ A comment is useful for explaining or clarifying the contents of a cell. Cells with comments attached to them have red comment triangles in the upper right corner of the cell. When the mouse pointer is passed over the comment triangle, a comment box is displayed.

➤ Each member in a workgroup can make changes to his or her own copy of a shared workbook. All those copies of the shared workbook then can be merged into one workbook.

➤ To select multiple worksheets that are adjacent to one another, click the first worksheet tab, press the Shift key, and then click the last worksheet tab. To select multiple copies of nonadjacent worksheets, press the Ctrl key and then click the worksheet tab for each worksheet to be selected. Once multiple worksheets are selected, commands carried out on the active worksheet affect all the selected worksheets. For example, if several worksheets are selected and the print command is issued, all the selected worksheets will be printed.

FEATURES summary

FEATURE	BUTTON	MENU/COMMANDS
Apply or remove a password to a workbook		Click File, Save As, Tools button, General Options
Hide a worksheet		Click Format, Sheet, Hide
Unhide a worksheet		Click Format, Sheet, Unhide
Protect a workbook		Click Tools, Protection, Protect Workbook
Remove workbook protection		Click Tools, Protection, Unprotect Workbook
Protect individual cells		Click Format, Cells, Protection tab
Protect a worksheet		Click Tools, Protection, Protect Sheet
Remove worksheet protection		Click Tools, Protection, Unprotect Sheet
Give specific users access to protected cells		Click Tools, Protection, Allow Users to Edit Ranges
Use a digital signature		Click Tools, Options, Security tab, Digital Signatures button
Set macro security level		Click Tools, Options, Security tab, Macro Security button
Track changes in a shared workbook		Click Tools, Track Changes, Highlight Changes
Accept or reject tracked changes		Click Tools, Track Changes, Accept or Reject Changes
Add a comment		Right-click the cell, click Insert Comment
Edit a comment		Right-click the cell, click Edit Comment
Delete a comment		Right-click the cell, click Delete Comment
Merge shared workbooks		Click Tools, Merge Workbooks

CONCEPTS check

Completion: On a blank sheet of paper, indicate the correct term, symbol, or command for each description.

1. This term refers to all the people working together on the same project.
2. The commands for protecting a workbook and worksheet are found on this menu.
3. This is what appears in the box when you enter a password.
4. When creating a password to be used for password protection, the password is always entered this many times.
5. If a worksheet is hidden, this is what must be protected in order to prevent other users from unhiding it.
6. When individual cells have been protected on a worksheet so that changes cannot be made to them, you also have to protect this.
7. The Highlight Changes command automatically turns this feature on.
8. List three sources for obtaining a digital certificate that enables you to create digital signatures.
9. Explain the differences between the three levels of macro security.
10. The option for tracking changes is found on this menu.
11. This term refers to boxes attached to individual cells which contain information regarding the specific cell to which they are attached.
12. Press this key to select multiple worksheets that are adjacent to one another.
13. Press this key to select multiple worksheets that are not adjacent to one another.
14. The command for merging shared workbooks is found on this menu.
15. List the benefits of sharing workbooks.
16. Explain what security issues you must consider when sharing a workbook.
17. List the Excel features that are not available in a shared workbook.

SKILLS check

Assessment 1

1. Open **ExcelWorksheet05**.
2. Save the worksheet using the Save As command and name it **eec7sc01**.
3. This workbook is the cash flow schedule for a ski shop that sells downhill and cross-country ski supplies.
4. Click File and then click Save As. Click the Tools button on the Save As dialog box and then click General Options. Assign the following password to the workbook: CM5!78sts.
5. Save and then close **eec7sc01**. You will be using this file in Assessment 2.

Assessment 2

1. Open **eec7sc01**. The password to open the file is CM5!78sts.
2. Save the worksheet using the Save As command and name it **eec7sc02**.
3. Select both worksheets. Create a custom header with your name displayed at the left margin and the file name displayed at the right margin.

4. The values in cells B9, C9, and D9 are linked to the *Commissions* worksheet, which is confidential. Hide the *Commissions* worksheet.
5. Protect the workbook by using the following password: 131!63C.
6. All the cells that currently have something entered in them contain formulas, which you want to protect, so these cells should remain locked. Select the cells that are empty, which would be cells B3 through D5, B10 through D13, and B19. Format these cells so that they are no longer locked.
7. Protect the worksheet using the following password: W89**25s.
8. Save the workbook using the same name (**eec7sc02**) and close it. You will be using this file in Assessment 3.

Assessment 3

1. Open **eec7sc02**. The password to open the file is CM5!78sts.
2. Save the worksheet using the Save As command and name it **eec7sc03**.
3. If necessary, edit the custom header so that the current name of the file (**eec7sc03**) is displayed at the right margin.
4. Click Tools, point to Protection, and then click Unprotect Workbook to remove the workbook protection. The password for the workbook protection is 131!63C.
5. Click File and then click Save As. Click the Tools button and then click General Options. Delete all the bullets from the *Password to open* box. Save the file, replacing the existing **eec7sc03** file.
6. Change the user name to your name. Make sure you jot down the current user name so that you can change it back at the end of the exercise.
7. Use the Highlight Changes command to turn the tracking feature on. You want to track all the changes made by everyone. The word *[Shared]* should appear in the title bar.
8. Resize the Excel window so that it appears on the left half of the desktop.
9. Open a second copy of the Excel program. Resize the second copy so that it is displayed on the right half of the desktop. Change the user name for this copy of Excel to Megan Bassett.
10. Open **eec7sc03** in the second copy of Excel. Both you and Megan have some of the figures that go into this worksheet. Type the following figures in the cells indicated on Megan's copy of Excel (the one on the right):

Cell	Value	Cell	Value
B3	36,540	C5	5,110
B4	6,000	D3	33,271
B5	2,658.50	D5	16,506
C3	43,960		

Save the workbook.
11. Click your copy of Excel (the one on the left). Save it so that you can see the changes made by Megan.
12. Type the following figures in the cells indicated on your copy of Excel (the one on the left):

Cell	Value	Cell	Value	Cell	Value
B10	24,500	C11	13,584	D11	13,072
B11	10,720	C12	6,589	D12	6,432
B12	6,280	D10	24,500	D13	2,000
C10	24,500				

Save the workbook.

13. Click Megan's copy of Excel (the one on the right). Save it so that you can see the changes that were made. Megan knows the loan/interest repayment in March is supposed to be $2,200. Change the value in cell D13 to 2,200. She also knows that the beginning cash balance in January was $750. Enter 750 in cell B19. Save the worksheet.
14. Change the user name back to the original entry. Save and exit Megan's copy of Excel.
15. Click your copy of Excel (the one on the left). Maximize the window. Save the worksheet to see the changes. Accept all the changes that were made to the worksheet.
16. Turn off the Track Changes option.
17. Unhide the *Commissions* worksheet.
18. Preview and print both the *Cash Flow* and the *Commissions* worksheets.
19. Change the user name back to what it was originally.
20. Save the workbook using the same file name (**eec7sc03**) and close it.

Assessment 4

1. Open **ExcelWorksheet06**.
2. Save the worksheet using the Save As command and name it **eec7sc04**.
3. Create a custom header with your name displayed at the left margin and the name of the file displayed at the right margin.
4. Attach a comment to cell A5. The comment should read as follows: This inventory reflects stock on hand as of December 15.
5. Designate this workbook as a shared workbook.
6. Save and then close the workbook.
7. Open the workbook and rename it **NewYorkInventory**.
8. Type the following values in the cells indicated:

Cell	Value	Cell	Value	Cell	Value
B8	5	B16	15	B23	19
B9	6	B17	35	B24	30
B10	10	B18	12	B25	18
B11	2	B19	8	B26	0
B12	1	B20	5	B27	28
B13	4	B21	14	B28	25
B14	7	B22	2	B29	6
B15	20				

9. Save the workbook using the same name (**NewYorkInventory**) and close it.
10. Open **eec7sc04**. Open the workbook and rename it **LosAngelesInventory**.
11. Type the following values in the cells indicated:

Cell	Value	Cell	Value	Cell	Value
E8	5	E16	25	E23	18
E9	10	E17	28	E24	22
E10	3	E18	35	E25	8
E11	18	E19	4	E26	5
E12	12	E20	6	E27	31
E13	10	E21	0	E28	24
E14	8	E22	13	E29	22
E15	36				

12. Save the workbook using the same name (**LosAngelesInventory**) and close it.
13. Open **eec7sc04**. Merge the **NewYorkInventory** workbook and the **LosAngelesInventory** workbook into the **eec7sc04** workbook.
14. Remove the workbook from shared use.

15. Edit the comment attached to cell A5 so the date is *December 31* rather than *December 15*. Save the workbook using the same name (**eec7sc04**).
16. Print and then close the workbook.

Assessment 5

1. Open **ExcelWorksheet07**.
2. Save the worksheet using the Save As command and name it **eec7sc05**.
3. Create a custom header with your name displayed at the left margin and the name of the file displayed at the right margin.
4. Protect cells B4 and B5 so that only specific users can have access to them. Use the password ST45 to protect the cells. Use the password B02fy to protect the worksheet.
5. Enter the following values in the cells indicated:

Cell	Value
B4	1,199,564
B5	681,805

6. Save and print the worksheet.
7. Enter the following values in the cells indicated:

Cell	Value
B4	1,713,660
B5	892,550

8. Save and print the worksheet.
9. Save the workbook using the same name (**eec7sc05**) and close it.

CHAPTER challenge

You work in the information systems department for a local bank. You have created a workbook named **PaymentCalculation** that calculates the monthly payment of any item. In the workbook, insert the comment "Amount has been changed to a positive number" in the cell containing the monthly payment. You place this workbook on the network, so that others may use it; however, you decide to protect the workbook and provide the password to only those authorized to use the workbook. In addition, you decide to protect the worksheet, but allow users to edit a given range. You will determine which range(s) users should be allowed to edit. Print the worksheet. Then write on the printout why you chose the range(s) for users to edit. Also, write on the printout all of the passwords used.

It is sometimes helpful to print out comments that have been entered into a worksheet. Use the Help feature to learn about printing comments. Then print the worksheet created in the first part of the Chapter Challenge so that the comment prints as displayed in the worksheet. Save the workbook again.

 You would like to post the workbook created in the first part of the Chapter Challenge to the company's intranet. Prepare the worksheet for the intranet by saving it as an HTML file named **PaymentCalculation**.

USING DATA FROM THE INTERNET AND OTHER SOURCES

PERFORMANCE OBJECTIVES

Upon successful completion of Chapter 8, you will be able to:

➤ Import data from text files
➤ Export data to text files
➤ Place a noninteractive worksheet on the Web
➤ Place an interactive worksheet on the Web
➤ Place an interactive chart on the Web
➤ Import data from a Web page into Excel
➤ Retrieve data from a Web page using Web Query
➤ Query a database using Microsoft Query
➤ Link an object in an Excel worksheet
➤ Embed an object in an Excel worksheet
➤ Use XML to share Excel data on the Web
➤ Structure workbooks using XML

EXCEL

In Chapter 7, you were introduced to the concept of workgroup computing. People working together in a workgroup on a particular project often share not only data found in Excel workbooks, but data from other applications as well. Data in an Excel workbook may need to be accessed by another application, or you may need to have the data from another application in an Excel workbook. When data from Excel is sent to another application, such as Word, the data is said to be exported from Excel. When data from another application, such as a Web browser, is sent to Excel, the data is said to be imported into Excel. Knowing how to import and export data to and from Excel enables you to share your Excel data across applications. One of the ways to accomplish this, which is covered in this chapter, is by linking or embedding objects.

Microsoft Excel includes many Web features. You can easily place worksheets and workbooks on the Web as well as import the data from a Web page into Excel. With the increasing popularity of intranets, which are described in this chapter, Excel data is frequently imported from and exported to Web pages as an easy way for people to share data.

Importing from and Exporting to Text Files

A text file is a file that contains only printable letters, numbers, and symbols, usually from the ASCII character set. There are no formatting codes in a text file. The strength of text files is that they are easily shared. The text file format is supported by nearly every application on every machine. The weakness of text files is that they cannot contain any formatting codes. If you need to share data with others, however, using text files can be a good solution.

Importing Data from Text Files

There are a number of reasons why you might have to import a text file. The source of the data might be a mainframe computer report, which has been saved as a text file so that it can be used on a personal computer. The data might come from an older application program, and the only way you might be able to open it in Excel is by saving the data from the older program as a text file. Data sent to you in e-mail messages might be in a text file format.

Excel provides automatic help when importing text files. There are two common formats for data that is arranged in rows and columns in a text file: a delimited text file and a fixed-width text file. A delimited text file uses a special character or delimiter, which is often a comma or a tab, to separate one column from the next. In Figure 8.1a, the delimiter is a comma. As shown in Figure 8.1b, the number of characters or spaces (or both) in each column in a fixed width text file is set.

FIGURE

8.1 *Two Common Text File Formats*

a. Delimited Text

```
Last Name, First Name, SS Number, Position, Hourly Wage
Dillard, Nancy, 555-90-2121, President, $75.00
Chung, Robert, 777-56-7654, Vice President, $55.00
Campbell, Norman, 444-78-7658, Designer, $38.00
Kimsey, C.J., 999-52-1014, Sales, $18.00
Simpsom, Katie, 555-68-3564, Designer, $29.00
```

b. Fixed-Width Text

```
Last Name    First Name    SS Number      Position         Hourly Wage
Dillard      Nancy         555-90-2121    President         $75.00
Chung        Robert        777-56-7654    Vice President    $55.00
Campbell     Norman        444-78-7658    Designer          $38.00
Kimsey       C.J.          999-52-1014    Sales             $18.00
Simpsom      Katie         555-68-3564    Designer          $29.00
```

EXCEL

To import a text file, click File and then click Open. The Open dialog box appears. Click the down-pointing arrow to the right of the *Files of type* box and then select *Text Files*. All the files with the extension *.txt* will be displayed. Usually text files end with the extension *.txt*. If the text file you are trying to open has a different extension, select *All Files* from the *Files of type* list box. Locate the file to open and then click Open. The Text Import Wizard - Step 1 of 3 dialog box, shown in Figure 8.2, is displayed. You can select whether the file is *Delimited* or *Fixed width*, although Excel will probably make the proper selection for you automatically. You can also enter a value in the *Start import at row* box if you want the first row of the data to be a row other than 1.

Text files can be imported into Excel so that they are refreshable, which means they can be updated to the most recent version of the original data. To import text so that it is refreshable, click Data, point to Get External Data, and click Import Text File. Locate and double-click the text file to be imported. Follow the directions in the Text Import Wizard. To refresh the data when the original text changes, click the Refresh Data button on the External Data toolbar.

QUICK STEPS

Import From a Text File
1. Click File.
2. Click Open.
3. Select *Text Files* from the *Files of type* list box.

FIGURE

| 8.2 | **The Text Import Wizard – Step 1 of 3 Dialog Box** |

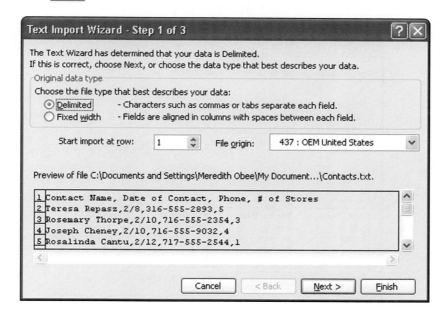

Click Next. The Text Import Wizard - Step 2 of 3 dialog box is displayed. As shown in Figure 8.3, the dialog box that is displayed depends on whether the file is delimited or fixed width. If the file is delimited, the Step 2 dialog box allows you to set what character should be used as the delimiter. You also can select the *Text qualifier*, which typically is the quotation mark. Any text entered between text qualifiers would be placed in one column. For example "Vice President" indicates that the words *Vice President* make up the contents of a column. If the file is fixed width, the Step 2 dialog box allows you to set the column breaks.

8.3 The Text Import Wizard – Step 2 of 3 Dialog Box

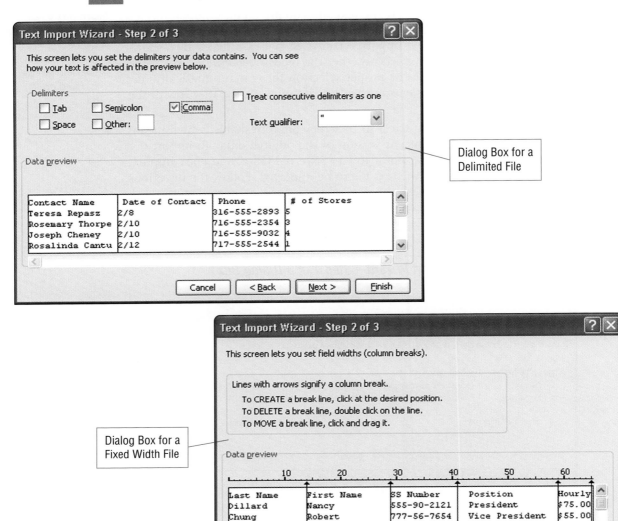

Dialog Box for a Delimited File

Dialog Box for a Fixed Width File

Click Next. The Text Import Wizard - Step 3 of 3 dialog box allows you to set the Data Format for each column. You can also select the *Do not import column (skip)* option if you do not want to import the data from a particular column or columns. Click Finish. The data is imported into an Excel worksheet.

Importing Data from Word Using Drag and Drop

Text from a Word document can be imported into an Excel workbook using drag and drop. To drag and drop between Word and Excel, arrange the windows so that you can see both applications. Select the text to be imported from the Word document. If you click on the selected text using the left mouse button and then drag it to a cell in an Excel worksheet, the text will be moved from the Word document to the Excel workbook. If you click on the selected text using the *right* mouse button and then drag it to a cell in an Excel worksheet, a shortcut menu appears, giving you the option of moving the text, copying the text, linking the document, creating a hyperlink, or creating a shortcut. You will practice this in Exercise 1 using this scenario: Taylor Made, a company owned and operated by Linda Taylor, designs and makes custom clothing. Sales representatives for Taylor Made call on owners or managers of clothing stores and boutiques who might be interested in carrying Taylor Made clothes. These sales representatives e-mail information on new contacts back to the main office. The e-mail messages are saved as text files, which are then imported into an Excel worksheet. You are going to import one of these text files into an Excel worksheet.

exercise 1

IMPORTING DATA FROM TEXT FILES

1. Open Excel.
2. Complete the following steps to open the file:
   a. Click File and then click Open.
   b. Click the down-pointing arrow to the right of the *Files of type* box and select *Text Files*.
   c. Open the **Contacts.txt** file from your data disk.
3. The Text Import Wizard - Step 1 of 3 dialog box is displayed. This is a delimited file, and the data can be imported starting at row 1, so click Next to accept the default settings on this dialog box.
4. The Text Import Wizard - Step 2 of 3 dialog box is displayed. Complete the following steps:
   a. Click the *Tab* check box to remove the checkmark.
   b. Click the *Comma* check box to select it and then click Next.

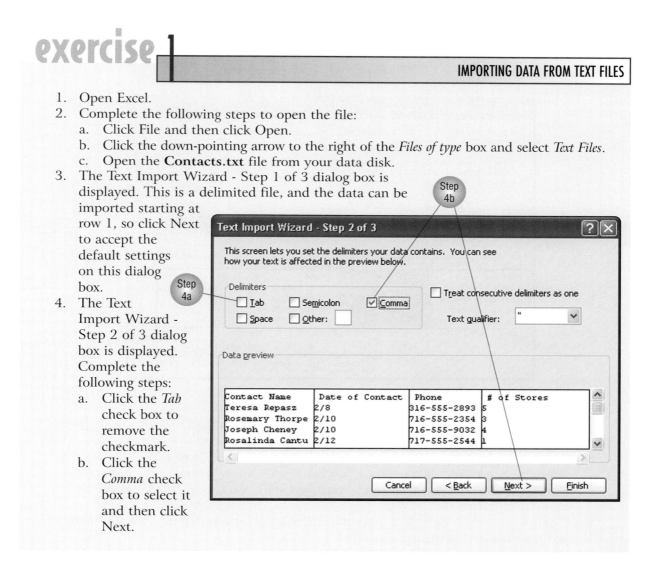

EXCEL

5. The Text Import Wizard - Step 3 of 3 dialog box is displayed. Complete the following steps:
   a. The first column in the *Data preview* area is selected. In the *Column data format* area, click the *Text* option.

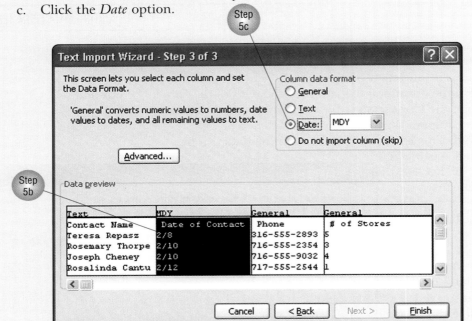

   b. Click the second column, *Date of Contact*, to select it.
   c. Click the *Date* option.

   d. Click the third column, *Phone*, to select it.
   e. Click the *Text* option.
   f. The last column, *# of Stores*, is already set as a *General* data format, which is what it should be. Click Finish.
6. Adjust the width of the columns so that all the data can be seen.
7. Click File and then click Save As. Click the down-pointing arrow to the right of the *Save as type* box and select *Microsoft Office Excel Workbook*. Change the file name to **eec8x01** and then click Save.
8. Create a custom header for the worksheet that displays your name at the left margin and the file name at the right margin.
9. Open Microsoft Word and open the **Memo.doc** file on your data disk. Arrange the windows for Word and Excel so that you can see both applications. To drag and drop data from the **Memo.doc** file in Word to the **eec8x01.xls** file in Excel, complete the following steps:

EXCEL

a. Select the name *Jane Mercereau* in the **Memo.doc** file.

b. Hold down the right mouse button on the name *Jane Mercereau* and drag it to cell A13 in the **eec8x01** file.

c. From the shortcut menu that appears, select Copy Here.

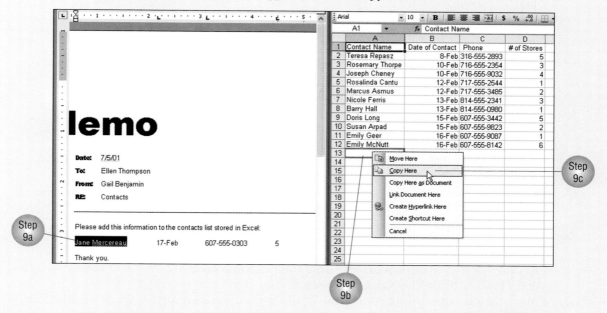

Step 9a

Step 9b

Step 9c

10. Repeat Steps 9a through 9c to drag and drop the date *17-Feb* to cell B13, the phone number *607-555-0303* to cell C13, and the number *5* to cell D13.

11. Save the workbook again using the same file name (**eec8x01**) and print it.

12. Close the workbook.

13. Close **Memo.doc** without saving changes and the exit Word.

Exporting Data to Text Files

There may be times when you want to share data with someone who does not have the Excel program. To do so, you can export the data in an Excel worksheet to a text file. To export a worksheet, open the worksheet, click File, and then click Save As. Enter a name for the file in the *File name* box. Click the down-pointing arrow to the right of the *Save as type* box. The option you select from this list depends on the application that is going to use the file. Table 8.1 explains some of the text file options found in this list. Once you have made your selection, click Save.

Export to a Text File
Click File and then Save As.

TABLE

8.1 *Text File Formats from the* Save as Type *List Box*

Option	Description
Text (Tab Delimited)	Columns are separated by tabs
CSV (Comma Delimited)	Columns are separated by commas
Formatted Text (Space Delimited)	Columns are a fixed width

1. Open **ExcelWorksheet01**.
2. Complete the following steps to save the file as a text file:
   a. Click File and then click Save As.
   b. Change the file name to **Sales**.
   c. Click the down-pointing arrow to the right of the *Save as type* box and then click *Text (Tab delimited)*.
   d. Click Save.
   e. At the Microsoft Office Excel dialog box warning you that the file may contain features that are not compatible with Text (Tab delimited), click Yes.
   f. At the Microsoft Office Excel dialog box, click Yes.
   g. Close the **Sales.txt** file. If a dialog box appears, asking if you want to save the changes you made, click Yes.
3. Open Microsoft Word and open the **Sales.txt** file. You may have to select *All Files (*.*)* from the *Files of type* selection box in order to display the **Sales.txt** file in the Open dialog box.
4. Select all the text in the document.
5. Set left tab stops at 1.5" and 2.75".
6. Save the file as a Word document using the file name **eec8x02**. You will have to select *Word Document* from the *Save as type* box on the Open dialog box.
7. Enter a header that prints your name at the left margin and the file name **eec8x02** at the right margin.
8. Save the Word file again using the same file name (**eec8x02**) and print it.
9. Exit Microsoft Word.

Accessing and Placing Data on the Web

Shortly after the World Wide Web appeared on the scene in the late 1980s, businesses began to take advantage of the capability to develop company intranets. An intranet is a local area or wide area network that provides an organization or business with services similar to those provided by the Internet without necessarily being connected to the Internet. Since about 1995, intranets have become increasingly popular in corporate computing because of the availability of inexpensive or, in some cases, free commercial browser and Web server software. An intranet is an excellent way to distribute information within a company. Employees find the graphical user interface of the Web easy to use. Intranets allow employees to easily access and share information. The HTML markup language used to create Web pages can be used on every desktop system. Therefore, even if some employees are using a Windows environment, some Macintosh, and others UNIX, all can access the company's intranet.

Excel incorporates many Web capabilities. You can export a workbook, worksheet, chart, or graph to HTML and then make it available on an HTTP site, on an FTP site, in a Web server, or on a network server. Users can then access the file using a Web browser. One of the advantages of putting Excel data on the Web is that people do not have to have Excel installed in order to interact with the data. All they need is a Web browser.

Worksheets you place on the Web should be no more than six columns wide. If the worksheet contains more than six columns, it may be too wide to fit in the browser window or the columns will be so narrow they will be hard to read. If possible, the worksheet should be no more than about twelve rows long. The larger the worksheet, the longer it will take to download.

Publishing Excel Worksheets as HTML

The data that you export to the Web can be either interactive or noninteractive. If the Excel data on the Web is interactive, users can enter, format, calculate, analyze, sort, and filter the data. If it is noninteractive, users will be able to view the data, but they will not be able to make any changes to it.

To publish Excel data on the Web, select the worksheet to be put on a Web page. Click File. You may have to expand the menu to see the *Save as Web Page* option. When the Save as Web Page option is displayed, select it. The Save As dialog box is displayed. Click Publish. The Publish As Web Page dialog box is displayed. In the *Choose* list box, you can select to publish a range of cells, all the items on an entire sheet, or previously published items. If the data is to be interactive, click the *Add interactivity with* check box. You can choose to have either *Spreadsheet functionality* or *PivotTable functionality*. Clicking Change displays the Set Title dialog box. Anything you enter here will be centered over the published data. In the *File name* box, you must select the drive, folder, Web folder, Web server, or FTP location where the Web page should be published or saved. Click the Browse button to help you find the proper location. To view the published Web page as it will appear on the Web, make sure the *Open published web page in browser* check box is selected. When all the selections have been made, click Publish.

QUICK STEPS

Export Excel Data to a Web Page
1. Click File and then Save As Web Page.
2. Click Publish.

If you get a message saying the file name cannot be accessed when you try to publish Excel data as a Web page, the amount of data you are trying to save might be too large, especially if the data is to be interactive. Break the worksheet up into two or more worksheets so that you can save a smaller amount of data in each.

exercise 3

PLACING A NONINTERACTIVE WORKSHEET ON THE WEB

1. Open **ExcelWorksheet03**.
2. Save the workbook using the Save As command and name it **eec8x03**.
3. Complete the following steps to save noninteractive data on the Web:
   a. Select cells A1 through D7.
   b. Click File and then click Save as Web Page.
   c. At the Save As dialog box, click Publish.

Step 3c

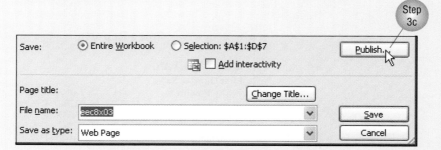

d. The default range of cells in the *Item to publish* area should be A1 through D7 on Sheet 1. Click Change.

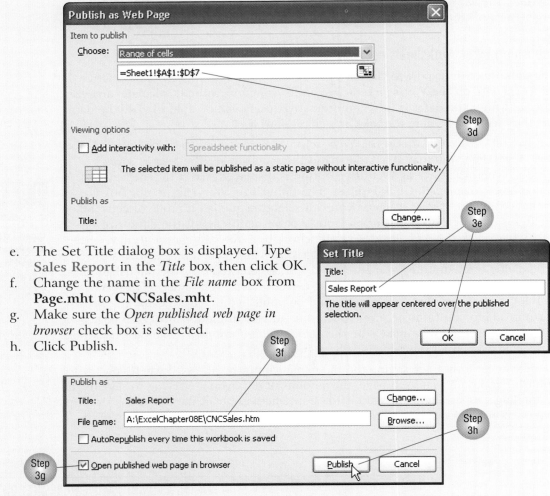

Step 3d

Step 3e

e. The Set Title dialog box is displayed. Type **Sales Report** in the *Title* box, then click OK.

f. Change the name in the *File name* box from **Page.mht** to **CNCSales.mht**.

g. Make sure the *Open published web page in browser* check box is selected.

h. Click Publish.

Step 3f

Step 3g

Step 3h

4. The Web page is displayed in Internet Explorer. Click the Print button to print the Web page.

5. Close Internet Explorer.

6. Save the workbook using the same file name (**eec8x03**) and close it.

Step 4

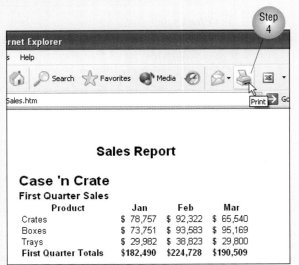

Sales Report

Case 'n Crate
First Quarter Sales

Product	Jan	Feb	Mar
Crates	$ 78,757	$ 92,322	$ 65,540
Boxes	$ 73,751	$ 93,583	$ 95,169
Trays	$ 29,982	$ 38,823	$ 29,800
First Quarter Totals	**$182,490**	**$224,728**	**$190,509**

EXCEL

exercise 4

1. Open **ExcelWorksheet04**.
2. Save the workbook using the Save As command and name it **eec8x04**.
3. Managers at Case 'N Crate need to compute sales representatives' earnings on a weekly basis. The sales representatives earn a commission based on their sales for the week. Those sales representatives who are a category 1 also receive a flat weekly salary of $200. This worksheet automatically calculates the earnings. The managers want it published on the company's intranet so they can use it to make the weekly calculations. Complete the following steps to save this worksheet as interactive data on the Web:
   a. Click File and then click Save as Web Page.
   b. At the Save As dialog box, click Publish.
   c. Make sure *Items on Sheet1* is selected in the *Choose* box.
   d. Click the *Add interactivity with* check box.

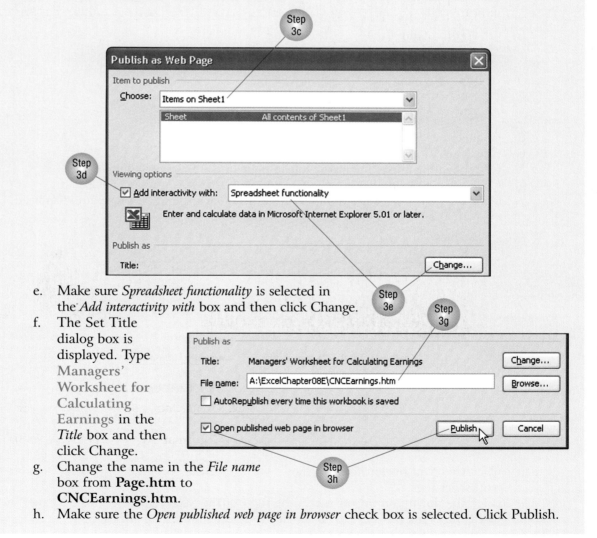

   e. Make sure *Spreadsheet functionality* is selected in the *Add interactivity with* box and then click Change.
   f. The Set Title dialog box is displayed. Type Managers' Worksheet for Calculating Earnings in the *Title* box and then click Change.
   g. Change the name in the *File name* box from **Page.htm** to **CNCEarnings.htm**.
   h. Make sure the *Open published web page in browser* check box is selected. Click Publish.

4. The Web page is displayed in Internet Explorer as an interactive data file. Complete the following steps to make changes to the worksheet:
   a. Click cell A5.
   b. To sort the worksheet by sales representatives, click the down-pointing arrow to the right of the Sort Ascending button and then click *Sales Rep* from the drop-down list.
   c. Type the following values in the cells indicated:

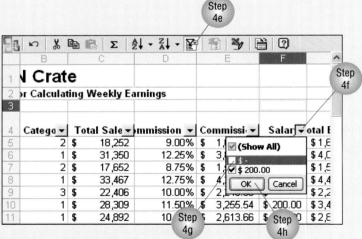

Cell	Value	Cell	Value
C5	18,252	C10	28,309
C6	31,350	C11	24,892
C7	17,652	C12	13,902
C8	33,467	C13	27,346
C9	22,406		

   d. Change the value in cell B6 to 1.
   e. Click the AutoFilter button.
   f. Click the down-pointing arrow to the right of the *Salary* column.
   g. Click the check box next to the *$* - option so that it is no longer selected.
   h. Click OK. Only the sales representatives who earn the $200 salary are displayed.

   i. Click the Print button to print the worksheet.
   j. Click the down-pointing arrow to the right of the Salary label.
   k. Click the check box next to *(Show All)* to select it and then click OK.
5. Close Internet Explorer.
6. Save the workbook using the same file name (**eec8x04**) and close it.

EXCEL

1. Open **ExcelWorksheet05**.
2. Save the workbook using the Save As command and name it **eec8x05**.
3. This chart can be used by the sales representatives at Case 'N Crate to track their first-quarter sales. Management would like this chart put on the company intranet so the sales representatives can chart their own sales. Complete these steps to save the chart on a Web page:
   a. Click File and then click Save as Web Page.
   b. At the Save As dialog box, click Publish.
   c. Select *Chart* from the *Choose* list box.
   d. Click the *Add interactivity with* check box.
   e. Make sure *Chart functionality* is selected in the *Add interactivity with* list box.
   f. Change the name in the *File name* box from **Page.htm** to **CNCChart.htm** and then click the Change button.
   g. The Set Title dialog box is displayed. Type Chart Your First Quarter Sales in the *Title* box and then click OK.
   h. Make sure the *Open published web page in browser* check box is selected and then click Publish.

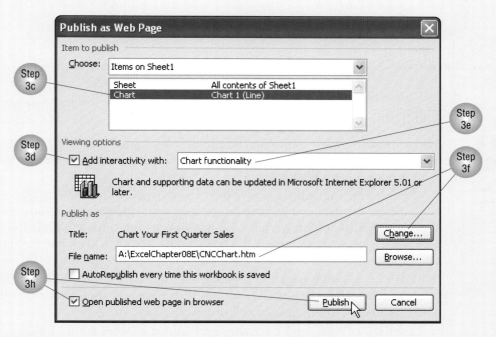

4. The Web page is displayed in Internet Explorer. The chart is interactive. Type the following values in the cells indicated to make changes to the chart:

Cell	Value	Cell	Value	Cell	Value
B2	1,895	C2	3,926	D2	4,053
B3	2,058	C3	8,502	D3	5,021
B4	7,358	C4	4,987	D4	7,932

5. Click the Print button to print the worksheet. Your chart should look like the screen below.

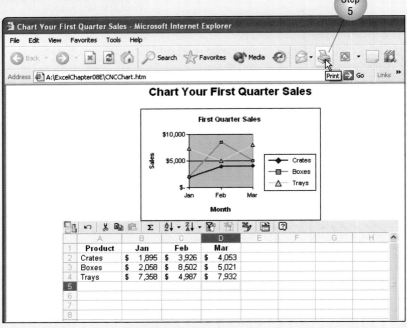

6. Close Internet Explorer.
7. Save the workbook using the same file name (**eec8x05**) and close it.

Importing Data from a Web Page into Excel

QUICK STEPS

Import Excel data from a Web Page
1. Right-click the data to be imported.
2. Click Copy.
3. Click a cell on the worksheet.
4. Click the Paste button.

There are many ways to import data from a Web page into Excel. Depending on which method you choose, some of the data might display differently in Excel than it does on the Web page.

Simply copying and pasting is one way to import data from a Web page into Excel. Select the data you want to import and right-click on any of the cells. From the shortcut menu that appears, click Copy. Click an appropriate cell on the worksheet into which you want to import the copied data and then click the Paste button on the Standard toolbar. The data from the Web page is copied into the worksheet.

Data from a Web page can be imported into Excel using drag and drop. First select the data to be imported from the Web page and then click the selected data and drag it to the desired cell in Excel.

The Object command from the Insert menu enables you to insert a Web page in an Excel worksheet. When the object is inserted, an icon for the Web page is displayed. Double-clicking the icon opens the Web page in Internet Explorer.

You can import data from a Web page into Excel from an Internet Explorer window. To do this, display the page that you want to export into Excel, right-click the mouse and then click Export to Microsoft Excel at the shortcut menu. Depending on the position of the mouse when you right-click the page, a different shortcut menu may appear. For example, if you right-click over a picture, the context-sensitive shortcut menu displays options for saving the picture. Within Excel, the imported data appears immediately allowing you to save the data as a permanent Excel Worksheet.

EXCEL

Another way to import data from a Web page into Excel is by using Web Query. Web Query allows you to query or retrieve text or data on a Web page. Web queries are particularly useful for retrieving data that is in tables. You can create a Web query by starting either in Excel or in the browser. If you start in Excel, click Data, select Import External Data, and then click New Web Query. In the New Web Query dialog box, enter the URL for the Web page from which you want to get data. Click Go. If you start in a browser, browse to the Web page containing the data you want to retrieve. Click the arrow next to the Edit with button and click Edit with Microsoft Excel.

When the Web page is displayed in the browser, yellow arrow buttons appear next to each table on the page, as shown in Figure 8.4. Click the arrow button next to the table you want to import. Click Import. The data can be returned either to the existing worksheet or to a new worksheet.

Run a Web Query
1. Click Data.
2. Click Import External Data.
3. Click New Web Query.

FIGURE

8.4 **The New Web Query Dialog Box**

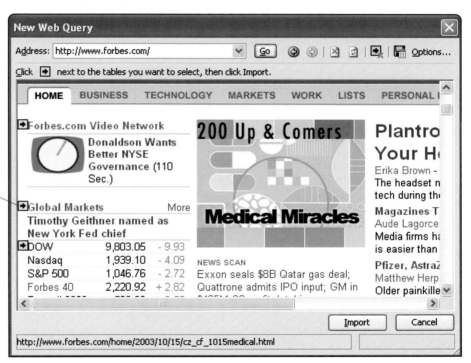

Yellow arrow buttons appear next to each table on a page. Clicking an arrow enables you to import the table to Excel.

The Web page data imported into Excel using a Web query can be easily refreshed with the latest information from the Web page. For example if you use Web Query to link to stock quote data on a Web page, that data can be updated in the workbook by clicking either the Refresh Data button or the Refresh All button on the External Data toolbar.

Refresh All   Refresh Data

Finally, you can open any *.html* file in Excel by using the Open command on the File menu. This method imports the entire Web page, although some content, such as *.gif* image files, might be lost.

exercise 6

1. Complete the following steps to use the copy and paste method to import data from a Web page into Excel:
   a. Open Internet Explorer (or Netscape). You do not have to be online.
   b. Click the File menu in Internet Explorer and then click Open.
   c. The Open dialog box appears. Click browse and locate the *sales_reps.html* file on your data disk and open it. Click Open and then OK at the Open dialog box.
   d. Open a new workbook in Excel. Arrange the windows so that you can see both the entire width of the table in the Web browser and at least cell A1 in Excel.
   e. The Web page lists the phone numbers of the sales representatives for Case 'N Crate. Click the First Name box in the upper left corner of the table and drag to the last telephone number in order to select the entire table.
   f. Click on the selected table in the Web browser and drag the mouse pointer to cell A1 in the Excel worksheet.
   g. Close Internet Explorer.
   h. Switch to the Excel worksheet and maximize it.
   i. Widen columns C and D so that the data in these columns is displayed on one line. Adjust the row height of all rows to 12.75".
   j. Create a custom header for the worksheet that displays your name at the left margin and the file name at the right margin.
   k. Save the worksheet using the file name **eec8x06a**.
   l. Print the worksheet and then close it.
2. Complete the following steps to use the Open command to import data from a Web page into Excel:
   a. In Excel, click File and then click Open.
   b. Locate the **sales_reps.html** file and open it.
   c. If the Case 'N Crate logo is covering the title *Sales Representatives*, click the logo to select it and drag it to the right so that it is no longer covering the title.
   d. Save the worksheet as an Excel workbook using the file name **eec8x06b**.
   e. Create a custom header for the worksheet that displays your name at the left margin and the file name at the right margin.
   f. Save the worksheet using the same file name.
3. Print the worksheet and then close it.

exercise 7

(Note: In order to complete this exercise you must be connected to the Internet.)

1. If necessary, open a new workbook in Excel and click cell A1.
2. Complete the following steps to run a Web Query:
   a. Click Data, select Import External Data, and then click New Web Query.
   b. The New Web Query dialog box is displayed. Enter the following URL: msn.com. Click Go.

EXCEL

c. Find the daily stock index on the home page and click the yellow arrow button next to it. When you click the button, the plus sign turns into a check mark. Click Import.

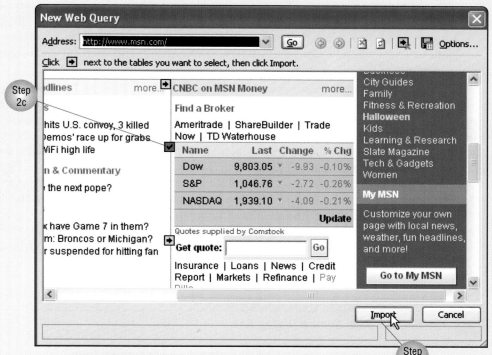

3. The Import Data dialog box is displayed. You want to put the data on the existing worksheet in cell A1. Click OK.
4. The External Data toolbar is displayed. Wait a couple of minutes. Click the Refresh Data button to update the stock index. If a Refresh Data dialog box appears, click OK. The numbers will automatically be updated.
5. Save the file using the file name **eec8x07**.
6. Enter a custom header that prints your name at the left margin and the name of the file at the right margin.
7. Print the worksheet.
8. Save and then close the file.

Using Microsoft Query

Another way to retrieve external data into Excel is by using Microsoft Query. Microsoft Query is a program that enables you to access databases, such as Microsoft Access, in order to retrieve data into a worksheet where it can then be analyzed in Excel. Whenever the database is updated with new information, Excel reports or summaries based on that data are automatically updated.

In order to retrieve data from a database into Excel, you create a query or question based on the data. For example, you might want to know last year's sales figures for a particular product. When creating the query, you select only the specific data you want to retrieve. There are three steps to using Query to retrieve data. First, you establish the data source of the data to be retrieved; second, you use the Query Wizard to select the specific data to be retrieved; and third, you return the data to Excel where it can be formatted, summarized, and used for creating reports.

Although you can work directly in Query, the easiest way to retrieve data using Microsoft Query is by using the Query Wizard. With the Query Wizard you can select the tables and fields to be included, sort the data, and do simple filtering before the data is returned to an Excel worksheet. In order to use Microsoft Query, it must be installed on your computer. Click the cell on the Excel worksheet where the external data range is to start. Click Data, point to Get External Data, and then click New Database Query. The Choose Data Source dialog box shown in Figure 8.5 is displayed. This dialog box is used for establishing the data source. On the Databases tab, make sure the *Use the Query Wizard to create/edit queries* check box is selected. Double-click the database from which the data is to be retrieved. The Select Database dialog box is displayed. Double-click the database file where the data is located. From this point you can follow the directions provided by the Query Wizard.

Query a Database
Click Data, point to Import External Data, and then click New Database Query.

8.5 **The Choose Data Source Dialog Box**

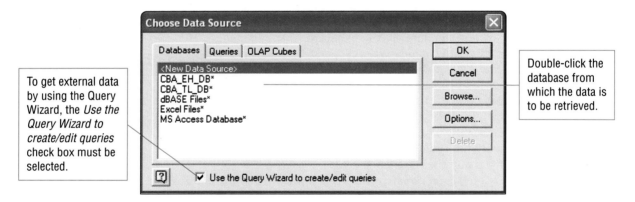

To get external data by using the Query Wizard, the *Use the Query Wizard to create/edit queries* check box must be selected.

Double-click the database from which the data is to be retrieved.

exercise 8

USING MICROSOFT QUERY TO QUERY A DATABASE

1. If necessary, open a new workbook in Excel and click cell A1.
2. Retrieve data from a Microsoft Access database using Microsoft Query by completing the following steps:
   a. Click Data, point to Import External Data, and then click New Database Query.

EXCEL

b. If necessary, click the Databases tab in the Choose Data Source dialog box.

c. Make sure the *Use the Query Wizard to create/edit queries* check box is selected.

d. Double-click the *MS Access Database** option.

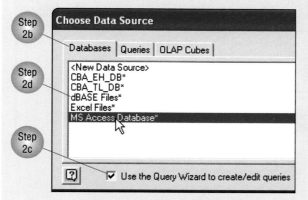

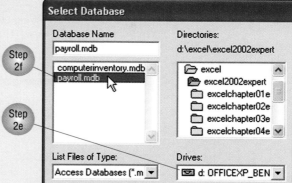

e. The Select Database dialog box is displayed. By default, the current drive and/or folder displayed is the location in which the student data files are stored. If necessary, change the drive and/or directory to the location of the student data files.

f. Double-click the *Payroll.mdb* option from the *Database Name* list.

g. The Query Wizard - Choose Columns dialog box is displayed. Click the plus sign next to *Employee Information*.

h. A list of all the fields in the Employee Information table is displayed. Click the *Firstname* option in the *Available tables and columns* list.

i. Click the greater than symbol. The *Firstname* option has now moved from the *Available tables and columns* list to the *Columns in your query* list.

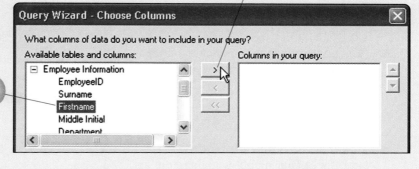

j. Click the *Surname* option in the *Available tables and columns* list and then click the greater than symbol.

k. Click the *HourlyRate* option in the *Available tables and columns* list and then click the greater than symbol. *Firstname, Surname,* and *HourlyRate* should all be listed in the *Columns in your query* list. Click Next.

l. The Query - Wizard Filter Data dialog box is displayed. You want to retrieve only those records of employees who earn more than $20.00 an hour. In the *Column to filter* box, click *HourlyRate*.

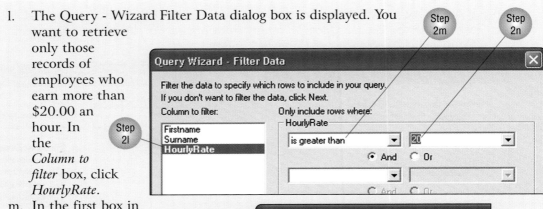

Step 2m

Step 2n

Step 2l

m. In the first box in the *Only include rows where* section, select *is greater than*.

n. Type **20** in the second box in the *Only include rows where* section and then click Next.

o. The Query Wizard - Sort Order dialog box is displayed. You want to sort the rows by Surname. Click the down-pointing arrow to the right of the *Sort by* box and click *Surname*, then click Next.

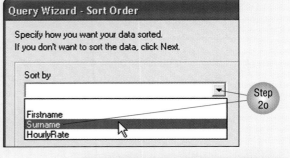

Step 2o

p. The Query Wizard - Finish dialog box is displayed. Make sure the *Return Data to Microsoft Office Excel* option is selected. Click Finish.

Step 2p

3. The Import Data dialog box is displayed. Make sure that the *Existing worksheet* option is selected and cell A1 is entered in the box. Click OK.

4. The appropriate data is retrieved into Excel. Format the figures in column C to display as currency with two decimal places.

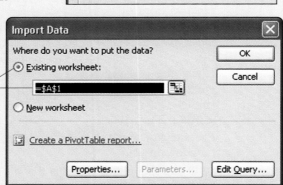

Step 3

5. Save the worksheet using the file name **eec8x08**.

6. Create a custom header for the worksheet that displays your name at the left margin and the file name at the right margin.

7. Print the worksheet.

8. Save the workbook using the same file name (**eec8x08**) and close it.

EXCEL

Linking and Embedding Objects

Another way of sharing Excel data with other applications is by copying the information as either a linked object or an embedded object. The information that is being copied is called the object. The file from which the object comes is called the source file. The file into which the object is being copied is called the destination file.

A linked object is stored with the source file. Any changes made to the object in the source file are automatically reflected in the destination file. An embedded object is stored with the destination file. If an object is embedded, there is no link to the source file. Therefore, any changes made to the object in the source file are not reflected in the destination file. However, you can edit an embedded object right in Excel by double-clicking on it. Double-clicking on an embedded object allows you to modify it using its original program while still in Excel. The commands and menus for the embedded object's original program are displayed even though you have not left Excel.

An important difference between linking and embedding objects is the size of the destination file. The size of the destination file is much larger if the object is embedded. Linking an object requires much less disk space for the destination file than embedding an object.

There is more than one way to link or embed an object in Excel. Using the Insert Object command provides you with the most control over the process. To insert a linked or embedded object, access the destination file, which is the worksheet where the object is to be placed. Click Insert and then click Object. The Object dialog box appears. To create a new object, click the Create New tab as shown in Figure 8.6. To insert an object from an existing file, click the Create from File tab shown in Figure 8.7.

QUICK STEPS

Insert a Linked or Embedded Object
Click Insert, and then Object.

FIGURE

8.6 *Object Dialog Box with the Create New Tab Selected*

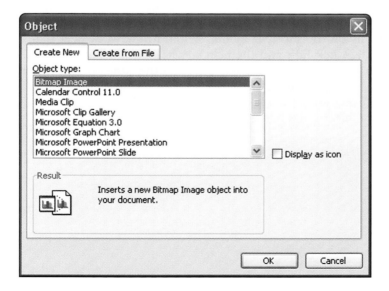

FIGURE

8.7   *Object Dialog Box with the Create from File Tab Selected*

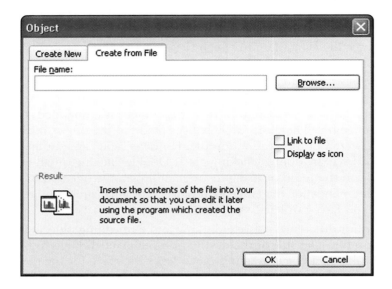

If you are creating a new embedded object, select the type of object you want to create from the *Object type* box. If you plan to put the workbook online, clicking the *Display as icon* check box will display the object as an icon that viewers can double-click to display the object. If you are inserting a linked or embedded object from an existing file, enter the name of the file in the *File name* box. If the *Link to file* check box is not selected, the object will be embedded. If it is selected, the object will be linked. Clicking the *Display as icon* check box will display the object as an icon to those viewing the workbook online.

In addition to inserting a linked object or embedded object from an existing file, you can copy information from an existing file as a linked or embedded object. First, select the information to be copied. Right-click the selected information and then click Copy on the shortcut menu. Switch to the worksheet that is to be the destination file. Click Edit and then click Paste Special. The Paste Special dialog box shown in Figure 8.8 is displayed. Selecting the *Paste* option from this dialog box copies the information as an embedded object. Selecting the *Paste link* option copies the information as a linked object. In the *As* box, make sure the option that has the word Object in its name is selected.

8.8 *Paste Special Dialog Box*

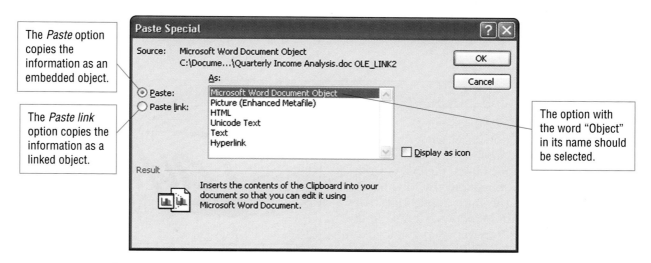

The *Paste* option copies the information as an embedded object.

The *Paste link* option copies the information as a linked object.

The option with the word "Object" in its name should be selected.

exercise 9

1. Open **ExcelWorksheet06**.
2. Save the worksheet using the Save As command and name it **eec8x09**.
3. Create a custom header that displays your name at the left margin and the file name at the right margin.
4. The figure for the proposed budget increase that needs to be entered into cell B10 can be found in the **Budget.doc** file. To insert text from the **Budget.doc** file into the **eec8x09** file, complete the following steps:
   a. Click cell A19.
   b. Click Insert and then click Object.
   c. The Object dialog box is displayed. Click the Create from File tab.
   d. Click the Browse button. From the Browse dialog box, select ***Budget.doc*** from your data disk, and then click Insert. Click the *Link to file* check box to select it and then click OK.
5. The linked object is inserted in the worksheet. Read the information that is displayed. Type **10** in cell B10. Save the workbook using the same file name (**eec8x09**) and print it.
6. Double-click the linked object. Word automatically opens and **Budget.doc** is the active file. Delete *10* and in its place type **08**. Save the file and exit Word.

7. If necessary, switch to the **eec8x09** workbook in Excel. The text in the linked object automatically changed from *10* to *08*. Type 08 in cell B10. Save the workbook using the same file name (**eec8x09**) and print it.
8. Close the workbook.

exercise 10

1. Open **ExcelWorksheet07**.
2. Save the worksheet using the Save As command and name it **eec8x10**.
3. The logo for Linda Taylor's custom-made clothing store, Taylor MADE, is stored in the Paint application that comes with Windows. Complete the following steps to insert the logo as an embedded object:
   a. Click cell A1.
   b. Click Insert and then click Object.
   c. The Object dialog box is displayed. Click the Create from File tab.
   d. Click the Browse button. From the Browse dialog box, select *Taylor.bmp* from your data disk and then click Insert.
   e. Make sure that the *Link to file* check box is clear and then click OK.
   f. Adjust the size of the image so that it is not covering any of the data.
   g. Save the worksheet.
4. The object is embedded in the worksheet. Double-click the image in the worksheet. All the commands and menus in the Paint program are now available for you to use. You can edit the image right from Excel. Complete the following steps to edit the image:
   a. Click the *Fill With Color* icon, the icon in the second column and the second row.
   b. On the bottom of the screen, click the orange color, the last color in the second row.
   c. Move the mouse pointer, which looks like a can of paint, over the white portion of the image and click. Click carefully in all the white spaces so that the entire background is orange.
   d. Click anywhere outside the image.

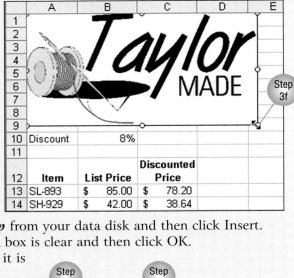

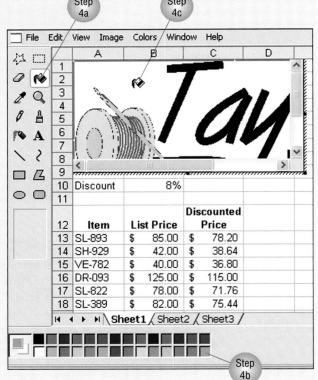

Chapter Eight

EXCEL

5. Create a custom header that displays your name at the left margin and the file name at the right margin.
6. Save the workbook using the same file name (**eec8x10**) and print it.
7. Close the workbook.

Using XML with Microsoft Excel 2003

XML, or Extensible Markup Language, is designed to improve the functionality of the Web by providing a more flexible way to identify information. XML is based on SGML, the same language on which HTML is based. Businesses are finding that HTML, currently the language most commonly used for documents on the Web, is limited in terms of the ways it can describe information. HTML focuses on the presentation of information, or on the way the information is formatted. XML focuses on the information itself. With an XML document, it is much easier to work with or manipulate data than it is with an HTML document. With XML, data from different applications are given a standardized format, making XML the data-exchange format of choice for many business applications. Since XML allows for much more flexibility in manipulating data and since it allows for easy data exchange, it is becoming an essential tool for business transactions.

QUICK STEPS

Open an .XML File in Excel
1. Click File and then Open.
2. Select *XML Files (*.xml)* from the *Files of type* list box.

With Excel 2003 you can create and analyze XML data. Excel 2003 can recognize and open any XML document. With the XML spreadsheet file format included with Excel 2003, you can also save an Excel spreadsheet as an XML file. Any XML document can be loaded into Excel by clicking File and then Open. Click the down-pointing arrow to the right of the *Files of type* box and click *XML Files (*.xml)*. Select the file to be opened and click Open. To save an Excel spreadsheet as an XML file, click File and then Save As. Click the down-pointing arrow to the right of the *Save as type* box and click *XML spreadsheet (*.xml)*.

Note: To complete exercises in the rest of this chapter, you will need to turn on the display of file extensions. If file extensions display, skip to Exercise 1. If not, complete the following steps to display file extensions:

1. *Display the Control Panel.*
2. *Double-click the* Folder Options *icon.*
3. *At the Folder Options dialog box, click the View tab.*
4. *At the Folder Options dialog box with the View tab selected, remove the check mark from the* Hide extensions for known file types *option.*
5. *Click the Apply button and then click the OK button.*
6. *Close the Control Panel.*

exercise 11

OPENING AN XML FILE IN EXCEL

1. Complete the following steps to open the **PhoneNumbers.xml** file on your student disk in Excel.
   a. Click File and then Open.
   b. Click *PhoneNumbers.xml* and then click Open.
2. The **PhoneNumbers.xml** file is opened in Excel. Save the file as an Excel worksheet (with the *.xls* extension). Name the worksheet file **eec9x11**.
3. Print and close the **eec8x11** worksheet file.

Using XML to Share Data

Since the early days of computing, both experts and users have recognized the need to exchange information among a variety of computer systems and software applications. However, word processors, spreadsheets, databases, web pages and e-mail applications, just to name a few, all use different file structures to store information. Over the past several decades the most popular approach to data exchange among different programs was to use structured text files. Structured text files come in several varieties such as the CSV (comma separated values) format and the fixed length field format, supported by Excel and Access. While there are many ways to construct these text files, they all have one important thing in common: the rows and columns are defined by plain text characters such as commas, quotation marks, tabs and line endings. Text files offer only a partial solution, however, since applications such as Word, Excel, or Access cannot successfully read text data files unless you specify in a dialog box the exact details of how the text file is organized.

The explosive growth of the Internet has significantly increased the number of users that want to exchange all types of information. One reason often cited for the rapid growth of the Internet is that, despite the dizzying variety of information on the web, it is all based on a common method of text formatting called HTML (Hypertext Markup Language). Because HTML is the standard for all web sites, users can go from site to site without having to think about or deal with different file formats on different sites. Many Internet pioneers wondered if, by using HTML as a model, a better method for exchanging complex sets of data could be developed. The result of their efforts is XML—*eXtensible Markup Language*.

XML Design

XML was created with the goal of doing for application files what HTML did for Web pages, that is, create a single type of file format that can be used to store data from anyprogram. If XML were fully implemented n Microsoft Office it would mean that you could save data from any Office program as an XML file and then open that same file (no conversion required) in any other program. Further, that file would be compatible with programs all over the Web that supported XML. At the moment such an ideal world is still in the future. But XML does support key features that one day may lead to a universal storage standard based on XML. There are three major aspects to the design of XML:

1. XML, like HTML, is 100% text. This is important because the basic protocol of the Internet, HTTP (Hypertext Transfer Protocol), was designed to transmit text information such as HTML documents. This makes XML fully compatible with data exchange on or off the Internet.

2. XML documents are highly structured. A single XML file can have a number of sections, each of which can contain different types of information. For example, a document can contain word processing format information which can be ignored but not deleted when that document is loaded into a spreadsheet application. This allows a single document to operate with multiple programs since each program uses only the sections of the document that make sense for that application.

3. XML is an extensible language, like human languages, in that allows for the invention of new terms. Computer languages have typically been created with a fixed vocabulary of keywords, which are the only

instructions that can be used in coding that language. In an extensible computer language, terms are restricted only by a set of rules, that is, a grammar, that defines how new terms can be added to code written in that language.

Rules Governing the Design of XML Documents

While XML is a powerful language, the basic rules that govern the creation of XML documents are fairly simple:

1. Each item of data should be enclosed in a ***tag***, which is simply a word that identifies the data. A starting tag is placed before an item begins and an ending tag is placed at the end of the item. Ending tags are identical to starting tags with the exception that a / appears before the tag name. The item below defines an *Actor* data item:

    `<Actor>Kevin Spacey</Actor>`

2. Each tagged item in an XML document is called an *element,* and groups of elements make up an XML document. Figure 8-9 shows a simple but complete XML document. It contains five data elements (character, film, year, actor and director) each enclosed by a pair of identifying tags.

FIGURE

8.9 **Sample XML Coding**

```
- <AFI>
 - <Performance>
     <Character>Erin Brockovich</Character>
     <Film>Erin Brockovich</Film>
     <Year>2000</Year>
     <Actor>Julia Roberts</Actor>
     <Director>Steven Soderbergh</Director>
   </Performance>
</AFI>
```

3. All related data items are grouped in containers, which help create an overall organization for the XML document. In Figure 8.9 note the tags <Performance> and, later in the document, </Performance>. These tags define the Performance element. The Performance element does not contain a specific item of data as do the character, film, year, actor and director elements. Rather, the Performance element acts as a container to group together all of the data items related to one performance as a unit.

4. All XML documents must have a ***root*** tag, which functions as the starting point of the document. In Figure 8.10, the AFI (American Film Institute) tag is the root tag. The root tag allows this document to expand so that it can contain any number of Performance groups.

5. XML documents are organized in a tree structure with the root tag as the starting point. Figure 8.10 pictures the American Film Institute document as a tree where the starting point is the root element. All of the elements can be located starting from the root element and traveling down the various branches of the document tree. The tree structure makes it possible for an XML-aware program to read a correctly composed XML file without any advance knowledge of the file's structure. The application starts at the root element, and reads through the document tags, assembling a complete picture of the document tree as it goes.

FIGURE

8.10 *XML Document Tree Structure*

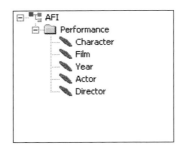

Advantages of Self-Documenting XML Files

The ability of an XML-aware program to read an XML file in its correct structure makes XML documents ***self-documenting***. A self-documenting file is one that carries both data and information about how the data in the file is organized. Eliminating the need for user intervention significantly streamlines the process of exchanging sophisticated sets of data among programs, especially those running on the Web. Excel 2003 can read an XML document and automatically extract a model of the document's data tree. Excel calls the outline of the document the ***document map***, as shown in Figure 8.11 automatically generated from the contents of even a simple XML document.

FIGURE

8.11 *Excel Map Generated from an XML Document*

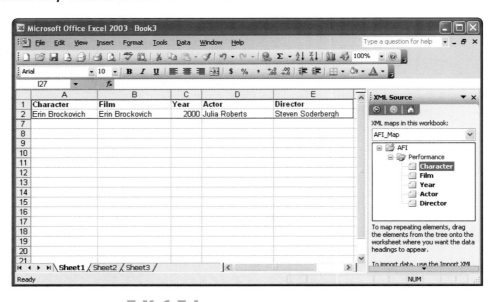

EXCEL

XML Schemas Provide Structure

While all XML files carry basic self-documentation, the XML standard provides a method for supplying more sophisticated information about the structure of an XML file in the form of an XML schema file. A *schema file*, usually indicated by an XSD extension, can be used to specify more detailed aspects of data structure such as data types, limits on values or lists of valid entries. A schema file also acts as a means for validating, or verifying, the information in an XML file. When a schema file is paired with an XML data file, the application loading the data can automatically validate the information being loaded by comparing the data to the requirements detailed in the schema file. For example, a schema can indicate that the data in a column should be a valid date. The schema would prevent loading data from a file if non-date information occurred in that column.

Note that the creation of XML schema files requires special skills and knowledge about XML. These files are generally prepared by programmers and distributed along with XML data files. In Excel 2003 the use of schema files is optional since Excel can generate its own schema (also called a map) if no schema file is available.

XML Namespaces

While extensibility is certainly a key feature of XML, it is not without its problems. Since anyone constructing an XML document can make up element names, it is possible, and even likely, that the same element names will appear in many different XML documents. For example, element names such as *date*, *type,* or *group* are likely to appears in many different data documents. In order to distinguish elements in different documents that have the same name, XML supports a concept called a *namespace*. A namespace acts as a prefix that identifies the source document of a given element. A namespace is assigned to the root element of an XML document using the *xmlns* attribute, as shown in the line below where the name *Example1* is assigned as the namespace for the document:

```
<Films xmlns="Example1">
```

Any element within that namespace can be referenced by adding the namespace as a prefix to the element name:

```
Example1:Actor
```

In practice, most namespaces used by XML designers take the form of Internet universal identifiers such as the one shown below. This can be a bit confusing because the name appears to refer to a site on the Internet. However, it is simply a name, like *Example1*, that identifies a namespace:

```
http://tempuri.org/performance.xsd
```

In Excel, namespaces are optional because Excel keeps track of XML documents by assigning then a name called a **map name**, based on the name of the root element automatically generated when the file is opened. If the root element already exists, Excel adds a number—for example, Film1—to the root name so that each document is uniquely identified.

Namespaces also play a role in XML schemas by identifying which schema match which documents. For example, suppose you are supplied with an XML document and an XML schema file. When both are opened in the same workbook, Excel uses the namespaces to match the schema file with the document or documents to which the schema should be applied. Conversely, if the schema namespace does not match the document namespace, then the schema will not be applied to the document.

Keep in mind the design of XML schemas and namespaces are of concern to XML professionals. Excel users simply take advantage of the XML features included in the document and schema files they use.

Working with XML Data in Excel 2003

Excel 2003 is designed to make working with XML data as simple as possible. It is not necessary to actually view the raw XML file. Instead, Excel displays the XML data as part of a normal spreadsheet display.

Information about the structure of the XML data can be viewed by opening the XML Source task pane. The task pane is interactive. Use it to drag and drop XML elements to different parts of the spreadsheet or remove XML elements from the spreadsheet. In the examples used in this section, the data consists of a list of the 400 most memorable heroes and villains in American movies compiled by the American Film Institute.

exercise 12

OPENING AND MODIFYING AN XML FILE

1. With a blank worksheet displayed, open the document named **afi2000s.xml**.
2. At the Open XML dialog box, click OK. (This message is an example of the self-documenting nature of XML documents.)
3. At the Microsoft Excel dialog box, click OK.
4. Excel loads the data from the XML file and places the data into the spreadsheet starting at cell A1 of the current worksheet as shown below.

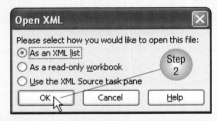

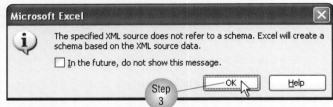

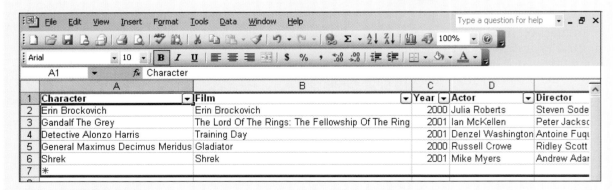

5. Excel has automatically created a schema map of the document when the data was loaded. To display the map, do the following:
   a. Press Ctrl + F1 to open the task pane.

b. Click the Other Task Panes button and then click XML Source at the drop-down list to display the XML Source task pane. The task pane shows the structure of the XML document as a tree of elements with AFI as the root element. Note that above the map box Excel has assigned the map a name, *AFI_Map*.

6. Change the name of the XML map by completing the following steps:

   a. Near the bottom of the task pane, click the XML Maps button.

   b. Excel displays the XML Maps dialog box. This dialog box lists all of the XML maps currently available.
   Each map has three items of information. Click the *Rename* button.

   c. With the insertion point position in the *Name* column, type Noted Performances.

   d. Click OK. The new name of the map appears in the task pane.

7. Excel can keep count of the number of records in an XML table. To display the total number of records, do the following:

   a. Close the task pane by pressing Ctrl + F1.

   b. If necessary, display the List toolbar by clicking View, pointing to Toolbars, and then clicking List.

   c. On the List toolbar, click the *Toggle Total Row* button. The label *Total* appears at the bottom of the *Character* column and the number *5* appears at the bottom of the *Director* column.

8. If you have several XML documents that share the same structure, you can combine the data into one large XML table. Perform the following steps to add additional Performances to the current table.

   a. Right-click on any part of the XML table.

   b. At the shortcut list, point to XML and then click XML Map Properties. Excel displays the properties dialog box for the current document map, *Noted Performances*.

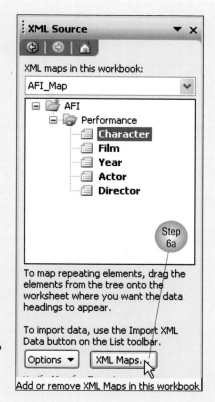

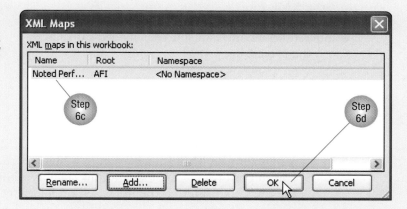

c. Options within the *When refreshing or importing data* section of the XML Map Properties dialog box control how new data is handled when it is added to the workbook. Click *Append new data to existing XML lists* to instruct Excel to add new data to the bottom of the current list and then click OK.

d. Click the Import XML Data button on the List toolbar.

e. Locate and then double-click the **afi1990s.xml** file. At the Microsoft Excel dialog box, click OK to have Excel create a schema. Excel adds the information from this file to the records that were already in the list.

f. Move to cell E71. It shows the new total of 68 records.

9. Save the combined 2000s and 1990s list as a new XML file by performing the following steps:

a. Click the Export XML Data button on the List toolbar.

b. Name the file *aficombined* and then click Export.

c. Close the spreadsheet.

d. Click No when asked to save the workbook. Note that data was already saved in the XML file.

10. Open the file **aficombined.xml**. Click OK in the next two dialog boxes. The combined 68 record data source is loaded into Excel.

11. Close the spreadsheet without saving changes.

XML Map Properties

Name: Noted Performances

XML schema validation
☐ Validate data against schema for import and export

Data source
☑ Save data source definition in workbook

Data formatting and layout
☑ Adjust column width
☑ Preserve column filter
☑ Preserve number formatting

Step 8c

When refreshing or importing data:
○ Overwrite existing data with new data
◉ Append new data to existing XML lists

[OK]   [Cancel]

Manipulating XML Data

In addition to simply loading and displaying XML data, Excel 2003 automatically recognizes the XML information as a highly structured data source. Excel allows you to perform database operations such as adding or deleting columns, sorting the rows, and filtering the list based on logical criteria.

If your XML data is supplied with schema files, (look for XSD extensions), you can start by loading the schema file and then importing data into the already loaded XML map. If you do not have a schema file Excel will generate a schema automatically by examining the elements included in the XML document itself.

Excel also automatically prepares the XML data for standard database operations such as sorting all of the rows by the values in a selected column or filtering the rows for those that match a specified set of criteria. Each column in the XML data list will automatically display a set of sorting and filtering options when you click a drop-down arrow next to the column heading. Further, you can use the element map to remove elements from the list so that you display only the column that you are interested in using.

1. With a blank spreadsheet open, display the XML Source task pane. If the task pane is not already visible, display it by pressing Ctrl + F1.
2. Click the XML Maps button in the task pane. The map list is empty.
3. Click the *Add* button. Locate and select the **voting.xsd** schema file and then click Open.
4. Click the *Rename* button and enter Heroes and Villains in the *Name* column and then click OK.
5. Excel displays the element tree in the XML Source task pane based on the information in the schema file even though no actual XML data has been loaded. Note that this schema contains additional elements, *Type* and *Rank*, which are not part of the XML data used in Exercise 12.
6. You are not required to display all of the elements, nor are you required to display them in the same order as they appear in the map. Organize the data display of elements on the spreadsheet by completing the following steps:
   a. Click *Film* in the map box and then drag the element to cell B2.
   b. Click *Character* in the map box and then drag the element to cell C2.
   c. Click *Actor* in the map box and then drag the element to cell D2. Note that the elements you have placed on the spreadsheet appear in bold in the map box.
7. You can now import data into the schema and the layout you have created by performing the following steps:
   a. Right-click cell D2. At the shortcut menu, point to XML and then click Import.
   b. Locate the file **afi400.xml** and then double-click the file name. The data loads and fills in the columns based on where you placed the elements on the spreadsheet.
8. Add another element to the spreadsheet. From the task pane map box, drag *Year* to A2. Note that no data appears in the column. It is necessary to have Excel import the data from an XML source. *(Note: Error flags will appear in the cells in column A. Since XML data is stored as text Excel is flagging the cells containing the years assuming this data should be stored as numbers. You can ignore the green error flags.)*
   a. Right-click cell A2. At the shortcut menu, point to XML and then click Import.
   b. Double click *afi400.xml*.
9. Sort the list by year from earliest to the most recent performance, by completing the following steps:
   a. Click in cell A2 and then click the down-pointing arrow at the right of *Year*.
   b. At the drop-down list, click *Sort Ascending*. (You may have to scroll up to see this option.)
10. Filter the list for occurrences of Humphrey Bogart in the *Actor* column by completing the following steps:
    a. Click in cell D2.
    b. Click the down-pointing arrow at the right of *Actor* to display the drop-down list.

c. Scroll down the list of names until you locate *Humphrey Bogart* and then click *Humphrey Bogart*. The list now displays the five performances that meet the specified criteria as shown below.

	A	B	C	D
1				
2	Year	Film	Character	Actor
49	1936	The Petrified Forest	Duke Mantee	Humphrey Bogart
91	1942	Casablanca	Rick Blaine	Humphrey Bogart
110	1946	The Big Sleep	Philip Marlowe	Humphrey Bogart
120	1948	The Treasure Of The Sierra Madre	Fred C. Dobbs	Humphrey Bogart
156	1954	The Caine Mutiny	Lt. Commander Philip Francis Queeg	Humphrey Bogart
401				

11. Restore the full display by completing the following steps:
    a. Click the drop-down list arrow in cell D2 to display the drop-down list.s
    b. Scroll up and then click *(All)*. The full list is now displayed.
12. Save the workbook and name it **eec8x13**.
13. Close **eec8x13**.

Data Entry and Data Validation

So far you have only loaded existing data from an XML source into an Excel spreadsheet. Excel allows you to modify and add information to an XML list and then save the revised data as an XML document.

When it comes to data entry, the issue of *validation* becomes important. Validation refers to a process whereby data in an XML document is compared to rules and restrictions written into an XML schema file. Validation ensures that the data entered into an element conforms to the rules written into the file by the schema developer.

For example, the AFI list of performances was created so that critics could rank their top 10 performances that AFI would compile and publish to find the top 10 most popular movie performances in American film. In order to facilitate ranking the performances, you might add a new element, *Rank*, to the schema. An XML schema can be used to ensure that only whole numbers, e.g. 1, 2, 3, ..., are entered into the Rank column. Below is a fragment taken from an XML schema that restricts the *Rank* element to positive integer values. The *minOccurs* attribute is set to zero to allow empty items in the *Rank* element as well as integers.

```
<xs:element name="Rank" type="xs:positiveInteger"
minOccurs="0"/>
```

Schema restrictions can be even more specific. Below is a section of a schema file that not only limits the entries to positive integers but also limits the value of the integers to the range of 1 to 10.

```
<xs:element name="Rank" minOccurs="0">
    <xs:simpleType>
        <xs:restriction base="positiveInteger">
            <xs:minInclusive value="1"/>
            <xs:maxInclusive value="10"/>
        </xs:restriction>
    </xs:simpleType>
</xs:element>
```

EXCEL

Schemas can also set rules and place restrictions on text entries. The schema section below limits the text entered into the *Type* element to either *Hero* or *Villain*. You can leave an entry blank because the minOccurs attribute is set to zero. Be aware that XML validation is case sensitive. Any entry must match the schema exactly, including case, in order to be valid.

```
<xs:element name="Type" minOccurs="0">
      <xs:simpleType>
            <xs:restriction base="xs:string">
                  <xs:enumeration value="Hero" />
                  <xs:enumeration value="Villain" />
            </xs:restriction>
      </xs:simpleType>
</xs:element>
```

In Excel, data validation is optional. By default, Excel will save XML data that does not meet the criteria established in a schema file. You do have the option to allow Excel to enforce schema validation rules and restrictions when data is imported or exported.

Validation is an important concept when the data being entered or edited is destined to be used by another application. Supplying a schema file along with a document file provides a way of checking the entries someone makes when you are not there to check it yourself. For example, if the schema specifies that a data item should be a date and the user enters 13/1/03 instead of 1/31/03, validation will prevent the user from saving the bad entry. The user will only be able to save the entries if the typo is corrected. Validation is to make sure that certain data items are not left blank, that numbers fall within a certain range, that the entry matches an item on a list of valid entries, and more.

On the other hand, if you are working though a project, you may want to skip validation until you have completed the document. This would allow you to save partially completed information that might not pass the validation test until you have time to go back and finish the entry. The fact that validation is turned off by default in Excel 2003 means that you must rely on the user to turn on validation before saving the final version of the data or else the validation rules included in the schema will not be applied.

Defining XML Source Task Pane View Options

You can define how you want to view information in the XML Source task pane using the Options button at the bottom of the task pane. With the XML Source task pane open, click the Options button to display the pop-up menu shown in Figure 8.12. By default, the options shown with check marks are active.

8.12 XML Source Task Pane View Options

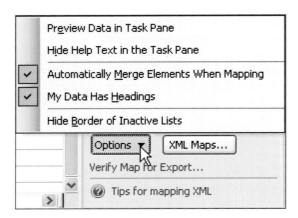

Click *Preview Data in Task Pane* at the Options pop-up menu and then click in the task pane outside the menu to remove the menu display. Next to each mapped element a sample of data from the associated list in the Excel worksheet displays as shown in Figure 8.13.

8.13 XML Source Task Pane with Preview Data View Option

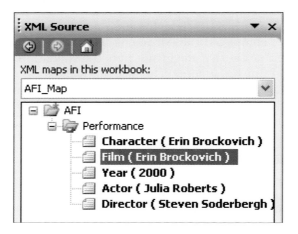

By default, help text displays below the element list box describing how to map elements from the hierarchical list to a cell in the worksheet and how to import XML data into the mapped list. Click *Hide Help Text in the Task Pane* at the Options pop-up menu to turn off the display of this text.

Dragging an element from the XML Source task pane to a cell adjacent to an existing XML list causes Excel to automatically expand the list to include the new element. To prevent the automatic inclusion of new elements into existing lists, click the Options button and then click *Automatically Merge Elements* When Mapping to remove the check mark.

By default, My Data Has Headings is active on the Options menu indicating that existing data can be used as column headings when you map elements to the worksheet. Dragging an element to a cell containing data will map the element but retain the existing text in the cell as the column heading. Remove the check mark if you do not want existing data used when mapping elements. When this option is turned off, dragging an element to a cell that contains text, causes the existing text to moved to the cell below.

To remove the border that displays around a list or a single mapped cell when the active cell is positioned outside the list, click Hide Border of Inactive Lists at the Options pop-up menu.

exercise 14

IMPORTING AN XML SCHEMA AND XML DATA; DEFINING XML SOURCE TASK PANE VIEW OPTIONS

1. At a blank workbook, display the XML Source task pane if it is not already open.
2. Import an existing XML schema file into Excel by completing the following steps:
   a. Click the XML Maps button at the bottom of the XML Source task pane.
   b. At the XML Maps dialog box, click the Add button.
   c. At the Select XML Source dialog box, double-click the file named ***voting.xsd***.
   d. Click OK to close the XML Maps dialog box. Excel loads the element tree into the XML Source task pane.
3. Map elements to the worksheet by completing the following steps:
   a. Drag the *Character* element to cell B2.
   b. Drag the *Film* element to cell C2.
   c. Drag the *Actor* element to cell D2.
   d. Drag the *Type* element to cell E2.
   e. Drag the *Rank* element to cell F2.
4. Import the XML data file you created and exported in Exercise 12 by completing the following steps:
   a. Right-click cell F2.
   b. At the shortcut menu, point to XML and then click Import.
   c. At the Import XML dialog box, double-click the file named ***aficombined.xml***.
5. Type your own column headings and map elements to cells with existing data by completing the following steps:
   a. Click the *Sheet2* tab to switch to a new worksheet.
   b. Make active cell B2 and then type Executive.
   c. Make active C2 and then type Released.
   d. Click the Options button at the bottom of the XML Source task pane.
   e. At the Options pop-up menu, click *My Data Has Headings* to remove the check mark. By deselecting this option, you are instructing Excel not to use the titles you have typed in cells B2 and C2 when you map an element to these cells.
   f. Click in the task pane outside the Options pop-up menu and then drag the *Director* element from the XML Source task pane to cell B2. Since *My Data Has*

Headings has been turned off, Excel moves the text *Executive* to cell B3 and inserts the element name *Director* in B2.

g. Click the Undo button on the Standard toolbar. *Executive* is restored to cell B2 and the *Director* element is no longer mapped.

h. Click the Options button at the bottom of the XML Source task pane.

i. At the Options drop-down list, click *My Data Has Headings* to insert a check mark making the option active and then click in the task pane outside the list.

j. Drag the *Director* element to cell B2. Notice this time the element is mapped however the existing text is retained as the column heading.

k. Drag the *Year* element to cell C2.

6. Import the XML file named **aficombined.xml** to the mapped elements in Sheet2. *(Note: Error flags will appear in the cells in column C. Since XML data is stored as text Excel is flagging the cells containing the years assuming this data should be stored as numbers. You can ignore the green error flags.)*

7. With *Sheet2* the active worksheet, create a custom header that prints your name at the left margin and the file name at the right margin.

8. Save the workbook and name it **eec8x14**.

9. Print only the first page of the *Sheet2* worksheet.

10. Close **eec8x14**.

Summary of XML Document Features in Excel 2003

Excel 2003 is capable of reading, manipulating and saving standard XML documents allowing easy exchange of data with users and systems that support XML. Because Excel can directly work with XML documents, translating data into data exchange formats such as CSV is not necessary.

- **Maps.** Excel displays the elements defined in an XML document as an interactive tree that can be used to drag and drop some or all of the XML elements to locations on a worksheet. You can also use the map to remove unwanted elements.

- **Schema**. A schema is an XML file that is designed to supply additional information to an XML-compatible application about an XML document. If you open an XML document without a schema, Excel automatically generates a schema based on the document element tree. If you are supplied with a schema file, you can use it to prepare, modify or validate XML documents.

- **Manipulation**. Excel automatically prepares XML data for database operations such as sorting rows and filtering rows based on one or more criteria. Each column heading has a drop list menu that lists sorting and filtering options.

- **Validation**. If you are supplied with a schema that contains validation rules you can have Excel apply those rules to the XML files that you are loading and/or saving. When validation is active, you will only be allowed to load or save XML data if it conforms to all of the rules specified in the schema. If you need to work with invalidated data you can turn off validation so that Excel will ignore the schema when saving or loading XML data.

CHAPTER summary

➤ Importing data to Excel refers to sending data from another application to an Excel workbook. Exporting data from Excel refers to sending Excel data to another application.

➤ A text file contains only printable letters, numbers, and symbols, usually from the ASCII character set. A text file contains no formatting codes. A text file is supported by practically every application on every computer platform.

➤ There are two common formats for data that is arranged in rows and columns in a text file. A delimited text file uses a special character called a delimiter to separate one column from the next. Commas and tabs are often used as delimiters. Each column has a set number of characters or spaces (or both) in a fixed width text file.

➤ An intranet provides the services similar to those provided by the Internet within a business or an organization. An intranet is not necessarily connected to the Internet. Intranets use the same Web browser and Web server software as the Internet.

➤ Excel data placed on a Web page can be either interactive or noninteractive. If it is interactive, users can enter, format, calculate, analyze, sort, and filter the data. If it is noninteractive, users will be able to view the data only. They cannot make any changes to it.

➤ Place Excel data on a Web page by clicking File, Save as Web page, and then clicking the Publish button on the Save As dialog box.

➤ You can import data from a Web page into Excel by copying and pasting, by using the Export to Excel button in the Web browser, by using a Web Query, or by using the Open command on the File menu in Excel.

➤ During the linking and embedding process, the information being copied is called the object. The file from which the object originates is called the source file. The file into which the object will be placed is called the destination file.

➤ A linked object is stored with the source file. Changes made to the object in the source file are automatically reflected in the destination file.

➤ An embedded object is stored with the destination file. Any changes made to the source file are not reflected in the destination file. Changes can be made to an embedded object in the destination file only.

➤ If an object is embedded in the destination file, the destination file will be significantly larger than if the object is linked to the destination file.

➤ Objects can be linked or embedded by using the Copy and Paste Special commands.

FEATURES summary

COMMAND	MENU/COMMANDS
Import from a text file	Click File, Open, select *Text Files* from the *Files of type* list box
Export to a text file	Click File, Save As, select *Text* from the *Save as type* list box
Export Excel data to a Web page	Click File, Save As Web Page, Publish
Import Excel data from a Web page	Right-click the data to be imported, click Copy, click a cell on the worksheet, click the Paste button
Run a Web Query	Click Data, Import External Data, New Web Query
Query a database	Click Data, Import External Data, New Database Query
Open an *.html* file in Excel	Click File, Open, select *All Web Pages* from the *Files of type* list box
Insert a linked or embedded object	Click Insert, Object, click the Create from File tab and check the Link to file checkbox
Copy a linked or embedded object	In the source file, right-click the object to be copied, click Copy. In the destination file, click Edit, Paste Special

CONCEPTS check

Completion: On a blank sheet of paper, indicate the correct term, symbol, or command for each description.

1. This term refers to sending data from Excel to another application.
2. The characters from a text file usually come from this character set.
3. This term refers to a text file that uses commas or another special character to separate the columns.
4. Text files usually end with this extension.
5. This term refers to a local area or wide area network that provides a business or organization with services similar to those provided by the Internet without necessarily being connected to the Internet.
6. This is the name of the markup language used to create Web pages.
7. This is the only software users need to access Excel data that has been placed on the Web.
8. This term describes Excel data on the Web that can be entered, formatted, calculated, analyzed, sorted, and filtered.
9. One way to import data from a Web page into Excel is to click this button from the Web page displaying the data to be imported.
10. This type of object is stored with the source file.
11. This type of object has to be edited in the destination file.

12. If you are linking an object by copying it, you have to click this option from the Edit menu in the destination file.
13. List the reasons why you might need to import a text file to Excel.
14. List the advantages of using a company intranet for distributing information.
15. You need to share Excel data with other applications, but the available storage space is limited. Explain whether you would choose to link or embed the data and why.

SKILLS check

Assessment 1

1. Someone has sent you some advertising figures as a text file. You need to import them into Excel. Open the **Advertising.txt** file. **Advertising.txt** is a fixed width file. The data in the first column is text. The remaining columns should be formatted as General.
2. Save the workbook as a Microsoft Excel workbook file using the Save As command. Name the file **eec8sc01**.
3. Create a custom header that displays your name at the left margin and the file name at the right margin.
4. Print the worksheet.
5. Save the workbook using the same file name (**eec8sc01**) and close it.

Assessment 2

1. Open **ExcelWorksheet08**.
2. This worksheet contains pricing information on some fabrics. Save this file as a text (tab delimited) file. Name the saved file **eec8sc02.txt**.
3. Close the **eec8sc02.txt** file.
4. Start Word and open the **eec8sc02.txt** file.
5. Select all the text in the document and, using the ruler, set left tab stops at 2.25″, 3″, 3.75″, 4.75″, and 5.75″.
6. Save the file as a Word document using the file name **eec8sc02.doc**.
7. Create a custom header for the Word document that prints your name at the left margin and the file name at the right margin, and then print **eec8sc02.doc**.
8. Save the document again using the same file name (**eec8sc02**) and close it.

Assessment 3

1. Open **ExcelWorksheet09**.
2. Save the workbook using the Save As command and name it **eec8sc03**.
3. Save cells A5 through E24 as a noninteractive Web page. The data should be published using the file name **Addresses**.
4. Print the Web page from Internet Explorer (or Netscape Navigator).
5. Close Internet Explorer.
6. Save the workbook again using the same file name (**eec8sc03**) and close it.

Assessment 4

1. Open **ExcelWorksheet10**.
2. Save the workbook using the Save As command and name it **eec8sc04a**.
3. Designers who help design clothes for Linda Taylor's company, Taylor Made, often need to calculate how much the fabric for their designs will cost. Linda Taylor wants this worksheet published on the company intranet so the designers can use it when needed. Select cells A3 through E15. Save this worksheet as interactive data on the

Web. When the Save As dialog box displays, click the option for saving only the selected range of cells. Set the title for the published data as Fabric Cost Calculations. The data should be published using the file name **FabricCost**.

4. When the Web page is displayed in Internet Explorer, delete the values in cells D2, D5, D9, and D10.
5. Type the following values in the cells indicated:

Cell	Value	Cell	Value
D3	35	D9	42
D5	18	D11	20

6. Print the Web page.
7. Delete the values in cells D3, D5, D9, and D11.
8. Sort the data in the *01-24 yards* column from the most expensive fabric to the least expensive fabric.
9. Filter the data so that only the fabrics that cost less than $100 a yard for 24 or fewer yards are displayed.
10. Type the following values in the cells indicated:

Cell	Value	Cell	Value
D5	12	D11	8
D8	26		

11. Print the Web page.
12. Change the filter so that all the fabrics are displayed.
13. Click the Export to Microsoft Office Excel button.
14. The worksheet is displayed in Excel. Save the workbook on your data disk. Change the file type to Microsoft Office Excel workbook. Use the file name **eec8sc04b**. Print the worksheet and close it. Close worksheet **eec8sc04a**.
15. Close Internet Explorer.

Assessment 5

1. Open **ExcelWorksheet11**.
2. Save the workbook using the Save As command and name it **eec8sc05**.
3. This file can be used by designers and the office management at Taylor Made to break down the design costs of individual designs. Linda Taylor would like it placed on the company's intranet. Save this chart as interactive data on the Web. Set the title for the published data as Calculating Design Costs. The data should be published using the file name **DesignCost**.
4. When the Web page is displayed in Internet Explorer, type the following values in the cells indicated:

Cell	Value	Cell	Value
B1	300	B4	782
B2	175	B5	679
B3	2560		

5. Print the Web page.
6. Close Internet Explorer.
7. Save the Excel workbook using the same file name (**eec8sc05**) and close it.

Assessment 6

1. Open Internet Explorer (or Netscape). You do not have to be online.
2. Open the **Employees.html** file. This is a list of the employees who work at Whitewater Canoe and Kayak Corporation, along with their titles and the number of years they have been employed there.

3. Open a new workbook in Excel. Arrange the windows so that you can see both the entire width of the table in Internet Explorer and at least cell A1 in Excel.
4. Select the entire table in Internet Explorer. Click on the selected table and drag it to cell A1 in Excel.
5. Close Internet Explorer. Maximize the Excel window.
6. Widen the columns as necessary so that all the data is displayed.
7. Adjust the row height of all the rows in the table to 12.75. Save the worksheet using the file name **eec8sc06a**.
8. Create a custom header for the worksheet that displays your name at the left margin and the name of the file at the right margin.
9. Print the worksheet. Save and close it.
10. From Excel, open the **Employees.html** file.
11. Adjust the height of row 1 so the company logo fits in it.
12. Save the worksheet as an Excel Workbook using the file name **eec8sc06b**.
13. Create a custom header for the worksheet that displays your name at the left margin and the name of the file at the right margin.
14. Print the worksheet. Save and close it.
15. Open Internet Explorer.
16. Open the **Vacation.mht** file in Internet Explorer.
17. This interactive worksheet calculates the number of vacation days for which employees are eligible. Type 15 in cell B3 to see how it works.
18. Export the table to Excel using the Export to Microsoft Office Excel button.
19. Save the data on your data disk as an Excel workbook using the file name **eec8sc06c**.
20. Create a custom header for the worksheet that displays your name at the left margin and the name of the file at the right margin.
21. Print the worksheet. Save and close it.
22. Close Internet Explorer.

Assessment 7

1. Use Microsoft Query to extract data from the Access file named **CoumputerInventory.mdb** as follows:
   - From the Product List table, include the fields named *PartName, SupplierNo,* and *ListPrice*.
   - From the Suppliers table, include the field named *SupplierName*.
2. Filter the data that is retrieved so that only those records are retrieved where the supplier name equals ComputerWay or Jorge Computers.
3. Sort the data by SupplierName and then by PartName.
4. Return the data to Microsoft Excel.
5. Format the figures in column C as currency with two decimal places.
6. Save the worksheet using the file name **eec8sc07**.
7. Create a custom header for the worksheet that displays your name at the left margin and the name of the file at the right margin.
8. Save the worksheet again using the same file name (**eec8sc07**) and print it.
9. Close the worksheet.

Assessment 8

1. Open **ExcelWorksheet12**.
2. Save the worksheet using the Save As command and name it **eec8sc08**.
3. Create a custom header that displays your name at the left margin and the file name at the right margin.
4. The logo for Copper Clad Incorporated can be opened through the Paint application that comes with Windows. Insert **Copper.bmp** as a linked file.

5. Adjust the size of the logo so that it fits in rows 1 through 8.
6. Save the file using the same file name (**eec8sc08**) and print it.
7. Close the workbook.

Assessment 9

1. Open **ExcelWorksheet13**.
2. Save the worksheet with Save As and name it **eec8sc09**.
3. Insert the logo for Copper Clad Incorporated as an embedded object in cell A1. The file name for the object is ***Copper.bmp***.
4. Resize the logo so that the bottom of the embedded object aligns with the bottom of row 7.
5. Double-click over the logo to edit the image using Paint tools within Excel.
6. Click Image on the Menu bar and then click Invert Colors.
7. Click in the worksheet area outside the logo to exit Paint editing mode.
8. Create a custom header that displays your name at the left margin and the file name at the right margin.
9. Save the file using the same name (**eec8sc09**) and then print it.
10. Close the workbook.

CHAPTER challenge

You work in the accounting department for Everyday Books, a book company that sells books at a wholesale price to area retailers. At the July meeting, awards will be given to sales reps who have achieved specific goals. A coworker in the organization has been storing this information in a table named Sales Reps in an Access database named **EverydayBooks**. You would like to import the data into Excel since you may be using the data for other purposes at a later time. Begin the process by using Excel's New Database Query feature to import the sales reps with an annual salary of at least $50,000 and bonuses of $4,000 or more. Include all of the fields. Sort the records in ascending order by the sales reps' names. Save the workbook as **Bonuses**. Create another database query that includes only the sales reps and their sales. Sort them in descending order by sales. Place the information in a new sheet in the **Bonuses** workbook. Name the sheet tab appropriately. Then prepare the worksheet to be placed on the Web as an interactive worksheet. Open the worksheet in your browser and calculate the average sales for the sales reps. Print the worksheet while in the browser.

Since your coworker will continue to use Access and update any changes made to the Sales Reps table, you would like the queries you created based on the Sales Reps table to be refreshed in your Excel workbook. Use the Help feature to learn about the refresh control. Then set the properties of the **Bonuses** workbook so that the data is refreshed each time the file is opened. Save the workbook again.

A PowerPoint presentation will be created for the July meeting. The presentation will include the worksheets created in the first part of the Chapter Challenge. Begin the presentation by linking the two sheets to separate slides in PowerPoint. Format the slides appropriately. Save the presentation as **JulyMeeting**.

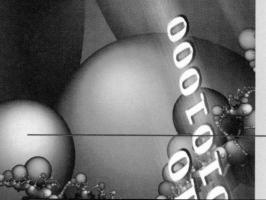

WORKPLACE Ready

Interpreting and Integrating Data

ASSESSING proficiency

Unit02E
EXCEL

In this unit, you have learned how to use PivotTables, PivotCharts, Goal Seek, Solver, and Scenario Manager. You learned how to project values by performing "what-if" analysis. You learned how to record, run, and edit macros; assign macros to command buttons; create custom toolbars; and use the auditing toolbar. You learned how to share workbooks; change workbook properties; apply and remove passwords, workbook protection, and worksheet protection; use digital signatures; merge workbooks; import and export data from text files; place a noninteractive and an interactive worksheet on the Web; import data from an Access database and a Web page; use Web Query; and link and embed objects. And you learned how to structure workbooks using XML.

Assessment 1

1. Open **ExcelWorksheet10**.
2. Save the workbook using the Save As command and name it **eeu2pa01**.
3. Create a PivotTable report that uses the data in cells A3 through G30. Place the PivotTable on a new worksheet. Rename the new worksheet **PivotTable**.
4. Create a custom header for the *PivotTable* worksheet that has your name left-aligned and the file name right-aligned.
5. Drag the Country button into the *Drop Row Fields Here* area.
6. Drag the Item button to the *Drop Row Fields Here* area, to the right of the Country button. When the PivotTable is displayed, the *Item* field should be to the right of the *Country* field.
7. Drag the Profit button to the *Drop Data Items Here* area.
8. Format the values in the *Total* column as currency with no decimal places.
9. Display only China and Saudi Arabia. Print the PivotTable worksheet.
10. Display all the countries. Print the PivotTable worksheet.
11. Save the workbook using the same name (**eeu2pa01**) and close it.

Assessment 2

1. Open **ExcelWorksheet11**.
2. Save the workbook using the Save As command and name it **eeu2pa02**.
3. There are three different work schedules for the employees of the Books Galore bookstore. Each employee gets two days off in a row. At the top of the Employee Schedule worksheet are the three schedules. The zeros represent the days off for that schedule and the ones represent the days worked. Cells C7 through I7 display the total staff needed for that day.

Cells C8 through I8 display the average number of customers who come into the store on a particular day. Cells C9 through I9 display the number of employees needed for each day based on a staff-to-customer ratio of 1 employee for every 80 customers who come into the store in a day. Cell B11 displays that ratio. The owner of the bookstore wants a comparison of two staff-to-customer ratios. Her goal is to find the lowest total payroll cost while adequately staffing the bookstore. Click cell B13 and enter the daily salary amount for one employee, which would be the average hourly salary times the average hours worked in a day. The average hourly salary is $10 and the average hours worked in a day is eight.

4. Click cell A16. Enter the total payroll amount. The total payroll amount would be the total staff needed, which is found in cell B7, times the daily salary, which is found in cell B13.

5. Use Solver to find the minimum payroll amount. The target cell is the total payroll, which is found in cell A16. You want the target cell to be equal to the minimum value. The cells that can be changed are cells B3 through B5. The following constraints must be applied:

> The value in cells that can change (B3:B5) must be an integer.
> The value in cells that can change (B3:B5) must be greater than or equal to zero.
> The total staff (C7:I7) must be greater than or equal to the staffing demand (C9:I9).

When Solver finds a solution, save it as a scenario. Name the scenario Staff/Customer Ratio of 1 to 80. Be sure to click the *Restore Original Values* option before leaving the Solver Results dialog box.

6. Change the staff/customer ratio to 1 to 100.

7. Use Solver to find the schedule that finds the minimum payroll amount at this new higher ratio. The constraints all stay the same as in Step 6. Save the results as a scenario. Name this scenario Staff/Customer Ratio of 1 to 100. Be sure to click the *Restore Original Values* option before leaving the Solver Results dialog box.

8. Use the Scenarios command to print a summary in landscape orientation of each saved scenario. In the Scenario Manager dialog box, click *Staff/Customer Ratio of 1 to 80* and then click Summary. The report type you want is scenario summary, and the result cell is A16.

9. Create a custom header that has your name left-aligned and the file name-right aligned for the *Scenario Summary* worksheet. Change the orientation of the page to landscape.

10. Save the workbook using the same name (**eeu2pa02**) and print it.

11. Close the **eeu2pa02** workbook.

Assessment 3

1. Open **ExcelWorksheets13**.
2. Save the workbook using the Save As command and name it **eeu2pa03**.
3. Create a custom header that has your name left-aligned and the file name right-aligned.
4. This worksheet lists some basic information on many of the cruises offered by the travel agency Travel Advantage. You want to create two filters for the list, save them as macros, and create a third macro that displays all the records. Then you will customize a toolbar by creating three buttons to run each of the macros. Click anywhere in the list. Display the Visual

Basic toolbar and then click the Record Macro button. When the Record Macro dialog box is displayed, name the macro *Under_1500*. Enter the letter **u** in the *Shortcut key* box. Click OK.

5. Use AutoFilter to display cruises on which the average price is less than $1,500.
6. Click the Stop Recording button.
7. Follow Steps 4 through 6 to create a second macro that turns off the AutoFilter feature. Name the macro *Display_all* and enter **d** as a shortcut key.
8. Follow Steps 4 through 6 to create a third macro that displays all the cruises that provide children's activities. Name the macro *Children* and enter **c** as a shortcut key.
9. Press Ctrl + d to display all the records.
10. Display the Forms toolbar. Click the Button button on the toolbar. When the mouse pointer turns into a crosshair, click and drag in the shaded blue area at the top of the worksheet to place the button. Assign the Under_1500 macro to this button. The button should be .40 inch high and .85 inch wide. Change the name on the button to *Cruises Under $1500*.
11. Create a second button and place it in the blue shaded area next to the first button. Assign the Children macro to this button. The button should be .40 inch high and .85 inch wide. Change the name on the button to *Activities for Children*.
12. Create a third button and place it in the blue shaded area next to the second button. Assign the Display_all macro to this button. The button should be .40 inch high and .85 inch wide. Change the name on the button to *Display All*.
13. Click the Activities for Children button. Print the *Cruises* worksheet.
14. Click the Display All button.
15. Click the Cruises Under $1500 button. Print the *Cruises* worksheet.
16. Click the Display All button.
17. Save the workbook using the same name (**eeu2pa03**) and close it.

Assessment 4

1. Open **ExcelWorksheet14**.
2. Save the workbook using the Save As command and name it **eeu2pa04**.
3. Create a custom header that has your name left-aligned and the file name right-aligned.
4. Redwood Community College offers some computer classes at two extensions. The head of the Computer Science Department on the main campus wants the enrollment figures for both extensions. A different instructor is in charge of each extension. You want to set up this worksheet as a shared worksheet so that each instructor can enter the appropriate enrollment figures. Then you will merge the two worksheets. Before you do that, however, you want to enter a comment. Attach the following comment to cell C10:

   > Since this is the first semester this course is being offered at the extensions, enrollment figures are expected to be low.

   Resize the comment box so that all the text is displayed.
5. Set up the **eeu2pa04** workbook as a shared workbook.
6. Start a second copy of Excel and open the **eeu2pa04** workbook. Save this

copy of the workbook using the Save As command and name it **NorthBranch**.

7. Type the following values in the cells indicated:

Cell	Value
B5	185
B6	78
B7	123
B8	118
B9	69
B10	35

8. Save the workbook using the same name (**NorthBranch**). Exit from the second copy of Excel.
9. Switch to the **eeu2pa04** workbook.
10. Save this copy of the workbook using the Save As command and name it **WestBranch**.
11. Type the following values in the cells indicated:

Cell	Value
C5	210
C6	96
C7	162
C8	149
C9	112
C10	58

12. Save the workbook using the same name (**WestBranch**) and close it.
13. Open **eeu2pa04**. Merge the **NorthBranch** and **WestBranch** workbooks into the **eeu2pa04** workbook.
14. Remove the workbook from shared use.
15. Save the workbook using the same name (**eeu2pa05**) and print it.
16. Close the workbook.

Assessment 5

1. Open **ExcelWorksheet15**.
2. Save the workbook using the Save As command and name it **eeu2pa05**.
3. Create a custom header that has your name left-aligned and the file name right-aligned.
4. This worksheet has several errors in it. Use the Formula Auditing toolbar to find and correct the errors.
5. Save the workbook using the same name (**eeu2pa05**) and print it.
6. Close the workbook.

WRITING activities

The following activities give you the opportunity to practice your writing skills along with demonstrating an understanding of some of the important Word and Excel features you have mastered in this and previous units. Use correct grammar, appropriate word choices, and clear sentence constructions.

Activity 1

The owner of the Waterfront Café wants to be able to project the amount of money the restaurant might make on any one night, depending on how many people are seated during the night and the average price each person spends on a meal. Prepare a worksheet that includes an appropriate title and a header with your Sname at the left margin and the file name at the right margin. Save the workbook using the file name **eeu2act01**. Use the Scenarios command to set up a scenario for holidays (which is when the restaurant tends to do very well), average nights, and slow nights. Use the following information for setting up the scenarios:

- The operating expense is $2,800, which is what it costs per evening to operate the restaurant.

- On holidays, the restaurant typically seats 725 people in an evening, and the average cost of each meal is $14.

- On an average night, the restaurant typically seats 600 people, and the average cost of each meal is $10.

- On a slow night, the restaurant typically seats 475 people, and the average cost of each meal is $8.

Each scenario should include the income for the evening, which would be the total amount of money taken in (the cost of each meal times the number of people seated) minus the operating expense for the evening.

Display and print each one of the scenarios (holidays, average nights, and slow nights). Create a scenario summary. On the Scenario Summary worksheet, create a custom header that prints your name at the left margin and the file name at the right margin. Print the Scenario Summary worksheet. Save the workbook again using the same file name (**eeu2act01**) and close it.

Activity 2

Import the text file **Sheet Music.txt** into an Excel worksheet starting in cell A1. The data in the **Sheet Music.txt** file is delimited. Tabs were used as the delimiters. The data format for all of the columns is text, except for the last column, *Price*, which is general. Save the file as an Excel workbook using the file name **eeu2act02** This is a partial list of the Little Music Shop's sheet music inventory. Format the headings *Song Title*, *Artist*, *Instrument*, *Level*, and *Price* as bold. Sheet music by the Beatles has become quite popular. Adjust the width of the columns as needed. Use conditional formatting so that every "Beatles" entry is displayed as bold and red. Since you will be adding more records to this list, make sure the conditional formatting applies to the entire worksheet.

Create three drop-down lists for entering data into the list. One drop-down list is for the *Instrument* column, one for the *Level* column, and one for the *Price* column. There should be two items on the drop-down list for the *Instrument* column: *Piano* and *Guitar*. There should be three items on the drop-down list for the *Level* column: *Easy*, *Intermediate*, and *Hard*. There should be four items on the drop-down list for the Price column: *$1.95*, *$2.50*, *$3.25*, and *$3.95*. Include appropriate input and error messages for each drop-down list.

Add the following records to the list:

Song Title	Artist	Instrument	Level	Price
Can You Feel the Love Tonight?	John, Elton	Piano	Easy	$1.95
Can You Feel the Love Tonight?	John, Elton	Piano	Intermediate	$2.50
Can You Feel the Love Tonight?	John, Elton	Guitar	Easy	$2.50
Can You Feel the Love Tonight?	John, Elton	Guitar	Intermediate	$3.25
Can't Buy Me Love	Beatles	Guitar	Intermediate	$2.50
Can't Buy Me Love	Beatles	Piano	Intermediate	$2.50

Sort this list first by song title, next by instrument, and finally by level. Create a custom header that includes your name at the left margin and the file name at the right margin. Save the workbook again using the same file name (**eeu2act02**) and print it. Close the workbook.

Activity 3

Open workbook **eeu2act02**. Using the Save As command, name the workbook **eeu2act03**. Insert four rows above the list for a criteria range. Copy the labels for the list to the first blank row. Name the range of cells that includes the labels and the first blank row under them (A1:E2) *Criteria*. Create a macro that uses Advanced Filter to filter the list to a new location, starting in G5. Extract from the records all the songs by the Beatles written for the guitar. Include as part of the macro optimizing the column widths for the extracted records and deleting the words *Beatles* and *Guitar* from the criteria range. Create a second macro that deletes anything entered in the range of cells G5 through K100. Create a third macro that uses Advanced Filter to filter the list to a new location, starting in G5. Extract from the records all the songs written for the piano that are easy. Include as part of the macro optimizing the column widths for the extracted records and deleting the words *Piano* and *Easy* from the criteria range.

Create a command button on the worksheet for each macro. Give each button an appropriate name. Filter the list using the command button that displays all the songs by the Beatles for the guitar. Print the list. Delete the extracted records using the appropriate command button. Filter the list using the command button that displays all the songs for the piano that are easy. Print the list. Delete the extracted records using the appropriate command button.

A music teacher has requested a list of sheet music that is for guitar and by the Beatles. Filter the list again using the appropriate command button. Start Word. Write a business letter to the instructor thanking him for his inquiry. The address for The Little Music Shop is 459 Sundance Square, Boulder, Colorado 80301. If you want, you can use The Little Music Shop's logo, which is the file **Lilmusic.tif**, as part of the letterhead. The name and address of the teacher requesting the information is Rodman Bates, 2285 10th Street, Boulder, Colorado 80301. Copy the filtered list from Excel into the business letter. Save the completed letter and name it **Wordeeu2act03**. Print and then close **Wordeeu2act03**. Display all the records in Excel using the appropriate command button. Save the list again using the same file name (**eeu2act03**) and close it.

INTERNET project

The Books Galore bookstore is starting a special reading group for mothers and their daughters who are ages 9 to 12. Make sure you are connected to the Internet and then explore the following two sites:

- www.amazon.com
- www.barnesandnoble.com

Each of these sites provides a special section for "Kids." In each of these sections, you can search for books that are of particular interest to children ages 9 to 12. The reading group is going to focus on historical adventure books. Use the keywords *adventure* and *history* to search these Web sites for books that would appeal to girls ages 9 to 12. Select at least five books you think the mothers and daughters would enjoy reading. Take notes on the name of the book, the author, a brief description of what the book is about, and the price.

In Word prepare an announcement for the reading group. The announcement should include the name of each book and a brief description of what the book is about. If you want, you can use the Books Galore logo, which is the file **Booksgal.tif**, as part of the announcement. The reading group is going to meet from 7:00 P.M. to 8:30 P.M. the first Monday of the month from October through February and is open to mothers and their daughters ages 9 to 12. The reading group will meet at Books Galore. The address of Books Galore is 138 Waterhouse Street, Cambridge, Massachusetts. The telephone number is (607) 555-1221. Print the announcement.

In Excel prepare a worksheet that lists each book's title, author, and price. Books Galore wants to put this worksheet on their Web site. Publish this worksheet on the Web as a noninteractive worksheet. Provide it with an appropriate title. Print the Web page.

JOB study

You have been asked to review the first quarter report for Thaxton Industries, and to prepare a revised report presentation to company management. Open the Worksheet **FURNITURE** that you created in Unit 1. Click the *Qtr 1* worksheet tab. Trace precedents to determine if there are errors in the formulas or functions. Turn off Trace Precedents. Create a macro, called Thaxton, which will select the print area for the Year-End worksheet as all the cells containing data; change the page layout to landscape; and change the number of copies to 2. Save the file as **THAXTON**. Assign this macro to a command button to be placed on the Standard toolbar. Edit the macro to change the background color of the title, Thaxton Industries, to green with white lettering. Save the files and print your copies.

INDEX

pivoting, 197
PivotTable and PivotChart
    Report button, 198
PivotTable and PivotChart
    Report Wizard, 214
    PivotTable and
        PivotChart Wizard
        Layout dialog box, 211
PivotChart report created
    with, 215
PivotTable diagram, 199,
    200
PivotTable Field dialog box,
    210
PivotTable Field List, 199
PivotTable lists, 242
PivotTable Options dialog
    box, 210
PivotTable reports, 196, 242
    AutoFormat and
        formatting of, 213-
        214
    data organization in, 198
    filtering, 200-203
    formatting, 205-207
    formatting and sorting,
        203-204
    grand totals/subtotals
        removed from, 210,
        211-213
    hiding detail in, 209,
        211
    hiding/filtering items in,
        242
    managing, 209-211
    PivotChart reports
        created from, 216-
        218, 242
    sorting and filtering,
        207-209
PivotTable sort and top 10
    dialog, 205
PivotTable toolbar, 199, 200
PivotTable Wizard, 211,
    242
PMT function, 103-104,
    121
    Function Arguments
        dialog box for, 101
Polynomial trendlines, 235
Portrait orientation, 29
Power trendlines, 235
Precedents, 267, 277
    tracing, 269, 271-273
Predesigned formats, 26, 56
Predesigned templates, 67
Print Preview button, 303
Problems: Solver and
    defining/solving of,
    229-231
Profit and loss worksheets,
    65-66
Projecting values, 235-236,
    243
Protected ranges: specific
    users given access to,
    291-292
Protecting workbooks,
    284-294
Protect Sheet dialog box,
    288
Protect Sheet warning box,
    288
Protect Workbook dialog
    box, 286
Publish As Web Page dialog
    box, 319
PV function, 105-106, 122

Q
Query Wizard, 328

R
RAND function, 107, 108,
    122
Random numbers:
    calculating, 107
Range, 107
    in COUNTIF function,
        110
    in lists, 129
    in SUMIF function, 107
Range names, 122
    in formulas, 113
Ranges
    access to protected,
        291-292
    naming of, 112-113
Reading group project, 361
Record Macro button, 250
Record Macro dialog box,
    250, 251, 276
Records
    deleting, 145-146
    editing, 144-145
    extraction of unique,
        159-161
    finding, 143-144
    finding, editing, and
        deleting, 145-146
    lists, 171
    modifying, 143-146
Reference functions,
    113-114, 122
Refresh All button, 325
Refresh Data button, 325
Regression analysis, 243
    performing, 239
    using, 240-241
Regression dialog box, 239,
    240
Relative cell reference, 277
Relative Reference button,
    251, 277
Relative references, 251
Remove All Arrows button,
    269
Remove Dependent button,
    269
Remove Precedent button,
    269
Reports: PivotTable, 196
Reset Picture button, 48
Resetting images, 48
Reset Window Position
    button, 74
Resizing
    images, 48, 56
    pictures, 47
Restrictions: with Solver,
    227, 242
Root tags: in XML
    documents, 337
Rotating
    images, 45
    PivotTables, 242
Rotating tools: using, 44-47,
    49
ROUND function, 106-107,
    108, 122
Row fields: in PivotTable
    report, 214
Row heights: adjusting, 13,
    56
Rows
    hiding and unhiding,
        34-35
    in lists, 129, 165, 171
    of PivotTable, 242

Run Macro button, 252,
    254, 277
Run Sub/User Form button,
    255

S
Sales Invoice template, 66,
    89
Save As dialog box, 89
Save As Type list box: text
    file formats from, 317
Save Options dialog box,
    284, 285
Scenario Manager, 195,
    232, 243
Scenario Manager dialog
    box, 232
Scenarios, 242
    creating, 232-234, 243
Schema files: XML, 339
Schemas
    restrictions in XML, 344-
        345
    in XML, 348
Scientific formats
    applying, 13-15, 56
    in number formatting, 8
Scientific notation, 8-9
Security
    for macros, 293-294
    for workbooks, 304
Select Changes to Accept or
    Reject dialog box, 295
Select Files to Merge Into
    Current Workbook
    dialog box, 300
Selfcert.exe tool, 292
Self-documenting XML files,
    338
Sensitivity Report: in Solver,
    228
SGML, 335
Shading, 21
    applying, 17-19
Share Workbook dialog box
    with Advanced tab
        selected, 84
    with Editing tab selected,
        83
Sharing workbooks, 304
    benefits/limitations of,
        284
Sheets
    hiding and unhiding,
        34-35
    renaming, 38, 39-42
Sheets in new workbook
    option, 20
Shortcut key: for macros,
    250, 276
Show Detail button, 209,
    242
Show Detail Level button,
    151
Show Detail symbol, 171
Show Field List button, 199
Sines, 106
Solver, 195, 242
    data analysis with,
        227-231
Solver Parameters dialog
    box, 227, 228
Solver Results dialog box,
    228
Sort Ascending button, 139
Sort Descending button,
    139
Sort dialog box, 139
Sorting
    lists, 139-143

multilevel, 139-143
PivotTable reports,
    203-204, 207-209
Sort Options dialog box,
    141
Source data, 242
    for PivotTable, 197
Source file, 331, 349
Standard toolbar: Format
    Painter button on, 17
Statements: for macros, 255
Statistical functions,
    110-113
Stock research, 190
Stop Recording toolbar, 251,
    277
Storage: of lists in
    worksheets, 165
Store Macro in drop-down
    menu, 251
Style dialog box, 16, 56
Style name box, 16
Styles, 56
    creating, applying, and
        editing, 16
    using, 21
Subtotal dialog box, 151
Subtotaling lists, 151-155
Subtotals: removing from
    PivotTable report, 210,
    211-213
SUM function, 148, 171,
    197, 242
SUMIF function, 107, 109,
    122
Summary formulas, 147
Sum_range: and SUMIF
    function, 107
Synchronous Scrolling
    button, 74

T
Tab color: selecting, 38
Tags: in XML documents,
    337
Templates, 65, 89
    editing, 71-72, 89
    features summary, 90
    new, 68-70, 89
    predesigned, 67
    use of existing, 67-68
    using, 65-72
Templates on Office Online
    button, 67
Text file formats
    common, 312
    from Save As Type list
        box, 317
Text files, 349
    exporting data to, 312,
        317-318
    importing data from,
        312, 315-317
Text Import Wizard
    Step 1 of 3 dialog box,
        313
    step 2 of 3 dialog box,
        314
Text strings: formatting, 28
Thaxton Industries first
    quarter report, 361
Tiled option: for arranging
    windows in desktop, 74
Timecard template, 66, 89
Time formatting codes, 11
Toolbars
    customizing, 261-267
    docked and floating,
        260, 277

hiding and displaying, 261

shading applied with, 19

Top 10 AutoFilter dialog box, 156

Trace Dependents button, 269

Trace Error button, 269

Trace Precedents button, 269

Tracer arrows, 269

displaying, 267

Tracing

dependents and precedents, 269, 271-273

errors, 269

Tracked changes: accepting/rejecting, 295, 304

Tree structure: in XML documents, 338

Trendlines, 195, 243

creating, 237-239

creating on charts, 235-236

types of, 235

Trigonometric functions, 106-109

.txt extension: text files ending with, 313

Type box, 9, 10

Type list box, 56

U

Underscore characters: in range names, 112, 122

Unhide dialog box, 35, 287

Unique records: extracting, 159-161

Unprotect Sheet dialog box, 288

Unprotect Workbook dialog box, 286

V

Validation, 344-345

of XML data in Excel, 349

Validation command, 270

Values projection, 235-236, 243

VBA. *See* Visual Basic for Applications

VeriSign, Inc., 292

Vertical option: for arranging windows in desktop, 74

Viruses: and macro security, 293

Visual Basic editor, 254

Visual Basic for Applications, 250, 276

Visual Basic toolbar, 250, 277

VLOOKUP function, 113-116, 122

W

Watch Window button, 271

Web. *See* World Wide Web

Web browsers, 222, 318

Web pages, 318

Excel data placed on, 349

importing data from, into Excel, 326

interactive PivotTables saved as, 242

PivotTable reports saved as, 222

Web Query, 325, 326-327

What-if analysis, 225, 242, 243

Word: importing data from using drag and drop, 314-315

Workbook computing, 311

Workbook properties

defining, 75

managing, 72-74

Workbook Properties dialog box, 72

with Summary tab selected, 73

tab contents, 73

Workbook protection: applying/removing, 286

Workbooks

advanced options for sharing of, 84

auditing, 267-276

benefits/limitations with sharing of, 284

comparing side by side, 74, 75

digital signatures for authentication of, 292

features summary, 90, 305

linking, 80-83

merging, 300-302, 304

multiple, 74

passwords assigned to, 284, 304

protecting, 284-294

running macros and, 252

shared, 83-89, 304

tracking changes in, 294-299

Workgroup computing, 283

Workgroup features, 83

Workgroups, 304

collaborating with, 283-310

security features with, 283

sharing features with, 283

Working folder: default, 20, 25

Work in progress: advanced formatting and functions, 181-191

Workplace ready: interpreting and integrating data, 355-361

Worksheet pages: selecting printing order for, 38

Worksheet protection: applying/removing, 286

Worksheets

adjusting layout of, 28-32, 30

auditing, 271-276

borders and shading in, 17-19

comments added to cells in, 299

data analysis in, 195

data consolidation in, 89

exporting, 317-318

features summary, 57-58, 277-278, 305

formatting features for, 7-8

formatting for, with styles, 16

furniture company, 190-191

graphics inserted into, 42-43, 56

hiding, 286, 304

interactive, placed on Web, 321-322

layout of large, 56

lists stored in, 165

managing and auditing, 249-282

multiple, 303, 304

noninteractive, placed on Web, 319-320

outlining, 147-151, 171

protecting, 289-291

setting default number of, 20, 25

on Web, 319

zeros turned off in, 19

Workspaces

creating, 89

using, 75, 80-83

World Wide Web

accessing and placing data on, 318-324

interactive charts placed on, 323-324

interactive PivotTables created for, 222-225

interactive worksheets published on, 321-322

noninteractive worksheets placed on, 319-320

X

.xls extension: workbooks saved with, 69

.xlt extension, 69

.xlw extension, 89

XML. *See* Extensible Markup Language

XML coding: simple, 337

XML data

importing, 347

manipulating, 342-344

working in with Excel, 340

XML document features: summary in Excel, 348-349

XML documents: manipulating in Excel, 348

XML files

opening and modifying, 340-342

opening in Excel, 335

self-documenting, 338

xmlns attribute, 339

XML schemas

importing, 347

structure of, 339

XML Source task pane, 340

view options, 345-348

Z

Zeros: turning off, 19, 21